The Adirondacks'
Moose River Plains

–Vol. 1–

Life Around the Indian Clearing

W J O'Hern

William J. O'Hern

The Adirondacks'
Moose River Plains
–Vol. 1–
Life Around the Indian Clearing

The book and cover design and typesetting
were created by Nancy Did It! (www.NancyDidIt.com)

Cover photo by Dante Tranquille,
courtesy of Town of Webb Historical Association

Find us on

Facebook Adirondack Author William "Jay" O'Hern

In the
Adirondacks

Camden, New York • www.AdirondackBooksOnline.com

Printed in the United States of America by Versa Press, Inc.
ISBN 978-0-9890328-9-6

PERMISSIONS

Long quotations from "French Lewie" by Gerald Kenwell are reprinted with permission from the New York State *Conservationist*, August–September 1952.

Grateful acknowledgement is made to reprint with permission from the New York State *Conservationist* magazine Gerald Kenwell's letter that appeared in the article "Our Forest Preserve," Vol. 6; No. 4, February–March 1952.

Grateful acknowledgement is made to Farrand N. Benedict Jr., Julia Peterson, Helen Dutton, and Anne Mead, the descendants of Abner Benedict, for granting permission to publish a portion of the Benedict papers that appears as "Pine Tree Camp Vacation on the Moose River Plains in 1873."

Grateful acknowledgement is made to Barbara McMartin and Nancy Long, Barbara's daughter, for granting permission to use long quotes from McMartin's *To the Lake of the Skies: The Benedicts in the Adirondacks*, (Lake View Press, 1996). I was thrilled to learn from Barbara that my introducing her to the Benedict letters provided her a wealth of inspiration that lead to her significant Benedict family Adirondack history.

Grateful acknowledgement is made to The Adirondack Experience, the Museum at Blue Mountain Lake for permission to reproduce quotations of Arpad Geyza Gerster from *Notes Collected in the Adirondacks 1897 & 1898*, copyright The Adirondack Experience, 2010, and for permission to reprint photograph PO26386.

Grateful acknowledgement is made to The Adirondack Experience, the Museum at Bue Mountain Lake, and to Jerry Pepper to quote from Dr. John C.A. Gerster's November 14, 1962, letter to Kenneth Durant.

"Sleeping in the Woods at Kenwells," September 2, 1899, and "September in the Woods: The Oswego Colony is Still at Kenwell's House," September 16, 1899, first appeared in the Oswego *Daily Palladium*.

Grateful acknowledgement is made to Katy Z. Allen and posthumously to Katy's mother, Mary North Allen, for permission to reproduce passages and photos from Arthur W. North's "The Log of the Walkaheaps" and from Mary North Allen's memoir, *Falling Light and Waters Turning: Adventures in Being Human*.

Grateful acknowledgement is made to Martha C. Leonard and posthumously to Martha's father, Almy D. Coggeshall, for permission to reproduce photos found in Coggeshall's 1933 "North Recreational Adventure: Being a Journal of a Three Weeks' Hike Through the Adirondacks."

Grateful acknowledgement is made to Ron Johns, Executive Editor of the *Observer-Dispatch*, and to the *Observer-Dispatch* newspaper for permission to reproduce long passages of E.A. Spears's 1938 article "In the Lore of the North Country, French Lewey Was a Pioneer of the Adirondacks."

Grateful acknowledgement is made to Patti Bateman Quinn for permission to use selected images from the Johnson Family Collection of photographs of Kamp Kill Kare, stored in the Hamilton County historian's archives in Lake Pleasant, N.Y.

Grateful acknowledgement is made to William Ingersoll for permission to quote from the Moose River Plains chapter introduction found in the first (1988) edition of *Discover the West Central Adirondacks*.

Grateful acknowledgement is made to Elsie Wilkins and *North Country Life* for permission to reprint "Woods Loafer."

CONTENTS

The mountain scrambler will find peaks with their elevations of 4,000+ feet impressive if they climb to a rocky outlook. On a clear day, lakes and rivers can be seen through the forest winding below and far off panoramas of distant ranges can be viewed. *Courtesy Earl M. Kreuzer*

EPIGRAPH

The Adirondacks, the Oldest Mountains Await

The Adirondacks, consisting most famously of rocky peaks, sheer cliffs and narrow valleys, also have millions of acres of undulating hills, wooded slopes and sparkling lakes. The Iroquois derisively gave the name Adirondack (meaning "tree-eater) to some of the Algonquins, their enemies.

Forty-three mountains have elevations of 4,000 feet or higher. Mount Marcy, with an altitude of 5,344 feet, is the highest. Near Marcy's summit is Lake Tear-of-the-Clouds, the source of the Hudson River.

Used for centuries as a native hunting territory, the vast wilderness was not penetrated by white men until the late 18th century. Mining began at the end of that century; Adirondack mines have yielded such ores as iron, zinc, titanium, talc, wollastonite and garnet.

The great wealth of Adirondack forests supplied demands for timber in the second half of the 19th century and the first decades of the 20th. Alarmed over the denuding of this natural treasure, New York State set up the Forest Preserve in 1885. The Adirondack Park today includes more than two million state-owned (Forest Preserve) acres within its total of 6.1 million acres.

Railroad construction after 1871 turned remote forest retreats into popular summer resorts. The opening of automobile highways in the 20th century made the area accessible for all to enjoy the rugged beauty of the Adirondacks. The Moose River Plains are representative of the pros and cons of that increased accessibility.

Beaver Lake, Moose River Plains, 1949. "Let us…be visionary enough to preserve inviolate at least a few places where primitive forces may be felt and seen without the influence of man." —Paul Schafer, *Ten Critical Years in the History of the Adirondacks: 1945–1955.* Photo by Dante O. Tranquille. Courtesy Town of Webb Historical Association

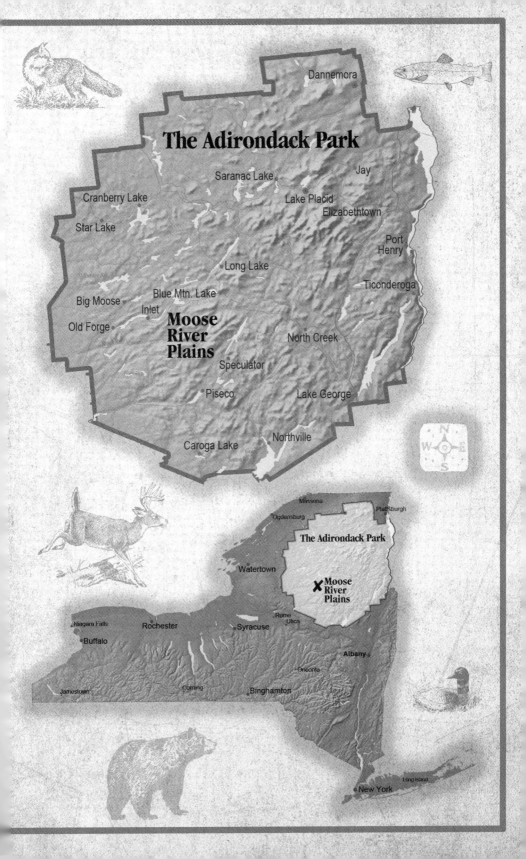

The Adirondack Park

Dannemora

Jay

Saranac Lake

Lake Placid

Elizabethtown

Cranberry Lake

Star Lake

Port
Henry

Long Lake

Ticonderoga

Blue Mtn. Lake

Big Moose

Inlet

Moose River Plains

Old Forge

North Creek

Speculator

Lake George

Piseco

Northville

Caroga Lake

Massena

Plattsburgh

Ogdensburg

The Adirondack Park

Watertown

X Moose
River
Plains

Niagara Falls

Rochester

Rome
Utica

Syracuse

Buffalo

Albany

Oneonta

Corning

Jamestown

Binghamton

Long Island

New York

DEDICATION

To WINFRED C. "SLIM" MURDOCK, who knew the way the Moose River Plains used to be. Slim shared his artifacts and enchanted me with incredibly detailed facts about people and places he was in contact with throughout the eight years of freighting using his Uncle Gerald Kenwell's pack horses, from 1928 to 1936.

Each time Slim and I would drive over the road through the Moose River Recreation Area he would exclaim, "Oh Bub, you have no idea how revisiting touches a soft spot with me. Some of the happiest times of my life, and some of the hardest work, took place in the Otter Brook Valley, especially in the company of Gerald Kenwell, to me, one of the greatest guides who ever lived."

OPPOSITE. **Winfred C. "Slim" Murdock, circa 1929. Nothing meant more to Slim than the time spent in the Moose River Plains where he claimed, "I fed the black flies for over 40 years."** *Courtesy Winfred C. Murdock*

PREFACE

Memories of Those Who Experienced Life in the Moose River Plains

The Adirondacks' Moose River Plains, Volume 1, is the first in a series of three major informal histories about the vast territory once referred to as the Indian Clearing country. Its story continues with Volumes 2 and 3. Until now, there has been no recognized recorded work about this remote territory other than bits of meager accounts scattered in early newspapers and travel magazines, period pieces such as Wallace's *Guide to the Adirondacks*, occasional references in out-of-print books, individuals' journals and various other vintage works.

My task was to gather as much material as possible, including untapped first-person accounts, then sift and sort the data and pull it together into a wide-ranging and unified history that looks back at a past time that otherwise would never be known. Here was a book ripe for the writing, a book about people, with enough of the background and other data to explain how and why The Plains has been such a beloved area.

Memories of those who experienced life in the Moose River Plains and narratives by others who knew old-time personalities connected with the south branch of the Moose River help to connect the reader with times past and allow people and events to be re-created through the images in readers' minds. This trip back in time is enriched by historical photographs which so many generously shared.

Equally refreshing is the vitality of gleanings from early Conservation Department biologists, who spent years on deer studies. Their investigations help explain why this country was once labeled The Land of Deer. Intertwined throughout this Adirondack history are stories of millionaires and powerful politicians, of conservationists and rogue hunters, and especially the stories of the first pioneers to settle in the territory, and their descendants.

The histories of the 1890s pioneer Kenwell family's Sportsman's Home and the latter-day triangle of the three foremost camps—Gerald Kenwell's Otter Brook Camp, Charles Chapin's Camp Nit on Beaver Lake (later owned and operated by Alan and Margaret Wilcox) and the ever-popular Hot Top Camp, later owned by Len Harwood—offer insight into the reasons why the area drew throngs of the early sporting crowd to the immense and magnificent Plains.

The Moose River Plains "is a land roughly forty miles long by twenty-five miles wide, dotted with lakes and ponds and threaded with rivers and streams. It is heavily forested and without clearings, except for the unique natural Moose River Plains which are situated near the heart of this region.

...The mountains are not tall, but present rounding contours which dip gracefully into the myriad lakes and ponds of every description. Spruce and balsam dominate the long reaches of valley, with pine and hardwoods covering the ridges and hills."

—From an informative letter written on September 25, 1945 by Paul Schaefer and Edmund H. Richard regarding the impending tragedy should the proposed multi-purpose Higley Mountain and Panther Mountain reservoirs be constructed. *Photo by Dante O. Tranquille. Courtesy Town of Webb Historical Association*

Camping parties, local guides and camp diary entries resurrect events and characters long associated with the Moose River Plains country. Character sketches of long-time packers, campers, forest rangers and game protectors, bush pilots, and sport enthusiasts interweave to tell their human story of the Plains. The narrative portions of the work aim to present this informal history in a casual story-telling manner.

A corduroy road is made by placing logs close together to allow access over wet areas. Evidence of the corduroy roads the Gould Paper Company built have disappeared over time. Two of the longest spans the author found were near Twin Lakes and the headwaters of Benedict Stream and Pine Grove Creek. *Photo by Dante O. Tranquille. Courtesy Town of Webb Historical Association*

The whereabouts of the earliest Gould Paper Company lumber camps, dams and logging activities reveal a robust timber cutting operation during the opening years of the 20th century. Gould's logging operations and lumbermen's goings-on take center stage in place of dry statistics dealing with acres cut and yearly cord totals.

The Adirondacks' Moose River Plains, Volumes 1, 2 and 3 comprise the vast social history I have assembled over a 50-year period. The reintroduction of beaver; treasured remembrances of the legendary trinity of principal

camps; and dozens of smaller sporting camps; the narrative of The Plains'
connection to the well-known Henry Ward Beecher, the famed Brooklyn
clergyman, and the nephew of author Harriet Beecher Stowe; "French"
Louie Seymour; the outlawed activities of poachers and meat hunters; the
decade-long fight to protect the Moose River valley from being intention-
ally flooded; the devastating effects of the November 1950 land hurricane;
and New York State's purchase of vast portions of once privately-owned land
are so enormous and far-ranging that it is only possible to complete this
history in three volumes.

I venture to guess that this broad, comprehensive social history will be
the only recorded work of its kind. I never intended to produce an exhaustive formal history. Rather, I followed my passion for a people story.

This enterprise has had the generous help of many people, mainly those
who with their generations before them have been associated with the south
branch of the Moose River country, and other people who over long decades
have known The Plains as their work and preferred vacation scene. My deep
obligation has been acknowledged in appropriate places in the text, but
here I once again extend my thanks for the patience with which each and
every person endured my inquiries.

Only a memory. Harold Scott's float plane at Beaver Lake lodge's dock.
Courtesy Margaret Wilcox (The Beaver Lake Collection)

Beaver Lake, Moose River Plains, 1949. Justice Harold Hinman of the Third Appellate Division on January 15, 1930 stated the following interpretation of Article VII, Section 7 of the Constitution (changed to Article XIV, Section 1, in 1938) in the following words:

"Giving to the phrase 'forever kept as wild forest lands' the significance which the term 'wild forest' bears, as we must conclude that the idea intended was a health resort and playground with the attributes of a wild forest park as distinguished from other parks too common to our civilization. We must preserve it in its wild state, its trees, its rocks, its streams. It was to be a great resort for the free use of the people in which nature is given free rein. Its uses for health and pleasure must not be inconsistent with its preservation as forest lands in a wild state. It must always retain the character of a wilderness. Hunting, fishing, tramping, mountain climbing, snowshoeing, skiing or skating find an ideal setting in nature's wilderness. It is essentially a quiet and healthful retreat from the turmoil and artificialities of a busy urban life." *Photo by Dante O. Tranquille. Courtesy Town of Webb Historical Association*

INTRODUCTION

The Big Plains, the Indian Clearing

For many years, the Moose River Plains country of the central Adirondack Mountains has been a much-frequented and favorite haunt of mine, as it has been for rod and gun enthusiasts, campers and paddlers. In its early days, Kenwell's Sportsman's Home, the only habitation on The Plains, became widely known to the sporting crowd. As its fine reputation grew, people in need of rest and quiet and the health-giving and strength-restoring benefits of the wilderness arrived by spring wagons[1] to Cedar River Flow, where they traveled by buckboard or rode horses the last miles through a vast wild land to the bank of the south branch of the Moose River. People who arrived at Kenwell's by way of Limekiln Lake walked or came on horseback.

In the 1940s, it was believed that in Moose River Plains were remnants of the state's original white pine and spruce forests, and a deer herd estimated by the Conservation Department to number more than 2,000 animals. And it was a land that held superb recreational value. *Courtesy Meredith Ferlage*

The wilderness covered thousands of square miles. A large portion of it was in its primitive state and unblemished by the inroads of civilization. The Plains, often called the Indian Clearing, contained innumerable small and large lakes and streams abounding in trout. There were forest glades and low-mountain fastnesses where the majestic buck, graceful doe and spotted fawn were frequently seen and often hunted, acts that are illegal today. Its prairie-like scenery has been described as *magnificent* and *unsurpassed*. No section of this great wilderness was more attractive from an artistic, healthful, or sporting point of view than that embracing the headwaters of the Black, Moose, and nearby Cedar Rivers and the West Canada Creek.

2nd from Lt., Leon S. Miller; 3rd from Lt., Milo Leach. Henry Thibado (with cigarette) poses with a number of unidentified Miller Camp party members and guides.

"One particular nasty day at Miller's Bear Pond Camp when the weather was not favorable for the party to hunt," said Alfred Thibado, "Bert Bonna [sic] and my dad [Henry] decided to hunt. They did not carry rifles because guides were not allowed to do so by law, or hunt. But since the Miller party was not going out, two of Miller's guests loaned Dad and Bert their rifles. Bert didn't see anything but Dad got a buck.

"When they arrived back at camp the rifles were returned and thanks were offered. Dad mentioned he had fired the rifle to see how it would shoot and offered to clean it for the owner before its return. Immediately, and rather gleefully, Bert blurted, 'Henry did not just discharge the gun without a reason. Henry's got a deer.'

"No one inquired, however. You see, he would have been obligated to hand over the deer to the party. But because no one asked for the meat, Dad got to keep it."
Photo taken by A.P. Ford. Courtesy Norton Bus Bird

The valley of the south branch of the Moose River is long and gently sloping as are the other tributary streams such as the Red and the Indian rivers, the Sumner Stream, Benedict Brook, Pine Grove Brook and others. *Courtesy Meredith Ferlage*

The Adirondacks' Moose River Plains, Vol. 1 is a focus-driven story. There are references to the land's natural beauty—its varied terrain; its flora and fauna; the unique landscape. But the low forested mountains and prairie-like plains make up only one color of the country. The history of The Plains I strove to accent was of the people who lived on and enjoyed the recreation it had to offer. It was, for me, a uniqueness of personable characters whose sayings and doings constitute an unusual and fascinating body of fact, legend and folklore. Here in Vol. 1 are the pioneering Kenwells and their guiding business, the restoration of beaver in the south branch of the Moose River territory, an influential lieutenant governor of New York state, a cheese-making industrialist who began the Kraft Cheese Company and a car-wheel millionaire who was a devotee of outdoor sports, Gerald Kenwell's popular hunting and fishing camp, Beaver Lake's camp caretakers, the New York State Conservation Department's early deer biologists and their assistants whose body of work has lent so much toward the understanding of what is known about deer management today, the first surveyors, and a team of women naturalists who came in the 1870s.

"You might say Henry Thibado was for years a mythical figure to me," Mart Allen said about the early Inlet native and Moose River Plains figure. "The country where Henry lived and the nature of his work intrigued me to no end." But for all the admiration, Allen admitted, "I only knew Thibado through my Uncle Stan. I thought of him as a mysterious figure."

Allen's uncle, Stan Narewski, was one of a handful of old-timers Mart grew up around who remembered what Allen considered to be legendary native Adirondack figures—men and women who first appeared in the Fulton Chain in the latter 1890s and early 1900s, walking beside others who traveled over rough, hard trails, scraping together a living while being paid little for their service and labor.

Now-retired forest ranger Allen began living in Thendara, N.Y., with his wife and family in 1958. He remembers Henry Thibado as a great hunter and pioneer who carved out his own meager existence in those hardscrabble days, but still loved the wilderness.

Bill Apgar (Lt.) and Alfred "Tip" Thibado with a day's catch of trout.
From an early age the cousins were the best of friends. *Courtesy Tom Thibado*

The Thibado family. Back row, left to right: Ella, Hattie, Henry, Elizabeth (Betty), Alfred (Tip). Front row: Bernie, Charles, Dora (Dora Burnett when she married). *Courtesy Tom Thibado*

Allen, a twenty-year columnist for the *Adirondack Express,* a weekly hometown newspaper, used his long-running "To Make a Long Story Short" column to introduce and tip his hat toward countless Adirondack people, described in his book, *Adirondack Character Builds a Community* (2012), as those "Who settled the Adirondacks in Old Forge and the surrounding area…. They are people who tamed the last great wilderness of the east, refining and taking the rough edges off what had for centuries been a hostile environment….

"Those early Adirondack settlers persisted, doggedly eking out a living until, somewhere in the middle of the last century, technology began to make life much more tolerable. It made it possible to thoroughly enjoy nature's bounties in all four seasons. The advances in technology made it possible for Adirondack residents to finally share every facet of the good life along with their neighbors to the south."

Ninety-three year old (in 2020) Allen remembers: "Henry Thibado was a native and teamster who toted supplies and hunting gear in and deer out of the Moose River Plains back in the 1930s and '40s. I turned to his daughter Dora Burnett and his nephew Bill Apgar to fill in the gaps.

"Henry and Hattie Thibado had six children, three girls and three boys. The girls were Bette, Ella and Dora; the boys Alfred, Charlie and Bernie. The family lived in Inlet, and Henry, like most of his neighbors, did what he had to do to provide for his family. In those days and in that area it could be caretaking, guiding, cutting ice, carpentry work, and in Henry's case, working as a teamster with his trusty team.

"Much of his teamster duties centered on The Plains which, depending on the destination, was accessed through the trail from Seventh Lake Mountain by Bear Pond or Fawn Lake Mountain. A jumper was used for the Seventh Lake trail and a wagon for the Fawn Lake road.

"The jumper was a sled-type conveyance that was usually pulled by a single horse. Dora told me the whole family was constantly on the lookout for hardwood trees with just the right natural bend for replacement runners.

Mart continues, "Bill Apgar and Cousin Alfred (or 'Tip,' as he was known) were the best of friends and 'partners in crime,' so to speak. They were usually in trouble with Uncle Henry and Aunt Hattie over one boyhood prank or another. Bill recalled one such time.

"'We were back in camp and Uncle Henry had left us with the horses to water. A steep bank ran down to the stream and water normally was carried up to the horses.

"'Tip had a better idea that seemed a whole lot easier than lugging up heavy water pails. We would lead the horses to the water, which we did. Down the hill we tumbled, we and the horses, head over heels. Luckily, the horses were not injured. The only exception was a damaged horse harness.

"'Uncle Henry was not pleased with our decision. We ended up needing to lead the horses a considerable distance along the creek and through the brush to get back up the hill.'"

Allen concluded, "After all these years, my original impression of Henry Thibado and the Moose River Plains has not been a disappointment. This has been a good place to live and raise a family. People like Henry Thibado and his family have proven it."

Allen's personal memories mirror those of the many other people whose lives and activities constitute this informal social history.

Bill Apgar holding an old saw from his former upper Red River camp in May 1987. Apgar remembered: "Tip and I had many good times at my camp. The old Indian, Art Lucas, knew how to build a camp and keep it hidden. Two of the many tricks he used were to selectively cut the trees for the building low on the stump and then cover the stub with earth and forest duff. Then he used the natural ledges and foliage growing on it to camouflage it from view by building in a low visibility area.

"One fall day when I was at camp, Floyd Puffer came over to thank me for fifty dollars he had earned the day before. Seems an inexperienced deer hunter from Utica had been tying colored Christmas ribbon on branches and shrubs to mark his way into the forested Seventh Lake Mountain territory from Route 28. I came close behind untying the markers. When I caught up with the hunter, he expressed how tricky the woods were to travel in but that he had no problem because he was so good with a map and compass.

"I chuckled wildly to myself. Later that night I heard a series of gunshots. I knew they were from the 'experienced' hunter who was signaling he was lost to whoever heard, and that he needed direction from someone. That someone who came to his aid was **Puffer.**" *Photo by author*

AUTHOR'S NOTE

Gordy and Inez Rudd's Red & White Grocery Store

Before the small, independently owned and operated Red & White[2] country food stores, with their signature red dot logo, spread throughout the Adirondack Park's towns, there was usually one family member who distinguished herself as the best baker. Family members might claim her pies, cakes, doughnuts and salt-rising bread could equal or exceed any commercially produced product.

This was in the days when "Saratoga potatoes" originally appeared in the American diet. Anne Gertrude Sneller, who was my mother's English teacher in 1927 at North High School in Syracuse, remembered those days in her autobiography, *A Vanished World*. In that world, her Aunt Welt was one of the women in her church who could be trusted to make the new potato goodies. There were no commercial Saratoga potatoes (not yet called "chips") in the 1870s, so Aunt Welt and two other women were always selected to furnish them for church functions.

"I watched Aunt Welt the first time she ever made them," Anne Sneller wrote. "There was a large kettle of fresh fine lard boiling away over the wood fire; clean white towels covered the kitchen table; and, standing like a priestess before it, Aunt Welt cut the pared potatoes so thin they were transparent. Next she laid the slices in rows on the white cloths to absorb any bit of moisture, and, when all was ready, she dropped the slices into the boiling fat, leaving them only long enough to reach the right shade of golden brown. Then out they came, crisp and delectable, and were spread again on the cloths. A few less perfectly perfect ones were put aside to taste for salt and flavor, and I was allowed to sample these and report. The report was always favorable."

OPPOSITE: **Gordon "Gordy" and Inez were proprietors of their own small, independent Red & White grocery store in the Adirondack Mountains.** *Courtesy Gregory L. Rudd*

These seemingly unconnected thoughts of the country store and snack foods like potato chips come to mind because I clearly recall shopping at Rudds' Red & White store in Inlet, when my family camped each summer at nearby Eighth Lake Campground from the late 1940s through the early 1960s.

Rudd's Red & White grocery store was often the most sociable place in the rural Inlet community. Circa 1956. *Courtesy Gregory L. Rudd*

Rudds' storefront was filled with cases of soda pop, crates of watermelon and cantaloupes, bushel baskets and crates spilling over with vegetables and fruit, and sacks of potatoes. The shelves inside were lined with canned goods, packaged foods, commercial bread, and sweet breads. Mom and Dad swore by the quality of the meat Gordon "Gordy" Rudd kept inside the glass case in the butcher section of the store. I always hoped the grocery basket would also contain a big box of Jean's Potato Chips.

"There were no superhighways or streetlights, and visits of the mail boat, pickle boat, bakery and meat trucks were major events back in the 1920s when the Adirondacks were among the most popular vacation areas in the state. But no one ever complained of being bored with nothing to do." —Marion B.A. Tubbs, "Memories of Inlet," Syracuse *Post-Standard*, August 19, 1970. *Courtesy Town of Inlet Historical Society*

I remember Gordon telling my father about the Moose River Plains, about three miles from Eighth Lake Campground. Once the private lumber road opened to the public, my parents took a drive through The Plains, while my sister and I sat in the back seat hand-cranking the windows up to prevent clouds of dust from invading each time a car passed us on the narrow, bumpy dirt track.

The typical community store included a wide array of dry and canned goods sections, beverages, fresh produce, meats, smoking items, personal care products, and an array of convenience items. Wide-eyed children peered through the glass display at a selection of hard candies, candy bars, chewing gum, and sparklers that added gaiety for children building their own campground memories spent during Fourth of July weekend. There are still a few old country stores surviving throughout the rural North Country, but now they are without the wood-burning stove and a few sturdy rocking chairs around which once the weather, politics, local news, and hunting and fishing tips were exchanged. *Courtesy Gregory L. Rudd*

Evelyn Rudd outside Rudd's Red & White store. Buying and selling habits changed as roads improved, railroads became widespread and motor vehicles became commonplace. Farm products could be transported by rail and truck. The old-time Adirondack store may be for the most part a thing of the past, but nobody would deny how well it served its purpose and answered the needs of a growing mountain community. *Courtesy Gregory L. Rudd*

Aug 1935	21	2 Bread		24	
		1 Butter		35	
		C of Lima		14	
		C of Wheat		25	
		1 Bread		05	
	23	2 Bread		24	
		sugar		31	
		8 Chips		23	
		1 Potatoes		29	
		Peaches		23	
		2 C. Beef		48	
	24	Carrots		10	
		3 Bread		36	
		2 milk		26	
		1 Butter		35	
		2 cigarettes		20	
		Cookies		57	
		2 C Beef		24	
	25	1 coffee		33	
		1 peas		17	
		1 P. Butter		25	
		2 Bread		24	

Rudd's Red & White store sales slip. *Courtesy Gregory L. Rudd*

I don't recall if we took a picnic lunch on that first trip. I do recall that the backcountry was not like the woods I was used to, where we pitched our tent in the campground. We began at the gate at Limekiln Lake outside Inlet, turned east at the junction to the Indian Clearing or Big Plains, drove past Cedar River Flow and exited onto Route 30 at Indian Lake. At that point we drove to Blue Mountain Lake, where we turned south onto Route 28 and back to our Eighth Lake campsite. It was a long drive. I remember it as a wild but interesting territory.

I never forgot that deep wildland core of backwoods. The Plains was my destination when I had my first deer hunting experience in the latter years of the 1960s.

Armed with the state's official pamphlet, a general map and guide called "Moose River Recreation Area," and two dated 1954 U.S. Geological Survey maps (Old Forge and West Canada Lake), I quickly became a Moose River Plains enthusiast.

The official guide says the state purchased the core of this area "from the Gould Paper Company[3] in December 1963. Past logging activity and road development have had a great influence on both the natural resources of the area and use by the general public."

Gould Paper Company's 1960s "Access Map Moose River Area" provided an outstanding guide to the network of primary woods roads and secondary woods roads to follow to otherwise hard-to-reach places. Those same endpoints require good bushwhacking skills today because the network of logging roads is all grown over.

Throughout the end of the 1960s, the 1970s and 1980s, it seemed I not only doggedly covered every foot of the Moose River Country, but ferreted out historical information about the many man-made structures that used to exist back there. I talked to those who knew the country like the backs of their hands and knew its stories and historic background. A distant goal was, and still is, to assemble a complete accounting of the Moose River Plains. *Life Around the Indian Clearing* is only a small part of a much larger project.

My notes remind me that on March 20, 1988, I interviewed Gordy and Inez Rudd. Gordy talked about his illegal camps built back in the deep woodland of the Moose River Plains and how various rangers like Ernest

Blue tried to sucker him into disclosing that he had camps on state property. His last camp was on Gould Paper Company's property near the outlet of Bear Pond, so close to the border of J.P. Morgan's property that Gordy said he "could read the writing on Morgan's posted signs."

Gordy started a high proportion of his stories with "Well I remember..." "They were good men..." and "I'll tell you another place." His vocabulary was clear and straightforward and the pauses gave the effect of considered judgment. He liked to talk about the various Moose River Plains camps and the occupants, and he liked to listen. From him I learned the location of the Puffer Camp along the Red River. He also confirmed that the so-called cave along a high cliff face where I had found Indian Head pennies and some metal plates and cups was definitely what was locally known as the Bear Hunter's Cave.

Gordy's camps were built from timber cut in the vicinity. Most were considered temporary, with a canvas tarp for a roof, but he assured me that no matter how cold it might be, the occupants all slept comfortably, "like bugs in a rug," and ate far better than those who relied on salt pork and Johnny-cake. Owning the local grocery store was a plus when it came to good eating!

Besides my parents preference for the high-quality meat at Rudds' Red and White, I believe they enjoyed the family-store owners' friendliness and conversation, something I also learned to appreciate.

What follows are two recipes found in my mother's cookbook. She must have named them for a favorite memory of our Eighth Lake camping vacations. I still spend a lot of time back on The Plains bushwhacking, hiking, paddling, mountain biking, and camping. There are still places to explore, favorite scenic spots to revisit, and old sites I continue to find, like the recent discoveries of Camp Pauline near the outlet of Sumner Stream, the site of Adirondack guide Phil Christy's old Mosquito Camp, and the elusive remains of Camp English and Camp Savage.

OPPOSITE: **Lt. to Rt. The author stands beside his sister Judy and father, William Joseph "Cowboy" O'Hern II at their Eighth Lake campsite. The box of Jean's Potato Chips on the picnic table was purchased from Rudd's grocery store.** *Photo by Marjorie Z. O'Hern. Author's collection*

Rudd's Red & White Steak

This was an old standby iron skillet favorite at camp, at home and in the campground. I named it after Inez and Gordon Rudds' Red & White store in Inlet where we bought our meat when tent camping in the Fulton Chain. (Mom's note reports it cost $1.79 to purchase the ingredients in 1953.)

Ingredients:
3 pounds rolled boneless beef chuck
1 tablespoon salt
1/2 teaspoon pepper
flour
3 medium onions, sliced
1 large green pepper, sliced
fat (amount is left to the cook's discretion)
19-ounce can of tomatoes
1/2 teaspoon thyme
1/2 teaspoon celery salt
1 tablespoon prepared mustard
3/4 cup cooked peas

Directions: Wipe meat with damp cloth; slice in 6 steaks. Season with salt and pepper, and dredge with flour. In skillet, cook onions and pepper in melted fat until tender. Remove from skillet. Put meat in skillet and brown on both sides, turning carefully. Top meat with onions and pepper. Add tomatoes and seasonings; cover and simmer about 1 1/2 hours until meat is tender. Add peas. Makes 6 servings.

Fulton Chain Beef Stew 'n' Herb Dumplings

This was another cast iron pan recipe. Mom said it was "A solid meal with feather-light dumplings." The ingredients cost $2.00 in 1953. When camping at Eighth Lake Campground, we used to purchase fresh vegetables and fruit from both Kalil's Grocery and Rudds' Red & White store.

Ingredients:
3 pounds boneless beef chuck
flour [amount is left to cook's discretion.]
1 medium onion, chopped
3 tablespoons fat
1 bay leaf
1 teaspoon celery seed
1 tablespoon salt
1/2 teaspoon pepper
1 pound green beans, cut
herb dumplings

Directions: Wipe meat with damp cloth; cut in 11/2-inch cubes; roll in flour. Brown with onion in fat in large, heavy kettle. Add bay leaf, celery seed, salt, pepper, and 3 cups of water; cover; simmer for 11/2 hours. Add beans, and cook for 15 minutes longer, or until meat and beans are tender. If desired, thicken stew with flour mixed with a little cold water. Drop dumpling batter from tablespoon into gently boiling stew. Cover; cook for 15 minutes. Serves 6 to 8 people.

Herb Dumplings

Ingredients:
3 cups sifted cake flour
11/4 teaspoon baking powder
1 teaspoon salt
2 tablespoons shortening
2 tablespoons chopped fresh herbs, or 2 teaspoons
    dried herbs, or 1 teaspoon poultry seasoning
1 cup milk, minus 1 tablespoon

Directions: Sift dry ingredients. Blend in shortening with fork. Add herbs and milk. Mix lightly just until flour is moistened.

October 19, 1922. Adirondack guide George Fallon's hunting party's camp on the Moose River Plains. *Courtesy Joan Davis*

Part One

Adirondack Mountains

Moose River Plains

Early Adirondack Camping

Woodsloafer

A woodsloafer needs no other reason,
For there is the lake, and here is the season;
And in the deep woods, and out on the stream
A woodsloafer is stopping to dream.

Here is the place where the river parts,
Here is the spot where the inlet starts;
There swim the trout of yesteryear,
There run the amber-spotted deer.

Here is his boat by the water's edge
And under a spruce, near a rocky ledge,
There is his tent by the drifting stream.
This is the pathway to his dream.

The noisy world is a mist blown by;
All that he hears is the plover's cry.
He smells pond lilies' night perfume;
His compass is the crescent moon.

Now that it's summer, the perfect season,
A woodsloafer needs no other reason.

—Elsie Wilkins, Utica, N.Y. Summer 1956

Chapter One

Squatting and Camping
on State Land

ATWELL, NEW YORK, is a small, remote Adirondack hamlet that sits at the headwaters of the mighty Black River. The basin in which it resides, first known as Lake Sophia, received its new name from renowned hermit Atwell Martin, who called the wilderness home after the Army Corps of Engineers built a dam at the foot of the lake in the 1850s. Martin's name became part of the headwaters' cartographic history.

Some old-time natives held that posted signs had the same effect on them as a red flag waved at a bull. *Courtesy Robert J. Elinskas*

OPPOSITE: **Wild land is an integral part of a balanced, civilized territory, just as tilled land and city blocks form the other integral parts. The primeval influence is an integral part of a balanced, civilized mental state just as the influence of the rural wayside and city street compose the other basic elements of such a state.... I enjoy the high lights of Broadway as also the aroma of the new-mown hayfield, and with them both the frog chorus of the dank and distant muskeg. All three elements are needed, urban, rural and primeval, if a molecule of human living is truly to survive. —Benton MacKaye, president, The Wilderness Society, 1946.** *Courtesy Meredith Flerlage*

Atwell was not an easy Adirondack neighborhood to reach over what was once a deplorable, pitchy, winding dirt road, and the area was never one that carried widespread name recognition. Yet today's sportspeople, campers

George Wandover stands by his Gooseneck Lake cabin built on Forest Preserve property, circa 1890s. According to the law on private parks dating back to 1871, private preserves must be posted every forty rods and defaced signs must be renewed each year. It needs only the imagination to recognize how simple it was for an irate group of hunters to wreck these signs. The Adirondack League Club started out by using very durable signs of heavy metal that were highly enameled. They were quickly appropriated by the woodsmen and adapted to all sorts of uses from reflectors on lanterns used in jacklighting deer to the sardonic humor of roofing outhouses in use at the turn of the century. With the disappearance of the expensive porcelain enameled signs, cheaper ones made of cloth were used, but the hunters seemed to find as many uses for cloth as they did for tin. *Courtesy Edward Blankman (The Lloyd Blankman Collection)*

4

and tourists have the same devotion to the bodies of water, forest and wildlife surrounding Atwell and reaching on into the wild Moose River Plains that others do to more high-profile Adirondack locations. Atwell appears very quaint and beautiful to me because of the surviving tiny old-time log and clapboard camps and cottages sited along the lake. Atwell wears a colorful coat indeed, but what I learned when I rented Nat Foster Lodge was a bit of hidden history, an attitude of general disdain toward the Adirondack League Club (ALC), a large private preserve, and New York State's Conservation Commission[4] over questions of land access and use.

August 16, 1904. The Rev. A.L. Byron-Curtiss stands next to 37 legal-sized trout caught in the Middle Branch of the Black River. The Reverend said he read the Adirondack League Club's "No Trespassing" signs as saying, "Good Fishing and Hunting Here!"
Entries in The Reverend's early camp journals make light sport of his trespass and poaching on ALC's, Gould Paper Company's and state-owned land. It's an example of the degree some would go to in order to thumb their nose at any regulation of their freedom of movement. *Courtesy Thomas and Doris Kilbourn*

"The Dirty Dozen," a group of trouble-makers in the Atwell-Forestport area as far back as 1897, regularly stepped outside the law. Their focus was "dedicated to the promotion of minor irritations, insofar as these might

5

discourage attempts at over-zealous enforcement of the [ALC's] trespass laws," Thomas C. O'Donnell wrote in his history of the area.

ABOVE AND OPPOSITE: **Occupancy of small and large illegal buildings on Forest Preserve land went unchecked for years.** *Courtesy Town of Webb Historical Society*

Charles B. Sperry reported that his grandfather, Charles T. Sperry, "was embroiled many times in trespassing disputes with the Adirondack League Club." The posted warnings informed the public they were not welcome on private preserve land. Up to that time, vast tracts of remote wilderness land dotted with lakes, streams and rivers had been freely used by natives, guides and sports who came to camp, hunt and fish. Their freedom to use the land was reduced and finally eliminated due to purchases by prominent and wealthy families and clubs, "who were attracted to the idea of traveling to the mountains to experience nature and outdoor activities in extremely private yet luxurious surrounding," wrote Wesley Haynes and James Jacobs in *The Adirondack Camp in American Architecture.*

Raymond S. Spears addressed a letter to the editor of *Forest and Stream* in 1898 questioning the closing of the ALC's vast sportsmen's possessions that stretched from West Canada Creek to Moose River, and "north further than I know about. The League is getting pretty gay. Now they forbid any one going across their land. They have a man at North Lake to stop any one."

Spears's letter seems to show an understanding that the first thing most new landowners do is post signs to inform the public they are not welcome— that these are no longer Adirondack lands but lands of such-and-such party. Spears went on to question the closure of such old and long-popular routes as the old Bisby trails, which he believed were former "Indian paths," stretching from the northern end of North Lake to Canachagala Lake and blazed more than forty years before his letter. These had been "a public highway for hunters, fishermen and campers of every class, from pure market-profit seekers to the beauty hunters, and recreators[sic]."

Posted warnings such as "No Trespassing—Violators will be prosecuted to the full extent of the law" and "Lines patrolled—Keep Out!" infuriated neighboring landowners, central Adirondack guides and sports who had previously used the open land. Sperry continued, "The no trespassing signs had the same effect on my grandfather as a red flag to a bull."

There was also resentment toward New York State's Conservation Commission and its legal maneuverings when the Commission began questioning the legality of long-time squatters' camps such as Kenwell's Sportsman's Hostelry, sited beside the south branch of the Moose River, and a short distance beyond, the Wilks D. Dodge, Rev. Byron-Curtiss, Charles T. Sperry, and George E.C. Kenyon camps, and Camp Cozy, constructed by Emily Mitchell Wires's grandparents sometime around 1870 to, according to Wires, "serve as a stop-over on the way to and from Horn Lake." These camps are all examples of squatters' structures that came under state scrutiny. The allegation was that the camps were on state land, and worse, that the state had been "tipped off," in the case of the North Lake reservoir buildings, by fractious ALC staff.

N.Y.S. Game Protector Maynard Phelps. In 1899 J.W. Pond, chief fish and game protector of the state, traveled throughout the Adirondacks to learn first-hand how the laws were being enforced. He learned the laws for the most part was being upheld but found that the further one got back in the woods the less the laws were observed.
Courtesy Edward Blankman (The Lloyd Blankman Collection)

The Sperrys assert their original cabin was built on land purchased during the 1880s from Atwell Martin, the original hermit of North Lake. Charles B. Sperry reported, "My grandfather, Charles T. Sperry, purchased his original camp site from Atwell. I have seen the original deed whereby Atwell purchased that land from another party, although no money was paid.

Little or big, the state burned all camps on Forest Preserve land.
Courtesy Lyons Falls History Association

"That deed was in my grandfather's possession. It listed the items by which Atwell Martin paid for the land with …cornmeal, bear traps, salt pork, sugar, salt and coffee, axes, knives, and so forth—acceptable items in payment of such a transaction at that time."

"At that time" meant in the early 1850s. This misguided and illegal selling of public lands, often by squatters making sales to outsiders, later led to complexities that arose when the Conservation Commissioner determined that, whatever might be done regarding present occupants of state lands, no further occupations would occur if the commission could prevent it.

By 1915, when Governor Whitman appointed George D. Pratt, Treasurer of Pratt Institute and President of the Camp Fire Club of America, to fill the important post of New York's Conservation Commissioner, a new stimulus was given to the whole conservation movement with which Commissioner Pratt has been closely identified.

Following the turn of the century, maps, brochures and information on how to hunt and fish became widely available. The monopoly guides once had on knowing how to get around and care for themselves in the wilds diminished. Where once the general public pursued their outdoor activities with little regard—hounding, jacking, luring with salt and meat baits, snubbing trespass laws, building on Forest Preserve land, cutting wood on State land and even operating illegal stills—better education and public opinion put values into the sport, improving personal income for Adirondackers, raising families' standard of living and leading, with tighter law enforcement, to a successful result. The Adirondack Mountains were going to be regulated, but that regulation would ensure the region's preservation. *Courtesy C.V. Latimer Jr. M.D.*

Among the important accomplishments of the Pratt administration was its management of the "squatter" problem. Historian Alfred L. Donaldson wrote in 1921 in *A History of the Adirondacks Vol. 2*, "For years there have been hundreds of cases of illegal occupancy of State lands, of which the authorities were fully aware, but the situation has been complicated by title uncertainty, political influence, and purely human sympathy. The result has been a Gordian knot, which no commissioner made any serious attempt to cut until it reached Mr. Pratt. He, however, by using both firmness and tact, succeeded in eliminating some seven hundred cases out of a heritage of over nine hundred."

A typical open camp or lean-to on state-owned property, 1919. Central Adirondack guide George Fallon built this for his hunting and fishing parties. *Courtesy Joan Davis*

"After some investigation," I reported in *Under an Adirondack Influence* (The Forager Press, 2008), "several of the camp owners concluded that the allegation was probably true. A number of owners hired an attorney in 1917, and with his help submitted a Record of Occupancy claim to the State of New York Conservation Commission. This in effect gave the camp owners a reprieve. At least until the state made a ruling."

These were some of the same difficulties folks were facing throughout the mixture of private and state-owned Forest Preserve land throughout the Adirondack Park.

To many of the residents and the guides who relied for a portion of their living on the millions of acres of Forest Preserve lands that were protected by law, residents might have appeared to some like lost souls simply looking for a way to eke out a living in order to live beyond poverty. The Conservation

Commission's move probably felt like the gates of hell opening, trying to swallow the freedom to use Forest Preserve land that they had always enjoyed.

An article in *The Evening Post* on Saturday, July 1, 1916, summarized the problem of squatters in the Adirondack Park. The writer, Raymond S. Spears, was a special correspondent. His father, Eldridge A. Spears, was a well-known journalist for the *New York Sun* newspaper. The Spears family owned a camp at North Woods, near Hinckley reservoir, and their son John R. was also a noted writer. Both Raymond and John had traveled the Adirondacks extensively. As reported in *Under an Adirondack Influence*, the brothers "had visited the woodsman-hermit 'French Louie' Seymour, who lived deep in the West Canada Lakes country. The Speares were ardent champions of preservation of the Adirondack forest and were interested in the folklore and legends of the Great Northern Woods." They and their father always had plenty to talk about around a summer evening campfire when they visited Rev. A.L. Byron-Curtiss, owner of Nat Foster Lodge.

It was the discovery of Byron-Curtiss's vast collection of diaries, correspondence and personal writing that brought my attention to his legal battle over the ownership of the land his original Atwell camp rested on. His individual crusade to save the camp mirrored those of hundreds of other early camp owners.

On May 16, 1922, Ranger Ernest W. Blue received this order from C. R. Pettis, Superintendent, Division of Lands and Forests in Old Forge. "...watch your opportunity and when [Byron-Curtiss's] camp is not personally occupied tear it down and so report..."

On June 6, 1922, Charley Brown, a friend who watched over Nat Foster Lodge, called Byron-Curtiss to report that rangers from the Conservation Commission had torn down his beloved shanty, where he had enjoyed over twenty pleasurable summers.

Activity like that had been taking place throughout the state-owned Adirondack land for years. Raymond Spears's report brings the entire matter into focus. The headline read:

OPPOSITE. **Raymond Spears pointed to the guides and the packs of sports they led, and often built permanent camps for, as being partly at fault for land squatting. Adirondack guides often joined forces to develop new trails.** *Courtesy North Elba-Lake Placid Historical Society*

**"TENT ERA NOW AT HAND IN THE ADIRONDACKS:
No More Permanent Camps on State Lands."** Guides Resentful
over Destruction of their shacks by the Conservation Commission—Boat Houses also Destroyed—Source of Revenue in the
Past is no More—Trappers feel the working of the Law the Most.

According to all accounts some Adirondack guides are very
resentful against the Conservation Commission because of the
order, promulgated some time ago, that all permanent structures
on state land in the Adirondacks be destroyed.

It was not uncommon for guides to hunt while ignoring the State's regulations of deer
hunting, which became over the years more stringent and correspondingly more repug-
nant to them; thus, the more solitude the better, so it's understandable they would seek
a place back in and on a complete squatter basis. *Courtesy Town of Webb Historical Association*

Spears reported about a large number of sporting camps and homes that
had been torn down and/or burned once the buildings were proven to have
been built on state land. Among those affected were "outlying" and "guides'
camps erected in the backwoods—camps which the owners had grown to
believe were theirs until the roofs toppled in."

Clarence Petty outside his Coreys, N.Y. childhood home, November 1995. Petty recalled his family once lived in a squatter's shanty on state land until the Forest, Fish and Game Commission decided squatters seriously impacted the land as a result of their illegal timber cutting. Petty said his father's good friend, Game Warden Jason Vosburgh, stopped by one day to deliver the message that he was sorry, but it was his duty to inform the Petty family that "all squatters have gotta get off state land." *Photo by the author*

Clarence Petty said in a September 2002 interview with Brad Edmondson, "I lived on state land at that time, and my father built his cabins wherever it was convenient, and it happened to be on state land." That was long before anyone gave a thought to occupying state land. Petty's parents' first home was a large canvas tent on a wooden platform on state property in 1901. They were among hundreds labeled "squatters" less than twenty years later, when Governor Whitman appointed George D. Pratt to the position of Conservation Commissioner.

Under the subtitle "Squatter problem solved," Alfred L. Donaldson, in *A History of the Adirondacks, Part II* (Harbor Hill Books, 1977) quotes from the state's 1915 report:

> Among the notable advances of the Pratt administration has
> been its handling of the 'squatter' problem. For years, there

have been hundreds of cases of illegal occupancy of State lands, of which the authorities were fully aware, but the situation has been complicated by title uncertainty, political influence, and purely human sympathy. The result has been a Gordian knot, which no commissioner made any serious attempt to cut until it reached Mr. Pratt. He, however, by using both firmness and tact, succeeded in eliminating some seven hundred cases out of a heritage of over nine hundred.

Adirondack guide Eugene Scrafford's Eighth Lake hotel. Tip Thibado recalled: "My father remembers Stafford's hotel at Eighth Lake. The state of New York wanted that building out of there since the land was in their possession, but because the owners had built, maintained and operated it for quite a while without the state ever questioning the fact that it was on public land, the owners claimed squatters' rights, that as long as they maintained possession of it they believed they could keep it. On the off-tourist season they always had a caretaker—well really a guard—stationed to watch over it. Well, the state hired a man to lure the guard down to Seventh Lake one year and while he was occupied, game protectors burned the wooden two-story frame structure down. This was long before the Civilian Conservation Corps camp was built there in 1933." *Courtesy Irene Blakeman Lerdahl Collection, Inlet Historical Society*

A popular open camp design. *Courtesy Lyons Falls History Association*

The Spears article makes clear people might have considered the Forest Preserve a "gift" that belonged to them and not the bureaucracy of the State of New York.

> Judging from the outcry, perhaps hundreds of camps have been burned by the forest patrols of the Conservation Commission. The camps have included some very fine cottages in which various politicians, wealthy city men and similar people of self-assumed importance had squatted [on] the public playground. These fancy camps have been in prominence in courts and on State lands for time out of mind, the first noteworthy ones being on Lake George where, under a lease system thirty years ago certain favored ones caught their hooks into the public play land as the saying is, and held on through thick and thin from that time.

The commission did not view the value of outlying camps as problematic. By and large the camps were small—eight-by-ten feet. Log walls were generally spruce. Roof shingles were split from blocks of spruce. A hand-split board door and a four-pane window sash completed the simple shelter that was well-chinked with moss and clay. A stove was brought in from some near-by logging camp or carried in from the settlements. A few dishes and cooking utensils and a few old blankets and quilts comprised the usual furnishings. The typical camp could last ten or fifteen years under the best of circumstances.

Cost of Private Camps

Spears described the occupants' use of the shanties:

> Such camps are used by fishing parties during the summer, hunters during the autumn and by trappers during the winter. A city man ordering such a camp constructed would have to pay from sixty to one hundred dollars for a small private camp of this type. Perhaps the total outlay of a guide or woodsman on such a camp of this kind would be fifteen dollars and two or three days of packing in the ten or fifteen dollars' worth of articles…say eight days at three dollars a day or thirty-four dollars all told.

A sportsman identified only as "F.B." came yearly to the Adirondacks from Hartford, Connecticut. In a *Forest and Stream* story he described the log cabin that his guide, Uncle Chauncey Smith, had erected for his hunting and fishing parties as "not an inviting spot for camping, although a great many parties seek its shelter, as it saves building one… ." The camp had lasted fifteen years by the time F.B. arrived in 1874.

> Pushing open the door to the main building, we enter. It certainly is not very inviting. Everything smells mouldy [sic] and looks dirty. An old stove, early worn out, stands at one end of the room, while the middle is graced by a rough board table with seats. A match, one or two old candlesticks and a few old

broken dishes stand on it, and from pegs driven into the wall hang old powder horns, minus the powder, rusty guns, frying pans, and all the odds and ends that could be thought of. Leading out from the back of the room are two closets or cells, with bunks like a steamboat, with dirty ticks filled with hay and covered with damp mould [sic]. In the rear we found some bunks filled with freshly cut hay from grass which grows around the cabin, and as the glass was out of the one window in the room, the air was much better. There was also an old stove in this room, and as the punkies and mosquitoes were plenty, we started a smudge in the hopes of smoking them out.

State land was clearly posted. *Courtesy Town of Webb Historical Association*

The Forest and Stream's "No More Permanent Camps" article continues:

These little camps were formerly constructed wherever the woodsman guided or wherever the sportsman wanted them. There were many of them along Moose River from Canacha-gala Stillwater up to the Pine Plains, a distance of fifteen miles or so. They ranged in size and importance from mere bark lean-tos to commodious structures like the old Kenwell place and Beecher Camp at the head of The Plains Stillwater.

A son of Henry Ward Beecher had a camp at the head of The Plains Stillwater twenty years ago (1896). It was a peeled-log, hewed-log, shingled-roof structure. A beautiful large fireplace was in one end under an old-fashioned plastered stone chimney. The camp was furnished with numerous luxuries for the deep woods and some of the best hunting in the Adirondacks was had within shouting distance of the door.

A later-day state-built lean-to. *Dante O. Tranquille photo. Courtesy Town of Webb Historical Association*

A clearly-posted notice identifying State Lands. *Courtesy Town of Webb Historical Association*

It was a two-or-three day journey to get to this noted camp.
It was one of several camps including the White Camp two
miles down the stillwater, the Natural Dam camp, a half-a-mile
below the White camp, and two or three temporary camps and
rare tent sites. Upstream from the Beecher camp were a number
of camps which were built and then rotted down in due course
in the [Wellington] Kenwell neighborhood.

Politicians in the Adirondacks

It was here that the State began to show its hand under the
remarkable political regime which developed in Adirondack
affairs in the [18]90s, when the downstate politicians appeared
in the wilderness, when the State began to buy land for its

Park. [Lt. Governor of New York] Woodruff obtained the Sumner Lake tract, which was soon surrounded by tens of thousands of acres of State land including The Plains, where the old Kenwell Hotel and Beecher's camp were located. The patrons of Kenwell's camp hunted the State lands below Woodruff's private preserve [Kamp Kill Kare]. The parties of hunters who came into The Plains and killed deer down the stillwater from Beecher's camp made the deer on the State land around Woodruff's camp "wild" and hard to get.

An unidentified member of George Fallon's hunting party snapped this photo in late October 1918. Fallon often guided sportsmen in the Moose River Plains. The location is somewhere along the Brown's Tract road. *Courtesy Joan Davis*

The State accordingly burned the old Beecher camp and Kenwell was hunted out of the establishment, which he had made notable among Adirondack sportsmen. That is to say the public was practically driven from that part of the State's preserve. Incidentally, numerous trails and roads leading across the barrier to private preserves were closed, and people seeking to visit State lands were told to "go around," where there were no trails to go around, and no way of getting around.

According to Spears's understanding, the state's policy burning of camps on state land seems to have begun when politicians and influential preserve owners wanted to "keep the public away from camps placed on private lands of questionable title in the midst of vast tracts of state land bought at exorbitant price from people who sometimes doubtless had less title and claim to the land than the state which paid for it." He cited as examples "the Upper Saranac Lake region and in the Fulton Chain country."

He pointed out:

> In those land and woods-grabbing days, guides frequently appeared as offenders. There are accounts in the old reports which show that the guides squatted on State lots. They also served the men who went into the woods seeking lands to take over from the State's possession, for many of them used to boast of the assistance they rendered in locating various land-tracts. For years, the guides who helped Adirondack visitors most in violating the law against jacking, summer deer-killing, and wanton killing were among the most noted and best-paid of the servers of summer and autumn visitors.

"Raquette Lake—Eagle Bay Boulevard." Leaving an Adirondack hunting vacation in October 1918 had challenges in the past. *Courtesy Joan Davis*

Clarence Petty weighed in on Spears's finding.

> My father was dependent on "sports" coming in, and my
> brother and I were guides here. We depended on people com-
> ing in from outside and we were getting money from those
> people. We weren't getting it from the land sub-dividers and
> the people that wanted development here. Now I could see
> when they had logging here and they were getting money from
> the sawing of logs and the mines were working. We were taking
> stuff out of the area, which is nonrenewable resources, really.
> We often think of forestry as a renewable resource, which it is,
> but we don't live long enough to plant a tree and wait 120 years
> until that gets to timber, so it's really not a renewable resource
> in a way. It takes 35 years just to get a tree up to pulp size. So
> I see these people, the majority of them coming around to the
> realization that this area is valuable as a magnet for people coming
> from outside.

Car-camping in the Forest Preserve. *Courtesy Lyons Falls History Association*

Tent camping at Seventh Lake, summer 1929. *Courtesy Town of Webb Historical Association*

By 1906, the *Journal of Outdoor Life* estimated there were "upwards of 1,000 men who render service to summer visitors in the capacity of guides and oarsmen. As a class they are fine-looking men, well built, and generally intelligent. The guides of the southern Adirondacks have an association of which the name is the Brown's Tract Guides' Association, and the guides of the northern Adirondacks, including the Saranacs, the St. Regis, Long Lake, Lake Placid, and other waters are organized under an association called the Adirondack Guides' Association. The objects of these organizations are to promote and facilitate travel; secure competent and reliable guides;

to aid in the enforcement of the fish and game laws, and to secure wise and practical legislation upon all subjects affecting the interests of the Adirondack region."

Spears pointed to the guides and the packs of sports they led as being partly at fault.

The advent of travel trailers brought a new level of camping comfort.
Dante O. Tranquille photo. Courtesy Town of Webb Historical Association

In one way, the Adirondack guides were at the bottom of the State land-squatting. From their little camps they took the visitors out into the woods and the squatting continued to wax until large hotels were put on State lands and on private lands of questionable ownership. The presence of these woodsmen's places on State lands suggested to visitors that they too could build on them, and there is no doubt but what the years of litigation and squatting on Raquette Lake began in the work of the woodsmen and guides themselves in seizing State lands there, first by little hunting camps and then by permanent hotels, which were joined by the huge and picturesque cottages which to this day are one of the vexatious problems of the Conservation Commission.

Conservation Commission Active

When Chief Game Protector John B. Burnham[5] under Commissioner [James S.] Whipple undertook to eject Raquette Lake squatters, money was supplied to the "poor guides" for the purpose of saving them from the pain and anguish of relinquishing their camps and homes upon State lands. The activity of the Conservation Commission has been very great for the past few months. The local forest patrols have gone into the woods and destroyed the camps, which they could find. They burned boat houses, as the one on Metcalf Lake, and they swept the woods around Fulton Chain, where there have been many offenders in the line of more or less permanent structures on public land. Little or no trouble was experienced for the reason that none of the camps destroyed was occupied at the time.

The little structures were cold when the patrols arrived between the winter trapping and the spring fishing. It was simply a matter of dragging the boats out from under the trees, taking out all the camping outfits, hanging up the quilts and blankets, leaning the folding cots against the trees and starting a fire in the corners with the dry firewood left for the next comer. The dry camps burned rapidly, and in their destruction, a difficult question was answered.

But the owners of these camps, the guides who built them and in some measure the patrons of the guides, have taken common cause in declaring that the restoring of the wilderness to its primitive condition, as the Constitution says it must be kept, is "red tape," and that the Commission is not using "common-sense" in the matter.

It was exactly thus that the old timber thieves and game hogs and fish hogs argued when the law was invoked against them. In the old days, the victims of enforced laws declared that they would burn the woods. There is little doubt that violators have destroyed tens of thousands of acres of green timber in the Adirondacks in the past. But the members of the guides' fraternity in the Adirondacks do not say they will burn the woods. What they say is that if the woods catch fire, they will not lift a finger to put the fires out, not to save the woods for the Conservation Commission to protect.

Petty again weighed in on the lifestyle of making a living and surviving at the turn of the last century. He witnessed many game law violations.

My brother and I used to go into the town hall when they had these game law violations back in the teens, 1912, '13, '14, and there were outlaws galore. It was considered smart if you could outsmart a game warden. Game wardens were targets. Everybody was against the game wardens. It took over a quarter of a century before they started taking game law cases out of the Adirondacks and started getting convictions. There was one guy in Saranac Lake who was a notorious game law violator. He'd kill deer out of season, catch trout out of the lake when you're not supposed to in the winter, do all kinds of things, and that was considered smart.

Spears's article concludes:

> Yet the fact is now recognized by intelligent sportsmen and
> guides that a permanent structure of any kind on State land
> gives the owner of that structure undue privileges. It is his camp,
> and he takes his parties into it for the summer months, and
> others who camp in that locality are regarded as and made to
> feel like trespassers by the guide and his parties.

Hounding (pursuing game with dogs) was a common form of hunting. Some Adirondack
guides continued to channel clients and their savvy-snouted, trail-toughened working
gun dogs to remote areas in the mountains, such as the Moose River Plains, long after
the passage of the Curtis Hounding Law of 1884–85. *Courtesy North Elba Historical Society*

Removing Permanent Structures

The only solution to the problems is that adapted by the Conservation Commission. The permanent structures on State land
must go as fast as the law will permit. Their places must be taken
by tents. The tent may be pitched anywhere: the heat required
for cooking and warming is amply supplied by dead and down
timber. This dead and down timber gives a bad smoke and is
less useful than the green hardwoods that used to be cut—yet
the tent can be pitched beside the wind-and snow-felled
birches and other hardwoods. The big firewood gashes cut in

the woods around permanent camps have long been a disgrace to the administration of the State lands. The tents used will prevent the cutting of these little clearings, for every year the tent will be pitched near wood and moved from site to site so that none will be able to claim any place as his own, and yet the wood will be free to all.

The Adirondack State land camping must be done in tents in the future. The tents will cost the guides who supply them to their patrons from $10.00 to $50.00, according to the kind of tent supplied. Often the patrons will furnish their own tents, and the guides, in order to preserve the tents year after year, will find that they must carry galvanized iron barrels or other receptacles into the wood to hold them.

Those who will suffer most by the destruction of the permanent camps on State lands are the trappers, and no doubt most of them will find means to escape the burden. Some will build little hidden camps deep in gullies and swamps; others will simply locate on private lands in outlying club preserve shelters.

I believe Spears's article in *The Evening Post* is a tidy digest of a toothy issue New York State had to address. This battle to protect New York State's "forever wild" land resulted in hard feelings, finger-pointing and sharp name-calling, alleged arson, and accusations, but in the end it kept state land protected, and today trees in the natural forest "grow, fall, rot, and provide food for the next generation of trees," wrote William Chapman White in *Adirondack Country*—an Adirondack book worthy of being the backbone for collectors' bookshelves.

Restoration of state land led the Conservation Commission's administration to deliberate a new way of outdoor recreation that included three of the public's most popular pastimes—fishing, hunting, and camping. The *Report of the Conservation Commission* for 1919 signified a distinct and sudden swing in viewpoint to a significant willingness to educate the public through lectures, news articles, educational materials, and the Commission's illustrated monthly magazine—*The Conservationist*. In addition, this year marked the first time private funds were used to help the state purchase additional land that would be added to the Forest Preserve—"the most important public vacation grounds in the United States," the report stated.[6]

New rules were made, open camps were erected during the teens by the Adirondack Camp & Trail Association over the mountains in the vicinity of Lake Placid, and new regulations by Commissioner Pratt encouraged a fuller use of the Forest Preserve and urged users to guard against the danger of many camp fires improperly placed.

The automobile created new ways to vacation. It spurred road-building projects and designated roadside campsites complete with fireplaces to help prevent forest fires. There were simple wooden tent platforms on state land. After 1922, the Adirondack Mountain Club (ADK) and state workers began to establish marked hiking trails. State-built public campsites that included indispensable water and sewage facilities followed.

Some descendants of guides, trappers, and camp and cottage owners who were squatters on property they did not own may still bear grudges against the state for destroying what they felt was theirs. For the most part, though, as environmental awareness and knowledge increase, most people understand why the state's actions were necessary to avoid exploitation of an incomparable treasure of wilderness.

It did not take long for those who love the Adirondacks to adjust to the "new tent era" headlined in Spears's article. The very word "camp" took on new meaning, and tent camping was just the beginning of a whole new way to enjoy the magnificent mountains, imposing forests, and sparkling waters.

An addendum: It is not the purpose of this chapter to analyze the issue of state lands that were squatted on, to question and examine how the Kenwells came to acquire the property on which they developed their Sportsman's Home on The Plains, or to offer any scholarly research.

Two (among other) interesting newspaper articles that shed further light and focus on these issues are "Lands Lost Through Negligence," *The Evening Post*, New York, Thursday, December 7, 1905, and "Did State Help to Entertain Guests of the Woodruffs?" *The Thrice-A-Week World*, Wednesday, August 31, 1910.

In the Adirondacks

Pine Tree campers on the Indian Clearing. *Drawing by Sheri Amsel*

The Indian Clearing, also referred to as the Big Plains, is a popular location to pick blueberries, watch birds and butterflies and look at wildflowers. *William J. O'Hern photo*

Chapter Two

Pine Tree Camp, Moose River Plains in 1873

TRY DEFINING VACATION. Simply, *taking a vacation is often* a necessary break in life's routine. But, when I attempted to widen the definition beyond my center of expectations, I wasn't surprised to find there is no one easy definition. A single person's vacation is different from a couple's vacation, and a couple's vacation time is different from that of couples who vacation with children. Personal preferences influence what constitutes a vacation, as do one's financial resources.

And, what is the "ideal" spot?

A vacation can be like riding a rollercoaster with lots of ups, downs, twists and turns! I learned a bit about a remarkable Adirondack vacation when I met with Farrand N. Benedict Jr. at his East Lake Road home in Skaneateles, New York. On that day he handed me a copy of a collection of handwritten letters that described an unbelievable arrangement of trips in 1873 made by a collection of ladies who planned to connect at "the lake of the skies," their expression for Blue Mountain Lake.

In the spring of 1873, a group of idealistic and scientific-minded women who chose to assume names related to goddesses or characters from Greek and Roman mythology decided to leave civilization on an adventurous botanical expedition to study nature—particularly botany in the heart of the Adirondacks' millions-of-acres of wild land. Guided by thirteen of the most reputable guides of the day, Themis (Miss Steele), the head of the botanists, drew up plans to split the women into four groups:

1. The Schroon River Section
2. The Saranac Party
3. The Moose River Party
4. The Lake Pleasant Section

She wrote of the teams:

> Ladies are much better qualified for the varied and arduous
> duties of such an expedition by their power of observation, their
> patient and persevering industry, no less than by their delicate
> touch in the manipulation of instruments and the minute organs
> of plants and by their intuitive sense of the beautiful.

I was most interested in the Lake Pleasant and Moose River parties that Amanda Benedict reported because of my experience with that area of the Adirondacks—in fact I felt a sense of connectedness with the troupe's vacation routes, having bushwhacked through much of the same territory.

In 1873, by the time the women were working their way along the tributaries of the Hudson, Black and Moose rivers, the wilderness had not yet been opened by a system of roads. People were still sprinkled through-

The Expedition

**A page from the report:
"The Journey" prepared by the women
in the Lake Pleasant party.**

out the wilderness in isolated cabins and clustered in small settlements through-out the mountains. The majority of men supported themselves logging and guiding vacationing "sports," hunters and anglers, who had most often been enamored by the writings of William H.H. Murray's *Adventures in the Wilderness* in 1869. There are numerous references to Murray's book in the letters written by the leaders of the four expedition groups, as well as to an earlier work, attributed to C.H. Burt in the *Adirondack Bibliography*, titled *Opening of the Adirondacks*, written in 1865.

Recognizing that my interest in the letters primarily centered about the events along the south branch of the Moose River and the Indian Plains, I contacted Barbara McMartin because of her enthusiastic interest in botany.

34

A page from the expedition's table of contents.

Barbara was a keen observer of fungi, lichens, ferns, wild flowers-really anything related to plant investigation and geology. There would be no one else more perfectly suited to take the material and do it justice.

After exhaustive investigation and years of work, McMartin wrote *To the Lake of the Skies: The Benedicts in the Adirondacks.* Her book brought to light two never-before-published manuscripts that give new insight into

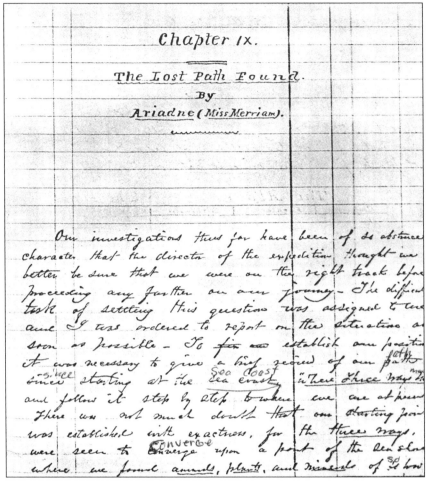

A page from **The Lost Path report.**

the Adirondacks of the 19th century. One is a beautiful personal memoir that resonates with deep love for the wilderness; the other is an extraordinary tale of a harrowing women's expedition that penetrates trackless forests in search of scientific knowledge. These very different works are by and about members of the Benedict family, who were involved in almost every aspect of the Adirondack region, from early surveys and land acquisition to the most cherished of summer vacations.

McMartin's work is also a tribute to Benedict family members who had safeguarded the papers for years.

Miss Coulter (Electra) wrote: "Very soon after leaving the Lake [Pleasant], the great northern forests closed about us and all signs of habitation had disappeared, and, for once, we felt that our safety and perhaps our lives depended upon our own exertions and the care of our trusty guides."

I often think of her description during my backpacks, which have taken me through the woodland where once part of the old Albany Road existed.

A page from the report prepared by the Lake Pleasant party.

A member of the Chapin party piggybacks a lady across the south branch of the Moose River, circa 1896. "'Indian Clearing' is about three miles in extent by one mile in breadth. It is almost entirely covered with huckleberry brush, which yield large quantities of berries in their season. It possesses an interest from the fact that there is a legend respecting it that it was made by the Iroquois Indians prior to the French and Indian War. The most probable theory of its existence is that it resulted from one of the tremendous forest fires which occasionally sweep over such wilderness regions. But, whatever may have been the cause of its existence, it certainly requires but little effort of the imagination, as one floats over the murky depths of the 'upper' or 'lower stillwater' and listens to the weird hooting of the owl, the croak of the raven or the splashing of trout, to picture this as once one of the favorite stamping-grounds of the scalp-lifters, or in fancy to see the traditional birch-bark canoe and painted warrior, plumed with eagles' feathers, gliding down the winding stream." —Joseph W. Shurter, written during a Fall 1871 three-week deer hunting expedition. *Photo by Charles Chapin, Courtesy Margaret Wilson*

The Albany Road was a blazed track during the time of the War of 1812. "French" Louie Seymour, the woodsman of the West Canadas and the Cedar Lakes, made his way over portions of the route on his treks from Speculator into that lake-speckled territory.

The south branch of the Moose River above Rock Dam appears as charmingly wild as it was in 1873. "Most of the magnificent tracts Farrand Benedict acquired are now prized parts of the Forest Preserve, lying in the Pigeon Lake and Blue Ridge wilderness areas and the Moose River Plains." —Barbara McMartin, *To the Lake of the Skies* [Lake View Press, 1996]. *Courtesy Jason Harter*

What follows is the June 6th, 1873 letter that describes the women's wildwood camp made along the stream north of the Indian Plains. Without exception, the letter addressed to "My Dear Themis" tells of a tale of the not-so-simple life the small party endured together, told with grace and eloquence, from an early vacation the central Adirondacks.

Pine Tree Camp Vacation
NO. 2 Moose River Party of Exploration, June 6, 1873

My Dear Themis.
We awoke in the morning with leisure to enjoy the wild and peculiar scenery of the surroundings of the Big Pine under which our camp was pitched. There was a beautiful mountain

stream on both sides of our camp, which united into one forming the South Branch of the Moose River. The one on the north
led to the ford where the Lake Pleasant party were probably
encamping at this very time, up which Jerome Wood started this
morning with a letter from Circe, and Daphne. The other
stream led to Indian and Squaw Lakes.

An unidentified woman stands among a bloom of wildflowers on the Indian Clearing,
circa 1893. Barbara McMartin wrote in *To the Lake of the Skies*: "The route chosen for
the western group, to leave the valley of the Moose, is perplexing. The western or lower
ford on the Moose was near the confluence of the South Branch of the Moose and the
Indian rivers. A modern traveler would continue up the Moose and follow the Moose River
Plains Road north and northeast to Limekiln Lake. The letter describing this portion
refers to steep climbs made shortly after leaving the Moose. No matter whether they
went over or around Mitchell Ponds Mountain, or one of the other intervening hills, they
would have encountered the sharp ridges with cliffs as they described. It was neither an
easy trip nor a route to be lightly chosen." *Photo by Charles Chapin, Courtesy Margaret Wilcox*

Thus far we had had nothing but trout to vary the pork, bread,
and potatoes brought from Black River, so Higby proposed a
hunt on Indian Lake for a deer. Amatheia and Circe accompanied
him on their exploration, leaving Arathusa and myself in camp.
I will not attempt to describe the sensations we experienced

that day that we were alone under the pine in the forks of the Moose. We were literally "Monarchs of all we surveyed" and "Our rights there were none to dispute." But we could not sympathize with Selkirk in his expression "Oh! Solitude where are the charms that Sages have seen in thy face?"

For although we were in the midst of scenery as wild as any on the island of Juan Fernandez, still we were surrounded with friends. After the hunters left us, we could not resist taking a ramble over The Plains and along the stream. You many judge the felicity of such a ramble when I tell you within 500 feet of our pine we saw fresh tracks of deer, moose, bears, and wolves, but what is very strange to say, they did not frighten us in the least.

We returned from our ramble to the camp to prepare dinner which probably would have been done with more care had we expected company; for before our dinner was half prepared a

Typical period outdoor dress for the women in the Lake Pleasant party.
Courtesy Carolyn Browne Malkin and Robert C. Browne

41

flock of little cross-bills lighted under our pine as though they felt they had more right to the position than we.

About the time the potatoes were done we were startled by the yelping and growling of a wild animal in the distance and soon we heard the breaking of brush and sticks; then a beautiful deer plunged into the stream and crossed The Plains near the camp with a fierce wolf in hot pursuit. The poor thing, which was running for life, was but a short distance in advance of the wolf, and would soon fall sacrifice to its hunger. In a few moments more they entered the forest north of The Plains, when an angry growl followed by a piteous bleating of the defenseless deer told us that the deed was done.

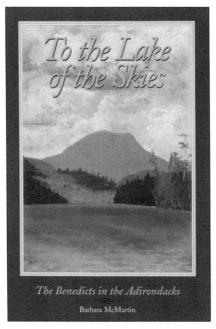

To the Lake of the Skies: The Benedicts in the Adirondacks by Barbara McMartin (Lake View Press, 1996) tells the entire extraordinary tale of the harrowing women's expedition.

This was not the kind of company we would have chosen to have so near us while alone, and we felt relieved when it was out of our sight. Although there was no danger to be apprehensive at that time of day, in camp near a fire, yet we cast longing glances up the river to see if Wood was in sight. After this slight interruption to our kitchen affairs, we took off the potatoes, made the tea, and sat down to dinner with our nerves a little unsettled.

Our next visitor was a large black bear, who was so sociably inclined that we thought at one time, he would take a seat at the table with us. We saw him come to the river to drink but a short distance below us. He then went in to bathe and turned his course up the stream directly towards our camp to see who were trespassing on his grounds. Both rifles and all the pistols were with the other members of our party and we had not even a broom-stick to defend ourselves with. After he approached so near that we could see the expression of his face, we left the table, walked boldly to the stream and followed it down, looking the bear so sternly in eyes that he came to the conclusion that his [illegible] was better than his company. Our visitor, when he saw our amiable expressions, turned about, left the stream, entered the woods where he first came in, and left us alone again.

Arethusa now came to the conclusion that she would not allow her dinner to be interrupted by any more practiced observations in natural history, so we finished our prolonged and excited meal of cold tea and potatoes.

It was now three o'clock in the afternoon, and the exciting scenes of the last few hours made us feel thankful that we were within an hour of the time set for Wood to return from up the river. We amused ourselves feeding the crossbills with the crumbs from the table, and with putting the camp in order for the return of the hunters who would be back about 6 o'clock.

The beautiful pine under which our camp was pitched was caught in the shadow of the high hills at the west before 6 o'clock and in another half hour the same shadow had crossed The Plains and climbed the hills to the southeast, making us visibly conscious that the shades of evening were upon us. When the sunlight had given place to the mysterious evening shade, we really felt for the first time that we were alone in one of the most retired regions of North America and this thought, which under other circumstances would have been highly pleasing, now impressed us with an indescribable fear.

We again cast a longing look up the south branch along the trail on which Wood was expected, and another to the south along the stream which came from the lakes where our hunters had gone, but not a sign of either party could be seen.

If the sense of fear could at this time have been banished from our minds, we might have enjoyed a scene that was worthy the attention of the poet and painter. The last rays of the sun were lingering on the top of the distant Cedar River Mountains, through which Electra and her party had passed a day or two since, and in ten minutes more we were in the embrace of night. Our studies had often brought us in contact with the myths and legends of the ancients, and we could now partially understand why the Greeks supposed Night to be the daughter of that most mysterious of all their mythical personages, Chaos, and, also why they made her the mother of Fates, Dreams, Sleep and Death.

The peculiar sensation of helpfulness felt by us in the presence of this invisible personage, when it seemed to drop from heaven to assume the control of nature, has been finely expressed by one of our own poets:

I heard the trailing garments of the Night
Sweep through her marble halls!
I saw her sable skirts all fringed with light
From the celestial walls!
I felt her presence, by its spell of night,
Stoop o'er me from above;
The calm, majestic presence of the Night,
As of one I love.

The change from day to night appeared to have influenced all forms of animated nature, and for a time these reigned in the forest about us, the stillness almost of death. We would not have been conscious that nature had a voice, had it not been for the babbling of the streams, and the pensive sighing of the wind through the strings of the Aeolian harps in the branches of the pine over our heads. For a time we were lost in the silent contemplation of our situation till the evening twilight had completely faded into darkness, when gradually we began to hear the usual sounds of the night. A bat flitted around the camp; a whip-poor-will was heard a little distance off, which carried our thoughts homeward; and some night-moths hovered around our fire, which again served to attract our attention from the wildness of our position.

It was now ten o'clock and thoughts of supper had not entered our mind. We were first startled by the hooting of an owl close by, and a little while after by the angry snarling growl of a wolf which was probably the same one we had seen chasing the deer, who was evidently enjoying the fruits of his chase. By this time we had become intensely excited. Soon we heard a heavy splash into the stream below and we immediately thought of the bear who, probably remembering his old friends, was coming to the Pine Tree for his supper. By this time we felt much more like Selkirk when he said,

> *Better dwell in the midst of alarms,*
> *Than to reign in this horrible place.*

It was now long after ten and it was as dark as it would be any time during the night. We looked again up the two branches of the Moose, but saw no one approaching. Then came another fierce screeching from the owl, an angry snarl from the wolf over the dead body of the poor deer, and a frightful yell from a panther from the direction where we had been looking for Wood. Has the great Adirondack hunter encountered a panther and been overcome? A wild scream from that same animal was the only reply.

We had heard that wild beasts will not go over a fire for its victims so Arethusa proposed making a circle about our camp, and while we were building the circle of fires we heard another fearful yowl in the direction from which we expected the hunters and from that direction there were heard frequent repetitions of that same frightful noise which impressed us more and with the thought that the panther had probably struck the path of our associates.

Again we heard the same noise and then a screech like that of a human being, then a report of a rifle and another screech like a person in agony, the report of a pistol but not a second report. Again the scream of the panther and again the rifle. By this time we were almost frantic with terror, for probably the wild beast or beasts, for they may have been several, which had killed Wood on his way back from the South Branch had encountered our hunters, perhaps killed Amatheia and was then having a deadly conflict with the other two.

After the second report of the rifle we did not hear a sound for half an hour. And exactly at midnight by our watch we heard the report of a pistol and saw a dim light up the stream, then another light and a report of a rifle. Our hunters, or at any rate a part of them, were returning on the bank of the stream by the aid of torches. In a little while we could hear their voices and then we noticed that there were two female figures returning with the hunters.

In five minutes more our lost hunters were back, bringing with them some fine speckled trout and rabbit, a small saddle of venison and a panther. The panther had struck their track, and smelling the fresh blood of the deer had come sufficiently close for Higby to get a shot at him, which was the report of the rifle that we had heard. Although the Panther was then mortally wounded, he was [not] killed, and Higby took one of the pistols and gave a final shot; then the panther gave his dying groan, which we took for that of Amatheia or Circe. It is not necessary for me to say that I felt so relieved when we found that they were back safely and the rest of the night was spent in preparing supper of trout and venison. We finished our supper just as the first light of morning was breaking the East, and we had fully made up our minds that the next time they went hunting we would form a part of the party. Just as Higby had washed the last dish, there appeared above the eastern hills the long lost Wood, seen coming down the South Branch toward our Pine Tree.

Wood's Story. "Well Wood," said Circe, "what is the news from the South Branch?"

"Perhaps this letter will give the news," said Wood, handing a letter written on birch bark of which the following is a copy. [The content of the letter isn't available.].

We were greatly disappointed that Wood had not seen our associates; and this disappointment was not any the less after reading the letter from Clymene. Their being nearly out of provisions in so wild a country was perhaps a sufficient reason for their being in such haste to meet the guides on Raquette Lake. There might have been other reasons for such haste which perhaps they thought best not to state.

We did not understand why the letter had been written by Clymene instead of Daphne. We read it over and over again and became more and more convinced that there was [something] beside the want of provisions for their hasty departure.

Wood, having traveled all night, had not been to breakfast and we noticed while the guides were preparing it that they were conversing with each other in a low and inaudible tone of voice, and we soon caught enough of their conversation to learn that Wood was somewhat concerned about the safety of the Lake Pleasant party.

☆ ☆ ☆

Amanda Benedict's narrative ends with the reader asking the question that begs an answer: What happened to the Lake Pleasant party? One can rest assured the guides saw to it that the women came through with flying colors.

The entire story of Amanda's botanical expedition is found in the second section of Barbara McMartin's *To the Lake of the Skies*. It had been Benedict's dream after she founded a female academy in New York City to send student and teacher on a remarkable botanical expedition throughout the Adirondack Mountains to gather samples and make drawings in order to document the plants and animals. McMartin explained, Amanda Benedict's 1873 mission "started from the cardinal points to rendezvous at Blue Mountain Lake, the 'lake of the skies.' Letters from expedition members describe encounters with wolves, difficult hikes over unnamed mountains, tumulous weather, and other wild adventures. Helping the women were thirteen of the most famous guides of the time and their participation in the women's expedition enlivens this new chapter to Adirondack history."

I found Amanda's Pine Tree Camp report to be historically interesting because her party camped on the Indian Clearing 101 years after surveyor Archibald Campbell, "with a supporting retinue of Indians crossed just above The Plains," wrote David Beetle in *Up Old Forge Way*," when he laid the Totten-Crossfield lines." Campbell's string of blazes was the base upon which later surveys were based.

Isaac and Wellington Kenwell were aware of two unsuccessful attempts to settle on The Plains in the years before and after the Benedict's botanical expedition camped on the Indian Clearing. In an April 10, 1935 letter addressed to W.P. Wessler on his son-in-law, Herb Palmatier's business stationary. Isaac evidently responded to a series of historical questions Wessler had inquired about. He organized the seven-page letter with subtitles, the first two pages dealt with The Plains. The excerpts appear here as he penned them.

Under the heading "Moose River Clearing," Kenwell wrote: "My first trip to the Morehouse was in Sept. 1867 the first mention of the clearing was when Archabald Campbell one of the English Surveyors who run the west line of the Totten and Crossfield Purchase of 50 Townships purchased from the Indians for the sum of 3 cents (illegible) Campbell it an old clearing this was the first white man to see the clearing."

Page two of Isaac's letter was headed "Indian Clearing on the Moose River." He wrote: "In the year 1844 Mr. Lyman Homes (sic) of the Town of Lake Pleasant moved his family coming in on the old Military Road cutting a road from the Military Road down the outlet of Lake [Little

Moose Lake] (illegible) coming to the head of the clearing on the Same Stream he built a Log Hose on the North Side of the Same Stream and Expected to Raise cattle and do farm work But the climate and Sandy Soil discouraged him and he left the Clearing in 1846. In 1890 I was looking over the place (illegible)…"

Bits and pieces that can be made out indicate he talked about his brother Wellington who moved there. "My Brother who lived at Inlet built a House and Barn about two miles farther down the Moose River and (illegible), (perhaps "below") where the Otter Creek enters with the Moose River (illegible) my Brother sold the place to the State and moved to Inlet.

"I Believe that the Indian Clearing was caused by fire its Length from west to east is a little of three miles long and about 1½ miles wide and there is two Small Ponds in it much of the clearing is over grown I do not Believe that today that 200 acres (illegible) the clearing is mostly quite level no hills on it the old road from Cedar River was cut out in 1867 Charles Ruseau (sic) lumbered just above the clearing in the 1872."

Beetle reported that Piseco pioneer farmer known only as Moore, according to Wellington Kenwell, moved on to The Plains with his wife, two daughters, a few oxen, and a milk cow. His goal was to "farm it." One winter and summer later, he abandoned his ambition. The plow he left behind and a small clearing he had tilled at the north end of The Plains were visible for years.

The Moores' brief tenure was followed by the appearance of an enterprising band of market hunters who, for a short time, supplied Saratoga hotels and other downstate marketplaces with deer meat.

No giant pine trees grow on the Indian Clearing today. The prairie-like plains has seen several widespread fires. I have enjoyed wandering here, there and everywhere, crisscrossing the great clearing looking for telltale signs of the past. During the 1980s, pioneering species had still not grown so thick and extensive as to hide portions of the ruts that wagon wheels had ground into the unpromising earth. Those ruts are not as visible today. Knowing about the Pine Tree Camp party's harrowing memoir and other historical facts all helps to resonate in my mind what it might have been like to penetrate the once trackless Indian Clearing territory.

Chapter Three

Wandering Through the Past

BEYOND MY INDIAN CLEARING WANDERINGS I have attempted to trace the Pine Tree Camp party's route to The Big Plains as well as wandered, explored, and investigated extensively throughout the Moose River Plains.

More years ago than I even want to believe have passed since I began a quest to follow every primary and secondary woods road the Gould Paper Company established in what I am going to greatly generalize as the Moose River Plains Territory—a vast area that stretches well-beyond the wild blueberry-studded central plain in the Moose River Recreation Area

Former Gould Paper Company gate at the Limekiln Lake entrance to The Plains.
Courtesy Wayne Blanchard

50

west toward North Lake, east toward Cedar River Flow and southward into the West Canada Wilderness. The definition does not abide by the official Department of Environmental Conservation designations.

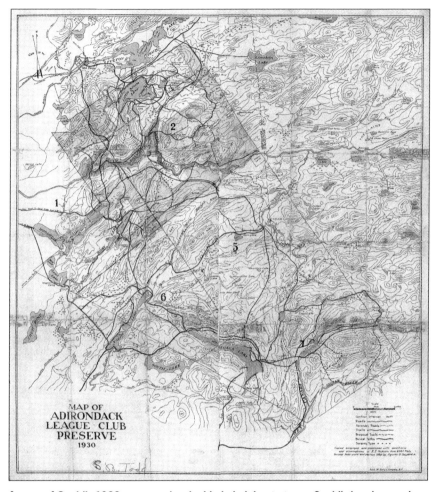

A copy of Gould's 1930 map was invaluable in helping to trace Gould's logging roads and the locations of the company's former lumber camps. *Courtesy John Todd*

My primary sources of information for these routes were the paper company's system of roads. John B. Todd, who was woodlands manager for the Gould Paper Company, and Scudder B. Todd marked the earliest routes on the 1930 map of the Adirondack League Club Preserve. Other forest avenues appear on a 1960s access map of the Moose River area. In addition to those, I have all the Lyons Falls Pulp and Paper survey maps that Daniel P. McGough, who was the Resource Manager, gave me when his company closed down.

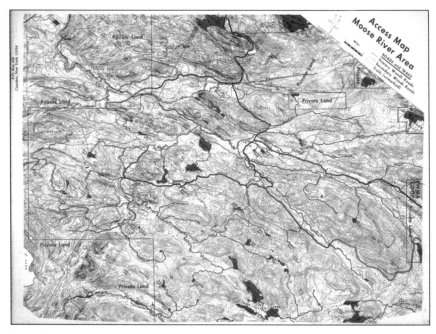

The 1960s access map to the Moose River Plains area provided details of Gould Paper Company's primary and secondary woods roads, trails and other places the author found of interest to explore. Author's collection

Of course, I avoided trespassing over private land unless I was given permission. My wanderings eventually included tracing unofficial trails such as the ones that Wellington Kenwell developed that connected Beaver and Squaw Lake and Beaver Lake and the south branch of the Moose River. Those footpath continued to be used until the 1960s. Then there is an interesting loop that connected Gerald Kenwell's Otter Brook Camp to Len Hardwood's Hot Top Camp near Bear Paw Creek. There is enough of that pathway still visible, in the fall, that an occasional deer hunter can follow it. I have also enjoyed the adventurous Kenwells' trails that led to Falls Pond and a hunter's camp on Twin Lakes.

I mention my investigative outings because the hundreds of vintage snapshots I have collected and stacks of slides taken during decades of exploration document particular places and untold stories. Many others remind me of an event such as crossing a hurrying Adirondack stream which, rushing and tumbling among rocks and boulders on its way to the south branch of the Moose River, had come perilously near to pitching me over. There were times I emerged all wet and dripping from a long bushwhack to set about my camp-making in the chill twilight. And as I write, there comes the picture of a certain canoe trip during high water that took me down the Red River, hurdling over six beaver dams before reaching the Moose River.

Otter Brook Camp, 1944. Located deep in the forest, 17 miles from the nearest highway. The log-constructed ranch-like layout served as both Gerald Kenwell's wilderness home and a comfortable shelter for hundreds of fishing, hunting, horseback riding parties and many Conservation Department personnel.

By 1953 the lithe, bronzed, sinewy Kenwell, often referred to as the "Mayor of Otter Brook," lived alone in his everyman's home castle and liked it. He came out of the woods thrice annually for the sole purpose of getting supplies from the Village of Inlet.

Courtesy Jack Tanck

I continue to enjoy an almost annual autumn pilgrimage starting at Otter Brook, near the location where Gerald Kenwell and Allen Wilcox constructed the first bridge to cross Moose River just above Kenwell's parents' hostelry and in sight of Fred Hynes' grave. Nearby the notorious band of dudes who called themselves The Governors had a camp near Ice House Pond.

Hot Top Camp, 1944. Len Harwood's wilderness retreat was popular among sportsmen and Conservation Department personnel. Located near Bear Paw Creek, the former site is a short hike off the main Moose River access road. *Courtesy Jack Tanck*

Paddling the Moose downriver beyond the old Wheelock logging dam furnishes a feeling of what it might have been like when for days at a time the only sign of civilization was perhaps nothing more than a blazed tree marking the start of a fur trail.

The romantic and healthful possibilities of a vacation in the Moose River Plains over a century ago, the lure of finding every Gould logging camp

Shawn Hansen, Inlet Town Highway superintendent stands at Moose River Plains campsite number 39. The spot marks where the Kenwell-Harwood loop trail crossed the main road. It continued on the other side to a clearing where Hot Top camp once stood. A sharp-eyed trekker will still see Harwood's spring-fed well along the unmarked bulldozed track. *Photo by the author*

site and my little safaris to locate an array of former locations of trap line and sportsmen's camps have kept me busy as I contemplated, steeped in idealistic association with the history I have collected.

Old time guide Phil Christy who maintained Mosquito Camp downriver beyond Kenwell's hotel hostelry had always counseled his clients that an experienced woodsman makes and breaks camp early. It's a piece of advice I have long followed, eating breakfast and being well on my way when the sun was yet sending its long yellow rays sideways across the tree trunks. I've relived in silence this little drama of the Moose River Plains wild. The principal actors have all passed on, but portions of their woodland lives continually replay in my mind.

Today's occasional bushwhacker following the grown-in bulldozed track that ends at a clearing where Len Harwood's Hot Top camp once stood might chance on to this hand-dug spring and wonder what history it could tell. *Photo and courtesy Shawn Hansen*

The Department of Environmental Conservation has done nothing to document the history of this wonderland of lakes, rivers, and forest that belongs to the people of the State. I have always hoped some of its informal history might be permanently etched on historical placards dispersed around its vast territory and connected with marked trails, but the sands of time are emptying that dreamy hourglass idea as more and more of the region is designated as "wilderness," a term that indicates there will be no trace of man found.

Remains of a horse-drawn wagon Gerald Kenwell used to draw supplies into Otter Brook Camp. *Author's photo*

Perhaps soon only the forest will have a monopoly, and when travelers move through the great wilderness, often stopping to rest and adjust packs, no one will ever know, save for some mention in a little guidebook or a chapter in an out-of-print book, about the magnificent human habitation that once constituted the Moose River Plains Territory.

Gerald Kenwell discusses construction with Alan Wilcox of a bridge they were building over the south branch of the Moose River. *Courtesy Ora Kenwell*

(Lt. to Rt.) Unknown child, Julia Price, Phil Christy, Lelia Barker, and Irene Craigue. Long-time legendary guide Phil Christy enjoyed reliving the old days and his recalling his physical abilities. Of his prized guide-boat he said, "It'll go through the water like a snake and climb a wave like a puffball—six mile an hour an' never sweat a hair!" Christy was one of Wellington Kenwell's earliest guides. *Town of Webb Historical Association P7008*

John Farr inspects a sleigh iron at Cellar Pond. There are all sorts of artifacts left strewn throughout the Moose River Plains. The old relics all have stories to tell.
Courtesy John Hanson

ABOVE AND OPPOSITE: **The popular Otter Brook launch site to reach the Moose River is at the Beaver Lake road barrier.** *Author's photos*

60

In the distance, the rocky cliffs on the backside of Mitchell Mountain rise above the south branch of the Moose River. Open outcrops provide panoramic viewpoints to hardy bushwhackers. *Author's photo*

The author kneels by a portion of a former sawmill once located at the top of the rise at Beaver Lake. A powerful storm known as the November 25, 1950 "Big Blow" toppled massive white pine trees in the area of Beaver Lake. Alan Wilcox cleared a road from Otter Brook outlet to Beaver Lake and set up a saw mill. Lumber cut from the trees was transported to Wilcox's Mohawk hotel on Fourth Lake for use in a variety of construction projects. The current 2.3 miles of yellow-blazed trail that starts at a parking area and road barrier just west of the Moose River bridge follows the old road to the northern shoreline of the lake. The lake is named for its odd shape which resembles a beaver. *Author photo*

Part Two

Adirondack Mountains

Moose River Plains

THE PIONEERING KENWELL'S

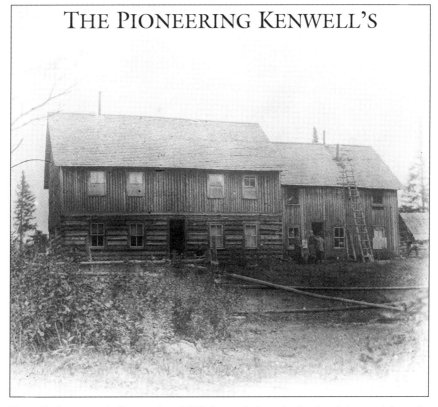

Kenwell's Sportsman's Home, circa 1895, located along the banks of the south branch of the Moose River a short distance from the Indian Clearing or Big Plains. Wellington and Eliza Kenwell operated this successful hostelry in what was a game-filled wilderness in the Moose River Plains country, miles from the nearest civilization. *Courtesy Ora Kenwell*

63

Chapter Four

Kenwell's Primitive Adirondack Hostelry

TO ENJOY THE FREEDOM of being nearly a day and a half's journey from the nearest settlement and over fifty miles from the railhead at North Creek was for many late 19th-century sportsmen and women all things Adirondack. Kenwell's Sportsman's Home was the perfect destination, with an appealing touch of pioneer life.

The Sportsman's Home was one of hundreds of hotels and boarding houses that guidebook writer Edwin R. Wallace listed in his descriptive

Guests at Kenwell's Sportsman's Home. The guide standing by the horse on the right is believed to be Louie Porter. The once treeless "prairie" known as Big Indian Clearing (aka The Big Plains, The Plains, or Moose River Plains) circa 1892. The South Branch of the Moose River was a popular destination for early hunters who supplied the Saratoga market with venison. *Photo by Wellington Kenwell, Courtesy of Ora Kenwell*

DESCRIPTIVE GUIDE

TO THE

ADIRONDACKS

AND

HAND-BOOK OF TRAVEL

TO

SARATOGA SPRINGS; SCHROON LAKE; LAKES
LUZERNE, GEORGE AND CHAMPLAIN; THE
AUSABLE CHASM; THE THOUSAND
ISLANDS; MASSENA SPRINGS,
AND TRENTON FALLS.

—BY E. R. WALLACE.—

EIGHTH EDITION.

REVISED AND CORRECTED BY THE AUTHOR.

CONTAINING NUMEROUS MAPS AND ILLUSTRATIONS.

SYRACUSE, N. Y.
THE AUTHOR, PUBLISHER.
1880.

Wallace's *Guide to the Adirondacks* was the gold standard for travelers. Copies of the rare guidebooks are sought by book collectors. *Photo by the Author*

Little Moose Lake is the headwaters of the south branch of the Moose River. Manbury Mountain is in the distance. Tracing the original route Wellington Kenwell took from the lake to the Big Plains was one of the author's bushwhacks. *Author's photo*

travel guide and directory of hotels and boarding houses throughout the Adirondacks. He touted the "Land of the Thousand Lakes" in the "revised and enlarged" 1894 edition.

> Some 14 m W. of "Wakley's" is a locality of great interest, called the "Indian Clearing," (accessible by rough road via [Little] Moose L., 4 m.) a cleared space of about 1,000 acres (3x½), perfectly free from stone, stump or tree. How, when, or by whom made, none living know—none live to tell. It is not supposed to have been the work of the beaver. Near this singular, solitary clearing (¾ m. distant,) [the south branch of the] Moose River courses its way—here, and for miles hence, a

Stillwater. It is crossed by several smaller crystal streams teeming with rarely molested trout. Here, the enthusiastic angler may test his skill until his ambition is gratified to the utmost. On every side are numerous and nameless lakes and ponds, embosomed hills richly clad in pine, spruce and hard wood, never desecrated by the hand of man with the invading axe. It is a charming section, full of primeval and romantic beauty. Game in fair quantities is still obtainable, and deer which frequently pasture in this natural deer-park, may sometimes be sighted in the day-time.

On the border of the [Indian] "Clearing" and on Sumner Stream (outlet of Sumner or Fonda L.) just above its confluence with Moose River, is located the "Sportsman's Home" (P.O., Indian Lake) where comfortable quarters are found. Boats also are kept here and at the neighboring waters, for the use of guests.

North E. of this point are Bear and Lost Ponds; and S. E. is Falls P., all distant several miles.

West a mile or two, are the 3 Mitchell Ponds (headwaters of Red River, a branch of Moose River) wild and lonely enough. Near here Verplanck Colvin, and Jack Sheppard,[7] the distinguished guide, killed a panther some years since.

South W. of Sportsman's Home, from 2 to 3 m, are the secluded sheets, Beaver, Squaw and Indian Lakes, where is found some of the finest sporting the region offers.

In this vicinity are Balsam Lake (W), Muskrat P. (E.), Horn, Beetle and Odor [Stink today] Lakes.

Sportsmen who visit this interesting district are rarely disappointed with the result. To reach "Wakley's" and Sportsman's Home, special conveyance is required from Cedar River Hotel. Stage fare from North Creek to the Latter, $1.75 or $2.00.

Price of Board Meals: 50 cents, $1.00–1.50, 5–7 days

—As reported in Wallace's *Guide to the Adirondacks,* (The Author, Publisher, 1894).

"Fabulous folk, the Kenwells," wrote *Utica Observer-Dispatch* reporter David H. Beetle, author of *Up Old Forge Way* (Utica Observer-Dispatch, Inc., 1948) fifty-four years later.

Wellington Kenwell, famous guide, insightful businessman, popular hotel-keeper and sportsman, was also a prominent figure in Inlet, New York's early politics. Kenwell is credited, as reported in ...*A Backward Look at 6th and 7th Lake* (Sixth and Seventh Lakes Improvement Association, 1989), with spearheading the circulation of a petition to appeal to the Town of Morehouse "to permit the community of Inlet to break away and form its own town government."

With all Wellington's laurels, including receiving top billing as an all-around Adirondack pioneer native, it was his wife, Eliza, who stole the show by being "a mother to the woodsmen and to the tourists," according to Foster Disinger, who shared his admiration of her with a reporter at *The Binghamton Press*. Both Disinger and A.M. Talbott, an outdoor columnist for the *Buffalo Courier-Express*, had known the Kenwells from their early days at South Branch. Disinger said countless other Southern Tier men in Binghamton, Endicott and Johnson City had a high regard for the one-time school teacher who made the change to a pioneer life with her husband and children when the family moved to the Indian Clearing along the south branch of the Moose River.

Records are imprecise as to how long Wellington and Eliza Kenwell were living at and running Little Moose Lake hostelry (near Indian Lake), where Wellington acted as a hunter and guide before the family pulled up stakes to relocate. (Kenwell's clients included Grover Cleveland.)

In the fall of 1890, Wellington procured a crude log building situated within earshot of the south branch of the Moose River. In 1898, Seth Aldrich's heirs sold Aldrich's three-quarter interest to Wellington Kenwell for $40. Information varies as to prior possession and title. *The Saratogian* newspaper paper trail tells us it had been built and occupied formerly by a J.P. "Pa" Brown[8] and that Si and Fred Brown acted as guides from the log building on the "Big Indian Clearing" during the summers of the early 1880s. In his "Deer Hunting in the Adirondacks" report in the "Game Bag and Gun" column of the April 12, 1883 issue of *Forest and Stream* magazine,

Joseph W. Shurter also told of being at the camp in 1881. Shurter wrote: "There is also a so-called "Sportsman's Home located at Indian Clearing, J.P. Brown proprietor. But the best plan for parties…who desire sport and good fare at reasonable expense is to camp."

Bryan Rudes (Lt.) and Bill Zullo inspect a decaying log structure veiled in a thicket of spruce above the northeast shore of Little Moose Lake in 2012. Our conclusion led us to speculate this was a barn from the original hostelry, latter-day Elijah Camp period. *Photo by author*

In "Famous Guide Choked to Death: While Eating His Supper in Utica's Hotel. Frank Gray a Mystery" (*Utica Herald-Dispatch*, Tuesday evening, January 19, 1909) the death announcement reads in part: "…Frank Gray who had lived alone 'over a score of years' had once owned a camp on the Moose River about 10 miles from the head of Fourth Lake, now called Kenwell's Camp. Mr. Gray owned the property and it was known as Gray's Camp; he was a trapper and hunter and acted as a guide to fishing and hounding parties in that region."

Sources do not agree the land had been occupied by a squatter. It is not this writer's intention to judge if the Kenwells had a legal deed to their property. There were many aggravated cases throughout the Raquette Lake country, and Kenwell's was one of them. I simply find noteworthy the numerous papers I've read that went between the State of New York and the Kenwells, the dealings of Timothy Woodruff to secure miles of unoccupied property as a buffer around his Kamp Kill Kare preserve (formerly called Kamp Kisabella), and the amount of cash the Kenwells received to vacate the property. They make for interesting reading.

Little Moose Lake hostelry, where Wellington and Eliza Kenwell worked.
Courtesy Indian Lake Museum

The following extract from the article, "Lands Lost Through Negligence," *The Evening Post*, New York, Thursday, December 7, 1905, offers a nod that the Kenwells might have had a questionable claim. "...Throughout the Adirondacks are dozens of 'camps' on State lands, especially in northern Hamilton County and in northern Herkimer County where leading politicians are said to have resorts on excellent lake sites. A few are also said to be along Piseco Lake. A notable instance of long-continued use of State land is Kenwell's Hotel on the south branch of the Moose River. This is on Lot 56, Township 4. By delaying long enough, it will be impossible for dozens of so-called cancellations made by State comptrollers in the late [18]80s,

THE PRESIDENT FISHING

President Grover Cleveland was known to enjoy camping out in the Adirondacks in the most comfortable way for his short periods of rest and recreation. *Courtesy Indian Lake Museum*

and early '90s, to become legalized through adverse possession. This affects thousands of acres of Adirondack forest land, including some of the best lands in the mountain country."

J.P. "Pa" Brown's log building, purchased by the Kenwells in 1890.
Courtesy the Town of Webb Historical Association

Whatever the future may have held, with two hired men the team made several trips to the newly-purchased property. They combined hunting with advance preparations that included re-chinking log walls, roof repair, putting aside firewood and doing interior improvements to make the place as comfortable as one could for the arrival of the family during the later winter-early spring of 1891.

Six months following the birth of their daughter, Laura, the pioneering Kenwells took advantage of the crusted snow conditions. With carefully loaded bobsleds, the family began a long trek through the wilderness.

In an undated interview with reporter Dick Long, Gerald Kenwell spoke about his parents, Wellington and Eliza, and their reason to move the family to the Indian Clearing along the south branch of the Moose River, where they established a hunting and fishing camp that gained a reputation as a preeminent sportsmen's hostelry smack dab in the middle of deer country. This was an era in outdoor history when health, recreation and sporting kicked into high gear. Hiking and climbing were becoming popular. Camping and water sports, hunting and fishing were all the rage. Crowds began to flock into the woods, and with them place names were frequently altered. Maps that once referred to "The North Woods" changed to "The Adirondacks." "John Brown's Tract" and "Fulton Chain" were replaced by Old Forge and Thendara. Newton Corners became Speculator, Sageville Courthouse was now named Lake Pleasant, Otter Creek was now Otter Brook and the Indian Clearing became the Big Plains—known today as the Moose River Plains.

Gerald tells of his parents' motive to settle into the middle of one of the most remote sections of the central Adirondacks. "My mother had developed bronchial trouble and our doctor had advised my father to move to a section that had many balsam trees, which would be favorable to her recovery."

The sensation of remoteness and inaccessibility of today's Moose River Plains is no comparison to what the "Land of Deer" was like in the Kenwells' time.

For ten years Eliza, Wellington and their two children, Gerald and Laura, lived at South Branch, miles from their nearest neighbor at a place on the map simply called "Kenwells."

Kenwells was a twenty room sportsmen's boarding house. The hostelry was on the "Little Plains" within sight of the Moose River. The place has been described by hunters and anglers as a sportsmen's paradise. Sports sought adventure in the woods and on the water, and all were pleased to return to the Kenwells' genuine primitive lodge.

Arpad Geyza Gerster was one of the hundreds of sportsmen who stayed at Kenwell's House. Gerster, a noted New York City physician, owned a camp at Raquette Lake. His marvelous diary entries, notes and sketches of vacation days in the Adirondacks at the close of the nineteenth century are entertaining and detailed. His August 16 and 17, 1898, posts that appear in *Notes Collected in the Adirondack 1897 & 1898* (The Adirondack Museum, 2010) tell about the Kenwells.

Trip to Moose River, South Branch
August 15–17, 1898
We rise at 4:30 for an early breakfast. The day is warm and hazy. Start at 6:30 in two boats, which are left at South Inlet Falls. Then Charley [Jones] & Jerome [Wood] shoulder their pack baskets containing provisions & camp kit, while John, his friend Butts and I get our knapsacks, as we begin our long tramp, reaching Shedd Lake camp at 9:00 A.M., whence we ferry ourselves across the lake to the old Sumner carry. At Sumner Lake a blast of the signal horn, suspended to one of the old cedars, summons Lieut. Governor Woodruff and George Bentley, who explain to us where to find the key to the Stillwater camp shanty, and how to find our way to the Rousseau Shanty.

We put across and start down the inlet at 11 A.M., reaching the upper Stillwater at 11:45. Near the fishing hole Jerome goes ashore from the punt and cooks lunch while we hook 15 small trout. We disembarked at the foot of the stillwater and

OPPOSITE: **A rare Moose River Plains pioneer Kenwell family portrait of Wellington, Eliza, Gerald and Laura. According to Margaret Wilcox, this photograph of the couple with six-month-old daughter Laura, and four-year-old son Gerald was taken soon after the Kenwells had established their Sportsman's Home hostelry.**
Courtesy of Margaret Wilcox (The Camp Nit Collection)

started downstream at 3 P.M. over a well-trodden blazed trail, reaching the middle stillwater at 3:45. A deer was heard jumping on the other side of the stream. The punt on this stillwater was too small to hold us all, wherefore two trips were taken. On the right bank, upon a knoll between this and the next stillwater, Woodruff has built a good, warm camp and store shanty, well stocked with firewood, dry provisions, blankets and camp kit, where we established ourselves for the night. A good fire was soon going, a balsam bed was laid, blankets spread, and Jerome's art evolved a fine supper of beefsteaks, trout and tea.

Lumber for building came by horse and wagon from the sawmill at Headquarters, a small settlement at Cedar River Flow. *Courtesy Roy E. Wires*

The place itself would be very pretty, if John Jones, the artificer of the camp, had not converted the surroundings into a howling wilderness of slash, stumps and chips, which he invariable does whenever left to his own savage instincts. There is a spring nearby, but its water had a bad metallic taste, and we preferred the warmer water of the stream. Right over against the camp is a huge flat-faced boulder, forming the back of the fireplace, the top of the boulder being occupied by a large and sturdy old-time spruce. We found a spare punt in the camp. Sapsuckers were singing their monotonous note, and two venison hawks came flitting no one knows whence, to forage. Before a glorious fire we turned in on the sweet-smelling balsam bed.

Aug. 16: Up at 5 o'clock, fine day, air from S. Before sunrise, go on stillwater with Charley. We hear a deer snort, but could not see him. We left camp at 7:45, crossing the stream by the camp to the left shore, following a blazed line for 30 minutes, reaching the lower stillwater at 8:15. Near its lower end is an island; take the South or left-hand side channel. We left the punt at the lower end, starting hence over the old corduroy road on the left bank, over a terribly bad trail, with most treacherous walking, rocks and logs being invisible in the tall grass and weeds. The stream is very fine and must afford excellent fishing in the spring and early summer. About 1½ mile from the stillwater the trail crosses over to the right bank, where a huge spruce was felled across stream for a footbridge. Here the boys informed me of the loss of the butt of one of our steel fishing rods.

After a rest & drink we floundered along the right bank until we entered a large beaver meadow, at the lower end of which we found first, to the right of the trail on the hill another of Gov. Woodruff's bark shanties, then we crossed the stream in the meadow, where it is about to make a great bend to the left. Here the path again enters the woods, passes over a knoll, and descends into a small hollow, crossing a fine spring brook, near which is the Rousseau Shanty, an old landmark. It is an untidy, spidery, breakdown, abandoned lumber shanty, the habitation of a huge colony of blue hornets, whose nest is attached to one of the rafters. We found a campfire smoldering *in the shanty* under some kettles, and the place occupied by two, rather grimy looking hunters, who were a sight of dirtiness, and begged us for a piece of soap, which we furnished.

We fished down the Sumner from here for about ½ mile till we reached a dam, above which we boiled the kettle, and had luncheon, consisting of some excellent country sausages, put up in tins. Jerome and I start from here over the old wagon road—infinitely better walking than before—while the boys & Charley fish downstream, the two parties to meet at the head of the *Indian clearing*, 1½ mile from the dam. The boys took 8 trout. A slight shower passed over us. Not to have the boys linger too long, I send Jerome for them, and we start together down the large open tract, three miles long by ½ mile wide, which was once the home of a large group of Indians, now nearly extinct, the last wretched remains of whom I have seen near the Old Forge and on the Blue Mt. Lake road, teaming and freighting. The country has been uncultivated for many— 60 or 70 years—and is overgrown with small bushes, blueberries mainly, and a coarse wild grass, affording an excellent ground for deerstalking or "stillhunting" as the pursuit is called in these parts. We passed a barn filled with hay in the middle of the clearing, and then turning to the South—heretofore our course, that of Sumner Stream was invariable S.W.—we passed over a small knoll, and made Wellington Kenwill's place, situated on the bank of the Moose River, ¼ of a mile above the forks of the Sumner. Our caravan was watched with interest by the people, and at the threshold good looking, kind Mrs. Kenwill met us, stating, that having learned (from Woodruff's) of our approach, she had reserved the best room for us—six of her boarders were sleeping in the barn—in grateful commemoration of a little medical service I had bestowed on her little boy Gerald nine years ago, when they were living on Raquette Lake. The gratitude of the good woman pleased me more than the fact that we secured shelter.

The Kenwells also used a horse-drawn jumper to draw supplies into The Plains. A jumper can best be described as a land sled. It was fashioned from materials obtained from the forest. For that reason, a teamster could repair a broken runner, usually on the spot. *Courtesy Indian Lake Museum*

Gerald had grown up to be a fine fellow of twelve, with keen honest blue eyes, and a cheery way of talking and acting. His bare legs and feet were sunburnt to a rich nutbrown, and a quick friendship was established between my whileom [sic] patient and his doctor. In ten minutes he had me down to the river, showed me all the boats and told me of all good holes from trout fishing. His little sister, a pretty, chubby child of seven in curlpapers and two little braided pigtails, gravely pumped some water from the well before the house, and made a stately and dignified presentation of the beverage to me. [page 152]

The place is a genuine, old-fashioned, primitive Adirondack "place," half home, half farmhouse and the rest "hotel," and with homemade furniture, unplanned boards for ceiling, walls and floor, and peeled rough rafters supporting things overhead. In the "parlor" a few rickety chairs, a stove and organ, the dining room jamful and in open communication with the breezy but clean kitchen, in which everything is done honestly and publicly before our eyes, the good housewife having no reason to hide any of the mysteries of her art. Children, guests, dogs, and hired girls roam where they please, and the air of the place is altogether delightful to a [illegible] and despiser of pretentious "Hostelry" of these days, which has the bad sides of both city and country hotels, and the good sides of none. We found the food, principally venison, excellent and abundant, and the place scrupulously clean. Over a creaky staircase covered with rag carpet we ascended to our room, containing two huge, "homemade" beds, deer's antlers serving over the washstands for towel racks. The only drawback to the place was the crowd of unfledged schoolboys in impossible sweaters, infesting the pleasant places with their continuous shooting at nothing, and their noisy ways, so unsuitable to the woods. Especially when this species of biped invades the woods in mass, in flocks of ten and twenty, matters are apt to become intolerable.

Aug 17: The whole house was creaking, floors, beams, and beds, whenever anyone turned about in bed during the night. Two racks from ours, was a part of the house arranged as a sort of barracks, with 10 or 12 beds, and a number of hammocks strung in between, where the young fellows slept. From here proceeded a medley of strange night-noises, which could be heard and movements which could be felt. Before breakfast I took a couple of towels and a rod and had Jerome paddle me down to the mouth of Sumner Stream, which I here learned to know from source to mouth. [page 153]

Dr. Gerster referred to Mrs. Kenwell as "the good housewife."

With the number of guests that came to the Kenwells' hostelry, daily housework could not have been successfully completed without domestic help. Records at the Hamilton County historian's office tell "servants with them (the Kenwells) in 1900, the last year they operated the hostelry, were Louis Stevenson and Raymond Norton." In addition to home help, the Kenwells retained a number of guides. Among the noted woodsmen who worked at Kenwells were Lewis Porter and Phil Christy. Porter, a young, lean, strong man just barely into his twenties, turned his summer pack work into an education as he learned the fine art of operating with amateur sportsmen and women. This early exposure led to "Lou" launching his own guide service. Christy became so popular as a fishing and hunting guide that he ultimately spun off from employment at the Sportsman's hostelry to establish his own two camps—Mosquito Camp near the Big Plains at the head of the south branch of the Moose River and Cozy Parlor at Natural Dam, about 20 miles above Old Forge. Phil's reputation was shared with the world in the June 1938 edition of *The National Geographic Magazine* when Frederick G. Vosburgh interviewed the old-style woodsman. The Old Forge guide told Vosburgh he might be an old-timer at 83, but offered to hold his rifle upside down and still outshoot any ordinary man, adding he was also nimble enough, "to kick the hat off your head before you can turn around."

In old age, Phil liked to reminisce, saying he began following the trout streams and deer trails at the age of eleven in a boat he had built. Christy could boast that during his long experience in the woods, he had guided five U.S. presidents—Harrison, McKinley, Cleveland, Teddy Roosevelt and Harding, as well as notables from Europe.

Foster Disinger spoke of Eliza Kenwell as a talented and kindly woman. She was known to offer a temporary remedy for a toothache and she "could set a broken leg if a tree fell on a lumberjack. She could nurse them through sickness; in a country where doctors were virtually unknown, her services were invaluable." These were all valuable assets to wilderness boarders who desired to "rough it," yet took comfort in the amenities the proprietors provided.

Eliza also racked up acclaim for her culinary expertise. Her table fare, always excellent, provided scrumptious meals. Her pantry was supplied with berries from the clearings, vegetables from the kitchen garden, wild game, and beef, chicken, and lamb from farm animals that ranged on a natural meadow where coarse blue-joint hay was cut by hand with a cradle blade.

One sport described how he had just finished a breakfast of coffee, bacon, potatoes and bread and was asked if he didn't now want an Adirondack short-cake. Upon inquiring, he learned it consisted of a stack of three 10-inch flapjacks with butter and maple syrup in between. He exclaimed, "I could eat no more without undressing." Eliza replied, "I would rather see you go hungry than to see you go naked."

Kenwells' guests were particularity fond of the way trout were prepared by Eliza. The old standby method was to simply fry the fish in salt pork. Eliza thought differently. She believed trout should be cooked with nothing that could impair their delicate flavor. Her method was to rinse them, dry them on a towel and then place the fish into sweet butter and fry them at just the right heat—which nothing but experience could determine—and serve them smoking hot.

Disinger shared that shortly before Eliza's death in 1920 "a multimillionaire who had eaten her pancakes as a small boy visited her to get some of the cakes. And every boy for miles around came to Mrs. Kenwell with his troubles."

Chapter Five

Problems with New York's Forest, Fish and Game Commission

WELLINGTON AND ELIZA KENWELL came of a hardy and courageous stock as did most of the men and women who ventured into the Adirondack wilderness. They and their brood went into their log and board cabin determined to make a good home and business for themselves, but after nearly a decade of living along the south branch of the Moose River, their lives and livelihood collided with the New York State Forest, Fish and Game Commission.

Hess Camp at the head of Fourth Lake. *Courtesy Winfred Murdock*

83

The Kenwells had problems of their own following construction of the two-story Sportsman's hostelry. By October 1900, announcements in the *Lewis County Democrat* and *Utica Daily Press* reported the Kenwells had moved to Inlet, where they leased Hess Camp at "the head of Fourth Lake, in the midst of unsurpassed fishing grounds. This hotel is up to date in every respect. Open fireplaces, comfortable rooms, and sumptuous table [fare]. Rates from September 1, $10 per week."

One question that remains to be answered is if Camp Pauline was also known as Camp Anne, the small log camp downriver from the Kenwell's home on the Little Plains. This camp was located on a bit of high ground located near the outlet where Sumner Stream empties into the Moose River. *Courtesy Town of Webb Historical Association*

The move was not made as a cure for Eliza. It can be reasonably assumed that either the source of irritation to her lungs, whether it had been tobacco smoke, dust, fumes, vapors or some other air pollution was removed, or the bacterial infection that irritated them had passed, because no other mention of it was ever made.

Their problem had to do with the State of New York's Forest, Fish and Game Commission. During the several years following their purchase of The Plains property, the commission had determined the Kenwells were squatters on land owned by William West Durant. In 1896 the state Forest Preserve Board purchased 24,000 acres from Durant. The sale included Sumner Lake, though a choice 1,030-acre section around the lake in the middle of the tract was left out of the transaction. In 1898, Timothy L. Woodruff, lieutenant governor of New York and a member of the Board, purchased the preserve from Durant for $12,360. It included Camp Omonsom, a camp which Durant had commissioned Josh Smith and Jerry Little to build for him and Dr. Arpad Gerster sometime before 1888.[9]

Timothy and Cora Woodruff changed the name of the lake to Kora. In 1899, a reporter from the *Albany Argus* described Woodruff's new Adirondack Kamp Kill Kare residence as "a palatial log home in the heart of the hills."

A short explanation of the events that conspired to vacate the Kenwells is found in correspondence between the Forest, Fish and Game Commission and Wellington Kenwell. It is obvious from the verbiage and volley of letters that Woodruff didn't want Wellington on the property.

The Commission's letter dated March 19, 1901 provides much insight into the action taken against the Kenwells.

Mr. Wellington Kenwell,
Inlet, N.Y.

My Dear Sir:
Governor Woodruff has to-day informed me that you are negotiating for the sale or lease of the property which you have been occupying for several years on the south branch of the Moose River. Parties with whom you have been negotiating have been to see him in reference to your title, and he has been compelled to advise them that your title is not good to those lands. While

the Forest Preserve Board has heretofore been willing to permit you to continue occupying that property, the Board is unwilling to permit strangers to either purchase or lease it from you and establish themselves upon that land. The State has, for several years, been the actual, legal owner under at least two valid and effective tax sales. The bottom title or deed which you acquired a few years ago is insufficient in law to give you any good title against the claim of the State. Governor Woodruff has directed me to suggest to you that if you desire to quit claim such interest as you may have in that property, the Board will be willing to allow you a reasonable and moderate sum for the improvements which you have made upon it, and has authorized me to negotiate with you for the purpose of reaching a settlement.

The Forest, Fish and Game Commission hereby certifies that an action has heretofore been commenced in the Supreme Court against Wellington Kenwell and Eliza E. Kenwell, his wife, under the direction of this Board, in the name of the People of the State of New York, to recover possession of about one hundred and fifty-nine acres of land in Lot Fifty-Six (56) Township Four (4), Moose River Tract, Hamilton County, together with the improvements thereon claimed to be owned by said Wellington Kenwell and now occupied by him; that said Wellington Kenwell has heretofore made an offer in writing to settle and compromise such suit, and to execute and deliver to the People of the State his quit claim deed of said land, and surrender possession thereof to the State for the sum of Fifteen Hundred Dollars. That this Board has, at a regular meeting, by resolution duly adopted, accepted said offer, and has entered into an agreement with said Wellington Kenwell and Eliza E. Kenwell to settle and compromise such suit upon the terms aforesaid, and that said Wellington Kenwell and Eliza E. Kenwell have become entitled to receive the sum of Fifteen Hundred Dollars, the amount agreed upon in such settlement as provided by Chapter 135 of the Laws of 1898, upon the delivery of a quit claim deed of said lands.

Timothy L. Woodruff and Charles H. Babcock,
Forest, Fish and Game Commission

Kenwell's store and transportation company, Sixth Lake, Fulton Chain of Lakes.
Courtesy Ora Kenwell

Several days later Wellington Kenwell had not taken action. It might be assumed that based on the language in the Commission's March 22, 1901 letter to Kenwell, he might have been stalling or trying to wrangle a more favorable settlement. This may have been the purpose of his telegram advising that he and Eliza would be unable to come to Albany. The Forest, Fish and Game Commission replied to Kenwell's telegram.

My Dear Sir:

I have yours of the 21st. I am sorry that you are unable to come to Albany, as I made the suggestion in the hope that you might be willing to meet the Department in a friendly way and endeavor to agree upon some satisfactory basis of settlement of the conflicting interests. You will, of course, understand that the State claims to be the absolute owner of the land which you also claim to own. If necessary, or if forced to take extreme measures, the State will have no other course upon to it than to take the matter into the Supreme Court for a judicial determination. This would be expensive for you, but not very expensive for the State. Out of consideration for you and your interests, Governor Woodruff directed me to endeavor to arrange the matter with you in such a way that you would be able to get a fair return for the value of the improvements which you have put upon the land. We cannot, of course, name any figures on a postal card, as you requested, and I doubt if the matter can be arranged satisfactorily by correspondence. Had I the time I should be glad to visit you at your camp, and talk the matter over with you there. This will be impossible, and because of the impossibility, it seems to me the wiser course to ask you to come to Albany and see me. I trust you may find it convenient to adopt this course, and visit me here at an early day.

I trust that Mrs. Kenwell and the children are in good health and hope to see them personally before many months.

The Commission's language indicates they were trying to act fairly while at the same time urging Kenwell to put an end to his wobbling on the issue as quickly as possible. "You might, if you desire, take a train which will bring you into Albany on Friday evening," a subsequent letter on March 24 directed. "I can give you such time as may be necessary on Saturday morning, and you might be able to leave Albany on your return trip on Saturday forenoon at 11:15, arriving at home again Saturday evening…"

Further correspondence on March 26, 1901 continues the saga. "... I am very sorry [Mr. Kenwell] to learn of the continued bad luck from which you have been suffering... Of course you will understand that there is now a new Commission which has charge of all these matters, and while the disposition continues the same towards you as it has been in the past, the difficulties of carrying out the former policy of the Board have been somewhat increased.

The stark scene shows the destruction of the forest land that bordered the channel that connected Sixth and Seventh lakes following the dam construction at Sixth Lake.
Scene from a post card in the Author's collection

"...If you are financially embarrassed, temporarily, and desire it I can send you some money for traveling expenses if it will be an accommodation to you..."

Eventually the State of New York settled amicably with the Kenwells. On April 13, 1903 the Commission learned Chief Protector Winslow, along with R.B. Nichols, had made sure a Mr. Gray, who had been farming on the old Kenwell property, was removed and that the former Kenwell buildings were destroyed "by fire or otherwise, taking all necessary precautions that no fire escape to the land beyond the building." At the same time, Winslow and Nichols also razed "an old house" known only as Camp Anne situated on Sumner Stream—where it enters the Moose River a short distance downstream from the Kenwells' former place.

This early picture was taken from the bank overlooking the dock at the head of Seventh Lake. Boats had to carefully steer around the flooded headwaters. From Sixth Lake landing, Kenwell's "Alisca" transported sightseers and shore dinner parties across Sixth Lake and Seventh Lake. Note all the dead trees in Seventh Lake. It resulted from the shore-line flooding when, in 1880, the Sixth Lake Dam was constructed. Edwin R. Wallace wrote in his *Guide to the Adirondacks* 1894 edition: "The Sixth and once lovely Seventh Lake now presents a scene of desolation. A dam has now been placed at the foot of the former, and ghostly dead trees now skirt the once bright and verdant shore.... The silver beach at the head of Seventh, so long the boast of that locality, has disappeared. Its inlets and outlets, from pleasant streams have become dismal swamps...." *Courtesy Ora Kenwell*

Once the Kenwells left the Moose River Plains and moved to Inlet, boarders who had hunted and fished in days past in the South Branch country continued to patronize the Kenwells, first at the Hess Camp they leased, and later at Kenwells' boarding house, store, small saloon and ice cream parlor, and store at Sixth Lake Dam.

Dock at Seventh Lake. At the time this picture was taken many of the stumps had been removed. Seventh Lake island appears in the background. *Courtesy Ora Kenwell*

Years later, when Frederick C. "Ted" Aber, Jr. and Stella King were gathering information for their *History of Hamilton Country* (1965) Riley Johnson offered his opinion. "Jack Murphy built a house at Sixth Lake dam and beat everyone out of everything in a year and took off for Canada. Then Wellington bought it..." By this time, Aber and King could not decisively determine if Johnson was correct. Wellington and Gerald had passed and no one he inquired knew for sure. Thus Aber added in a letter to me dated April 4, 1986: "From an interview I had with the late Riley Johnson, who also told about the Kenwells on Sixth Lake—only trouble is his material jumps and [the] sequence is sometimes hard to follow (and like other sources, he, too, had mistakes." It's possible it will never be known for sure who built the Sixth Lake Dam house. One fact is visually clear, however. The building and business enterprise shown in several snapshots illustrate an appealing stop for tourists.

Kenwell's Sportsman's Home on the Little Plains was paradise. *Courtesy the Town of Webb Historical Associati*

Post cards sold at the store shows autos lined up advertised as "Kenwell Transportation Co." Vacationists could also hire sightseeing boats at Kenwell's Sixth Lake Landing. Boats took campers, and tourists who desired to shore dinner parties, "across Sixth and Seventh Lakes." Travelers who chose to make a one-mile trek over a footpath to Eighth Lake[10] found a small steamboat christened Ella awaited to take them on a journey around the final Fulton Chain of Lakes.

While Eliza Kenwell was at ease cooking and entertaining notable men and women, leading politicians, writers, artists, and socialites, she was no slacker in the administrative end of operating a business. Eliza ably handled financial affairs, and when it became necessary she filed a $400 claim against the State of New York for damages to her property from overflow due to the state's raising the Sixth Lake Dam at the outlet of the lake.

Wellington Kenwell freely admitted to writer A.M. Talbott (complete name unknown) one day that his "wife could beat him fishing any time she tried." Talbott quoted his friend in his "In the Open" weekly column in Buffalo's *Courier-Express*. Eliza was capable of "bringing home a four-pounder if he had a three, and not needing to go beyond the [South Branch] Stillwater to do it."

Eliza and Wellington's son, Gerald, often spoke about his early childhood in the pioneer setting on the Moose River Plains. The family was often the victim of hard winters. Gerald said that during those early years of farming and homesteading his father "built his own tote road fifty-five miles to the nearest store" [in North Creek]. Gerald was referring to the tote trail developed across the blue-joint grassland on The Plains. Wellington had competent men in his employment. It was across this prairie-forest route that supplies and guests would travel from the railroad depot at North Creek to Headquarters House on the Cedar River and on to Kenwells.

Even today, before vegetation springs to life over The Plains, a section of ruts made by those wagon wheels can be spotted by a careful eye.

When the Eagle Bay train station on the Raquette Lake Railroad opened, the Kenwells began having provisions hauled by competent packer-guides like Louis Porter and Phil Christy over this much shorter supply route.

Hal Boyle, who wrote "Boyle's Notebook," a weekly column that appeared in Amsterdam's *Evening Recorder*, reported a conversation he had with Wellington. Once "some young men asked the elder Kenwell what was the most fearsome sound he had heard in the woods: A bear's growl? A wolf's howl? The cry of a panther?

"'Twasn't any of them,' allowed the old man. 'The wuss noise I ever heard was one winter about the end of February when I woke up and heard my wife scraping the bottom of the flour barrel.' Knew I'd have to snowshoe fifty-five miles for more flour.'"

Eliza Kenwell could remind Wellington of this story as a seriously good way to get her husband motivated to head for more supplies. Wellington knew that on his return he would enjoy the fruits of his long overland trek in the form of more of Eliza's specialty baked goods. She always had the family's best interests at heart! There was no way she'd let them be anything less than well fed.

☆ ☆ ☆

Despite the time and labor involved in "putting food by," Eliza might have looked at making extra-good preserves, conserves, jams and jellies as one of the delights of homesteading at South Branch. She was known to can only those things that were garden surplus and a few specialties that made it possible for her to set a more interesting and individual table. According to her great-grandson, Paul Birmingham, people of privilege were often guests at the Sportsman's Home. It's quite conceivable that customers who came from an urban culture to vacation in a far-off place of beauty and tranquility were delighted to find the combination of hostess Eliza's table setting, meals, and refined etiquette.

The paradise guests enjoyed at Kenwell's Sportsman's Home was the result of a joint effort between Wellington and Eliza and the cooperation of Mother Nature. Guests enjoyed the diversions of fishing, hunting, and simply gazing at true wild beauty. Wellington made sure the accommodations were comfortable, and Eliza made sure her guests left the table smiling.

Chapter Six

A Tutor Arrives on The Plains

WINFRED "SLIM" MURDOCK had a lot of admiration for his Uncle Gerald. He shared, "Gerald's parents made sure they had a tutor for their kids during their homesteading days. A short time after they settled The Plains, they advertised for a live-in teacher. John Gale Hun applied and got the job. Hun told the Kenwells his parents were descendants of a Dutch family that was among the early settlers of Albany, N.Y. I remember Gerald saying Hun was an intelligent young man."

Gerald's and his parents' reminiscences about their tutor reveal how lucky the Kenwells were to secure Hun's employment as a private teacher soon after he graduated from Albany Academy.

John Hun took a personal interest in each child and everyone found him an interesting person. He had a wonderful sense of humor—"always a twinkle in his eye," according to how Slim remembers.

His teaching style while on The Plains mirrored his style as a headmaster later in life. Gerald remembered he had a very informal technique and he was always able to put a restless child at ease. "If Laura or I came to see him during a time of day we weren't being tutored, as likely as not we'd find him sitting with his legs draped over the arm of his favorite chair as he read. If he went to speak to me in my room, he would think nothing of stretching out on my bed while we talked."

Hun and Gerald used to have signals. If Gerald came to him when he was in the workshop where he spent some of his spare time—with axle grease on his hands—Hun would gesture "Just a minute" with an upheld finger. He was more formal with Wellington and Eliza.

Hun had a dynamic personality which was reflected in his interest in other people. That trait was what made him such a brilliant teacher later in life and what made him recognize good teaching in others.

Edith Johnson worked for Hun after he left his early Adirondack teaching job. She said, "He felt that a teacher should learn his own method—that what one teacher might accomplish in one way another might do just as effectively in another way.

"Dr. Hun was a man of many interests and managed to find time for all of them…. He loved to spend time with his tools creating all kinds of gadgets and time-saving inventions. But most of all, he loved fishing and made trips into the wilds of Canada and the Adirondacks each year."

Mr. John Poe, a life-long friend of Hun said, "John was imaginative and highly individualistic.

"He loathed a stuffed shirt, and he could deflate one faster than anyone I ever saw…he never paraded his efforts on behalf of others."

The Kenwells saw in Hun that he was sincerely interested in his students as individuals rather than just as people to be taught.

The only known image of John Hun. From an unlabeled clipping about Kenwell's tutor.
Courtesy Winfred Murdock

Hun demonstrated he had an unusual capacity for making a subject even as difficult as mathematics come alive for students in terms of their own environment and knowledge, generating a genuine interest in the subject.

Hun taught intelligent mathematics. Students were required to know why as well as how a problem was worked. Slim said his uncle's tutor made classes interesting—with unexpected material being introduced constantly. "Uncle Gerald had no time to nod."

The interest John Hun took in his first students was phenomenal.

In 1895, Hun left the Kenwells to enroll in Williams College, from which he graduated in 1899. Hun went on to obtain his doctorate of philosophy at Johns Hopkins University and soon after became a member of the faculty of Princeton University, serving there until 1914, when he resigned to found the Math School of Princeton. Hun and the Kenwells remained in contact throughout the years. Gerald showed me the textbooks on plane and spherical trigonometry that Hun authored.

Mrs. Gordon McAllen Baker added some additional insight and background about John Gale Hun, her maternal grandfather, and questioned if her grandfather's love of the outdoors and tutoring of the Kenwells' children was a contributing factor to his purchase of property in the Adirondacks.

"Grandfather came to Princeton University as an instructor in mathematics right after graduating from Johns Hopkins.

"From memorabilia I have, it's clear Grandfather had a wonderful time at Williams College. One of his good friends was Herbert Lehman, later Governor of New York. Grandfather died in 1945. He was very bright. He was also utterly charming and an outrageous gambler. I am told that he would gamble on almost anything—from poker or bridge hands to the stock market. Many of his students have said that he was the most incredible teacher they ever had.

"His purpose in starting the Hun Tutoring School in Princeton in 1914 was to help those university students who were having a hard time in math. He was appalled at the lack of basic competence in math in those students he was teaching at the university. The Hun School eventually evolved into a preparatory school—still with its main thrust toward students wishing to enter Princeton. Over the years this thrust changed, of course, with students applying to many different colleges. The school had an amazing charisma, as he did. 'Send your boy to Johnny Hun—he'll pull him through.' I have heard that sort of statement time after time anytime I meet a member of that generation who discovers my relationship to John Hun.

"In the mid-1920s Grandfather bought a summer home in Keene Valley, New York. Although he enjoyed his time in the shadows of the High Peaks of Essex County, he actually preferred the wilds of Canada for fishing trips."

Twists and Turns of Research: Finding Mrs. Baker

Sometimes researching a shot-in-the-dark results in an unexpected but welcome surprise. What led me to Dr. John Gale Hun's granddaughter, Mrs. Gordon Baker, who lived in Portland, Oregon, was just that.

On a hunch I sent a letter of inquiry to the chancellor of Princeton University. In turn he directed me to Earle Coleman, the university's archivist. Coleman told me (in 1988) the Hun School of Princeton is still in business. He provided a sufficient address and said that between that contact or one at Williams College and Johns Hopkins University, someone would be able to assist me in locating a living relative of Dr. Hun.

A group of musical guests at Kenwell's. The song "'Round the Hunting Lodge at Kenwell's" was a popular tune. *Courtesy Margaret Wilcox (The Camp Nit Collection)*

So, it was a wonderful surprise to hear from Mrs. Baker and to see all the information she had copied and included about her grandfather as well as her excitement when she learned about the Kenwell family and the Moose River Plains.

But surprising me beyond belief was this line in her first correspondence: "In Princeton Grandfather Hun met Leslie Stafford Crawford, a graduate

98

of Smith College. She was secretary to Dr. Henry Van Dyke. They were married in Westfield, MA in 1906."

Margaret Wilcox, owner of The Mohawk on Fourth Lake had loaned me journals connected to Camp Nit on the shore of Beaver Lake in the Moose River Plains. Wellington had built the camp both he and his son, Gerald, referred to as the "Waldorf in the Woods" following the turn of the 19th century.

I immediately recognized the name Leslie Stafford Crawford and immediately sent Baker photocopies of the camp's September 11 and 14, 1908 entries that showed her name, and with permission from Margaret Wilcox I included a yellowed snapshot of Crawford that was in the register.

Barker was intrigued. "That's my Grandmother's name written by her— it's her handwriting," she replied. "It's a charming picture. I'm pleased to have it though I don't quite understand how Mr. Chapin [owner of Camp Nit] came to have it. This is all quite intriguing! I'm enclosing for you a copy of the back side of a clipping titled 'Echoes of Camp Life,' perhaps you will be able to decipher something that will tell where the undated newspaper clipping came from."

The column reads:

> The members of the W.F. Williams Adirondack camping party have plenty to talk about these days and the memory of their experiences in camp are very pleasant. A new Camp was built by the party three miles below Kenwell's on the Moose River and the party was there nearly six weeks. Gilman took the prize for champion fly casting and Rice stuck to his nightrobe in the woods regardless of cost. Alex and Faick shot the first deer, a fine buck. The camp was dedicated to the great god Twitch with impressive ceremonies, and flashlight photographs of the god were taken with ceremonies. Hun saw 38 deer and missed eight, and vowed that he would remain until he shot one with his "Savage" [rifle] or become a savage himself. Several terrific thunder storms were experienced while in camp. W.F. Williams shot a deer on Indian River and narrowly escaped losing his life

in Moose River with the deer on his back. The Canadian canoe trip which two or three of the party were to make was given up on account of a break in the large canoe. The camp was broken August 23. Simmons, Benson, Gilman, How, Rice, Faick, and Vandeveer coming out, and Hun and Williams remaining. They returned a few days later, but not until Hun had "killed his deer." The following ode was composed by the camp poet and set to the ancient music of 'On the Banks of the Wabash.'

'Round the hunting lodge at Kenwell's wave the alders,
In the distant, very distant, lurk the deer;
I have been there every summer since my childhood,

And I always swear I won't come back next year;
But every season comes to me the picture
Of waving pines and woodlands fair and sweet,
And I forget the punkies and mosquitoes,
The loss of sleep and blisters on my feet.

Chorus:
Oh, the moon shines fair and bright upon the South Branch,
From the streams tramps Gilly on his weary way,
Through his thirsty lips his hungry teeth are gleaming,
As he says, 'What have we got to eat today?'"

Mrs. Baker didn't recognize all the names but felt many might have been fellow professors from Princeton.

It was obvious to me Hun's friendship with Wellington Kenwell had resulted in Kenwell's arrangement of a rental for the large camping party with the owner of Camp Nit.

The crown jewel to this whole historic footnote was when Tom Gates showed me in 2018 a leather-bound photograph album he acquired at an auction. Included was the party identified in the "Echoes of Camp Life" newspaper.

Chapter Seven

Wilderness and Governor Black

From an undated and unidentified newspaper

"Distanced from the strains of Albany, now far behind him, Governor Frank S. Black stepped off the Pullman car at the Eagle Bay station and boarded a rickety tote wagon pulled by a large Belgian workhorse. Gerald Kenwell, a nine-year-old Adirondack native, had been entrusted to help escort the governor of New York to his father's 'Sportsman's Home' located along the south branch of the Moose River. This was one of the most remote corners of the newly-formed Adirondack Park.

"At Limekiln Lake the party disembarked to begin the long 15-mile walk into camp. In the governor's easy conversational style, he joked with the entourage of Inlet guides and big-city aides, demonstrating how his own particular gait was thought to help reduce the risk of a heart attack; young Gerald related they were not far from Limekiln Falls—the very spot where Nat Foster, the well-known trapper immortalized in Cooper's *Leatherstocking Tales* killed 13 panthers many years ago."

A JANUARY 20, 1897, *Garden and Forest* weekly article, "The North Woods" reads, "It is now twenty-five years since the passage of an act by the New York State Legislature, providing for the appointment of seven Commissioners of Parks for the state, who were directed to inquire into the expediency of 'providing for vesting in the state the title to the timbered regions lying within the counties of Lewis, Essex, Clinton, Franklin, St. Lawrence, Herkimer and Hamilton, and converting the same into a public park. That is, as long ago as 1872 there was a general recognition of the value of this region for its timber-supply, for its usefulness in preserving and maintaining the water supply of the canals and streams of the state, for furnishing hydraulic power, and for the attraction of its picturesque scenery, its numerous lakes and its abundant game offered to the invalid, the tourist and the sportsman. This record also demonstrates that even then the attacks on the timber of this region had been so merciless that the Legislature had been driven to take some active interest in its preservation. In the documents prepared by these commissioners, of whom the Hon. Horatio Seymour was President, it is set forth that this broad area, once owned by the state, had been largely conveyed to purchasers who had bought it for the timber and bark it carried; that a single tract embracing more than a quarter of a million acres had been conveyed to a corporation for five cents an acre under a scheme of speculation that was little less than fraudulent, and that the state then owned but a small fraction of the territory, and this was in detached parcels. The report also declares that the lands originally bought for their timber had been largely abandoned after this [the timber] was removed as not being worth to the holders the taxes on wild land, so that large blocks had been repeatedly sold for arrears of taxes or left in the possession of the state as not worth these claims until, in the course of time, another growth had made them desirable, when they were again bought from the state, again to be abandoned when stripped of everything worth carrying away."

Governor Black was among many outspoken voices of this era who worked to save the forests of New York. It's reasonable to believe his vacation in the Moose River Plains with the Kenwells went a long way to help foster his desire to protect the state's forests.

Governor Frank Swett Black. From "Ex. Gov. Black Dies at His Troy Home," March 22, 1913, *The New York Times*.

OPPOSITE: **Governor Black valued protection for Adirondack land.**

In Governor Black's first annual message to the state legislature, he made clear that he came to believe more money was needed to secure North Woods land forever for the state—and the sooner the better. He said the cost alarmed commissioners twenty-five years earlier, but wisely reasoned "the land would cost more today, and many times as much twenty-five years hence, but in the end the state must own the North Woods, if there are any woods to own, so that every dictate of wisdom suggests that their devastation should be arrested at the earliest possible moment.

"A question too long neglected is the preservation of our forests," he said. "The state either through indifference or false economy, has been stripped of its most valuable timber lands, has allowed its water-supply to be seriously impaired, and permitted the most wonderful sanitarium of the world to be defaced and partially destroyed. Every element of economy and foresight is outraged by this course."

In the *Garden and Forest* article Black was quoted as saying "that private individuals, taking advantage of the state's neglect, have taken possession of more than three-fourths of the area of the entire Adirondack region, and that more than five-sevenths of the proposed Adirondack Park, which includes some 2,800,000 acres, are now held as private preserves or owned by lumbermen, much of the land being exposed to appalling and disgraceful devastation by fire and axe...."

Black continued: "More than four hundred and fifty million feet of wood and timber are cut, and more than one hundred thousand acres are stripped every year.... Every year the loss to the state grows large, in all cases difficult, and in some cases impossible to recover.... Not long ago the state appropriated a million dollars to preserve the beauties of Niagara Falls. That subject is without significance compared to the Adirondack forests. Every consideration of health, pleasure, economy and safety urges the speedy consideration of this subject, and such consideration should include appropriations adequate to ascertain the nature of the titles adverse to the state, to recover where the titles are insufficient, and to purchase where they are valid. Any other course would be false and unwise economy...."

It would be grand if Wellington Kenwell had kept a journal or if his Sportsman's Home register's guest remarks shed more light on the governor's vacation with the Kenwells. Sadly, neither has surfaced. The only tangible remarks were recorded by David Beetle on the day he interviewed both father and son for an article about the south branch of the Moose River country that would appear in a 1946 edition of the Utica *Observer-Dispatch*.

Governor Black saw first-hand the need to regulate logging. *Courtesy Jim Fram*

Gerald recalled, "I remember that the arrival of the governor was a big occasion. He would come all the way from North Creek, accompanied by four guides from that area. There were usually about 16 in his group and my boyish enthusiasm was increased by the presence of a Civil War general by the name of Tillingast in his party. And of course people of this kind kept us in touch with what was going on in the outside world."

The solitude sought by Governor Black at the turn of the century can still be experienced today but with the ease of a well-maintained seasonal dirt road. His appreciation for wilderness and his influence on its preservation left a legacy for all to enjoy.

He would have approved of this statement made decades later:

> "Wilderness serves all the people; particularly those who penetrate it gain its fullest reward. But even the wilderness beyond the road furnishes a tremendous setting and a tremendous background for others. People view and enjoy and are inspired by the wilderness—five, ten, twenty miles away. Destroy that background: lumber off even a part of it and the wilderness disappears. And there will also disappear the pleasure of those whose only contact with the wilderness is experienced as they look outward and over it from a window from the road," said Sharon J. Mauhs, Conservation Commissioner, State of New York in her speech before the Oneida Lake Association at its annual meeting in Syracuse, April 23, 1958.

Today the preservation of the Adirondack Park has more proponents than ever. If not for those like Governor Black who spoke up early and loudly, there might have been nothing left to preserve.

Chapter Eight

Sleeping in the Woods
at Kenwell's Camp, 1899

THE FULTON CHAIN OF LAKES and distant Kenwell House formerly
located on the Moose River Plains appealed to and charmed a range of visitors. Many who came to the Adirondacks were interested in the health of
the deer population and fishing conditions.

Guide-boats were swift and stable. *Courtesy Margaret Wilcox (The Camp Nit Collection)*

The Adirondack winter of 1898–99 was particularly cold. Vacationers who came to Kenwell's during the late spring and summer of 1899 learned that early-arriving guests had reported seeing decaying bodies of deer as well as many other rotting carcasses within a radius of five miles of the camp, which they "detected by their sense of smell, but did not see them." Wellington Kenwell, as well as his guides, reported they had probably seen at least one hundred bodies of deer that had perished from starvation. According to Kenwell, it was "owing to the deep snow and extreme cold" of the past winter.

Kenwell said that on one occasion when he went to the barn that stood on the Indian Clearing, he found several deer inside feeding on the dry grass which he stored inside after cutting it from the prairie-like field. He also reported seeing deer "come up close to the house in the cold weather." Kenwell told guests he chopped balsam trees down for the "nearly famished" animals that "would begin to feed on the farest end of the tree almost as soon as it touched the ground."

In spite of the winter-kill, guests found deer "plentiful in the region now." Kenwell said he, "never saw a locality in the woods" where deer were so abundant. In spite of the slow spring warming and melting of ice and snow, long after the opening of legal fishing, by June the bodies of water threw off their winter ties and the waters began "to yield their usual abundance" of "speckled beauties, and many a fine specimen" had been recorded in Kenwell's register.

Fishing, hunting, and boating were not the only drawing cards to a quiet, restful outing at Kenwell's. Devotees of the south branch reported the sweet boiling spring water was another attraction. "Icy, cool spring water bubbles right out of the ground," one unidentified customer reported in his hometown newspaper. "Liquors are not sold but the most refreshing

OPPOSITE: **The Sportsman's Home provided guide-boats for guests. Gerald Kenwell was proficient with these handcrafted boats at an early age.** *The Syracuse Herald American,* **July 27, 1958 says of him: "Gerald Kenwell, born in Indian Lake in 1887, may well have been the youngest guide ever employed in the spring of 1896 when he was only nine years old, he took his first party into the Moose River region. Among them was Mr. Mert Lewis, then Attorney General of the State of New York."** Courtesy Margaret Wilcox (The Camp Nit Collection)

of spring water and the richest of cream and fresh milk is always at the disposal of the guests."

An example of the sense of relaxation one gained at Kenwell's is this report in *The Albany Evening Journal*, Thursday, August 31, 1899, "Secretary Angle's Return: Out of the North Woods When the 'Tenderfeet' Entered."

> Secretary Clarence B. Angle of the Civil Service Commission returned from his vacation in the North Woods. Mr. Angle started his vacation as an invalid, having succumbed to overwork last spring, but for the past few weeks he has been resting and building up and now he is as brown as an Indian. He was at Kenwell's camp, about twelve miles above Fourth Lake of the Fulton Chain. He had some good luck fishing and landed one trout that weighed a pound and three-quarters on the south branch of the Moose River. He was finally driven out of the woods by the 'tenderfeet,' who poured in in droves as soon as the deer season opened. He said that a fisherman could not feel safe unless he got behind a large rock, as the favorite weapon of the [inexperienced and] experienced hunter this season…is of the new high-powered rifles that…send a ball through any ordinary…tree trunk."

Just two days later, Kenwell's again made news in *The Oswego Daily Palladium*, Saturday Evening, September 2, 1899. The column read: "Sleeping in the Woods at Kenwells, 1899: A party of Oswegoians in the Adirondacks"

> Kenwell's House, Adirondack, Aug. 30—(Special) Foot-sore and weary, after a journey of 12 miles over one of the roughest trails that exists on the green earth of ours I find myself in the midst of an Oswego colony who are enjoying themselves killing deer and bears and taking brook trout from the many streams in the neighborhood; shut away from the outside world, sleeping upon pine boughs in an open camp and eating the roughest of fare excepting when we take dinner with my host Kenwell. "If

you want a few days rest go into the heart of the Adirondacks," said my friend, and I followed his advice. At the Fifth Lake I found Tim O'Hara, a famous guide, and he told me it would cost five [dollars] to reach Kenwell's, the famous resort on the Moose River, where Lieutenant-governor [of New York state] Tim Woodruff is spending his vacation and resting from the arduous duties of state. We started at sunup with the guide in the lead. I brought up the rear with white laundered shirt, cuffs, high collar, patent leather shoes, straw hat and my new summer suit from Ould's [sic].

A Rough Road

It takes seven hours to cover the 12 miles over the usual trail, so you can gain some idea of the road one encounters. I thought I knew something about hills, but I must confess that those of my experience were never in it for a single moment with those we met on our way to Kenwell's House.

"I can make this route shorter," said Tim O'Hara, "if you would prefer to go that way. It would take only about four hours to make it and the conditions of the trail are about the same."

"You're the doctor, Tim my boy," I said, "anything that you recommend goes with me."

How I wish I had never said it for the words were no sooner out of my mouth then he struck off at a lashing stride through a virgin forest. There was no apparent track to guide him but he kept right on while I struggled in the rear covered with perspiration and cursing myself for a fool to go looking for recreation in a trackless wilderness.

As Hot as Hades

The heat was almost unbearable, the mosquitoes and punkies tortured me almost unto death, as I pantingly tried to keep the sturdy young guide in sight. First I divested myself of my coat, then my vest came off, and then my starchless collar and cuffs

were removed, and last of all my white-laundered shirt. We made the clearing in four hours but I was the toughest-looking wreck that struck that camp in many days.

Friends Didn't Recognize Me

The first man I saw puffing away on a big pipe was my old friend Pat Grace. He has been here since early in July and his beard and hair haven't been touched by razor or shears since he left The Inlet. I called to him and he didn't know me and I was obliged to tell him who I was. The punkies had found me out and my face, neck and arms were covered with big blotches. When I boasted that we had made the trip that usually takes seven hours in four they gave me the laugh and told me that was one of the guide's tricks. He was used to such work and by taking the cross country march he had earned his five dollars in four hours and was ready for another job. I saw it all then but I was too nearly in a state of collapse to make any "kick"; besides I remembered my magnanimous instructions that "everything went."

What Kenwells Is Like?

Kenwell's House I found to be a rambling log house, covered with climbers, and the interior furnished very comfortably. The Kenwells have been hunters, guides and trappers in these parts for generations. They know every path without being obliged to the blazed trees and shoot, hunt and fish in the good old Davey Crockett style. Every room was occupied and I was told I could only obtain accommodations in the open camp. That suited me, and after a bath in the cool waters of the Moose River I was ready for dinner. When I walked into the dining

Kenwell's guests fished from and tried their hand at rowing guide-boats on the still water of the south branch of the Moose River downstream from the Sportsman's Home. It has been a long-accepted legend that the Adirondack guide-boat was invented by Mitchell Sabattis, an Abenaki Indian and guide. *Courtesy Margaret Wilcox (The Camp Nit Collection)*

room I was greeted by salvos of applause from a table at the far end of the dining room. And turning I beheld the Oswego colony consisting of Mr. Grace, his son, Will, M. J. Kirwin, the eastside grocer, Bart Dowdle, John H. McDowell of Syracuse and his son Kenyon, James Surton and Martin O'Melia. How did they laugh at my blotched and swollen face, but their greeting was as welcome and as hearty as it could be.

A Delightful Place

After dinner I was escorted out to my bed chamber. Imagine four bed posts standing straight with a ridge pole a few feet higher with birch bark tacked up against it. A couch of pine boughs with the rich odor of balsam were arranged under this shed. The sides were open and that, I was informed, was my open camp. I was too tired to make any complaint for my thin-soled shoes had blistered my feet terribly, so I stretched myself out on the couch of boughs and slept the sleep until the sun was an hour or two high. A dip in the river and we were ready for breakfast. And how [good] did brook trout and fried bacon taste. It seemed as if I had never had anything taste quite so good despite the fact that I had been troubled with dyspepsia.

Visit Neighboring Camps

After breakfast, with Gerald Kenwell, the twelve-year-old son of the proprietor as my guide, we went down to Beecher Camp, where a son of the famous preacher Henry Ward Beecher spends the latter days of summer. Then we went over to Camp Woodruff [along the Sumner stream], where Tim Woodruff, our lieutenant governor, holds forth and where he is expected on Saturday—to-day. Both are open camps; by that I mean that anyone is permitted to occupy them and use the utensils when the owners are not here. The latter are never disturbed and are always left in good condition as found. The guides see to it that the campers do not omit this small obligation.

114

One Woman at Kenwells

There is only one lady at Kenwells, Miss Maynard of Hartford, Connecticut. The trail is so rough that ladies will not chance it, but Miss Maynard was looking for a quiet retreat in the heart of the mountains and she found it. She is a teacher and the sturdy little Kenwells [Gerald and Laura] have enjoyed and profited by her visit among them and it is with reluctance that all who have been here look forward to her departure for she expects to leave in a short time to resume her duties among the youth of Long Island where she is engaged in her profession.

Lakes, rivers and streams teemed with fish. *Courtesy the Indian Lake Museum*

Deer Shooting

There are plenty of deer and bear in this neighborhood. Wednesday last, Bart Dowdle, Gerald Kenwell and myself went across Helldiver Lake in a boat to try to get a shot at a bunch that were reported on the opposite shore, while "Mike" Kirwin and "Pat" Grace with Tim O'Hara to guide them went out to The Plains for bear. As we rounded a point we came upon a fine big buck standing near the edge of the lake. In an attack of pure fright, Bart Dowdle was in the bow of the boat and gave the signal. We were within fifty yards of the noble fellow, who didn't fear our approach. We were also on the windward side of him. "Stand up and shoot quick," whispered young Gerald. Bart stood up, placed his rifle to his shoulder and then began to tremble and shake as if he had a chill. "It was 'deer fright,'" the guide said, and Bart had it so bad that he dropped his gun into the lake, the deer got away, we all swore and Dorsey has been ordered to ship a Winchester, with a strap attached to it, by express.[11] The guides told us afterwards that 'deer fright' was usual among those taking their first lessons among the mountains.

Killed Two Bears

Grace and Kirwin had better luck. Towards dusk they struck fresh bear tracks up in The Plains. The latter is a space covered with brush and berry bushes. O'Hara left the two and going about a mile around started in through the dense growth. The scheme worked, for soon an old black bear and a cub about two-thirds grown came out into the clearing. Mr. Grace took the big one and Kirwin fired at the cub. The former sent a bullet right though the old one's head and she died almost instantly, but what Kirwin shot broke the cub's shoulder. The latter made a lively fight. Kirwin though it would be a nice thing to take him back alive to Oswego, but in the struggle he lost the better part of his wardrobe and he found it necessary to dispatch his cubship with his hunting knife. We have been eating bear steak and venison all day.

Lost in the Woods

John H. McDowell went out the other day without a guide or a compass looking for deer and was lost in the woods. The guides sounded whistles and tin horns all night and about three o'clock in the morning found him about nine miles from camp, almost exhausted. He had killed one deer, but was unable to get him back to camp. The guides go out for him in the morning.

Oswego Visitors

John H. McDowell came into camp yesterday with a guide but could not be induced to stay. Mr. C.H. Bond and Mrs. Bond are at a cottage on Fourth Lake.

Lines By An Oswego Man

While looking over the register to-day I came across the following lines written by Henry M. Blossom Jr. of St. Louis, an old Oswego boy. They are on the punkies that infest the woods in August and the song is supposed to be sung to the tune of "On the Banks of the Walbeak." "Will" Grace and "Jim" Betton have attempted it with mandolin accompaniment, but with different success. It is entitled "On the Banks of the South Branch" and begins:

> Round the hunting lodge at Kenwell's wave the alders
> In the distant, very distant lurk the deer
> I have been there every summer since my childhood
> And I always swear I won't come back next year...

Will Stay Till Snow Flies

With the exception of Sutton, the party here say they will remain until snow flies. They are having a big banquet and the Oswego friends are looking forward to a big feast of venison, wild partridge and duck—and plenty.

Chapter Nine

September 1899 in the Woods at Kenwell's Camp

"SEPTEMBER IN THE WOODS: The Oswego Colony is still at Kenwell's House." This is how the author, identified only as "D.K.L.," describes his September vacation at the Sportsman's Home. The Plains or Indian Clearing was one of the most touted areas in the Adirondacks for early sporting enthusiasts and vacationers.

Gerald and Laura Kenwell under a ladder. Gerald said his family kept in contact with their former tutor long after Gerald's youthful days afield with John Hun. *Courtesy of TOWHA*

The following narrative is written in the flowery style common in newspapers of more than a century ago. It's not the kind of writing most of today's readers are accustomed to, but its old-fashioned elegance adds authenticity to what a century-ago vacation was like in a region now so familiar to Adirondack fishermen, hunters, paddlers, nature lovers, mountain bikers and all those who drive over the rough, bumpy road hoping to catch a glimpse of Harold, a huge bull moose immersed shoulder-high in Helldiver Pond, feeding on tender vegetation.

Hunting was a big part of vacation plans in the Moose River Plains.
Courtesy the Indian Lake Museum

This is a nostalgic look for those who like to tag along with the Adirondack sports enthusiasts of the late 19th century. The story is a rare look at life at Kenwell's Camp written for *The Oswego Daily Palladium's* Saturday evening edition on September 16, 1899.

Out of Past. This is a contemporary record of how deer jacking was done when that sort of thing was legal. The lantern, placed well-forward in the bow of the boat so that it would not reveal the hunters, was beamed toward the shore after the hunters had located a deer by the sound of splashing in the water. The light picked up the eyes of the deer. While the animal remained spellbound by the light the man in the stern paddled noiselessly until within easy range. Then the man in the bow lined up his sights in the light of the lantern, and fired. *Courtesy John Knox*

Beyond this memory, the only other published visit to Kenwell's I have read is found in Arpad G. Gerster's *Notes Collected in the Adirondacks 1897 & 1898* (The Adirondack Museum, 2010).

> The Oswego colony here is growing less in numerical strength, the last to depart being Mr. M.J. Kirwin. Those remaining are Patrick Grace and son Will, and Bart Dowdle. They have said that they intended to remain until snow flies; the first snow has come and gone but they show no inclination to leave behind

OPPOSITE: **Guests Kate Wilson and Pauline Ste. Marie sharpen their aim on the open firing range.** *Courtesy the Indian Lake Museum*

120

the glorious September weather that we are enjoying. Thursday night last the first snow of the season put in an appearance, but it did not remain long. It was a cold night and when the visitors got down at 6 A.M. they found it necessary, for the second time this season, to remove the ice from the water buckets before they could arrange their morning toilets. The lavatory at Kenwell's is a large bucket of clear spring water with individual basins and fresh towels.

All bucks. Deer takes like this were common on The Plains. Courtesy the Indian Lake Museum

New Visitors Daily

While some of the old visitors have gone out, new ones are arriving every day. This morning Jerry Hayes of Syracuse put in an appearance astride a big Army mule that came from the barracks at Plattsburgh. Mr. Hayes is one of the best-known commercial travelers in northern and central N.Y. He and Mrs. Hayes, and their son have been spending a few weeks at The Inlet and he came up here for a few days' shooting, partridge, duck and deer being plentiful. Besides, he wanted to get away from the mad portion of the community of Inlet. "Tim" O'Hara, the guide, says that the gentlemen's game that was in vogue there during the summer has given way to one in which it is found necessary to count the cards after every deal, and that was too trying, even for the nerves of a Syracuse traveling man. Mr. Hayes has a fine naphtha yacht at The Inlet, which will hereafter accompany him on his Summer pilgrimages to this region. His many Oswego friends will be pleased to learn that he is enjoying excellent health.

Unloaded rifles were stored in one room in the Sportsman's Home.
Courtesy the Indian Lake Museum

Miss Maynard's Deer

Miss Maynard went out Wednesday morning, taking with her the finest pair of antlers that have gone from the mountains in several years. The man who looks after the chores at Kenwell's, and incidentally the herd of Jerseys that furnish the richest of cream and milk for the guests, came in Monday morning and reported he had seen a fine big buck down in the pasture lot with the cows.

This successful hunter proudly poses. Period photos were sepia tinted and mounted on firm pressboard stock. *Courtesy the Indian Lake Museum*

"He will be back there tomorrow morning," said young Gerald Kenwell, and he invited Miss Maynard to go with him on the morrow and get a shot at the old fellow. She wanted to take her camera along to get a picture of the old fellow in his native wildness, but was assured that it would be useless to try for a picture because of the heavy mist, so she took her rifle instead, and after two visits to the pasture lot she and Gerald succeed in knocking over the stag. He was a handsome old monarch, with wide branching antlers that will hereafter grace the young lady's boudoir, a mute testimony to the prowess of this modern Diana with a rifle in the heart of the Adirondacks. But the campers were all sorry to see her depart.

It was not uncommon for guests at Kenwell's Camp to report a single sudden ripping sound, a series of loud snapping noises which reverberated throughout the building, or creaks and groans like a haunted house that would cause them to sit up in their beds, waiting for something more to happen, but nothing did. The next morning Wellington would point out a long crack that had widened, running lengthwise in a log beam.

Duck and Brant

Mr. Grace, his son and Bart Dowdle went to Falls Pond, about four miles from here, on Wednesday afternoon, where the guides reported that wild duck and brant were coming in quite plentiful. The latter are species of w.[sic] geese. The hunters had fairly good luck. They brought home twelve ducks and three brant. One of the latter is a beautiful specimen and was killed by Mr. Dowdle. He is being mounted by the "Hermit" who lives near Beecher Camp, and will be taken to Oswego to find a place in Mr. Dowdle's home. The health of the Oswego

party is excellent. They enjoy the clear, cool, bracing air of the mountains and tramp through the woods all day, with gun in hand, looking for game. Partridge are very plentiful and weigh from a pound to a pound and a half each. They are enormous size this season and as fat as butter.

Living High

The camp is living high. Trout are no longer taken, as the season has ended, but beyond that they are not plentiful and it is only occasionally that one can be taken with hook and line. They have returned to the deep pools and lakes to spend the Winter. But with bacon, fresh eggs, wild duck, venison, bear steaks, squirrels and partridges, we have managed to make a pretty good living and all have grown brown and fleshy. The Oswego party has all killed a deer. All the game laws permit the killing of but two deer by any one person during the hunting season; they are giving their attention now to other shooting until about ready to go out, when they each hope to be able to knock over another to take home with them.

No Accidents at Kenwells

While the papers tell of shooting accidents in other places, there have been none at Kenwell's House. As a matter of history, there has never been a serious shooting accident here. The reason is that parties go out in charge of experienced hunters, and the necessity of obeying the guides is impressed upon every man handling a gun. A week ago a party from Rochester went out and a young man who, despite multiple warnings, would get careless, had his gun taken from him by Frank Gray, the guide, and was turned back to camp at the first opportunity.

OPPOSITE: **The author kneels next to the Kenwell's well point, the only visible sign of Kenwell's Sportsman's Home, his homestead for nearly ten years. In early spring faint traces from the burned buildings used to be found. Fred Hynes grave site is in the distance.** *Photo by the author*

127

Learning to Paddle

Speaking of Frank Gray reminds me of a dunking Mr. Dowdle had in Helldiver Pond a few nights ago. He had been out with Gray learning to paddle a canvas-covered canoe. To a novice it is no easy trick, and Mr. Dowdle was but a few yards on his voyage before the canoe rolled over and he was in the water. The latter was warm enough, but his walk home in the cool air of the evening, a distance of nearly a mile, took all the romance out of the situation. He had to run to keep warm, and after changing his clothes he felt very comfortable wrapped in a heavy blanket in front of the huge campfire. The latter is lighted every night to dispel the chill that accompanies the setting sun.

Raced Against Time

Phil Christy, the sturdy guide, won a ten-dollar wager last Monday. He is a favorite guide of Lieutenant Governor Timmy Woodruff when that gentleman is after deer. The record from Kenwell's to The Inlet was held by an old guide, now laid up with rheumatism. The best record for the twelve miles with a hunting canoe on his head was three hours and old "Tom" Lawton held it. Christy started at daylight with Kenwell and "Tim" O'Hara following. He went so fast that he lost his watchers and landed at The Inlet in two hours and forty-five minutes after starting. An idea of the feat can be had when it is stated that the boat which he carried weighed eighty-two pounds. The trail is one of the roughest in the Adirondacks and it usually takes seven hours to make the journey. —D.K.L.

Chapter Ten

W.W. Hastings' October 1897
Quest for Adirondack Deer

THROUGHOUT THE LATE 1890S, the reputation of Wellington Kenwell's remote sporting camp, located along the banks of the south branch of
the Moose River, had popularized the Indian Clearing. Locals, including
guides, knew it remained highly favorable for deer, as no train came within
twenty miles of it. While Kenwell's camp was well-situated in the heart of the

**The Indian Clearing was a popular destination for local guides to take hunting parties.
Pictured is Louie Persons with two unidentified women hunters.** *Courtesy the Indian Lake Museum*

prairie-like plains, he did not have exclusive rights to the so-called Land of the Deer. Other guides also took their parties into the Indian Clearing in search of game, armed with Marlins, Bullards, and Winchesters. Throughout the summer and fall, these parties of sportsmen made the Adirondacks their headquarters. They were pleased to bag trophy bucks, but sports of the day also tested their marksmanship on otter as the swift creatures fished and caught frogs in the cover of the river flats. They also fired at hell-divers, loons, mink and other wildlife. Loon were a favored target because of their reputation for being difficult to bag—the prize most often ended up mounted among a collection of other birds and wildlife.

Indian Lake guides bound for the Indian Clearing entered past Headquarters at Cedar River Flow. *Courtesy the Indian Lake Museum*

W.W. Hastings was much like Governor Black and other city sports who had fallen under the spell of the central Adirondacks. Hastings was an occasional contributor to the popular *Forest & Stream* outdoor magazine. The epic adventure of Hastings's white-tail deer quest, which forms the content of his rambling "A Few Days in the Adirondacks," roused my interest because his

Headquarters dam. *Courtesy the Indian Lake Museum*

experience took him to the Indian Clearing. I imagine Hastings was typical of the ordinary sportsmen of the day who had no knowledge of the Adirondacks and thus relied on local boatmen and guides to take him where he wanted to go. His late autumn trip is not particularly amazing, nor does it include any novel experiences, and yet I find the charm of this man's simple story and its authentic atmosphere interesting. The portion of Hastings's story that relates to Adirondack brothers and guides Archie and Eri Delmarsh and Wellington Kenwell follows.

☆ ☆ ☆

Determined a hunting vacation in the Adirondacks was in order, W.W. Hastings outlined his tracks to reach the North Woods. He boarded the Empire State Express, changed train cars at Utica Station for Fulton Chain, and changed again for Old Forge. It was October 1897.

"The lakes were drawn low," wrote the hopeful deer hunter, "for repairs on the dam at Old Forge, hence the trips of the steamers were erratic. It

 131

was best to employ a boatman to reach Hess's Camp, at the upper end of Fourth Lake. We started off for the twelve-mile pull. Clouds began to gather and an October gale with rain came on with the darkness. The guide (Bob Dalton) admitted that we were in for it…."

Hours later guide and client found themselves riding wild waves. "In spite of the utmost care, the crest of the waves was spilled into the boat, and the guns were wet and the baggage afloat. Bailing was difficult. The wind made talking impossible," Hastings wrote, "and things grew rapidly worse. A glimmer of light shone out from the forest and the guide headed the boat for it. The change of course made confusion. We were carried inshore rapidly, tossed up only to come down upon a rock, and off one rock to land upon another. The result was a hole in the bottom of the canoe."

Fortunately the stranded men had landed at Dr. Miller's camp. The doctor offered refuge for the evening and the loan of a flat-bottom boat in the morning.

Archie Delmarsh, second from left, stands with a hunting party that had returned from deer hunting on The Plains. *Courtesy Archie Delmarsh III*

132

A very young Eri Delmarsh on the Indian Clearing. *Courtesy Archie Delmarsh III*

Hastings's narrative continues: "Thanking Doctor Miller in the morning, we departed…. Arriving at Hess's Inn, tired out, wet and hungry, an open fire and breakfast were very acceptable. …I strode away from the hotel for a walk. Skirting Fifth lake, I came upon a sawmill…. The smell of the new lumber recalled pleasant memories…. I wandered along to the dam at Sixth

Lake, where I could intercept a guide who had been recommended to me on his return from the woods.

Interior of a New York Central railroad car. Hastings left the rough woods life behind as he traveled home in comfort. *Courtesy Town of Webb Historical Association*

"…A noise in the brush across the brook attracted my attention, and soon a pack horse loaded with a deer comes into sight. I had inquired at the hotel for a guide named Archie Delmarsh, who had been highly recommended to me. I readily surmised that one of the parties following the pack horse was Delmarsh. I watched him as he forded the stream, noted the ease with which he climbed the bank, loaded as he was with pack basket and rifles….and said, 'I presume that you are Mr. Delmarsh?'

"'I am,' he said. I introduced myself, stated my desires, and the bargain was soon concluded. This guide, Delmarsh, is a fine fellow. An honest man, pleasant smile, broad shoulders, clean cut from head to foot, he stands

OPPOSITE: **Hastings' proud take.** *Courtesy Town of Webb Historical Association*

before you a young Hercules. A continued acquaintance with him vindicated first impressions. He proved to be a good cook, skillful hunter and a genial companion; his speech is free from ribald jests, and the stereotyped jokes of the camp were noticeably absent."

The next morning Delmarsh and Hastings started off for "the virgin forest." Hastings's description is colored with purple prose and rambling nature descriptions typically found in the writings of the day. But all indications are the ultimate destination seemed to be the old Beecher camp after a stop at an open camp Hastings said Delmarsh had recently left. "There were live coals under the back log. The fire has kept twenty-four hours, Delmarsh having left the noon before....

"Now for a still-hunt for deer before night comes on. This still-hunting is serious business. Stillness and 210 lbs. of clumsy humanity do not blend harmoniously in my case.... The guide tells me I carry the gun all right, but that I must be more quiet.

"...He led me away off two miles or more from camp; we came to a rock...[and he] told me to stand up there and look out; told me to keep my mouth shut and to breathe through my nose after dark, as the night air was bad for gregarious people. I mounted the rock and posed as Ajax Defying the Lightning, or as a plate of ice cream upon a sideboard.

"...It had grown dark before the guide returned He came upon me suddenly and with no warning. I advised him that he was careless, that he might be considered as a deer and get his solar-plexis disorganized by a bullet. He told me that he had considered that before leaving camp, and had prudently removed the cartridges from my rifle. I lifted my hat to this philosopher and allowed him to lead me by the hand back to camp. We passed near the place the next day and inadvertently found a spot where the dead grass had been matted down by some reclining form. By a kind of Sherlock Homes deduction, I was satisfied that Delmarsh had slept quietly through my four hours of watchfulness on the previous day. These Adirondack guides are slick...

"...Tuesday and Wednesday passed, and we were still hunting.... Friday came around in regular order.... With thirteen cartridges in my pocket just for luck, I started out in the rain. The leaves were damp under foot, and there was sufficient wind to cover any sound caused by passing through the undergrowth. Delmarsh waited around the camp until I had been gone thirty minutes or more. He then started off to the right for a valley between the mountains. I had reached the opening of the valley down in The Plain and paused for a moment to locate the ford of the stream that pelts down through the valley and empties into the river. Oh, my eyes! Across the river, and jumping as only a startled deer can jump, was the largest buck I ever seen in the Fulton Chain regions. My .380-55 handled itself grandly…. The first shot smote the hindquarters… The second shot spat the brush where the poor fellow went down….

Hastings departed Old Forge for Fulton Chain [Thendara today] to connect with the train that would transport him home. *Courtesy Town of Webb Historical Association*

"The weight at Fourth Lake after the dressing was 225 pounds. Allowing less than the usual one-third for shrinkage, it is safe to presume that the weight in life was 310 pounds.

Hastings' camping days were memorable experiences. *Courtesy Town of Webb Historical Association*

"Archie had heard the three shots and came down to see what the trouble was. Upon seeing the deer he said, 'If I had known that you could shoot I would not have untied that buck. I have kept him for the last five years in order to allow my guests to see one upon the last day.'

"Wellington Kenwell lived seven miles further on. We met him on the trail with two pack horses. This was luck. I could ride old Doctor and the deer could be packed upon the other horse…. I had mounted old Doctor;

Delmarsh passed up the pack-basket loaded with pots, kettles and pans. On top he placed a bag of buckwheat flour that he wished to save. I bade good-bye to the old camp and promised to come again.

"This old horse, Doctor, is a famous beast about thirty-seven years old. A big bay at one time, but now grizzled with age, he has carried many burdens and been faithful through all. His end is near; possibly at this writing he has passed over the great divide…. Two miles from camp he erred sadly and caused me much discomfiture. I forgave him. It was caused by a dimness of sight and the stiffness of old age. We were crossing a swamp where the mud is bottomless. The path was rudely corduroyed. The Doctor let one of his stern anchors down between the timbers and the old craft began to settle. With a tremendous effort to retrieve, and by reflex motion, I was bucked high in the air. I clutched at the treetops, looked longingly at the clouds, and came down next, then the rifle, then a shower of pots, tin plates, knives and forks; the buckwheat flour came down last and covered what the mud did not. Oh! I was right in it (the mud) and out of sight.

"Kenwell and Delmarsh pulled me out; one picked the mud from my best ear with a match, while the other scraped my bald head with a tin pan. I was a study in black and white and splatter work that would put in the shade the best efforts of Frederic Remington. I alternately spat mud and flour until I wondered whether I was a dump-cart or a gristmill. The Doctor was struggling to get up and slinging mud like a yellow journal editor. I asked Archie why he had saved that buckwheat flour, and he said, 'I have not saved it.' It angered me to think that anyone could joke at such a time. I twirled the coffeepot at him with a left in-shoot, but he ducked, saying 'Jog along boys, there's soap and water at the hotel and a complete Baxter street outfit.'

"We reached Fourth Lake safely. I gave old Doctor a cleaning, saw that he had his peck of oats, kissed his old muzzle, and we laughingly parted as good friends. A bath, supper, bed, and night's sleep were never more highly appreciated.

"In the morning Delmarsh was on hand and his bill was paid. I gave him an extra counterfeit ten-spot. The chap really seemed to like me and requested me to come in '98. I led him to the valley where the stream from Fifth Lake empties into the Fourth, and assuming an Aguinaldo attitude I whispered thus: 'In '98 I'll meet you, when the leaves turn, Archie; when the beech nuts are falling I'll meet you; down there where the canoes land. I'll meet you, stay for me there; I will not fail to meet thee…' his answer was pathetic. I could only catch two words between his sobs, 'rats' and 'crazy.'"

Delmarsh's brother and the deer took one canoe, Delmarsh and myself another, and we started for Old Forge, intending to catch the afternoon train and procure a berth in the Montreal sleeper at Fulton Chain and reach New York Sunday morning. The lakes were like mirrors; the mountains, trees and cottages were reflected perfectly. If you should stand on your head you could not tell t'other from which. I proposed a race; the boys agreed. Archie said there was an old buck in each canoe and the chances were even. It looked like his race until I called his attention to a stump ahead. While he was looking over his shoulder, I got out a sea-anchor in the way of a rubber boot. The stakes—my pipe and tobacco—and the race went to his brother. The race and the stillness of the water brought us to Old Forge in time for the noon train. By quick work with the express agent I made it…."

Hastings did not have to wait for the overnight train; he arrived in New York City at 10 P.M. When he picked up the morning paper he read of the disaster on the Hudson River Railroad. The entire train had gone into the river and with it the Montreal sleeper that he had intended to take. He said of the disaster, "I might have escaped—I might not have," before ending by telling readers that he did not believe whiskey had any place in a huntsman's camp: "Whiskey means locomotor ataxia for his legs, incipient paresis for his brain." Instead he stressed, "Extract of witch-hazel is of far more use, Ring off!"

Chapter Eleven

Wellington Kenwell's Guide Business

WELLINGTON KENWELL was 73 years old in 1930, and a veteran of the woods. To Clarence C. Smith, this Adirondack guide's life seemed remarkable. Smith admired the old-timer's accomplishments. At that time, he said, "Mr. Kenwell's reputation among his oldest neighbors is that of a truthful and dependable gentleman, and upon being offered a good cigar he politely refused with the remark that he never used tobacco."

When Smith sought out the native-born man for an interview that appeared in the September 1930 issue of *The Up-Stater* magazine Smith like many of the younger generation, held the popular conception of old mountain guides

Wellington Kenwell, a veteran of the woods.
Courtesy Ora Kenwell

Wellington Kenwell's courage and fortitude still presides over the south branch of the Moose River. *Courtesy Robert "Zeke" Cummins*

as "characters" who were inveterate truth-stretching story-tellers "along certain lines, notably fishing and hunting experiences, and were inseparably devoted to an old pipe which must have been used to lay down a smoke screen against punkies and mosquitoes during some portions of the year."

Smith confessed that notion was inaccurate, at least when it came to Wellington Kenwell. After decades spent, "sleeping out under the stars, following a trap line, stalking game, and guiding city sportsmen through the Adirondack wilderness," those qualities would "seem to qualify one to speak on his business of being a guide. And that is the undisputed record of Wellington Kenwell."

Born in Johnsburg, N.Y. on December 8, 1856, Wellington had hunted and fished when Saratoga, Amsterdam, Troy, Albany, and other city hotels bought wild Adirondack game from guides who took the meat on their back or used wagons or shipped via the railroad to the cities in exchange for supplies such as flour, sugar, cornmeal, tea, and tobacco–commodities they could not grow or gather back in the day. Native folks earned a subsistence living that utilized home-grown vegetables and wild foods and meat. The

A guide-boat was essential to guides. Wild game to hunt, trout to fish, and pleasant wilderness scenes were the inspirations that drew sports to the Adirondack Mountains.
Courtesy the Town of Webb Historical Association

nearest cities were the best markets and, of course, the Saratoga hotels were the best of all.

This all took place until hounding was outlawed and game laws intervened, including the one-deer transportation provision that prevented meat hunters from killing for the market. This enterprise was never a great commercial endeavor on the part of Adirondack natives. It was a matter of survival. Kenwell knew of one man at Indian Lake who from the 1860s through the 1870s had an icehouse for storing game—particularly fish. Occasionally a fellow would come by and buy some for resale. The meat hunters also sold to local establishments and to the sportsmen who came into the mountains and were disappointed with their hunt. Kenwell believed that the prime time for this kind of activity came to an end by the 1880s.

In 1887, two years after he married Eliza E. Porter of Indian Lake, Wellington, then 23, was assisting his brother, Isaac Kenwell, by performing a variety of jobs at his Raquette Lake Hotel on Tioga Point until it was destroyed by fire that year. Following the fire, the young couple moved to Little Moose Lake, where they managed a hostelry. There, Wellington continued his hunting activities and guided clients.

Smith believed Wellington's career warranted documentation. The following is an edited summary of his interview with Wellington. Kenwell was at the time of the interview living with his son Gerald in Inlet, N.Y.

Smith began by asking about Kenwell's occupation. Wellington replied, "This guide business, like a lot of other things, ain't what it used to be.

"Fifty years ago, parties coming into the woods usually planned to camp for a month or six weeks, and they were the finest people that America could produce. They were all true sportsmen. They would engage a guide because of his knowledge of the wilderness, but they never treated him as an inferior and the wealthiest of them were always ready to do their share of the hard work of making camp, cutting boughs for the beds, and other duties of the day. Usually a deep and abiding friendship would develop between the guide and his employer."

"Now there is something," mused Mr. Kenwell, picking up a field glass from the table, "that a very wealthy man in New York sent me the other day with a note that he had heard through a friend that I wanted a field glass to supplement my eyesight, which has had many years of constant use. Anything else that I want he would send me if he heard about it.

"In those days the sportsmen came in by stage and boat to Old Forge and then on horseback. Or if they came from the east, it was by rail to North Creek and then by seven-hour stage journey to Blue Mountain Lake and from there they carried supplies on their backs into the Raquette Lake country, where I was guiding at the time. A man had to have a genuine love of nature to undertake that.

"I know more about a man's real character after camping with him a few days than many, many months contact in civilization would disclose. Sleeping in an open camp in the wilderness, a man throws off his mask. He says what he really thinks. I was guiding a New York man, a banker and manufacturer, many years ago. I liked him and we became good friends. I told him about a big buck I had seen with a very peculiar formation of horns. They dropped forward and spread wide. To my surprise we killed that very buck in a short time. He immediately told me that he was satisfied with this hunting trip and would like to arrange to return at once. I urged him to stay, that the hunting season had just begun and game would be plenty. Then he told me that his wife had been in Europe since February and that he wanted to be 'Johnny-on-the-spot' when her boat arrived in New York. In all the time we had been acquainted he had never mentioned his wife before. We were accustomed to speak our innermost minds to each other, so I commented on this fact that in all our days in camp he had never before mentioned his wife, and predicted that they would separate. He laughed at the idea, and went to New York. It was many years before we met again and when we did I inquired whether he was in the woods again while his wife was in Europe. A shadow came over his face and he was evidently deeply touched. 'Wellington,' he said, 'your prophecy came true. I divorced her ten years ago. She stayed in France with another man.'

"Legal limitations on deer hunting and modern transportation have changed everything. There are still real sportsmen coming into the Adirondacks, but they stay only a short time and when they hire one of the younger generation of guides it is for a day or two to make short excursions from Headquarters, which they reach by automobile.

"And along with the sportsmen now come a horde of riff-raff, men who are not gentlemen at all, are not woodsmen, are not careful either in the use of fire or of rifles. Many of them are not ordinarily honest. In the old days it was the custom that anyone who came along in the woods could use another man's shack, leaving a note to tell who occupied it and when. A woodsman could leave his suit of clothes with his watch in the pocket and return six months later and find it. Now he is lucky if he doesn't have his pockets picked while he is wearing his clothes.

"Last fall I was walking up a woods road. Two men a little ahead of me separated and circled out into the woods on opposite sides of the road. Very shortly five men with rifles appeared over the hilltop in the road. One of the men in the woods stepped on a dry stick which cracked and the leader of this band of what I call outlaws jumped to the edge of the road, cocked his gun, and prepared to shoot. I shouted to him that it was a man in the woods but he answered, 'Hell no, it's a deer,' and continued to try to get a shot. Fortunately, no other stick cracked nor did the hunter show himself. If a glimpse had been obtained of him he would have been killed—and then the five of them probably would have sworn I told them to shoot. In the old days, a sportsman did not fire until he could see all of the game.

"Changing laws have limited the methods of hunting. We used to kill deer much earlier than the present season opens. There is probably no more exquisite scenery in the world than the Adirondacks in autumn when the leaves have first turned to every brilliant color imaginable. Men would come into the mountains to fish and loaf and enjoy the wonderful beauty of nature at that season, and would kill a deer occasionally but only what they needed to eat. When we wanted a deer I would hang a lantern near a drinking place and hood it with bark so the light would shine out in only one direction. The sportsman would conceal himself opposite that shaft of light so he could aim and fire toward it. The light attracted deer and it was easy and certain to get one. Later in the season dogs would be used. Both methods have been abolished and 'still hunting' is the only prevailing practice."

Clarence Smith then inquired, "But how about deer at present?"

Kenwell replied that they were just as abundant at that time as they had been twenty years earlier. "It isn't so much the hunter as the winter that kills

145

Wellington Kenwell was an authority on the white-tailed deer, the Moose River Plains' most important big game species. Deer made an important contribution to the welfare of the pioneers and, indirectly, to the development of our country. Through the years they have been the quarry of armies of hunters who valued them highly for food, clothing, recreation, or as trophies.

Limekiln camp owner, Grandpa Harter had a tale to tell about his fall 1953 prize **bucks.** *Courtesy Jason Harter*

the deer," the sage guide pointed out. "A sleet storm starves them to death. They increase so rapidly that two favorable winters will result in great numbers of them and then one bad winter will make them scarce. We are seeing more deer this year [1930] than we have before in a long time. Last week I saw seventeen deer in one bunch. I should say they average as well now in numbers as they did many years ago.

"The period in my memory when deer were most plentiful was in 1893 and 1894. One day in November 1894, another trapper and myself were covering a trap line and we agreed to count the number of deer that we might have shot on that day's walk. That meant that we would raise the gun, take aim, but not fire, as we did not need any deer. Assuming that if we had actually fired each time with the same amount of skill we ordinarily displayed, we would have killed seventy-six deer. On another day I actually counted seventy-five deer while walking two miles, but of course not all of them (were) in reasonable shooting distance."

"What about the bear, Wellington?" the interviewer asked. Smith himself was an avid outdoors man. He believed fly-fishing is the poetry of motion. He also felt that a sportsman of old without a good guide might easily be a month in the woods and never catch a trout, or see a deer or black bear.

Kenwell responded, "And the bear? He is a peculiar animal and never was very plentiful. He is treacherous and when supposed to be fairly tame never ought to be trusted, although of course in the open he will usually run away. He is a great roamer. Bear may appear suddenly in considerable numbers in a locality and then for the next twenty or thirty years only an odd one may be seen. In the meantime they appear in another locality. They wander over a wide territory and it is hard to say whether there are as many as there were a few years ago or not."

Smith concluded the meeting by asking whether Wellington had ever had a serious accident.

"No," the old-time guide answered, but added that he did have typhoid fever once. "Not knowing what was the matter," Smith related, Wellington "kept on his feet until the ninth day when he dropped exhausted in an old deserted shack and became delirious. Some passing hunter reported it and a minister from Boston came over with his guide, who he left at the shack to care for

Mr. Kenwell as best he could while the minister returned to civilization for a doctor, who had a journey of many miles through the wilderness to reach him."

"'Now there was a minister,' Smith said Kenwell remarked, 'who certainly practiced what he preached. That was Dr. Durea, well-known in Boston. He is dead now and I hope has received ample reward.'"

Eleven years following that interview Wellington Kenwell passed away on Friday, November 29, 1941, at the Inlet home of his son Gerald Kenwell. He had been in failing health for the previous three years, but was confined to his bed only two days before his death.

When camping in the Moose River Plains at a favorite spot along Beaver Lake, it is impossible for me not to have my thoughts turn from the lovely silence of evening when the smoke of my campfire is the only sign of life, to the opening years of the 20th century. Those first few years were a time of building. Charles T. Chapin had appointed Wellington Kenwell to oversee the erection of a custom-built log lodge on the shore of the lake. Chapin furnished Kenwell two large canvas wall tents as temporary shelter for the carpenters and for his occasional visits. Later, a small workers' quarters was assembled. That building became Wellington's camp. According to Chapin's camp register, the camp was positioned along the shoreline under the massive white pines. The cabin provided Wellington with a backcountry place long after he had evacuated the old Kenwell homestead on what the family referred to as the "Little Plains."

Evening is a time when nature seems to be at rest until a rising fish sometimes breaks from the lake. Shadows deepen. Faint reflections of the western sky begin to illuminate the lake. A silver moon comes out, and the air begins to feel cooler, yet no breeze ruffles the dark surface of the lake. At that moment, sometime in Wellington Kenwell's past, he would have gone out nightshooting on this jewel of a lake. With the vapor rising from the waters in misty wreaths, the solemn stars shinning above, guide and sport would seem to be gobbled up by the great blackness of the lake as they skirted the shore, when suddenly the guide would quietly whisper, "A deer! A deer in the lily pads!" as the light thrown by the jack lantern would shine on the quarry.

The old days and the old ways are remembered, but I prefer today's methods of hunting for sport.

Chapter Twelve

Did Eliza Kenwell's Kitchen Magic Help the Chapins to Buy Beaver Lake?

WELLINGTON KENWELL, famous guide and insightful Inlet business-man, received top billing as an all-round Adirondack pioneer native, but it was his wife, Eliza, who stole the show by being "a mother to the woods-men and to the tourists," according to Foster Disinger, who shared his admiration of her with a reporter at *The Binghamton Press*. Both Disinger and A.M. Talbott, an outdoor columnist for the *Buffalo Courier-Express*, had known the Kenwells from their early days at South Branch. Foster

Kenwell's boarding house at Sixth Lake Dam. Lt. to Rt.: Gerald, Laura, two unknown girls, Eliza. *Courtesy Winfred Murdock*

149

Disinger said countless other Southern Tier men in Binghamton, Endicott and Johnson City had a high regard for the one-time school teacher who made the change to a pioneer life with her husband and children in 1891 when the family moved to the Indian Clearing along the south branch of the Moose River.

For ten years Eliza and Wellington lived beside the South Branch, twelve miles from their nearest neighbor at a place on the map simply called "Kenwells."

Kenwell's was a twenty-room sportsmen's boarding house. The hostelry was on the Little Plains within sight of the Moose River. The place has been described by hunters and anglers as a sportsmen's paradise.

Disinger spoke of Eliza Kenwell as a talented and kindly woman. She was known to offer a temporary remedy for a toothache, and she "could set a broken leg if a tree fell on a lumberjack. She could nurse them through sickness; in a country where doctors were virtually unknown, her services were invaluable."

These were all valuable assets to wilderness boarders who desired to "rough it," yet took comfort in the amenities Wellington and Eliza Kenwell provided. They sought adventure in the woods and waters, and were pleased to return to the Kenwells' woodland lodge.

Louise Porter Payne can also attest to the uncomplicated camp life at Kenwells' South Branch camp. Louise remembered: "When I was a young girl my father [Lou Porter] used work for the Kenwells. He would take me with him to their hotel when Tom and Sam Breakey and he were hired to help ready the camp for guests or do carpenter work for Wellington and Eliza. Back in those days all the city women wore big pleated bloomers you know. I remember Mrs. Kenwell, who had been a school teacher, telling me that she was preparing food in the kitchen when Mrs. Chapin and two other ladies passed close by. The guests used to have to pass through the summer kitchen to get to the outhouse. Well, as they were walking by Mrs. Kenwell heard Mrs. Chapin make this remark. 'I really don't think it's quite necessary to wear these bloomers back here. The people at camp seem quite civilized.' Oh my but did Mrs. Kenwell bust out laughing when she repeated the remark she had overheard."

Eliza also racked up acclaim for her culinary expertise. Her table fare, always excellent, provided scrumptious meals. Her pantry was supplied with berries from the clearings, vegetables from the kitchen garden, and wild game, as well as beef, chicken, and lamb from farm animals that ranged on a natural meadow where coarse blue-joint hay was cut by hand with a cradle blade.

Disinger shared that shortly before Eliza's death in 1920 "a multimillionaire who had eaten her pancakes as a small boy visited her to get some of the cakes. And every boy for miles around came to Mrs. Kenwell with his troubles."

Hikers returning to the Sportsman's Home looked forward to Eliza's meals.
Courtesy Bruce Koenig

Once the Kenwells left the Moose River Plains and moved to Inlet, boarders who had hunted and fished in days past in the South Branch country continued to patronize the Kenwells, first at the Hess Camp they leased, and later at Kenwell's boarding house and store at Sixth Lake Dam.

While Eliza Kenwell was at ease cooking and entertaining notable men and women, leading politicians, writers, artists, and socialites, she was no slacker in the administrative end of operating a business. Eliza ably handled financial affairs, and when it became necessary she filed a $400 claim against the State of New York for damages to her Fulton Chain of Lakes property from overflow due to the state's raising the Sixth Lake Dam at the outlet of the lake.

Wellington Kenwell freely admitted to writer Talbott one day that his "wife could beat him fishing any time she tried." Talbott quoted his friend in his "In the Open" weekly column. Eliza was capable of "bringing home a four-pounder if he had a three, and not needing to go beyond the [South Branch] Stillwater to do it."

Eliza and Wellington's son, Gerald, often spoke about his early childhood in the pioneer setting on the Little Plains. The family was often the victim of hard winters. Gerald said that during those early years of farming and homesteading his father "built his own tote road fifty-five miles to the nearest store."

Hal Boyle, another journalist who wrote "Boyle's Notebook," a weekly column that appeared in Amsterdam's *Evening Recorder*, reported a conversation he had with Wellington. Once "some young men asked the elder Kenwell what was the most fearsome sound he had heard in the woods: A bear's growl? A wolf's howl? The cry of a panther?"

"'Twasn't any of them,' allowed the old man. 'The wuss noise I ever heard was one winter about the end of February when I woke up and heard my wife scraping the bottom of the flour barrel. Knew I'd have to snowshoe fifty-five miles for more flour.'"

Eliza's hint was a seriously good way to get her husband motivated to head for more supplies. Wellington knew that on his return he would enjoy the fruits of his long overland trek in the form of more of Eliza's specialty baked goods. She always had the family's best interests at heart! There was no way she'd let them be anything less than well fed.

Sports returning to Kenwell's on the Plains claimed Eliza's cooking beat the best hotel fare hands-down. *Courtesy Peter Costello*

☆ ☆ ☆

Canning and preserving was an essential part of life for early Adirondack pioneers living in remote rural locations. While once it was necessary to can, there came a time when it was not always economical to. If the same commercially-canned product could be bought for only a little more, it made sense, for the home-canner not only expends money for the equipment, but labor and time as well.

Despite the economics, "putting by" the products of one's home garden has a certain satisfaction, even today. Eliza might have looked at making extra-good preserves, conserves, jams and jellies as one of her delights of home-steading at South Branch.

She was known to can only those things that were garden surplus and a few specialties that made it possible for her to set a more interesting and in-dividual table. According to her great-grandson, Paul Birmingham, people of privilege were often guests at Kenwell's Sportsman's Home. It's conceiv-able, that coming from an urban culture for the opportunity to vacation in a place of beauty and tranquility, the combination of hostess Eliza's table setting, meals, and refined etiquette enhanced their customer's experience.

South Branch Summer Vegetables is a basic recipe for cooking whatever vegetables are at hand. Fresh vegetables from the Kenwells' garden, in a land where a sportsman didn't expect to find veggies, was one reason for Eliza's cooking fame.

South Branch Summer Vegetables
About 8 servings.
2 lb. Zucchini
¼ cup butter
½ cup thinly sliced onion
Dash of pepper
½ teaspoon dried oregano leaves
3 medium tomatoes, cut into eighths
1½ cup fresh corn kernels or 12-oz. can corn

Directions. Scrub zucchini and cut into slices ½-inch thick. In large skillet, sauté onion in butter until tender. Add zucchini, salt, pepper, oregano and tomatoes. Bring to a boil, then simmer until zucchini is almost tender. Add corn and cook another 2–3 minutes. You can make this with nearly any combination of vegetables you have, and in any quantity. For example, in wintertime, you can use canned tomatoes and corn with diced carrots, potatoes, and cabbage.

Mrs. Charles Chapin at Camp Nit on Beaver Lake, circa 1906. Mrs. Chapin's arrival at camp sitting in a wicker chair was as much a novel idea as it was a joke. It only happened the day the chair was delivered. Judging from Mrs. Chapin's shoes in this picture, her arrival might have been set up for a camera shot. It's doubtful she carried the dog in a pack basket over fourteen miles. *Courtesy Margaret Wilcox (The Camp Nit Collection)*

Eliza Kenwell might have picked up this recipe from one of the many French-Canadians who worked in logging camps.

Adirondack Lumberjack Meat Pie

1 pound ground lean pork (or venison, lamb, ground beef or other meat)

1 tsp. Salt

½ tsp. Pepper

¼ tsp. each ground cloves, cinnamon and nutmeg

2 tsp. cornstarch

1 c. water

Pastry for two-Crust Pie

Directions. Combine all ingredients through water. Simmer 30 minutes on stovetop. You should have a thick meaty filling. Pour into bottom pie crust. Put the top crust on and crimp edges. Cut decorative slits in the top crust. Bake at 425°F. for 10 minutes. Then reduce heat to 350°F. and bake 35 minutes. Let cool about ten minutes before cutting. Serves 6–8.

While Wellington was on his long treks for flour, Eliza had to make do. If she had cornmeal on hand, this recipe would replace flapjacks.

Standby Cornmeal Pancakes

Makes 4 servings.

2 eggs

2 cups milk

1 cup yellow cornmeal

½ tsp. Salt

3 tablespoons melted shortening (or bacon fat or lard)

Directions: Beat eggs and milk together until light. Stir in cornmeal, salt and shortening. Let stand 10 minutes. Cook on hot lightly-greased griddle or skillet, turning once, until lightly browned on both sides. Serve with homemade preserves or maple syrup.

Mrs. and Mr. Charles Chapin take a trail break. *Courtesy Margaret Wilcox (The Camp Nit Collection)*

When Wellington returned with flour and other supplies, everyone enjoyed Eliza's yeast baking.

Valentine Ridge Nut Bread

Makes 2 loaves.

First: 1 cup rolled oats

3 tablespoons shortening

½ cup sugar

1 tablespoon salt (Tip for new bakers: This is correct. Two packages of
yeast are coming up, and salt keeps it from getting carried away while
it's feeding on the half cup of sugar.)

1 cup boiling water

1 cup finely chopped nuts

6–7 cups flour

Directions. Put oatmeal, shortening, sugar and salt into large bowl.
Add boiling water and cover for a few minutes to soften oats.
Next. While the oatmeal softens, dissolve two packets active dry yeast in
one cup warm water.
Then. Stir ½ cup cold water into the oatmeal mixture to cool it. When
the oatmeal mixture is no more than lukewarm, stir in the yeast mixture.
Next. Add two cups of the flour and the nuts and beat well. Stir in 3
more cups of flour. Then work in one more cup with a dinner knife.
Knead in the bowl until all flour is taken up. Put out on floured board
and knead until smooth and elastic, adding necessary flour if dough is
sticky. Place in a greased bowl, cover with a damp towel, and let rise in a
warm place until double. Punch dough down and let it rise again. Then
shape into two large loaves for 9" x 5" loaf pans. Let rise once more.
Bake about 40 minutes at 375°. When done, loaves should sound hollow
when tapped.

Eliza would have known perfect, delicate conserves, jellies, and preserves could
only be made in small quantities. Cooking in large quantities causes the fruit
to cook unevenly and lose shape, and lengthens the period of cooking.

Indian Clearing Blackberry Jam

Ingredients:

6 cups of blackberries

½ cup of water

6 cups of sugar

Juice of two oranges

Juice of one lemon

Grated rind of one orange

Directions: Cook the berries with the water until soft. Rub through a sieve and add the sugar, the juice of the oranges and lemon, and the grated orange rind. Boil together until thick.

Tip: In testing whether or not jelly is "done," the spoon test is easy and reliable. Dip a clean silver spoon into the jam or jelly, hold it above the boiling mixture, and let the syrup run off. If it "sheets" or flakes off the spoon into a jellylike mass, it is ready to be skimmed for the last time and poured into glasses or jars.

Within a short span of time, the pioneering Kenwells had developed a comfortable home and a fine reputation as a back-county hotel. There is no documentation to point to when Charles Chapin and his wife were first guests at Kenwells'. The guest list included Civil War generals, leading manufacturers, downstate tycoons, writers, and New York State Governor Frank Black. It would be interesting to read the extent of their clienteles if the guest register ever surfaced.

What is known is that Charles Chapin's family did enjoy their annual pilgrimage to the Moose River Country and it was Wellington Kenwell who introduced the Chapins to Beaver Lake Country. This is how Mr. Chapin described the territory: "It is a charming section, full of primeval and romantic beauty. Game in fair quantities is still obtainable, and deer which frequently pasture in this natural deer–park may sometimes be sighted in the daytime. Here too, the crystal streams are teeming with rarely molested trout."

Eliza and Laura Kenwell
Courtesy Winfred Murdock

The Chapins were particularly fond of the way trout were prepared by Mrs. Kenwell. The old standby method was simply to fry them in salt pork. But as a good cook Eliza knew trout should be cooked with nothing that could impair their delicate flavor. She would quickly rinse them in cold water, wipe them on a dry towel, immerse them in sweet butter, and fry them in a skillet over just the right amount of heat which nothing but experience could determine and serve them piping hot.

"Food is not about impressing people. It's about making them feel comfortable," Ina Garten stated in *The Barefoot Contessa Cookbook*. That quote rings true about Eliza Kenwell's table fare too.

Slim Murdock repeats the following story that he says has been passed down over the years about sportsman at Kenwells. When he had just finished a breakfast of coffee, bacon, potatoes, and bread he was asked if he didn't now want an Adirondack shortcake. Upon inquiring as to what it was—(a stack of three, ten-inch flapjacks with butter and maple syrup in between), he exclaimed, "I could eat no more without undressing." At which Eliza replied, "I would rather see you go hungry than to see you go naked."

Part Three

Adirondack Mountains

Moose River Plains

EARLY CAMPS ON AND AROUND THE INDIAN CLEARING

Deserted buildings built by the Gould Paper Company provided shelter for sportspeople.
Author's Collection

161

Chapter Thirteen

Camps and Guides, an Adirondack Culture

THE BACKWOODS CAMPS came in many forms—the simplest shelters were old-time hunters' camps constructed from bark or brush, or pole-built for temporary shelter by guides or were a traditional canvas tent affair. Other sportspeople, vacationers, and recreationists who sought a woods experience but had more genteel tastes and wished to avoid living in the heart of the woods chose the comforts of a permanent cabin, a rented room, or a boarding house, or chose hotel life. For them, elegant hotels and inns featured covered verandas, barrooms, bedrooms, indoor bathrooms to wash off the mud and dust of forest travel, and dining rooms that offered enticing menus. Boarding houses, less elaborate and less expensive, still provided a level of comfort considerably above that of a rudimentary bark shelter.

Backwoods camps came in many forms—the simplest shelters were old-time hunters' camps constructed from material found in the surrounding forest. *Courtesy Maitland C. DeSormo*

162

A sportsman is toting a roll of tar paper into the Moose River Plains over the corduroy road that followed Fawn Lake's muddy shoreline. Tar paper was typically used for roofing and siding. *Courtesy Ray Hart*

163

The Indian Lake House offered comfortable accommodations.
Courtesy the Indian Lake Museum

A basic tent. Some early sports carried lighter models made of silk fabric.
Courtesy Authors Collection

The Cedar River House and the Indian Lake House provided comfortable accommodations for sportspeople who entered the Moose River Plains by way of Cedar River Flow. Courtesy the Indian Lake Museum

 165

ARTICLES AND ADVERTISING in newspapers and outdoor magazines of the day depicted the exciting experiences available for tourists and sportsmen who came to the Adirondack Mountains. Many "sports" stayed in fishing and hunting camps—often bark or pole lean-to's and tents provided by guides who selected campsites, felled trees and peeled bark for the shanties, fitted up enticing balsam bough beds on the floors, built shelves and racks, kept the campfires and smudges going night and day, prepared and cooked the meals, washed dishes, told yarns and, late nights or early mornings, left the sports to sleep while they slipped away to return with venison or fish. Those recreationists who preferred a less authentic woods life experience

Area guides often converted their homes into boarding houses such as this one along Fourth Lake in the central Adirondacks. Beyond offering home-like coziness for clients, they provided an additional source of income. *Courtesy Maitland C. DeSormo*

Proprietor H. Radley operated The Pauley Place, a welcoming no-frills boarding house.
Courtesy the Piseco Historical Society

but still wanted the feel of "roughing it" a bit chose public houses with unpapered pine board partitions rather than the fancy hotels and genteel boarding houses.

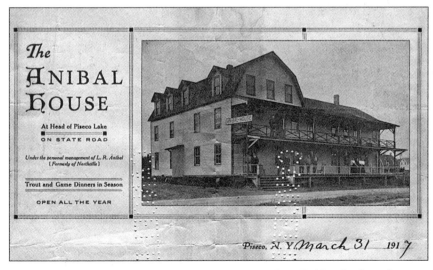

The Anibal House at Piseco provided luxuries one would not find in a backwoods environment. Courtesy the Piseco Historical Society

THE TERM "CAMP" is a loosely-used nomenclature in the Adirondacks. Depending on one's point of view, the term can conjure up images of anything from a shotgun-style shanty to an elaborate, fashionable lodge. My friend Roy Wires lives in a RV set up in Singing Waters, an RV park near Thendara, New York, from May to October. That is Roy's "camp," but his father, Edwin B. Wires, served as superintendent of Kamp Kill Kare, the Francis P. Garvan family "camp." The Wires family lived year-round there, overseeing the residence, the wildlife and its surrounding acreage.

In 1899, a reporter for the *Albany Argus* described Kamp Kill Kare, then owned by New York's Lieutenant Governor Timothy Woodruff, as a "palatial log home in the heart of the hills," Harvey H. Kaiser told in *Great Camps of the Adirondacks*. This is a view of Kill Kare's main house looking toward the "casino" end. It looks the same today. *Courtesy Author's Collection*

The superintendent's quarters at Kill Kare. Kamp Kill Kare's website (www.lakekora.com) describes the history of the private camp and the accommodations offered. It is not a typical "Let's drive to the Adirondacks and book a room for a few nights" situation. The rate for a minimum stay of four nights plus N.Y.S. sales tax would gobble up a considerable amount of a middle-class wage earner's yearly salary. Kaiser hit the nail on the head when he coined the phrase, "A Camp Is a Camp." *Courtesy Roy E. Wires*

KAMP KILL KARE {when later owned by the Garvin family) is described by Harvey H. Kaiser in *Great Camps of the Adirondacks* (and in Craig Gilborn's *Adirondack Camps: Homes Away From Home, 1850–1950*) as of "impeccable French Romanesque style," designed by John Russell Pope, better known for his Beaux Arts Classicism designs such as the National Gallery of Art in Washington." The scale of the Garvan camp is grand, "imaginative and continuous," wrote Kaiser in *Great Camps of the Adirondacks*. It is a "camp" with "a monumental town gate and extensive barn and service complex arranged around an interior court[yard]."

In *Kamp Kill Kare: Memories of Life in an Adirondack Great Camp*, Roy Wires describes his eleven years of helping his father oversee the massive log and masonry complex that included a service complex, "groves of pine trees towering above clipped lawns; a dairy; woodworking, metal, and machine shops; a guest house sited on an island in Lake Kora, and the main complex, which extends along the lake."

169

Abner Blakeman: An Unsung Moose River Guide

ABNER "AB" BLAKEMAN was one such Fulton Chain guide, carpenter and camp caretaker. His career mirrors many other guides whose lives remain relatively undocumented. One source that has some historical facts about Abner is *The Fulton Chain: Early Settlement, Roads, Steamboats, Railroads and Hotels* by Charles E. Herr (HerrStory Publications, 2017). One other source is a few century-old snapshots that have been handed down through the Blakeman family.

Abner is in good company when it comes to name recognition. How many people recognize the widely popular early 20th century guides in this line-up of Rocky Point guides? Lt. to Rt.: Milo Leach, George Burdick, Abner Blakeman, Tim O'Hara and **Henry Hart.** *Courtesy Town of Webb Historical Association*

Abner operated a few tent camps he'd rent to anglers and hunters between the Benedict and Sumner streams in the Moose River Plains during the early teens and 1920s. This picture shows one of his camps pitched for deer hunters. *Courtesy George Blakeman*

This typical scene shows backpackers skirting x. Food and equipment were carried in woven pack-baskets. Entering the Moose River Plains by way of Limekiln on foot meant many miles of hiking with heavy loads.

In the early days, sportspeople relied on guides to reach particular locations as well as for their safety, comfort and success. Every locale within the Adirondack Park had its guides. *Courtesy Edward Blankman (The Lloyd Blankman Collection)*

Abner snapped this picture of Henry Nelson holding the reins of Blakeman's pack horses. If you look closely you will see the horses are standing on a trail that has corduroy. A good guess suggests the scene is Fawn Lake. *Courtesy George Blakeman*

Abner Blakeman (left) and an unidentified client proudly stand by their catch of the day. It's unfortunate that stories of Abner's vast guide experiences have been lost to the passage of time. *Courtesy Irene Blakeman Collection*

172

Oral history about George Abner Blakeman (in middle) is sparse. I think this picture of him, in the company of deer hunter clients, gives the impression his clients found him to be a likeable man. *Courtesy Irene Blankman Collection*

173

Abner Blakeman (Rt.) stands with a client on The Plains. Sports often referred to their trek into the Moose River Plains as "entering the Badlands." *Courtesy George Blakeman*

Abner Blakeman and Allen Quest fishing on Fourth Lake. Clients relied on their guide's knowledge of where best to fish to be successful. *Courtesy Irene Blakeman Collection*

Abner Blakeman stands between two packhorses somewhere along the Kenwell trail. One of his responsibilities as a guide was to check on his clients and resupply them.
Courtesy George Blakeman

Phil Christy: One of the Sportsman's Home's Earliest Guides

PHILLIP HENRY "PHIL" CHRISTY was born in Montreal, Canada, on March 28, 1854. At the age of seven he moved with his family to the United States, where they made their home in Michigan. Several years after this the family moved to Port Leyden and then to Moose River Settlement, N.Y.

At the age of eleven, Phil said he began following the trout streams and deer trails, and in 1869, at age 15, he claimed he knew every square mile of the entire Adirondacks—which was quite a boast. In that year he also accepted his first professional employment as a guide.

Philip H. "Phil" Christy (1854–1947) was a popular guide at Kenwell's during his early 30s. Phil worked at lumber camps in the winter and spent the rest of the year leading parties of hunters and anglers throughout the central Adirondacks. He was known for his wit and story-telling. During the month of March 1892, he had the misfortune of having his face badly disfigured by Nellie, who he called "an ugly cow," who kicked over her bucket of milk. Christy said that had it not been for the timely assistance of Will McGarry, Nellie might have killed him.

On July 24, 1895, James Barrett drowned in Fourth Lake. Christy recovered Barrett's body between Gingerbread Point and Alexander's Camp.

OPPOSITE: **"Phil" Christy was heralded as the oldest central Adirondack guide when he died on September 11, 1947.** Photo appeared in The Adirondack Arrow on September 11, 1947. Courtesy Ora Kenwell

His first year of professional guiding proved successful, and patronage increased with his growing reputation. He said he gave his compass to a friend in 1875 and never carried one after that.

He claimed that his sense of direction never failed him. His initial experience as a guide occurred before highways, railroads, motorboats, game laws, licenses and resort hotels had penetrated the mountains.

Dapper Adirondack guide Phil Christy, center, spruced up for this portrait which included, from left, one of the Russell boys, Julia Price, Phil, Lelia Baker, and Irene Craigue. *Courtesy Town of Webb Historical Association, P7008*

On June 1, 1878 he married Bridget Rivett, also of Moose River Settlement, where the couple made their home for a number of years, and where Phil was employed in the woods by the Gould Paper Company.

Christy first came to Old Forge in 1880 when, according to Phil, "there was practically nothing there in the way of buildings." It's ironic that he explained, "I wanted to be near the center of things." At that time Old Forge had a total permanent population of 18, including men, women and children, but no roads, stores, schools or other conveniences—although its fame as a resort and hunting locale was growing. There Phil worked in the lumber woods and did some guide work.

In 1888 he moved his family to Old Forge, and in 1890 built his home on Main Street. For some time Christy operated a stage line between Fulton Chain (Thendara) railroad station and the boat landings at Old Forge. With the coming of the railroad, Phil took to guiding, and for many years was one of the most trusted guides employed by the Adirondack League Club.

Some of his most memorable times involved taking hunting parties to mainly two camps—Mosquito Camp at the Big Plains in the vicinity of the head of the south branch of the Moose River, and Cozy Parlor at Natural Dam on Moose River, about 20 miles above Old Forge.

On a late summer 1899 guided hunt, Mr. and Mrs. E. Stuart Williams of Rome, N.Y. were so appreciative of his services during their vacation at the Arrow Head on Fourth Lake that they shared their gratitude publicly in the September 4, 1899 edition of *The Rome Daily Sentinel*. The short column told how their 14-year-old son, S. Randall Williams, distinguished himself as a marksman by killing a 149-pound buck when the teenager was guided "on a hunting expedition…with Philip Christy as a guide on the Kenwell's hunting ground [The Big Plains] about 12 miles from the Arrow Head…."

Through his guiding and work in the woods during the off-season, Phil became well-known to many prominent sportsmen in the Eastern United States. During the course of over 70 years spent roaming the Adirondacks with hunting parties, he guided four United States Presidents—Harrison, McKinley, Teddy Roosevelt and Harding—plus a list of notables from England and continental Europe. Roosevelt, he said, was the most energetic of the presidential woodsmen, but Harrison was the best marksman. "They were all good sports, too," he added.

He claimed when in his prime he weighed no more than 145 pounds, was a crack shot, and could walk miles through the forests with a 60-pound pack or could shoulder a guide boat along the wooded winding carries of the mountains. In the fall he would shoulder a big buck deer and think little of hiking five miles with it.

He was a natural wit and famous storyteller. He often told of the days when guides hunted for the meat market. In those days meat hunters killed many deer in the Moose River Plains and in the Nick's Lake section. He also recalled the days of the old turkey shoots held in the heart of Old Forge, when the marksmen would line up at the site of the Given Drug Store and the target would be in the vicinity of where the Niccolls Memorial Church now stands. Those were the days, Christy said, "When a rifle was as common in a man's hand as a knife and fork."

Phil Christy may have been small and nimble, but he was a highly respected outdoorsman and skilled guide. Here in town, Phil is in the company of, from left, Julia Price, Irene Craigue, Lelia Baker, and Mary Jane Craigue. *Courtesy Town of Webb Historical Association, P5022D*

OPPOSITE: **83-year-old Phil Christy displays his marksmanship with his deer rifle upside down to *National Geographic* photographer-writer Frederick G. Vosburgh in 1938. Christy claimed he could still outshoot any ordinary man and was still nimble enough to "kick the hat off your head before you can turn around."** *Author's Collection*

One story Christy liked to tell was about the worse scare he ever got in the woods. Phil would tell, "You could call it a scare, but I certainly was startled the day I was sitting down on a log to eat my lunch. I stood my gun (that's Old Betsy) up against a tree and all of a sudden a deer came up in back of me and jumped right over me and out of sight. As the deer jumped he snorted and that was the first idea I had that there was a deer around. By the time I grabbed my gun, there wasn't any deer."

Asked about the largest deer he had ever shot, he once told, "About 1907 I shot one that weighed 286 pounds, and just 14 years later in 1921 I killed one that weighed 286. I guided Will Rogers of Rochester when he killed a buck that weighed 306 pounds, and we had to make a stretcher to carry it out of the woods."

During Christy's long career as a hunter and guide, he piled up an imposing set of statistics, according to his meticulous recordkeeping. He guided 4,000 hunters, 3,000 fishermen and had been instrumental in the killing of some 2,100 deer and the taking of more than a quarter million brook and lake trout. He also killed numerous black bear and panthers.

Christy used to say that modern-day hunters wanted luxury, weren't satisfied to sleep out in a tent in the woods, and that they were in too much of a hurry. In the old days most parties came for a month. He complained that "modern" hunters came in on the morning train, wanted to hunt for a day, and left on the night train.

In June 1938 Christy was written up in *The National Geographic* magazine, and in 1940 told of his guiding experiences on the radio program, "We the People."

And on September 11, 1941 in the *Daily Sentinel* he and other area old-timers were recognized for uncovering the location of a long-lost grave. The article in part read:

> The forgotten grave of Peter Waters, known as Drid, an Algo-
> nquin Indian, who fell victim to the marksmanship of Nathaniel
> Foster, Jr., famed Adirondack woodsman buried at Ava, in one
> of the last shootings that marked over a century of continual
> strife between the red men and white in the mountain area, has

been uncovered at Old Forge by a group of old-time guides, pathfinders of more than 60 years ago....

Drid was killed Sept. 17, 1833....

The guides who found the burial place were Emmet Marks, resident of Old Forge since 1872, William Weedmark, Ira Parsons, Phil Christy, Dennis Fraula, Jack Rivet and Peter Rivet, all of whom have resided in the Old Forge vicinity for 60 years or more. They recalled that the grave was once a respectable mound, shrubbed and marked with two small boulders and a wooden cross bearing the name of Peter Waters and the date of his death. In the years that followed the cross rotted away and the stones were covered with sand....

In 1943 Christy celebrated his 89th birthday as he renewed his fishing, trapping and hunting licenses in preparation for another busy year in the woods. He was featured in another *Sentinel* newspaper article titled "Dean of Adirondack Guides Sets Sights for Century Mark as Active Woodsman."

The article read in part:

> This season will mark his 74th consecutive year of Adirondack guiding, and leave him only 11 more seasons to go in order to achieve an unusual ambition.
>
> He wants to continue guiding without interruption until he reaches 100. On this 100th birthday, he says, he will not renew his guide's license. He plans to begin "easing off" then, doing just enough hunting and fishing to keep himself limber and in good physical condition...
>
> "After a guide's 100 he can't give the service people are accustomed to," he declared. "I believe in quitting before I'm licked too bad..."

Phil fell seven years short of the centurion mark. At the time of his death at the age of 93 he left his wife, Bridget; sons William, Jack, and Donald; two daughters, Mrs. Jay Barker and Mrs. Villiere; and 27 grandchildren and 29 great-grandchildren.

Christy's home still stands along a much busier Main Street.

VETERAN GUIDE DIES—Philip Christy, Adirondack guide for 75 years, died Saturday at the age of 92.

Philip Christy, 92, Adirondack Guide, Expires in Auto

OLD FORGE.—Philip Christy, 92, one of the best known Adirondack guides, whose parties had included those of five presidents, died Saturday afternoon in his daughter's car in Utica as they were starting back to Old Forge.

His daughter, Mrs. George Villiere, said she saw her father slumped in the car when they were starting home after a shopping trip. She drove to Saxton hospital, but he was dead on arrival. Death was due to a heart ailment.

Private services were conducted at 8 p. m. Sunday at the home in Main st. A requiem high mass will be celebrated at 9.30 a. m. Monday in St. Bartholomew's church. Burial will be in Riverview cemetery, Old Forge.

Born in Montreal, Canada, March 28, 1855, he was six years old when he moved to the Adirondacks with his parents. They settled at Moose River. When he first came to Old Forge there was but one house there.

He began following the trout streams and deer trails at the age of 11 in a boat he had built. During his long experience in the woods he guided five presidents — Harrison, McKinley, Cleveland, Teddy Roosevelt and Harding, as well as notables from Europe.

Hunting parties were taken mainly to two camps—Mosquito camp at Big Plains at the head of Moose river and Cozy Parlor at Natural Dam, about 20 miles above Old Forge.

Christy used to say that modern day hunters wanted luxury, instead of being satisfied to sleep out in a tent in the woods, and that they were in too much of a hurry. In the old days most parties came for a month. Hunters nowadays, he complained came in on the morning train, wanted to hunt for a day and left on the night train.

Several years ago Christy was written up in The National Geographic magazine and about seven

Miss Larche Wed to A. S. Traynor in Notre Dame Church

MALONE.—Miss Alice M. Larche, daughter of Mr. and Mrs. Damase Larche, 24 Bigelow st., became the bride of Harold S. Traynor, son of Mr. and Mrs. Carl Traynor, Brushton, at 9 a. m. Saturday in Notre Dame church.

Rev. Gerald Seguin performed the double ring ceremony. Miss Mary Ellen Durkin, Brushton, was maid of honor and Carl Michael Traynor was best man. The bride was given in marriage by her father.

The wedding breakfast was served at the home of the bride's parents. The couple will live at Tupper Lake. The bride was graduated from St. Joseph's academy and is employed in the canteen at Veterans' hospital at Sunmount. She is a former member of the junior CDA. Traynor attended Brushton high school and is also

Malone Game Club Schedules Outing

MALONE.—Many are expected to attend an outing of the Malone Fish and Game club at 7 p. m. Tuesday at the Company I range house at Bare Hill.

Hot dogs and sandwiches will be served by a committee headed by Warren Lockerby, treasurer of the organization. No formal program has been planned, but hunting equipment will be given away.

Use of the clubhouse has been made possible thru the co-operation of Company I, 105th infantry, NYNG of Malone. President Mark Chaffee urged members who have gasoline lantern to bring them to the outing as electric lighting is not available.

State Announces GI Scholarship

After three quarters of a century helping "sports" hunt, fish and enjoy the mountains, famed Adirondack Guide Phil Christy died due to a heart ailment while on a shopping trip in Utica with his daughter, Mrs. George Villiere.

184

Chapter Fourteen

Elijah Camp and Little Moose Lake Camp

TROY, N.Y. *Daily Times*. 1880. "UP NORTH-A telegraph line will soon be constructed between North Creek and Blue Mountain Lake. Elijah Camp, the noted guide, has built a hunter's lodge on [Little] Moose Lake. The trout fishing on Cedar River, above the drift wood, is unusually good. The brooks about Cedar Falls headquarters are overflowing with small trout..."

Wyoming County Times, November 28, 1880: "Elijah Camp claims to have found veins of both gold and silver in rock deposits along the Cedar River, about three miles north of Indian Lake in the Adirondacks. Camp has filed a claim in the secretary of state's office. He says the veins run north and south He claims five acres of land on each side of the river."

Poughkeepsie Daily Eagle, December 30, 1880: "Elijah Camp, an Indian guide, thinks he has discovered two Adirondack lakes never before visited by white men, about 10 miles west from North Creek and 13 miles south of Blue Mountain Lake.

The Evening Gazette, July 18, 1883: "AN ADIRONDACK ROMANCE: A Crafty Indian Maiden At Little Moose Lake Alleged To Have Drunkard And To Have Entrapped A Guileless Sing Sing Dude Into The Bonds Of Matrimony."

Utica Morning Herald, January 7, 1886: "The case of Elijah Camp, arrested for shooting a deer out of season at Moose Lake, is still pending."

The Auburn Bulletin, Wednesday, February 8, 1899: Saratoga, N.Y. "Elmer Osgood, the Adirondack guide who was murderously assaulted by the Indian guide, Elijah Camp, in a Hamilton County camp Monday, cannot survive the day."

The Warrensburg News, March 3, 1889: "CAMP HELD FOR GRAND JURY—Elijah Camp, of Indian Lake, who assaulted Elmer Osgood at a lumber camp near that place about three weeks ago, was arraigned before Justice C. D. Gilson..."

Elijah Camp (foot against post) at Little Moose Lake. *Courtesy Bill Zullo, Hamilton County Historian*

The Evening Telegram, Tuesday, June 18, 1901: "Adirondack Mountains Island camps; terms $8.00 a week. For further particulars address Elijah Camp, Indian Lake, Hamilton Co., N.Y."

The Warrensburg News, Thursday, April 21, 1904: Elijah Camp, an old resident of Indian Lake, died very suddenly on [April 8]

Sportsmen at Elijah Camp's Little Moose Lake. Circa 1883.
Courtesy Bill Zullo, Hamilton County Historian

of Neuralgia of the heart. He leaves a widow, two sons, Samuel and Gabriel Camp, and one daughter, Mrs. Emma Mead, all of Indian Lake. The deceased was about seventy years old and had lived in Indian Lake about forty years. The funeral was conducted by the Rev. William Rist of Newcomb, who preached a sermon from the text, 'What I say unto you, I say unto all, watch.' ''

Say what you will, as remote as Little Moose Lake might seem today, a hundred thirty-five years ago the pristine lake was well known, as well as its "half-breed" resident-guide, Elijah Camp.

Elijah, born in 1836, was the son of Englishman John Camp and his wife, Maria Benedict, daughter of the Indian, Sabael Benedict. (Maria's mother was Elizabeth Kennedy of the Oneida tribe.)

187

The prospect of work in the lumber industry brought Elijah to Indian Lake.[12] By the time he arrived, a trail was cut into Little Moose Lake. The otherwise wilderness territory was known for its deer hunting and trouty waters. Game laws were unknown then—the supply seemed endless. Market hunters regularly brought out venison and fish, sending them to hotels in Saratoga. Lumber camp cooks relied on venison as their main source of meat, and trout was taken by panfuls.

Lumbering, which came almost to a standstill during the Civil War, was again upset in 1876, when a raging fire burned all the timber between Beaver Meadow Brook and North River.

Elijah was a man with ideas. By 1880, the railroad at North Creek and roadbuilding let stage coaches and buckboards transport tourist and freight over the mountain began to bring change to the wilderness character of the region. Hotels on Indian Lake and Lewey Lake sprang up. Lumbering was still the chief industry, but by this time city dwellers—tourists known as "sports"—were coming in larger numbers to fish, hunt and vacation. Some bought property and hired camps to be constructed, where they returned summer after summer.

Recognizing the interest in the budding tourism industry, Elijah and his wife, Elizabeth, built and operated Hunter's Home on Little Moose Lake,[13] headwaters of the south branch of the Moose River. Elijah acted as guide; Elizabeth served as cook.

Hunter's Home at Little Moose Lake advertisement. *Courtesy Bill Zullo, Hamilton County Historian*

By 1880, Elijah was not a young man, but he was known to have the strength of a man of much younger years. He also had strong beliefs and opinions, and when anyone violated his principles, he knew how to strike back!

Elijah Camp holds an infant at his Little Moose Lake camp. *Courtesy Bill Zullo, Hamilton County Historian*

Old-timers talked of Elijah's talents. He was shrewd and canny, and he knew the environs of Little Moose Lake better than anyone else did. Sports were considerably impressed by this native's prowess with a rifle. It was said that he never missed a shot, and stories told in hunting camps and in hotel parlor rooms added confirmation that the Indian guide was a deer-killer of legendary proportions.

As a guide, Elijah was a handy man to have around. Men who walked behind him over the rough, hard trails—hunting, going to distant lakes to fish or across the wilderness forest to the Moose River country—quickly learned how important he was to their success.

Sportsmen talked about freedom when on vacation in the Adirondack Mountains, and it seemed to be something like heaven lodging at Hunter's

Home. Relaxing on the porch overlooking the lake, the sports sat beside Elijah listening to his stories, some nodding at intervals, as if they understood, more than the others, what the guide was saying about hunting stealth or fishing techniques.

W.C. Buell was a popular captain of the Laureate Boat Club in Troy, N.Y. and one of numerous sportsmen who came to the comfortable Hunter's Home. During Buell's hunting trip, "he saw an enormous deer feeding on lily pads," the Club captain's newspaper, *The Troy Daily Times*, reported on August 10, 1880.

Little Moose Lake by C.H. McBride. *Courtesy Bill Zullo, Hamilton County Historian*

Characteristic of the newspapers and sporting magazines of the day, the story goes on in embellished detail about the hunt. With the aid of his guide, Buell bagged a trophy buck. The deer, long known as the Monarch of the North Woods, was a 400-pound buck that had defied hunters for years.

With the aid of his guide, Buell gained a bit of Hunter's Home notoriety and returned victorious to the Laureate Boat Club with a head and rack that hung on the Club's wall for years afterward.

Further significant material about the camps and Hunter's Home is contained in letters dated between 1881 and 1890 found in the files of the former Hamilton County historian, Bill Zullo.

Two examples follow:

December 21, 1883
Northampton, Mass.

Friend Elijah:
I wish you and all your family a Merry Christmas and a "Happy New Year."

I often think of the pleasant days which I spent at Moose Lake and wish that I may be able to go there next year.

We have had considerable snow here, though I presume that you have had enough to cover up the tops of the trees. I suppose that this is one of the best times in the year for deer hunting, but for my part, I would rather be there when it is warmer than it is in December.

I have intended to ask you to send me a pair of buck's horns, as I find myself too poor this year so that I shall have to come up next year and shoot my own deer.

I have sent each of your family a Christmas card which I hope you will accept, together with my best wishes for yourself and family.

The cards have your names on and the fringed one is for Mrs. Mead.

Hoping that next summer will see our party again at Moose Lake.

I remain, Yours very truly,
Harry G. Townend [sic]

June 25, 1885.
The equitable Life Assurance Society,
No. 120 Broadway, New York.
Elijah Camp, Indian Lake.

Dear Sir: I propose, if all is well, to make my usual visit to Moose Lake this summer in company with Mr. Toffiel. We should be out the first week in August and stay the usual time, perhaps a little longer.

I should be glad to have you with me if convenient. We got along very nicely last year and I think we can again.

Please drop me a line and say how things are at the Lake and what arrangements are to be made this summer.

My respects to Mrs. Camp and all the family.

Very truly yours,
Francis W. Jackson

Elijah Camp's sports, who stayed in the log buildings that straddled the bluff of Little Moose Lake, enjoyed many successes, but perhaps no visitor to the Moose Lake country garnered more free newspaper publicity for Hunter's Home, situated twenty miles back in a pristine forest, than Gabriel Mead, who had inherited $125,000—a fortune in 1883.

"Camp has a daughter, Emma, now about seventeen years of age, who has been quite widely noted for her beauty of person and charming deportment," it was reported in the Port Jervis (N.Y.) *The Evening News* on July 18, 1883.

A lengthy saga outlines the story of an Adirondack romance and the objections of Mrs. Camp who "forbade the harboring" of any thought of matrimony. That was until December 24, 1882, "when [Elijah] Camp and his daughter, accompanied by Mead, went out to Indian Lake to prepare for the Christmas festivities. When they arrived there, both of the men began over-indulgence in fire water, and Mead told Camp, in substance, that if (Mead) was going to marry his (Camp's) daughter, now was the time. Previous of this, he had engaged Rev. G. W. Edgerton, of Indian Lake, to come up to Camp's and marry them, but Mrs. Camp's objection had so far prevented the celebration of the nuptials. Camp consented, and the forest maiden was nothing loth [sic] and the parson was hastily sent for. Rev. Mr. Edgerton came and soon bound in the silken ties the Sing Sing Rolfe and the Adirondack Pocahontas, the couple returned to Little Moose Lake, where Gabriel resided, enjoying the society and favors of his dusky bride."

By July 1883, the groom's father had enticed his son out of the woods on false pretenses, keeping Gabriel from returning to the mountains. "Soon after, Mrs. Emma Mead was served with a summons," continued *The Evening Gazette*, "and complaint in the name of Smith Lent, plaintiff's attorney, and verified by Gabriel Mead, as plaintiff in a suit for divorce at Sing Sing [New York]. The venue was laid to Westchester County, and the complaint alleges that Camp and his daughter, well knowing the reputed wealth of the plaintiff, plotted, conspired and contrived and did entrap him into marrying Emma Camp, while under duress, by taking advantage of his passion for intoxicants, and getting him so under the influence of alcohol that he was not of sound contracting mind at the time of the alleged marriage."

The determined Mead family's objection to the marriage put quite a spotlight on Little Moose Lake, and it's probable that it at least brought in more sports to Hunter's Home, even if Elijah's plan to profit from his daughter's marriage had been foiled.

Bill Zullo, provided me with the history of the area after Elijah Camp left, setting up residence on the Sabel Road, where he and his wife operated the Adirondack House.

Zullo said the information came to him in a letter from John Carroll, son of Jack.

The information in the correspondence told the original Little Moose Lake Club began on December 21, 1897, after a 99-year lease was signed between the Hudson River Pulp and Paper Company and a group headed by A. Pagenstecher Jr. from New York City. They referred to the lease as being in Township 7 of the Totten & Crossfield's purchase. An advertising poster announced that the log cabin establishment was called Elijah Camp. By 1900, guide David E. Farrington had become the new proprietor. He called his commercial business the Hunter's Home. The club was incorporated on December 1, 1931, and continued to be incorporated until the lease ran out in December 2006. The property has over a hundred years of private ownership history. In December 2006, New York State acquired the property.

Little Moose Lake lodge in 1929. *Courtesy Bill Zullo, Hamilton County Historian*

"Sometime prior to 1929, Dr. Richard Bunker of Hudson Falls was a member of the club and eventually bought the club in 1944. The officers of the club during 1948 were Dr. Richard Bunker, president (Hudson Falls); my father, vice president; E.C. Alden, secretary (Hudson Falls); and Leslie Bruso, treasurer (Hudson Falls). Other members were Norman Bruso (Fort Edward) and Howard Taylor (Hudson Falls).

"Dr. Bunker and Dad held their respective club positions until Bunker's death in 1974, at which time Dad and I were the only shareholders in the club. Dad had negotiated a lease extension from International Paper Company in 1985 that continued the lease from its original expiration date of December 1996 to December 2006. This involved surrender of acreage that left the club with 500 acres for the final 10 years. Dad told me that the original lease was for 10,100 acres. Over time, especially during the 1960s, the club negotiated deals with the state and the acreage was reduced."

The freedom to fish and hunt without restriction that Elijah Camp and his sports experienced would not be seen again. Regulations, of course, have made it possible for succeeding generations to enjoy what the wilderness offers while keeping it pristine for those who will follow.

The last time I hiked to Little Moose Lake, I sat on the deck of the abandoned camp and considered the history of the camps that had been built on the site. I braced myself to meet the onslaught of the wind that came off the lake. A scum of frothy bubbles accumulated along the shore below me. There was no sign of any human track, not even a scrap of food wrapper to indicate someone had recently been there. "Get going!" I told myself as I checked the time. I did not want to run out of daylight before reaching my car, which was parked along the road beside Silver Run Stream.

Little Moose Lake camp, date unknown. Over the years, due to fire, the camp was rebuilt, taking on a new appearance each time. *Courtesy Bill Zullo, Hamilton County Historian*

Chapter Fifteen

Lt. Gov. Woodruff's
Kamp Kill Kare

SOMETHING STRANGE was happening in the wilds near Raquette Lake. A sprawling, 1,000-acre[14] compound of pristine timber on the edge of a secluded lake was purchased by Teddy Roosevelt's lieutenant governor, Timothy L. Woodruff, in 1898.

Kamp Kill Kare was his and Cora Woodruff's Adirondack vacation retreat. In 1899, a reporter for the *Albany Argus* described it as a "palatial log home in the heart of the hills."

"Palatial" is a good description. The camp was indeed a grand affair. Beyond William West Durant's excellent choice of the setting and architectural appearance of the original buildings, the retreat appeared as impressive as "any forest villa in Europe," writer and guest Henry Wellington described it in "Kamp Kill Kare: The Home of Hon. Timothy L. Woodruff," in the February 1903 issue of *Field and Stream*.

Cora Woodruff stands on the porch at Lieutenant-governor Timothy L. Woodruff's Kamp Kill Kare, 1904. *From the April 9, 1904 issue of* Rider & Driver & Outdoor Sport Magazine, *Courtesy Roy E. Wires*

During the summer of 1901, a Venetian gondola began to ply the waters of the former Sumner Lake, renamed Lake Kora in honor of Woodruff's wife (the spelling presumably in keeping with "Kamp" and "Kare"). The fanciful gondola joined summer parties dotting the lake in canoes, on a barge, and in guide boats.

Mrs. Cora Woodruff in her gondola, named "Venice" on Lake Kora.
From the April 9, 1904 issue of Rider & Driver & Outdoor Sport Magazine, Courtesy Roy E. Wires

The Woodruffs were among the families of wealth and privilege to enjoy their affluence and leisure time in "camps" built in the Adirondack Mountains during the Gilded Age. The magnificent secluded buildings were an escape from the traffic, congestion, air pollution and summertime heat of their city homes. Beyond the healthful benefits of a vacation in the great northern woods, there were sporting opportunities in the unspoiled wilderness such as hiking, boating, hunting and fishing.

Statistically, Timothy Woodruff was a politician, but he was far more—historian, businessman, sports enthusiast and passionate admirer of the arts. The Woodruffs were enthusiastic hosts who enjoyed making their wilderness haven available to bigwigs, dignitaries and celebrities, welcoming all who came to Kill Kare to experience life in the Adirondacks as they wished. Reports by those who visited spoke of a range of activities from relaxing strolls to guide-led hikes along a section of an old military trail to a wide variety of social and sporting events to even an opportunity to "rough it" in a small camp Woodruff had constructed along Sumner Stream, a short distance by trail from Lake Kora's dam. The comfortable little fishing shanty with a rustic-type exterior was complete with guide boats to use on the Sumner Stillwater. This building was known as Boat House One. Near-by was Camp English.

The origin of Camp English's name is unknown, but perhaps it had something to do with Sir Thomas Lipton's sojourn at the Woodruffs' summer home. Reports written by John Westwood, the Baronet's secretary, were published in various newspapers of the day. He wrote that Sir Thomas found Mr. Woodruff to be "a jolly good fellow."

Governor Woodruff' camp at Lake Kora. *Courtesy Patti Bateman Quinn (The Johnson Family Collection)*

Mr. Westwood reported that Lipton, who was the founder of the Lipton Tea Co., commented to the Woodruffs, "Yes indeed, your Adirondacks are wonderful. They are so much different than the forests in England. No such variegated foliage over there and the timber is so much heavier. Why, the air in the Adirondacks is so fine I don't wonder that they consider the mountains a great health resort."

During Lipton's short stay at Kill Kare he hunted with "Commodore Todd, of the Atlantic Yacht Club," Westwood said, and "spent considerable time" with Charles Moore, who was a close friend of President William McKinley.

At the time of Lipton's departure from Raquette Lake, a good-size crowd of locals gathered at the train station as an unidentified preacher hushed them with a raised hand to announce, among other things, that Sir Thomas had "done more than any other person to exterminate the ill feeling created between Great Britain and America by the Revolution."

The remarks of others who had visited the Woodruffs' place also referred to it as a throne of the Earth where they wandered forest paths through a welcoming woodland, strolled over an enchanting ornamental wooden bridge to a pretty island cottage, and rested along the lip of clear, cold Sumner Stream as it tumbled from its outlet to continue its journey downstream through uncut woodland, passing through the Indian Clearing until its waters mixed with those of Benedict Creek, where both streams poured into the south branch of the Moose River.

Governor Woodruff and guests at Lake Kora. *Courtesy Patti Bateman Quinn (The Johnson Family Collection)*

One member of what he termed "the Brooklyn Pan-American expedition," which included William Cullen Bryant, Major P. Henry McNully and Herbert L. Bridgman, secretary of the Peary Arctic Club, reported his mid-autumn

1901 visit in *The Brooklyn Daily Eagle*. "Lieutenant Governor Woodruff led the way. The road runs through a canyon of magnificent trees, winding over the hills until it reaches the camp, on the shore of Lake Kora.... Here is one of the most beautiful spots to be found in all the Adirondack land. The Lieutenant Governor has built his unique and beautiful home without the help of architects or skilled workmen; but guided by Mrs. Woodruff's artistic taste, the axmen of the mountains have made a group of buildings that look more as if they had grown with the forest than like creations of the hand of man. The symmetrical logs of the spruce have been turned into massive walls, and the beech and birches, white and yellow, adorn the interiors. The skins of the deer and bear have become rugs and hangings, and implements of warfare and the chase furnish the decorations.

Bridge from mainland to the island in Lake Kora.
Courtesy Patti Bateman Quinn (The Johnson Family Collection)

"After luncheon Mr. Woodruff conducted a large number of the party on a two-mile walk through the forest, and at the end of the forward march, made a little address on the history of the great North Woods since the Revolutionary period. He said his interest in the acquisition of the territory by the state was so great that it gave him pleasure to bring here the residents of the cities in order that they might learn with him to live in the mountains, lakes and forests and to appreciate the necessity and wisdom of preserving them. The state, he said, had already acquired nearly one half of the Adirondack territory and he was urging an appropriation of at least $1,000,000 a year for the purpose of complete acquisition.

Governor Woodruff's sawmill. *Courtesy Patti Bateman Quinn (The Johnson Family Collection)*

"As head of the state [Forest Preserve] board, he had become greatly interested in the history of the old land titles, since the time after the revolution when Alexander Mac Comb [sic] had acquired by grant the 3,000,000 acres constituting the Adirondack regions. He became bankrupt and parted with the territory, which became, in time, much split up. One speculator met King Joseph Bonaparte at Marseilles after the overthrow of Napoleon and sold him an immense tract in Lewis County, where Bonaparte lived for six years…. Mr. Woodruff added that he had brought to the camp nearly every legislator who had been at Albany during his term of office and he hoped aroused an interest in the preservation of the North Woods, that would not die out until the work had been accomplished and the 1,500 lakes, nearly all of which were interlinked by streams, would set forever in the midst of the trees."

Woodruff served four years as president of the Forest Preserve Board, overseeing the work of purchasing state lands in the Adirondacks and Catskills. He led the board that recovered 90,000 acres of Adirondack land that had been lost by previous improper cancellations of the state's title; he worked tirelessly to prevent forest fires and the stealing of state timber, and for the protection of fish and wildlife. He advocated for game protectors to keep better track of all fishermen, hunters, tourists and camping parties on their sections, and was very interested in the plight of deer during the winter.

Friction between interlopers on Kamp Kill Kare's property and Woodruff's personal guides was quickly ended following the purchase of the Woodruffs' Adirondack playground. Fred "Mossy" Maxam[15] and Ernest C. Blanchard were Kill Kare's full-time guides. The men were well-respected among their community and made it known they were not about to let trespassers "bustin" their career. And it's not that far-fetched to suspect the woodsmen might have carried out that statement with a pointed rifle to apply an added effect.

Immediately surrounding the various buildings, reported Mr. Louis Rhead, who wrote a report of his trip, "Kamp Kill Kare Costs About $50,000 A Year," for the *Brooklyn Daily Eagle* in 1910, was a "virgin forest of magnificent trees, some nearly two hundred feet high and mostly of hard wood, where deer, bear, foxes and other wild animals are allowed to roam unmolested and free from pot hunters or sportsmen that shoot for the 'fun of killing.'"

Rhead heaped praise on the Woodruffs. "Paradise in wilderness," he gushed. "The Kamp proper is a collection of buildings that are separate, yet still connected with the large and commodious dining room, so that each party or number of guests occupies exclusive quarters, to assemble at meals or dine alone at their discretion. Three buildings, aside from their costly structure, evidence the most exquisite taste in architecture and appointments, with splendid bathrooms and every possible convenience of a city home, yet in character with their surroundings. Ingeniously designed and built of pine logs, the outside bark is left in its natural state, while indoors it is stripped off, the wood stained and varnished. The large and beautiful windows of plate glass are so placed as to afford from each of them a fascinating vista to look down on the dower gardens, winding paths and rustle bridges over various streams and arms of the lake. If necessary, these windows are curtained off to soften the light into a pale, delicate gold, the silk material blending in to match the tender green stained wood and rich carpets with appropriate wild animal skin rugs, all tending to make a general artistic ensemble, both comfortable to the body and pleasing to the eye, so far as it is possible for money to acquire and taste to achieve.

Mrs. Cora Woodruff and her cat. *Courtesy Patti Bateman Quinn (The Johnson Family Collection)*

"Most of the bedroom furniture is specially made of bent and twisted native wood; one piece in particular, a bed used by the owner, being a magnificent piece of work, constructed of picturesquely formed limbs and roots of wood, and at the head a complete tree, rising above to make a sort of canopy, every little twig of which is stripped of its bark then stained and varnished. Among the branches are ingeniously arranged various stuffed birds and climbing animals in the most natural attitudes that convey the impression to a marked degree that the sleeper is truly reposing in the 'great outdoors.' The room itself is large and about fifty feet high, while the canopied tree takes up most of the space above. To construct this exquisitely artistic

203

bed and the time expended in stripping the thousands of twigs and branches must have cost no little sum, but the unique results attained, it seems to me, are well worth the labor.

"Space forbids a detailed description of the splendid dining hall, with its walls arranged in blue china, enough, it would appear, to entertain an army. But the host and hostess at Kamp Kill Kare are royal entertainers and worthily do in deeds what the Kamp's name implies by frequently having at one time from thirty to fifty guests, and quite as many attendants to care for them."

Kamp Kill Kare's fish hatchery. *Courtesy Patti Bateman Quinn (The Johnson Family Collection)*

Kamp Kill Kare even had a fish hatchery that outranked any of the state-supported Fulton Chain hatcheries that Dr. Nash, Chairman of the Fish and Game Committee, was in charge of, sending thousands of brook trout eggs into the Adirondack mountains. The goal of the Committee was to raise and keep the eggs for propagation purposes in central Adirondack waters. Dr. Nash, who was an authority on questions of raising fish, declared that the Adirondack trout were the sweetest-flavored fish he had ever tasted.

On June 16, 1909, a Mr. Burke reported that the fingerlings in Kill Kare's hatchery were, "feeding well in water at 62 degrees. The average length of the fish was about 1½ inches. Some of the landlocked salmon planted in Kora Lake in the preserve of Hon. T.L.W. [Timothy L. Woodruff],

Woodruff's black bear at Kamp Kill Kare. *Courtesy Patti Bateman Quinn (The Johnson Family Collection)*

 205

Raquette Lake, N.Y., seem to have thrived according to his superintendent, Mr. E.S. Casselman. On August 8th, Mr. C. saw these salmon jumping all over the lake. He caught two with a small fly-hook, one of them 5½ in. long, and the other over 6½ inches. The fish were planted in the fall of 1908."

Woodruff's private hatchery and its game fish rivaled anything outside Canadian waters. Louis Rhead, himself an avid angler, reported that lakes within Kamp Kill Kare's preserve had been stocked with trout and land-locked salmon from, "Woodruff's private hatchery during the last two years [1909–1910]. This hatchery is said to be one of-the best equipped in the country.

"There are three lakes on the estate, the largest, Lake Kora. being three miles long, well stocked from the private hatchery with trout (fontinalis) and ouananiche (land-locked salmon),[16] the latter as yet but half grown, having been planted two years ago as an experiment, and crowned with success. The salmon have been planted by the state in various lakes in northern New York, so far with poor results, and Mr. Woodruff is to be congratulated that his able hatchery superintendent, Mr. Casselman, has succeeded so well in breeding from the eggs transported from Maine many thousands of this splendid game fish up to the time when the young fish are fully able to feed and protect themselves. Indeed, during my visit this spring, these young fish of ten inches long persistently rose to the flies that I cast after the speckled trout. In another year or two these young salmon will arrive at an adult state, and, if they continue to rise to the ar-tificial fly with equal vigor as they do now, Lake Kora will contain a game fish found in no other water in New York state and not matched in the state of Maine or elsewhere outside of Canada.

"I believe the ouananiche are only caught at the surface of the water on the fly in the Dominion of Canada, and that in Maine they are taken in deep water by trolling methods. According to the opinion of our state fish culturist, Dr. Tarleton Bean, the hatchery maintained by Mr. Woodruff is 'a better equipped and finer establishment of its kind than any other In New York state.' For the past two years Mr. Woodruff has been restocking the lakes and streams of his own and adjacent private property, as well as some of the state waters in the vicinity, with fry and fingerling trout of a superior selection. The output of the hatchery has not attained a magnitude beyond the requirements of a gradual, yet bountiful, restocking of neighboring waters, so that the excess of young fish raised is being sold for planting in waters within the limits of harmless transportation from Racquette Lake station."

For the owner or his guests who wished to hunt or fish, Kamp Kill Kare permanently employed guides who knew well how to go about providing the legitimate sport required.

The last known picture of Timothy L. Woodruff before his death, with the foreman of Woodruff's Adirondack summer home. *Courtesy Patti Bateman Quinn (The Johnson Family Collection)*

"Kare Killed at Kat. Here Kare is Killed." is the "Kill Kare" motto according to one Brooklyn Pan American expedition. One guest gushed about the amenities, from the "noon-day sun that tempered the air and the luncheon served outdoors by the lakeside and amid the trees" to the grand lawn, to Colonel William Hester, "who on behalf of the party presented Mrs. Woodruff with a box of beautiful orchids, as a present from her Brooklyn friends."

Kamp Kill Kare lived up to its motto no matter what it meant.[17] The unidentified writer concluded, "Even Maria the tame bear has no troubles, but rolls lazily about the vinegar barrel which forms her den in blissful happiness, eating chocolate caramels and occasionally nipping a guide's leg, when in need of healthier fodder. A family of deer roams in the wire-enclosed paddock and a bevy of red squirrels make merry in a cage commodious and so situated as to seem like home."

"It can well be imagined," said Louis Rhead, "both in summer and winter, that a paradise for pleasure and recreation such as this camp can be made in the midst of a veritable wilderness, and yet can be reached by the Empire State Express in eight hours' time from New York City. In such a place diversions are endless—gondolas and boats run by motive power to explore the miles of lakes, accommodations for swimming and diving, golf links and tennis courts, riding and driving, fishing and hunting, camping and sleeping out in the lean-tos, with freshly-cut, sweet-scented balsam boughs, kept in perfect order for any who desire to use them, not forgetting ample provision for indoor pleasure in bad weather. Finally, abundant provision for the larder of fresh vegetables and fruits grown on the place, and there are chickens and cows that supply fresh eggs, milk, cream and butter.

"Money goes a long way to procure such things: It also requires brains to do it right, and a competent head to direct a retinue of servants whereby the best is available at a nominal cost."

Woodruff cared for the well-being of the wildlife that lived throughout his spacious acres. In a Glens Falls, N.Y. *Daily Times* on January 14, 1901, he shared the care he had his guides provide for the white-tailed deer in "Feeding Deer in Winter."

"During the months of March and April of last year…when snow was nearly four feet deep on the level, and when the deer were in poor condition as a result of an unusually severe, protracted winter, I kept four men constantly employed in feeding deer in the vicinity of my camp. We tried hay, oats, and almost every kind of food given to domestic animals. This food they would not eat, but we soon discovered that they would eat the buds and twigs of the maple and other hard woods; also the tips of most of the evergreen branches or those trees….were cut off and thus placed within their reach. It is not necessary to cut down trees for this purpose and thus spoil good timber, as the deer feed only on the tender buds and smallest twigs."

The owner of Kamp Kill Kare was just as passionate in his capacity of president of the Forest Preserve Board in working toward the speedy recovery of state land where the titles were bogus or insufficient and to purchase additional acres of Adirondack forests where there were clear and valid titles. It is from that perspective that he spearheaded the removal of the

Wellington Kenwells, who the legal advisors to the board learned were on land that was the domain of the State.

It is hard not to believe that Woodruff also clearly had a personal motivation. It seemed clear there was more than one person at the time who nodded at Woodruff's interest in protecting his nearby estate from encroachment by sportspeople who vacationed at Kenwells' hostelry. The popular guesthouse was located a few miles down Sumner Stream from the outlet of Lake Kora.

Letters that passed between the board and Wellington Kenwell were legal and polite in tone, yet one cannot help but read into them the true nature of the business. Woodruff had discovered that Wellington and Eliza Kenwell's deeds for their lots in Township 4 of the Moose River Tract did not contain a clear title.

It was in Woodruff's personal best interest to work out a solution to remove the pioneering Kenwells. Without the Kenwells' footprint on The Plains, the territory suddenly became more inaccessible to sportspeople. Now, with a larger buffer of wilderness around Kamp Kill Kare, those awesome trophy fish and deer were all within Woodruff's domain.

Woodruff's purchase was an important moment in upstate New York history, for the Kenwells invested the compensation they received for their hostelry in real estate development and became founding residents of the Inlet community.

The times of the last years of the 19th century and of those family names of vast wealth —Woodruffs, Rockefellers, Astors, and Vanderbilts among them—and how the Golden Age magnates ventured into the Adirondacks in private railway cars, bringing family, friends, notable personalities and wisely-selected business connections up to enjoy their estates with them is long past.

Kamp Kill Kare's website speaks of the Woodruffs' park land estate as one of the most magnificent retreats: "By most accounts, Lake Kora was the grandest of all the Great Camps. …Tales of the camp under Woodruff's ownership are that of legendary hedonism in the woods, enjoying the greatest luxuries and most unexpected amusements: gondolas imported from Venice plying the lake, semi-tamed bears kept amongst the cabins, even telephone service as early as 1903. Subsequent owners (the Vanderbilts among them) also indulged certain eccentricities—at one time, tame deer visited each day for freshly made blueberry pancakes; for years, the baseball teams of Yale and Harvard were brought to the property for a few preseason games for the amusement of the owners and their guests.[18]

"And even today, a sense of uncommon merriment permeates; one of many elements that has remained unchanged since the property's first days. Most of the original buildings still stand, built with such care over a century ago—the logs and stone sourced from the property itself, the ironwork hewn in an ironmaker's workshop on site. The grand dining table, the hunting trophies, even the billiards table are all original to the property.

"There have certainly been some minor modifications over the years for guest comfort. There are, of course, now telephones in the accommodations and WiFi throughout the property. The spa facilities in the old icehouse certainly allow for comforts that the original vacationers weren't lucky enough to enjoy. Overall, however, the property retains its original appearance (and spirit) to an extraordinary degree.

"Lake Kora is one of very few Great Camps to have remained in private hands until the present day. Until recently, Lake Kora was seen and enjoyed by no one but its owners and a few well-placed friends who were fortunate enough to receive an invitation to visit. At this time, its new owner has made a considered decision to open this most captivating, private and historical estate to a limited number of rentals, during the finest weeks of the summer."

Unlike rough camps and mere tents in the woods that were found throughout the Moose River Plains, Kamp Kill Kare was designed to be more along the lines of the marble palaces in Newport, R.I, that many referred to as "cottages."

Kill Kare's stately compound, constructed from local timber and stone, was designed to "house several dozen visitors at once, with guests sometimes outnumbered by staff," continues the website. "Set in the remote, lake-studded woodlands of the Adirondack Mountains, it was here that these families could enjoy nature in its purest form and play at 'roughing it' in the epitome of rustic comfort—a dream no less desired in the modern age."

Chapter Sixteen

Dr. Gerster's Memories of Sumner Lake Before the Woodruffs

FOR DR. JOHN C.A. GERSTER (1882–1974), camping days and boyhood adventures he enjoyed at Raquette and Sumner lakes with his parents, Dr. Arpad G. and Anna Wynne Gerster, were priceless memories.

Throughout the fall and early winter 1962, Dr. Gerster and Kenneth Durant corresponded. Durant was then collecting historical material that eventually became part of his *The Adirondack Guide-Boat* book published in 1980. Gerster's first-person knowledge about his and his family's early days in the Adirondacks provided Durant a wealth of background information. Adirondacks.

Gerster knew the Kenwell family; he had lodged at Kenwell's hostelry on The Plains. In a July 27, 1958 *Syracuse Herald American* newspaper article, he told of Gerald Kenwell, speculating that Gerald, "may have been the youngest guide ever employed. In the spring of 1896, when he was only nine years old, he took his first party into the Moose River region. Among them was Mr. Mert Lewis, then Attorney General of the State of New York."

Durant wrote that by 1874, Dr. Arpad Gerster believed the days of "camping out were no longer necessary if one preferred hotel life, because few wilderness routes were without hotel facilities less than a day's journey apart." By 1890, "railroad and steamboat lines were bringing tourists into the north woods." Tourists hired guides at points of departure, who then whisked clients over the lakes and stopped by day's end for a hot meal and lodging in a boarding house or hotel.

OPPOSITE: **Dr. Arpad Gerster, 1897. Gerster said in his 1917 book *Recollections of a New York Surgeon*, he felt an increasing annoyance on early guide-led 1880s tours because, in his opinion, the guides showed too great an impatience to reach the next hotel dining room.** *Courtesy of The Adirondack Experience, the Museum at Blue Mountain Lake, PO26386*

213

Durant concluded it was not the outdoor experience John's father favored. He illustrated his point of view in his comments on page 276 in Arpad Gerster's 1917 *Recollections of a New York Surgeon*, Dr. Arpad Gerster felt increasing annoyance on such tours because, in his opinion, the guides showed too great an impatience to reach the next hotel dining room. 'Even in the eighties [1880s], the Adirondack guide began to change his character. From a woodsman, he was turning into a mere machine for transportation, losing his woodcraft, his leisurely and knowing ways.'"

As a boy, John Gerster felt nothing beat the feeling of exploring the water route between his parents' Oteetiwi camp [pronounced Oh-tee-tye-wye, as he clarified in his letters] on Raquette Lake and their lean-to campsite shared with William West Durant on Durant's private Sumner Lake. Kenneth Durant was the son of Fredrick C. Durant, builder of Camp Cedars and the Prospect House. That makes him William West Durant's cousin.

John reminisced about the family's passion for sleeping. "My father, mother and I were devoted to sleeping out of doors, in fact the only nights I can remember sleeping indoors, were nights just before the days we were to leave camp."

The Gersters' original camp on Raquette Lake was an "open camp" much like today's lean-to. John explained that it "had logs at the front and the back lying on flat stones at either end, and barely clearing the ground. On these were laid a row of birch stems (head and tail) forming the floor, and on these were placed carefully sorted balsam boughs freshly picked and brought in on stringers. The bough bed is made particularly thick and soft from where one's shoulders to one's hips are to engage contract. Beyond this the boughs can be less thickly and less carefully laid.

After a while the boughs begin losing their needles and a fresh layer is placed directly over the original one. As time goes on, and layer after layer of boughs have been laid, the bed accordingly becomes springier and springier. Finally, in the old camps at Sumner Lake—1888—the beds were fully 18 inches thick. At last, one had to 'clean house' (care being taken not

OPPOSITE: **Dr. Arpad G.C. Gerster had a camp on Raquette Lake, then later at Long Lake. While at Raquette Lake he was a good friend of woodsman-hermit Alvah Dunning. Dunning is seen on the far left of this S.R. Stoddard photo.** *Courtesy Maitland C. DeSormo*

215

to put on too many at one time) and there then the bare poles were once more covered with their first laying of green, fragrant boughs. ...

"...The bough bed, once completed, then was covered by a black rubber blanket—black side down, white side up—on this were laid regular blankets with one thickness under and one or more thicknesses over the sleeper...

"At bedtime, we changed into pajamas and dressing gowns and moccasins in our own bedrooms, and then, with oil lantern in hand, walked out to the open camp where a good fire (built and lit by our guide) was awaiting us (our beds on the fragrant balsam boughs were 'piled into,' after leaving footwear inside on boughs near the front, and hanging up dressing gowns) one promptly fell asleep by fire-light. If one were to awaken in the dark before daylight, one could see a red eye, a solitary glowing coal survivor of the bedtime fire and later, in the morning light, white ashes and a thin wisp of smoke marked the empty fireplace."

John recalled that when traveling a back-country footpath one summer with his father from Sumner Lake to Wellington Kenwell's hotel (near the confluence of Sumner Stream and the south branch of the Moose River) and back to Raquette Lake, they stopped and occupied a rough shelter for two nights known to all as the Sumner Stream camp. "It was just there for anyone to use," he said. That temporary shelter's floor was covered too with the customary balsam boughs for bedding.

John's November 14, 1962 letter to Kenneth Durant tells of his family's days before W.W. Durant built Kamp Kill Kare and Timothy Woodruff's occupation of the grand camp.

My parents went up to Sumner Lake for the simple primitive mode of life in an ideal spot. Sumner Lake was about 1 to 1-½ miles long running east and west and about ½ mile wide with a sand beach at the western end. The carry from Shedd [Sagamore] Lake came to the north shore and one took a guide boat to the camp near the eastern end on its north side, and, near it a little brook. Buildings: 1 bear house with cook stove and eating quarters. One open camp for sleeping—no plumbing. In short, we camped! And we loved it! About twice a week, a guide from

Raquette would bring (pack in) provisions and mail. No one but ourselves on the lake—one came and went in freedom and privacy—to observe and to enjoy undisturbed. We were able to keep warm and dry and properly fed and enjoy woods life free from intrusion.

Yes, this was the "open camp jointly maintained," etc. There were one or two guide boats available.

A Hungarian doctor guest was taken out after supper for a row by my father. It was a dead still evening. My mother and I remained on the dock at camp. When the gentleman returned and the guest had retired for the night, Father reported that his friend had become engaged—and Mother told him she knew it, because every word was audible to us one mile away.

Why the joint maintenance was not continued was due to Mr. Durant's extravagant tendencies—too rich for my father's mode of life. They remained fast friends, however.

Sumner [Lake] was visited often afterwards by parties of men, especially for hunting deer with hounds. Breakfast before dawn. Hunters silently departed for their appointed watch points in guide boats—no noise!—only whispers or hand signs—field glasses (binoculars to you) and Winchester 44s or Marlin 38s.

Meanwhile one or two guides, with one or two dogs each, left at daylight to designated areas to release said dogs in succession at fresh deer sign (tracks). The dogs chased the deer to water and then their job was done. Dogs either returned to camp or sometimes waited on shore to be picked up. Mike McGuire had a black dog name Speed who was so fast the deer went straight to water. Slower hounds produced less certain results—the deer might come in very quietly and coast along shore and so escape at the approach of guide boats before they could be cut off from landing again. Killed deer might sink and so be lost.

Occasionally a hound might drive a deer over the hill to a nearby lake—not to the intended one.

There was an island on Sumner Lake and on it a loon's nest—close to the water's edge—where the mother bird could slide into the water with ease and dispatch.

The Sumner stream (outlet) left the lake on its south shore. Years later my father and I, and my schoolmate, G.W. Butts, plus two guides, Jerome Wood and Charley Jones, went from Camp Oteetiwi, Big Island, Raquette Lake to Wellington Kenwell's on (the south) branch of (the) Moose River where Sumner Stream joins it. I have photos of the open camp facing a large boulder—and members of our party there. As I remember, there was a boat on a Stillwater to help travel for part of the way. Near Kenwell's we waked through an Indian clearing with scattered mounds. We stayed overnight and as the drinking water was under—suspicion—I drank a lot of tea and slept soundly, but, thrashed around in my sleep disturbing Butts, my roommate, no end.

All this idyllic region was ruined when Tim Woodruff acquired the property. No more woodland carries—a road was run in and Kamp Kill Kare on Lake Kora housed crowds of junketing politicians from Albany, guests of the Lt. Governor—shooting at glass bottles, etc. etc.

According to gossip, a dam was built by the state on the Sumner stream. For exactly what happened thereafter—see H.K.H.'s [Harold K. Hochschild's] *Township 34*.

The wealthy push nature away by leading exactly the same sort of over-sheltered artificial existence, no matter what the location may be—and, now even the Adirondack motels have wall-to-wall carpeting. For 10 months of the year lilac bushes are kept in green houses only to be brought out of doors for two months. THAT'S NOT CAMPING! One might just as well be at Mt. Kisco or Greenwich—the life is no different. Golf and tennis are games to enable people to share exercise in the open air where land is scarce, i.e. considerably populated. We once visited a so-called camp at Upper Saranac with a chicken-wire fenced and covered tennis court! Why tennis, when you can go camping and living in the woods. Tennis (or golf) is for when you can't go camping or sailing or cruising— good enough if something better does not offer, Selah!

P.S. I think my mother and our cook, Marie Papp, were the only two women to visit Sumner until after Durant sold it to Woodruff.

Throughout John's boyhood days there were a lot of waterways and woodland to explore that today have opened to the public. John saw the Sumner Lake property before its purchase by the Woodruffs. He enjoyed the property before the construction of the dam and the subsequent renaming of what he called "the sweet little lake" to Lake Kora. John's description of times past is the epitome of north woods history before road development came to the mountains.

By crow line, Sumner Lake was just over five miles from Big Island on Raquette Lake, but the windings of South Inlet and numerous carries from Camp Oteetiwi to the rustic campground accommodations at Sumner Lake required three guide boats, one kept at each carry, to reach the wilderness lake destination.

John lived through times that brought sweeping change to the mountains. He saw the coming of the railroads, lake steamers, roads and new people. The building of Kamp Kill Kare, which has continued to remain in private ownership to this day, may have been one of his greatest disappointments.

Chapter Seventeen

The Governor's Camp

DURING THE LATTER HALF of the nineteenth century, long-standing attitudes about game regulation and the natural environment began to change. New York's "history of environmental affairs…is the story of how New Yorkers decided to use their natural resources, and how they still struggle to use soil, timber, water, air, and wildlife in ways that do not decrease their value," wrote Brad Edmondson in "Environmental Affairs in New York State: An Historical Overview." [19]

Edmondson pointed out that New York's environmental movement "is mostly the story of well-educated city dwellers insisting on changes that have the greatest impact on rural residents," but that did not mean that all rural people pillaged a helpless Mother Nature.

As a growing awareness to set aside ideas "conquering" nature and instead begin to think about how the natural environment could be nurtured and preserved, New York State took the lead in what might be considered the formative environmental programs that the Department of Environmental Conservation still runs today.

To that end, in 1880, New York State "appointed the first officers to enforce its game laws. These 'game protectors,' who would later be called 'conservation officers,' were New York's first statewide law enforcement professionals, preceding the formation of the Division of State Police by 27 years," as reported on the "History of DEC" website.[20]

According to the website, "In 1885 the State Legislature established the Forest Preserve of New York State, setting aside land in the Adirondacks

There are none among us, in the twenty-first century, who remember The Governors. All that remain are legends, stories, and a handful of old snapshots. *Courtesy Margaret Wilcox (The Beaver Lake Collection)*

and Catskills to be protected as 'forever wild' and establishing regulations and guidelines governing the use of these lands. The year 1885 also marked the beginning of the forest ranger service in New York State.[21]

Wellington Kenwell rides over the Indian Clearing, circa 1890s. In spring, evidence of wagon wheels ruts that mark the original route across the Big Plains can be sighted from the air. *Courtesy Ora Kenwell*

"In 1895, the Fisheries, Game and Forest Commission was formed to take on functions related to fish and game regulations, hunting seasons, and poaching. This and several other small Commissions were combined in 1911 to become the Conservation Commission, which then later became the Conservation Department in 1926. The Conservation Department became one of the forerunners of the New York State Department of Environmental Conservation when it was formed in 1970."

By the mid-1880s, the headwaters of the Moose River Plains was still a large wild tract of land, particularly remote and a comparatively unvisited section of Herkimer and Hamilton counties that contained one of the best trout waters in the state. In earlier times, the south branch of the Moose River is believed to have been a destination along a water pathway for the Iroquois, who prior to the French and Indian War established a seasonal encampment on the Big Plains—thus the name Indian Clearing, where they hunted, fished and picked wild huckleberries, blueberries and black berries. Theories that may explain the existence of charred stumps and roots uncovered in the sandy, gravelly soil are that either the Native Americans burned off the cover to encourage the growth of berries or, more likely, that tremendous forest fires occasionally swept over such wilderness regions.

The south branch of the Moose River country had long been a favorite haunt of pot hunters—nonsporting huntsmen who took trout and shot deer for profit. Soon after the end of the Civil War, these procurers of meat moved into the headwaters of the Moose because it was one of the wildest and most remote locations in the Adirondacks. Bear, partridge, duck, and trout were plentiful and deer clustered thickly. The early pot hunters' main goal was to supply the growing Saratoga, N.Y., resort hotel trade's demand for wild game to list on their fancy menus.

Supplies for Kenwell's arrived by wagon from North Creek. *Courtesy Ora Kenwell*

The party known as The Governors from time-to-time participated in several unsportsmanlike practices of killing deer. *Courtesy Indian Lake Museum*

An aged Wellington Kenwell told Utica *Observer-Dispatch* reporter David H. Beetle during a lengthy interview that appeared in 1947 as "Kilroy Was Not Here," that the little pond now known as Icehouse Pond took its name from an ice house that had been thrown together for the purpose of storing deer meat until it was time to transport the venison to the North Creek railroad station, where it would then be taken by train to Saratoga, the Capital District and sometimes as far away as New York City. Kenwell admitted that he first learned about all the balsams that bordered The Plains from his early Saratoga hunting days. Kenwell had long ago realized that hunting laws were passed to protect and conserve a sustainable deer herd, not to interfere with anyone's hunting pleasure.

Joseph W. Shurter provides an informative description of traveling to "Moose River, the paradise of the deer-slayer," and camping on the Indian Clearing when his hounding party took a three-week outing during the fall of 1881, during which they killed a dozen deer, "three of which were magnificent specimens, beside a quantity of other game."

The Governors were a mid-to-late 1880s group of sportsmen from the Troy–Albany area who entered the forest from the Adirondack Railroad to North Creek, and then, it is assumed, traveled, according to numerous accounts, "fifty miles" by a very rough road to The Plains. Dick Burch, the well-known Blue Mountain Lake guide, and Tom Savage acted as their guides throughout the years they came to the Moose River Plains. Burch and Savage conducted themselves in a manner typical of some die-hard guides of the period.

Hounding for deer with dogs contributed to the butchery of Adirondack deer.
Courtesy Indian Lake Museum

225

While hounding, or hunting for deer with dogs, was illegal at the time, the practice continued among some guides who disagreed with the law or were comfortable doing whatever they needed to satisfy a customer's "buck fever." Perhaps this method of procuring venison was also endorsed for the guides' economic gain or when local residents were truly in need of food—one can only speculate.

The Dog House, Jock's Lake. It was said that "Dut" Barber had the best pack of deer hounds in the whole North Woods. The elimination of hounding deer and bear from the Adirondack Mountains was a drawn-out process. More laws were not the answer; public awareness and education proved to be bigger, more effective weapons.
Courtesy Edward Blankman (The Lloyd Blankman Collection)

Floating for deer and jacking deer were still legal ways to hunt at this time, but guides were beginning to hear about the growing shift in urban attitudes about nature conservation. As these ideas began to trickle down from sophisticated metropolitan-based residents, they began to make sense to many guides and sportsmen.

Preserves and private organizations such as the Bisby Club and later the Adirondack League Club spearheaded a movement on their sanctuaries to institute a policy that eventually carried over into accepted practice on state lands, too.[22] The preserves and clubs had control of a large territory, and they added their own rules to the state game laws that regulated the taking of game and fish. Private owners and members of clubs were convinced that jack-hunting and floating resulted in the wounding and maiming of more deer than were killed, and in the lingering deaths of more deer than were "reduced to possession."

Floating for deer at night with a jack-light carried connotations of insensitivity toward the killing of animals. And, this attitude began to reach a new maturity with guides and sportsmen and women. Sports still hunted, fished, and trapped, but they became more skillful at their craft and usually got their limit but did not exceed it, another law that was beginning to make sense to sportsmen who had respect for the environment and even for their prey.

Wellington Kenwell said he did not care for The Governors' conduct. Phil Christy, one of Kenwell's notable guides, was more blunt than Kenwell when he talked about the "Capital District gang," who hunted and fished out of a small camp built for them in the vicinity of Ice House Pond. Christy called the men "hooligans" and "the worst bunch of skunks I'd ever laid eyes on."

The resident Adirondackers based their opinion on the fact that The Governors' guides allowed the sports to recklessly blaze away at wildlife with utter disregard, they continued to take deer with dogs, and they secured venison using methods considered to be something like committing murder. At times with their Winchesters and Marlin repeaters shot off murderous rains of lead at targets with utter disregard for the cost of ammunition.

Savage and Burch, like Shurter's guides, believed "deer coursing," or as it was commonly termed, "hounding," was unquestionably a sportsmanlike way of hunting deer when practiced in the proper manner, meaning when a deer was driven to watchers, who were posted on ridges or shallow streams.

In addition to hounding, jacking and floating, The Governors picked off partridge at the side of trails and slaughtered squirrels, spruce grouse,

owls, bluejays, and ground hogs for target practice. And, this gang were a rowdy, raucous bunch who often dominated spring-holes where some of the largest trout could be caught and spent an inexorable amount of time discharging their shotguns in a state of wild excitement that produced blinding clouds of smoke. A final prominent trait of the disliked sportsmen was their love of boasting. They seemed to desire notoriety for these pleasures that were dear to them—all activities that interfered with Kenwell's paying guests.

After the passage of the Curtis Hounding Law during the winter of 1884–85, the deer population began to rebound in The Plains territory, but the passage of the law prohibiting the use of dogs for hunting deer did not deter or discourage those sportsmen who found the newly enacted game law unpopular. The remaining hunters who hounded were apparently greatly reduced by the new law, however, since not long after its passage magazine articles of the day reported the bottom had dropped out the hound market.

The Governors were not for-profit-only meat hunters who had previously exploited the area. The Governors represented a breed of sportsmen who enjoyed their independence, disregarded game laws, and found the headwaters of the Moose River an ideal location for secluded camps, where they hunted the rich pockets of game and the good game country beyond the sphere gone over by the general hunter, knowing their very seclusion ensured they would not come into much conflict with the law. The distant Plains not only proved advantageous to their pursuit of wild game, but also added zest to their illegal activities.

Along with The Governors and their guides, there were other pockets of dissent where a good many didn't observe the State's ban on hounding as a method of getting deer despite tremendous popular sentiment in favor

OPPOSITE: **The wooden grave marker and rail fence marked Fred Hynes's remains. The epitaph reads: Gone But Not Forgotten. In Memoriam. Sacred-to-the-Memory Of Fred Hynes. Departed – This Life Jan. 23,1885. God-Only-Knows-When-He-Was-Born. Died-In-A-Game-Of-Freeze-Out. There-Is-A-Pleasure-In-The-Snowy Wood, There-Is-A-Rapture-By-The-Frozen-Shore, There-Is-A-Dreariness-Where-None-Intrude, Moly-Hoses-Here-No-More. Erected By The Governors Oct. 5, 1892. It's-A-Hell-Of-A-Long-Time-Between-Drinks. Hard-Times-Can-Be-No-More.** From the Adams Collection. Courtesy Town of Webb Historical Association

of it. Harry Radford reported in his "Adirondack Department" column in *Field & Stream* that even by June 1901 New York State Assemblyman Graeff of Essex aimed to exempt his county and certain other sections of the wilderness, but the proposal was killed.

By 1892 there was an almost universally-growing sentiment against hounding. Articles in period magazines such as *The Angler & Hunter*, *Field & Stream*, *Forest & Stream*, and *Journal of the Outdoor Life* reported that Adirondack guides and woodsmen continued to be the most ardent lovers of deer-hounds.

While no picture has surfaced of The Governors' camp, it might have looked like this building. *Courtesy Tom Gates*

The editor of *Forest & Stream* wrote in the February 13, 1897, issue: "We print the following letter, which has come to us from an Adirondacks writer, not because we consider that it pictures a particularly enticing form of "sport," but because we believe that it describes accurately the mode there employed for teaching dogs to work on deer. It is the midwinter making ready for the midsummer tragedy of dogs, lake, boat, deer and Deerslayer with his rope."

The letter to which the editor refers came from Lem Lawson, an Adirondack native who lived in Skaberry Settlement. He described his love for training deer dogs, his interest in the sport, and how the silence of an early morning would be broken by the "music" of the yapping hounds driving a deer to water before a sharp crack of a hunter's rifle brought the animal down. It's not difficult to imagine why all Kenwell's guides despised the presence of The Governors when they appeared each fall to hunt with dogs.

> ...It don't take long to have a buck going; though it is better to start a doe, because they blat louder when the dogs get hold of them. Then the best shot in the party draws down on the started deer as soon as he can and bores a hole in its pouch or breaks a leg—anything, so that the beast will still be able to run away and bleed well.
>
> ...it's more fun to see two pups on a trail like that, and to hear their joyful far-reaching bay.... I like to lean up against a tree at such a time and listen to the sounds about me—the cracking of the trees, the swaying sign of the branches, the *chic-a-dee-dee-dee* of the birds and the eager shouts of my companions as they flounder along the trail behind the dogs...

Many decent sportsmen of the day would have found Lawson's inhumane description unsettling enough to make them think twice about hounding, but The Governors were not decent sportsmen.

The Governors continued their lethal pursuit of wild game, but did not go unpunished. For example, an October 1887 *Field & Stream* article reported four members of the Trojan party were pursued by State Game Protector Drew, who "was rewarded by bringing them to justice."

The "clever fellows" were running deer with dogs, which Drew said was "no worse than floating, but the game laws should be observed to the letter." He was also troubled by their guides' behavior. "From Blue Mountain to Raquette Lake, guides have brought their parties to the Moose River region," the article revealed, "and encouraged them in defying the law, or for a paltry sum allowed them to hunt in season or out, according to methods

231

which the law forbids. It is time a stop was put to this practice and the guides and sportsmen should rise up in arms against the poachers who unlawfully rob the woods of the game...."

Because the South Branch country was so vast and far-flung, jackers and hounders had less fear of a warden coming upon them. It made breaking the law tempting indeed. For that same reason the elimination of the scoundrels was slow, but even without arrests those disagreeable methods of hunting became almost extinct once the Kenwells established their hostelry. Wellington and his guides not only upheld game laws, but also instilled in their guests a disdain for the use of small caliber, long-range "murder-rifles," believing instead that there was no game that could not be taken with the old .38-.40 or .44-caliber guns. The belief was based on the fact that an accidental killing of a human being would inevitably occur if hunters all believed that to kill a deer or black bear they needed a rifle that would shoot through a half dozen trees. Such a long range was just too dangerous.

Man-driving grew more successful as the hunters learned how, and the illegal hounding practice was eventually phased out.

Beyond finding an abundance of sport with comparatively little labor, during The Governors' reign in the South Branch, the group erected a wooden tombstone in memory of Fred Hynes,[23] a Black logger who froze to death on January 25, 1885, during the Rousseau logging era. He was found dying in the snow by a lumberjack who was doctoring a sick horse near where the old Kenwell trail crossed the south branch of the Moose River. The unlucky man died, after being taken to a nearby lumber camp situated beside Otter Brook.[24] While his gravesite was common knowledge to all during that era, there was no official marking until The Governors uncharacteristically erected a wooden monument at the burial site complete with a rail fence that bordered the plot.

No documentation has been uncovered to learn why the Ice House camp occupants abandoned their camp following the 1894 hunting season. The close proximity of Kenwell's hunting lodge, pressure from the Kenwells, and the increased presence of game wardens is suspected. I also wouldn't discount the friction between Kenwell's guides and Dick Burch and Tom Savage.

Nothing succeeds like success. Nothing will so suddenly convince a man

OPPOSITE: **Gerald Kenwell inspects the marble marker at Fred Hynes' resting place on a small mound on the Little Plains within sight of his parents' former Sportsman's Home. 1950. One can only think how hopelessly lost Hynes felt. Surely, he suffered intensely from fright, exhaustion, hunger, thirst, and cold. No one who has not experienced the pitiable plight of the lost can appreciate the untold horrors of their position. I have always felt the Department of Environmental Conservation should carry on the gesture the Kenwells made with a small, permanent marker.** *Courtesy Ora Kenwell*

of the necessity of vacating property and obeying the game and fish laws as to have a game warden push a six-shooter into his face and take his gun and game away from him. I would bet ten to one that the herd of swine

The front cover from The Governors' complimentary dinner held at The Pafraets Dael in Troy, N.Y. on December 31, 1894 in honor of their guides, Dick Burch and Tom Savage.
Courtesy Winfred Murdock

who went by the handle "The Governors" met such a fate and decided to do no more hunting and fishing in the Indian Clearing's wilderness.

Deer hounding was certainly unsportsmanlike for many reasons. In fact, it was pure butchery. Charles Dudley Warner, in "Hunting of the Deer," entered an eloquent protest against this method of hunting. Harry V. Radford was another vocal opponent who led the resistance at the turn of the 20th century. The issue was eventually settled once and for all when New York Senator George R. Malby of St. Lawrence County succeeded in procuring passage of a law that was signed by Governor Odell. It extended the provisions of the existing anti-hounding law indefinitely and also prohibited the keeping of dogs for running deer within the Adirondack region.

Hounding, jacking, floating, luring with salt and meat baits, snubbing trespass laws, cutting wood on state land, and even operating illegal stills—these all were made illegal, and better education and public opinion put values into the sport, improved personal income for Adirondackers, raised their standard of living and led, with tighter law enforcement, to a successful result. The Adirondack Mountains were going to be regulated, but that regulation would ensure the region's preservation.

I wonder if the reality show *Ghost Hunters* would want to explore the hillock that stands alone on the Little Plains along the south branch of the Moose River. I have poked around the area, and have also slept near the old cemetery plot to be ready to begin a paddle down the Moose following the evaporation of morning dew shortly after dawn.

Before The Governors left their Ice House camp permanently, they used Fred Hynes's wooden grave marker as a target—blasting it into splinters, "riddling the monument with rifle and shotgun fire," said Gerald Kenwell, as a parting salvo. Apparently they wanted to destroy one of the few good things they had done. Soon after, Wellington Kenwell placed a small marble headstone that stood for years on the Little Plains within sight of his former Sportsman's Home. Today, there is no sign of the marble headstone. But ghosts and stories of the supernatural go hand-in-hand with the Adirondacks. The spirit of Fred Hynes is still reported to be active around the Little Plains. What a first-person story Hynes and The Governors could tell of their time there.

Chapter Eighteen

Lew Porter's Camp Strategy

MARY LOUISE PAYNE'S FATHER was born "Jesse Lewis" Porter. Somewhere along the way it was changed to "Lewis 'Lew' Henry." He worked as a packer for Wellington Kenwell when the Kenwells owned the Sportsman's Home along the south branch of the Moose River in the 1890s, so Louise knew quite a bit about the Moose River Plains and Inlet, New York's early days, although some of the memories she shared were learned from people who lived in the area before the Town of Inlet was formed in 1901.

The location was referred to as "Inlet on Fourth Lake" in articles in early sporting magazines. Following the Civil War, veterans began to trickle into the area. The history of Inlet tells that it developed to service the needs of many sportsmen after the middle of the 19th century.

In the late 1880s, trains like the legendary Empire State Express moved sportsmen from cities like New York and Buffalo to Utica, where they changed to trains for Old Forge. There, they boarded steamboats to carry them up the Fulton Chain of Lakes. Eagle Bay was a typical termination point where sports disembarked. Most had made arrangements with guides such as Archie George Delmarsh, his brother Eri and Abner Blakeman. These men led fishing and hunting parties into The Plains to guide-constructed open camps and little log cabins.

"A prominent feature of Adirondack life is the large number of guides, whose services are indispensable to the tourist in his journeyings through the wilderness. The fisherman and hunter, also, will find that success is largely dependent on the assistance of an intelligent, skillful guide," the 1893 State of New York Annual Report of the Forest Commission stated.

The late 19th century account continues on the subject of Adirondack guides of the period:

The guides are, for the most part, intelligent, sober, and industrious. That there should be some exceptions is natural; but they are few.

Soon after the ice goes out, which, in our northern lakes occurs often in May, the fishing season opens. The large number of sportsmen who throng into the woods in May and June, on every railroad and from every direction, furnish employment for a large number of guides. The guide provides a boat, furnishes bait, carries the boat over the trails leading to the neighboring ponds or streams, cleans the fish, and packs them

Left to Right: Louie "Lew" Porter, Mrs. William Payne, William Payne Jr. and Sr. Porter worked for the Kenwells when they conducted business on The Plains. During Wellington Kenwell's era, the services of a guide was of the upmost importance. *Indian Lake Museum*

237

properly in case the fisherman wishes to carry some of them home. He is of great assistance, also, in pointing out the exact, circumscribed spots in which it is necessary to cast a line in order to catch trout, places which a fisherman unacquainted with the locality would seldom find.

With the close of the spring fishing, the season for summer boarders and tourists commences, and the guide locates at or near a summer hotel. During the hotel season his principal employment, if in the Lake Region, consists in carrying tourists over the long, hundred-mile routes which traverse the wilderness in various directions. In the mountain region, the guides during the summer season are in demand for mountain climbing, camping-out parties, picnics, and brook fishing.

With the closing of the summer hotels, the hunting season opens, and the guides find employment with the deer hunters whose hounds make the woods echo until the leaves have fallen.

Many of the guides are retained for the entire season by cottagers or campers. Some of the most competent ones are hired by the year as gamekeepers or guides on private reserves and by sportsmen's clubs.

That was back before Louise's time. She was born in 1903.

☆ ☆ ☆

Louise always offered me something to eat when I interviewed her. Besides telling me wonderful stories of Camp Strategy, her father's camp, the guides she knew who worked in the Moose River Plains and of her early days in Inlet, New York, she gave me a tip about cooking I still carry on, and some of the mittens she knitted for my children are now being worn by my grandchildren.

Louise's cooking tip was simple. Peeling apples is time-consuming. To sidestep that, she ground up apples in the blender. I've tried that method. Not only does it save time but there is a lot of nutrition in the peels. However, I found it can be a messy job if I don't use the right kind of blender.

Lew Porter. *Courtesy Lewis H. Payne (The Payne Family Collection)*

Louise lived in Inlet's early Adirondack days. She had seen her share of traveling peddlers both on foot and with the later customary cart pulled by one horse. Peddlers brought smidgens of the outside world into the mountains. The traffickers furnished needed goods, and provided bits of social amenities and neighborly news or some word of more widespread national or state happenings to the isolated families.

Like Louise, Abram Kilborn also remembered the peddlers when he spoke with Marjorie L. Porter in 1952. Porter made it her life's mission to put together a remarkable collection of audio recordings of Adirondack Mountain ballads and lore.

Kilborn recalled that people of the mountains who had orchards would peel apples in the fall, string them and tie the long string to poles that were suspended between hooks. He said, "All the kitchen ceilings of the old houses had 'em. You ran a pole between the hooks and dried apples and such over the wood stoves and kitchen ranges." Apples were not the only thing dried. Pumpkins were cut in half. "You make a half moon," he pointed out with a laugh, "then hang 'em up there. It was free food for the flies. Did the same thing for turkey weed and sage. Put 'em in bunches today."

Jerky Rock near Lost Ponds. Norman Chapin is supported by a crutch. Lew is cooking.
Courtesy Lewis H. Payne (The Payne Family Collection)

One day, Kilborn told Mrs. Porter, a rag peddler came by. He bought and sold. This man traded for several strings of dried apples. "We didn't fight flies in those days, so we'd dry those apples you know, put 'em in a big bunch and sell 'em to the peddler and this particular one, Old Man Bartlett, he'd come along, pick them up and he'd take a row of them apples, throw 'em up on his cart and drive along through all the dust and dirt. I don't know what he'd done with 'em but he must of sold 'em, maybe to later be turned into some apple recipe."

Louise's tales of living in the mountains were typical of the older generations of people I have interviewed. But I found her simplest stories to be some of the most interesting, such as an offhand remark she made about bygone guides and loggers who tested their strength in an attempt to lift the trip-hammer and anvil, relics from the former iron industry in Old Forge that sat near the Forge House on the shore of Old Forge Pond. It's a shame that the tape recordings she made in the 1980s for the now-defunct Adirondack Discovery organization have never surfaced.

Then there were the sounds of steamboat whistles on the Fulton Chain, the stagecoach, the muddy stretches of road no one driving Route 28 today through the village of Inlet would ever believe was so difficult to traverse, and the guides who spun yarns and debated the merits of this or that brand of whiskey.

Louise's tales were those of many hardy souls who lived in the Adirondacks in the beginning of the 20th century. They saw hard times, devastating forest fires, wild animals, blizzards that caused families to be snowbound, and terrible accidents in the lumber woods, and they faced way more hardship than a modern generation could imagine.

The wig-wagging tails on white rear ends of leaping deer "like the flutter of white skirts at a picnic at the cry of snakes" were an ordinary sight for Louise when she traveled with her father into The Plains.

Louise remembered her father pointing out windfalls and spots where under the hemlock, spruce and balsam deer yarded in winter for protection, and the bone yards where some deer had died of old age or starvation.

Camp Savage was another tag for her father's shanty. Why? It was named after Lewis's favorite .303 Savage rifle.[25]

To reach the rough log shelter, one would pass over the acres of prairie—The Plains—"level as a floor," was the old saying. Sometime during the early part of 1889 the wild region had been completely burned over—"perhaps caused by a lighting strike," reported W.W. Hastings. Hastings's guides during that fall deer hunt were the Delmarshes—"Father Delmarsh, Archie's brother Eri, and his cousin, whom I chose to call Longfellow for obvious reasons," he wrote. Hastings observed that the great pine tree that stood near a habitual tent site on the waterless Indian Clearing no longer stood. The hooves of packhorses traversing the black, charred, crusted earth surely kicked up a sharp-tasting dust, but following the blaze, the blue-joint grass would grow greener and richer.

I found Hastings's report interesting because I frequently visit the Indian Clearing or Big Plains. The words are used interchangeably—along with "The Plains." It all depends on who is talking about the unusual flat land, a long-time opening in the forest, and a winter concentration area for an unusually large number of deer.

The first white man of record to see the Moose River Plains was Archibald Campbell. Campbell was a surveyor who was running out the western boundary of the Totten and Crossfield Purchase in 1772. Ralph Smith said in a 1954 *Conservationist* magazine that Campbell was guided "by Mohawk Indians who had hunted in this country and who could tell him which streams led where; he crossed the South Branch (calling it the Canada Kill) and encountered 'flat stony land, almost cleared.'"

I've found the best descriptions of The Plains and the probable reason for their non-forested appearance in the 1823 survey reports of Duncan McMartin, Jr. and later in an 1837 Gilbert and Griffin forest appraisers report. L.V. Lyon's 1819 writing about the forest of the Moose River country is also interesting:

> It was supposed that these lands had spruce timber on them of
> value, but on examination I find this species of timber as also
> the Fir or Balsam, to be nearly all dead on a large portion of the
> lands—the blight (or whatever it may be called) is attributed
> by the "hunters" to the leaves having been eaten off entirely by
> worms two years in succession some nine or ten years since.

While Hastings talked about "sharp-tasting dust," J.C. Finch, who was a brakeman on the Mohawk Division, was a registered guide who proudly claimed to have "shot 42 deer" since 1900.

Like Hastings, Finch also took train "No. 55" from Albany, "changed at Thendara, hiked the two miles to Old Forge, had a feed there and took passage on the steamer up the lakes to Inlet.

"W. Kenwell furnished a packhorse to take our luggage over the sixteen miles on the Big Plains, where we put up in a hunter's cabin situated in a nice balsam wood.

The Eagle Bay Hotel. Dock was a typical termination point.
Photo from The Great Adirondack Wilderness: Souvenir of the Fulton Chain Section

Oh, boy! Some place! I mean for black flies and mosquitoes…"

Louise claimed a similar recollection of hordes of insects and, in contrast to throngs of bugs, Harry Radford admitted that in 1901, he shot a deer on The Plains not because he was a good shot but only because "the deer were so thick."

Northeast of the Indian Clearing, well beyond the Moose River and Sumner Stream, is a secluded body of water in a wild region. Labeled "Lost

Pond" on Seneca Ray Stoddard's 1891 "Map of the Adirondack Wilderness," today the water goes by "Lost Ponds." Louise wrote, "It might be called that today but in my day it was called Rosseau's Ponds and Lost Grove Ponds. The name Rosseau came from a logger who worked back in there; the other name came from nearby Pine Grove Creek."

When I pressed Louise to recall the exact location of her dad's camp, her historical memory got a bit murky. Notes on vintage family photos of Camp Strategy, a.k.a. Camp Savage, report the hunting camp to be at "Rusoe Pond." Today, there is the remains of a dam on Sumner Stream that is typically referred to as Rousseau's dam. I do not believe that is the area referred to on the Payne family photos as "Rusoe Pond."

Lew Porter steadies his guide-boat on Lost Ponds. Camp Strategy is in the center of the background. *Courtesy Lewis H. Payne (The Payne Family Collection)*

I've learned from reading correspondence that Isaac Kenwell, Wellington's brother, wrote regarding the early history of The Plains that perhaps because of the logger referred to as Rousseau, Lost Pond (now Ponds) was more likely to have been Rousseau's Pond back in Lewis Porter's day. Several photos Louise allowed me to copy of Porter's camp were dated in the late 1890s and early 1900s. One image's caption mentions Lewis Porter's Camp

Strategy "near Lost Ponds or also known as Pine Grove Ponds" (Pine Grove Creek is nearby). Another photo dated 1917 reported it was a group picture of a hunting party from Miller's Camp at Bear Pond that arrived at Porter's camp at Lost Ponds. A third picture shows Camp Strategy with the notation: "Camp Strategy built by Lewis Porter over by Lost Ponds, near where The Governors used to have a crude boathouse." A recent meeting with Lewis's grandson Bill, and great grandson Lewis H. "Lou," and the discovery of an additional family photo confirmed Camp Strategy was located at Lost Ponds. The snapshot placed the camp on the opposite shore of the current launch site. There are enough identifying large rocks and height of land along the north shore to pinpoint the exact camp site. We plan to verify the spot with a visual ground search soon.

Another photo showing Lewis Porter with Norman D. Chapin and another unidentified man cooking deer meat beside "The Jerky Rock" really rang a bell in Louise's memory. She said, "The man (Chapin) hurt his leg. Dad fixed him a crutch."

I think that if someone was motivated to try to zero in on the location of Lewis's Camp Strategy, the best clue would be to take along a copy of the Jerky Rock snapshot and try to identify the terrain.

Louise's earliest memories might also be helpful to the would-be explorer.

"I was four or five years old the first time I went into camp," explained Louise. "My sister, 'Rilla' (Esther Aurilla), and our brother Richard would also go. We did a lot of walking to get in there. The route followed a path. It wasn't more than a narrow trail that packhorses had made. There wasn't any other camp nearby. "

Camp Strategy was a simply-constructed trapper-style cabin. Spruce, tamarack and cedar were preferred logs to use in log cabin building because they grow naturally straight, but there were other kinds of logs from which cabins were made too. Pine, poplar, hemlock and even hardwoods were used, but the hardwood variety was harder to work and did not last as long as that from conifers.

Lewis probably built his 12 by 14-foot cabin's sidewalls vertically because shorter logs were available. Logs are placed upright, also suggesting help to build the cabin was limited. It is also a faster method of putting up a shelter because it eliminates the need to notch at the corners. The bark would have been peeled from logs a few weeks before the cabin was built, however, to allow them to season and make them lighter to handle. It also eliminated wood-borers from hatching out under the bark. Moss and mud were typical chinking material as well as saplings that were nailed on to close off the space where logs joined.

Regardless of the short vertical walls and low ceiling that would crush the silk hat of a minister should he enter without removing it, according to its appearance in snapshots, Camp Strategy was a satisfactory building sited near the shoreline. Louise had memories of the camp, but lacked specifics when I spoke to her.

Lew's Camp Strategy at Lost Ponds. *Courtesy Lewis H. Payne (The Payne Family Collection)*

It was a typical guide-built camp-of-the-day constructed and fitted along the same lines as the ones the Delmarsh brothers put up for their fishing and hunting camps. Ted Harwood describes his uncle's Archie and Eri Delmarsh's camp as "the old Norton Camp. It stood along Norton Brook at the eastern head of the Big Plains above Helldiver Pond. Dad went in on his honeymoon. It was just before the wooded area on the right in the second opening."

OPPOSITE: **Lew on a guiding trip with an unknown man.** *Courtesy Lewis H. Payne (The Payne Family Collection)*

Strategy's roof was pitched and covered with boards and tarpaper. Louise said her dad was "a strong young man" and thinks even though he had good carpentry skills and could have roofed the camp with spruce shingles, he probably didn't have time. "When Dad was in his twenties he was a busy man." He packed for Kenwells because Wellington needed a young strong person to bring in supplies by horse. "It was the only way to deliver the needed sundries that the hunters and fishermen who were guests of the Kenwells wanted. Later on he packed for [Charles] Chapin after Wellington built Camp Nit over at Beaver Lake.

Lew's tent at Strategy, Lost Ponds. *Courtesy Lewis H. Payne (The Payne Family Collection)*

"I remember Mrs. and Mr. Chapin [Sr.] and their friends arriving [by train] in Eagle Bay and then being picked up by Wellington at the station, then being brought to his place on Sixth Lake opposite the dam where he and the men would ready horses and pack in the men and supplies to Camp Nit.

248

The women waited in comfort at his boarding house or small cottage out back until camp life could be made more comfortable for them back at the lake."

Louise assumed Camp Strategy's cook stove probably arrived on a jumper pulled by a horse. Typically, there would have been boards nailed on a tree trunk near the door to hold a wash basin. A bar of yellow soap provided the suds, and was also about the only thing hedgehogs did not chew in woodland camps. Table, benches and bunks were fashioned from wood. Inside illumination came from candles or kerosene lamps. Eggs, potatoes, flapjacks, fish, partridges and deer meat were typical food, along with condensed milk, maple syrup, coffee and tea. All were served on tinware.

I find it interesting how little has changed on The Plains from the days when Camp Strategy was in full swing. For instance, I seek out a lakeside camping ground far from the sounds of civilization. The quiet of the water and forest is a soothing stillness. To sit outstretched before a crackling fire of softwood, to breathe the invigorating mountain air, to hear the soft murmur among the evergreens high overhead, and the mysterious pulsating undertone of forest critters hidden from view in the darkened woodland— this is the joy of camping that is perennial.

Lewis' clients must have had similar feelings whether they did their snugg'lin sheltered in the cabin or slept on a bed of soft-tipped balsam boughs in a canvas wall tent erected nearby.

Many factors certainly determined Lewis Porter's camp location—the nearness of hunting grounds, of wild trout streams, of spring water, of fuel, the force and direction of winds, the character of the soil and undergrowth— and only a real son-of-the-forest, the guide who was reared in the Moose River Plains country, could have known all those things.

Lewis could strike out without a compass and find his way all day long on instinct. He had an ability to build brush shelters that didn't leak and bring in fresh venison, all for three dollars a day—although it was possible if he had a party of campers the set rate for one "sport" might not apply. His guide boat, guns, fishing tackle, pack-basket and pots and pans were ready at a moment's notice to take off with tenderfoot sportsmen who would look forward to him cooking a trout or venison meal complete with bacon and flapjacks.

Someday I think it might even be fun to roll out a batch of traditional camp baking powder biscuits to be cooked in a reflector oven using a whiskey bottle for a rolling pin. If the old-timers didn't concern themselves so much with sanitary utensils why should I fret when in a wilderness setting?

Whether campers slept as snug as bugs in a rug compared to my twenty-first century slumbering system is up for interpretation in my eyes. I can't imagine being rolled up in even the warmest horse blanket to be as comfy as I am in my hollow-filled sleeping bag, but perhaps balsam bough bedding and clean, new horse blankets provided insulation for a warm, comfortable night's sleep.

Lou's campers would have come into the Adirondacks with some personal gear—utensils, such as a compass, pocket knife, watch, lantern, wire nails, a few feet of cord, an axe and hammer, punky paste, simple medicines and surgeon's plaster, a deck of playing cards, a book or two, blankets and toilet articles. I'm reminded by notes in old-timers' diaries they never forgot "a baking-powder box full of angle-worms mixed with earth." And why? "More Adirondack trout were caught with angle-worms than with any other bait" back at the turn of the twentieth century. And, accepted practice was to carry a firearm of nothing smaller than a .45-70 in black powder. Fifty cartridges were considered enough for a three-week trip, even if one did some target shooting before leaving home.

What other memories of Camp Strategy did Louise carry with her until she passed in 1999 at the age of 95? Indian summer days on The Plains, autumn leaves falling as the colors mixed with the green of the balsam and spruce needles in kaleidoscopic changes? Firing her father's eight-pound rifle? Her father's hand-fashioned cabin?

"Oh, you know," Louise said with a start, "it's surprising what things I do remember and so many things I don't remember. I recall Camp Strategy was also called Camp Savage. The name was so often flip-flopped. I didn't go back there [into the Moose River Plains] as much after the camp burned."

OPPOSITE: **Lew Porter in the wilds of the Moose River Plains.** *Courtesy Lewis H. Payne (The Payne Family Collection.*

But she did recall the Kenwell horse trail. "The terrain was rolling and for the first few miles it went through rather ordinary forest country. Easterly to and along the north shore of Fawn Lake, then southeasterly to a crossing of the Red River." It was at that ford where a traveler began to get an inkling of what lay ahead. "The trees began to get bigger," she recalled. A.T. Shorey also remembered the view from that point. He said of the country, "It was like walking into a picture land of long, long ago."

Lew is standing spread-legged, showing where an old moose trail was cut into the Big Plains. *Courtesy Lewis H. Payne (The Payne Family Collection)*

As the horse trail turned more southerly and the Indian Clearing came in sight, huge pines would have dotted the landscape. Louise recalled around every bend was a new view to delight her eyesight. "Deer signs were everywhere." The Big Plains were also studded with ancient soaring white pine trees. "Dad's camp was like a lot of them back then. He built the camp on state land, and in the teens the state went around and did a lot of that kind of burning."

Similar to so many mountain people, Louise was referring to the conflict in the woods that occurred throughout the first decade of the 20th century about the natives' long-time, unfettered use of state land. While outlaw homes and camps were being removed, there was also ill-feeling over well-heeled citizens who were purchasing large tracts of land, then posting the land—prohibiting others from coming onto their property, such as guides who had long used the land for hunting, fishing, trapping and even for laid-back hikes.

Other than being somewhat aware of Lewis Porter's banding together with fellow Adirondack guides Arthur Blanchard, Frank R. Wood, Asa and William Payne, William Stevens, William Ballard, Andrew Sims and George Jenkins, Louise knew nothing more about the lawsuit the men brought against the State that was trying to dislodge the guides' valuable-to-them camps on State land—an action in accordance with a law passed by the State Legislature. Ted Abner, in "Conflict in the Woods," *Adirondack Folks* (1980), reported: "The first round was a victory for the guides, decreeing that the State must show ownership." Ultimately, however, the State prevailed.

Lou's younger images showed him sporting a double-bitted coffee-dunked strainer-type mustache. His grandson said, he "never remembered Grandpa with facial hair." Being a second generation of guides, the first being a product of the post-Civil War days when the Adirondack Mountains were a real rather than a preserved wilderness, perhaps Lou's wife had a preference and influence over her rugged husband-guide and man of many other talents. That would have been an interesting question I could have asked Louise about her mom.

Louise's recall of Camp Strategy was but a small part of our many conversations. Beyond her lifetime of recollections was her knowledge that she and her husband had raised a tight-knit loving family that still shares close ties to her part of the Adirondacks.

Chapter Nineteen

The Goffs of Seventh Lake

THE GUIDES IN THE FULTON CHAIN were more or less known to Isaac Channing Goff who co-owned a coal company in Cleveland, Ohio, and Harriet Goff when they built their camp, Meenahga (Iroquois for "blueberry"), on Goff Island in 1897. One notable guide, a hardy fellow, Lewis 'Lew' Porter, had been trapping in the big woods since he was 12. Lew's reputation as a top-notch carpenter and guide began when he worked for the Kenwells back on the Big Plains along the south branch of the Moose River. He had guided and earned the distinction of having had charge of important notable parties who vacationed at Kenwell's Sportsmens' Home. Lew knew the woods when it was necessary for even a guide to have a compass to travel about, and yet his sense of direction was so keen, appreciative members of parties he guided on deer hunting and fishing expeditions claimed Lew relied on nothing more to navigate the forest than his inborn sense of direction.

Isaac and Harriet Goff had been coming to the lake region of the western Adirondacks since 1891. In those days it was legal for a sportsman or guide to kill up to three deer in a season between August 15 and November 1. Pot hunters (those who sold venison to restaurants) were not allowed to hunt deer for the market at any time. These laws had a strong public backing in favor of their strict enforcement and resulted in a marked increase of the graceful wildwood creatures in Herkimer, Hamilton and Lewis counties. Fellow Fulton Chain vacationer Frank H. Taylor described the region poetically. "There are vast reaches of somber forests, plentifully dotted with lakelets, cool, deep and still, seldom disturbed by the reverberations of the rifle shot, where the occasional wanderer may paddle so closely to the feeding deer that they may be shot with the harmless trigger of the camera."

By 1891, the region had about 30 camps, several of which were guide-owned and offered vacationers room and board. Two or three of them actually rose to the dignity of being hotels. The greater number of these camps were on Fourth Lake, which was considered one of the most enchanting of the bodies of forest-bound lakes. The greater part of the forest not owned by the state was held by a number of clubs, notably the Adirondack League, Ne-ha-sa-ne and Fulton Chain Clubs, organizations which proposed to hold their domains as exclusive hunting territory for members and their friends and also to secure a profit from the land by cutting the abundant spruce timber which was in demand at the time for paper pulp.

August 15, 1932. (Lt. to Rt.) Houghton, Bill Goff, Shorty Lobb, and Lew Porter.
Courtesy Lewis H. Payne (The Payne Family Collection)

It's not known why the Goffs chose Seventh Lake as the location for their log camp. The area might have been suggested by Abner Blakeman, 34-year-old and so-called philosopher-guide who earned a reputation among sportsmen. Blakeman led pack-basket parties from Fourth Lake to nearby Fifth and Limekiln lakes when they were still dense silent retreats. He knew of the abundance of deer prints that could be found along the beaches of fine gravel and dry sand, and in the black soil of the woodland. He knew the towering groves of giant pines and was able to satisfy his clients' cases of "buck fever" whether they were hunting for prize photos or trophy antlers.

Over the years, names for the Fulton Chain island where the Goffs built Meenahga have been: Indian Pines Island, Seventh Lake Island and White Island, named for Green White, who is believed to have been the first non-Native American to have a trapper's shanty on the island that some old-time guides called "the lordly Seventh." Mary Goodwin Armstrong, in her August 30, 1990, interview with me, remembered that in the 1920s, when she accompanied her father delivering the mail by boat, they called the island "Cleveland Corner" because the camp residents were from Cleveland, Ohio. (The Goffs are credited with establishing the so-called "Ohio Colony" of camps clustered along the upper end of Seventh's Lake south shore.) One of the best places to view the island in Seventh Lake is from the motorist pull-off along Route 28 approximately three miles north of Inlet. From that vantage point the lake stretches before you. Black Bear Mountain's rocky quartz-veined summit rises in the background.

When it came time for the Goffs to decide on whom to put in charge of the building of their island camp, they chose Lew Porter. Porter and Blakeman were friends, and it's easy to assume the Goffs had inquired who they might employ.

Isaac Goff was a man of varied interests. He reportedly had mechanical skills and practical knowledge of construction, enjoyed music, wrote some poetry and prose, and did sketching and painting. Goff wrote this description of Lew:

> His face was pale, almost colorless. His hair straight and black, with a wayward lock hanging over his forehead. His nose, like his words, straight to the point. Eyes keen, quick and black, back under his brows. Lips, though silent, bespoke determination. Yet, a smile from them would light up his face as gentle as a

woman's. It was not often he spoke, nor often he smiled, though when at work he would frequently break forth in lusty song. His body was lithe and agile as a panther. If clothes make the man, to such heights of manhood Lew Porter had never aspired.

Lew Porter's great grandson, who carries his great-grandpa's first name, says he talked with his father, Jim Payne, about a story Isaac and his brother Fred used to tell of Lew single-handedly finding a man during a terrible storm. (You can read this account in the following chapter.)

Isaac, Harriet, and Fred Goff not only owned camps on Goff Island, but also property on Seventh Lake. Jim Payne, who said Isaac was known to all as 'Uncle Ike,' assumes *Seen and Overheard Uncle Ike-His Book*, may have been was written by Isaac, printed only for the Goff families on the island, and never published. It offers some rare and valuable insights into what life was like on their island, in Inlet and on Seventh Lake.

In addition to the contracting work Lew Porter did for Isaac and Fred Goff, the local craftsman teamed up with businessman Isaac during the winter of 1917 to survey and map Sixth and Seventh lakes. Their map of the area was still available in 1989 in the files of the Sixth and Seventh Lakes Improvement Association.

The Goffs, always interested in improving their island properties, hired area carpenter Billy Gilchrist in 1910 to build a lookout out from aesthetically twisted and curved tree trunks. The structure overhung the point of land by their boathouse on the southwestern end of the island.

In 1917, Gilchrist was called back to construct a tiered and pillared pergoda on the front of the island. It was modeled after a Japanese garden. Robert A. Maloney describes the structure in his book, *A Backward Look at 6th and 7th Lakes*. The full-sized pergola was a replica of one Fred had seen in Sorrento, Italy.

A pergola is similar to a trellis or an arbor. This was a giant undertaking involving forty 14-foot high pillars aligned in two rows with many overhead stringers intended to hold climbing vines. The pergola covered an area measuring 152 feet by 14 feet. To bring all of the materials—lumber, concrete, reinforcing steel—to an elevated island site when the nearest access road was at the Sixth Lake Dam was a monumental task. All materials of necessity were brought by boat and there were no Redi-Mix concrete trucks to conveniently spew forth their already prepared mixture. All sawing, digging and concrete mixing was done by hand. Unfortunately, harsh Adirondack winters and short summers proved hostile to the vegetation that was to cover the pergola. In 1960 the pergola was torn down, although the structure itself had weathered the climate quite well.

Lew Porter's great-grandson Lew Payne said of the edifice in 2016, "Fred and Lew would dig wildflowers and transplant them on the tiers. The pillars are long gone, but the foundation of the tiers are still there. Fred gave Lew a two-volume set of a book titled *Wildflowers of New York State*. They are large books with plates in them of the wildflowers of the state. They were passed from my grandmother, Louise, to me. They are one of my most prized possessions. Fred wrote a note to Lew in the front of the book. It reads. "'To my friend and partner in the wild flower business with sincere respect and best wishes.'"

The Goffs continued to bring progress to the area. A June 13, 1921, telegram written on Goff-Kirby Coal Company letterhead by Isaac C. Goff to Frank E. Tiffany, provided by Charlie Herr, Inlet's unofficial historian, indicates that Isaac by this time had contracted to have another large cottage constructed on another island. He descried Doll Island as a small island located a short distance from the mainland and "opposite the Seventh Lake House." Goff's newest cottage connected to the mainland by a bridge. In the telegram he told Tiffany he believed the Doll Island camp would be completed and available for Tiffany to manage (as a rental) about the first of July.

Goff described the vacation retreat as having, "...five bedrooms, a nice sitting room with fireplace, dining room, bathroom, etc.—all new and newly furnished." He told Tiffany, "...should you chance to hear of any desirable person wishing to rent such, I will be glad to hear. I ask $400.00 for July, August and September or $150.00 a month, preferring the season arrangement. I have one or two prospects but will avail myself of the first that is ready to close."

Following the investment cottage, Isaac Goff contracted to have telephone lines installed. Maloney said, "Placing telephone lines in the lake is a routine procedure today, but in the 1920s it was an innovative move.

"Following the death of Isaac Goff's son Harold, Camp Meenahga changed ownership and the Van Gorders took over Isaac's camp and the Glovers took over Frederick's camp in 1955. (I.C.'s brother Frederick's camp had been built in 1904.)

"Although Isaac Goff has been deceased for some time, he has left an indelible mark on the area and belongs in the ranks of those other early [Inlet] people who appreciated the beauty of the area."

Jim Payne, Lew Porter's grandson and a well-known area seaplane operator on the lake, knew Harold Goff. He recalled, "I used to carry all of his groceries from the dock up to Goff Island. Harold was very particular. He wanted me to always stay on the trails and not beeline straight to the camp.

"I recall Isaac owned the two camps on the end of Goff Island and sold one to Fred in 1904. Some of the other Ohio camp owners that came in to the lake were the Dennisons, Tallmadges, and Van Gorders—all had camps on the south shore of the lake."

Jim is currently [2020] the caretaker of the Goff Island camps. He reports that the original blueprint of the map Lew and Isaac developed is at the island. Jim's grandfather, Lew Porter, helped build the two camps on Goff Island.

The Paynes are proud of Lew Porter's contribution to the Goffs' many building projects and of his friendship with some of the early summer residents in Inlet, New York.

Chapter Twenty

Lew Porter's Heroic Deed

SOMETHING ALARMING was happening inside the Wood Hotel's bar room in Inlet, New York, one evening during the late summer of 1906. The Eagle Bay train station's agent burst into the tavern where a group of lumberjacks, guides, businessmen, and sportsmen had gathered for the evening during a storm that had begun to gather. Among them was Ohio businessman Isaac Channing Goff, an early camp owner and real estate investor who was also a bit of an amateur writer, and he remembered in his camp log book that the clouds had begun to hang "like a pall over mountain, forest and lake. The door opened and the riotous wind forced its way in along with the station agent, and resisted hard his attempt to shut it out.

Lew is standing on a large, old pine stump on The Plains which he called "Deer Lick."
Courtesy Lewis H. Payne (The Payne Family Collection)

OPPOSITE: **L.H. Porter was a man of action.** *Courtesy Lewis H. Payne (The Payne Family Collection)*

"So much of the wind as had rudely forced its entrance tossed the blue clouds of tobacco smoke which were drifting lazily about, into swift swirls and eddies, almost strangled the lights in the lamps, and then plunged into the fireplace and up the chimney, forcing the smoke out into our midst, that it might have room to escape and rejoin the furies it had so recently left," Goff wrote in a narrative that was romantic and poetic—a style of the time to which he was accustomed and had been using to record narratives in his *Seen and Overheard Uncle Ike-His Book* camp log book.

"Uncle Ike" continued his narrative. "The station agent held in his hands a message he had just received. 'John Sherman is dying. Please find his son.'"

The Woods Hotel, Inlet, N.Y. Photo from The Great Adirondack Wilderness: Souvenir of the Fulton Chain Section

Living in a small mountain town, the agent knew the movements of a stranger would likely be known at the tavern—the center where such local news items were received and from which they were distributed.

The agent looked around the big room for someone who knew the whereabouts of Sherman's son, when someone spoke up. "He's fishin' up at Mitchell Ponds with that guide and game constable, Ab Blakeman."

Again the agent waited, darting a glance around the room, hoping someone would volunteer to take the telegraph message.

"The waves were pounding on the shores" of Fourth Lake, Goff recorded. "The trees overhead were roaring like the ocean surf in a storm. Not a rent in the clouds above through which even a glint of a star could be seen to light one's way.

"The leaping flames from the crackling logs in the fireplace seemed to suggest to all but one, 'Wait till morning to search out and climb the mountain trails to Mitchell Ponds, to find John Sherman's son.'"

Then from a corner in the smoke-filled room a voice was heard. "His father's a dying, d'ye say?" asked Lewis Porter. "Why, I'll find John Sherman's son. Send word to Goff's camp. I may not be on the job 'til late tomorrow."

All the locals knew Lew Porter had been working since early morning cutting and sawing lumber, hewing logs, prying and lifting heavy framework, and spiking the cedar, spruce and hemlock logs for a new mountain lodge on Goff Island, and yet here was a modest, unassuming and retiring man, "in appearance," said Isaac Goff, "possibly least liable of ten men to be chosen to perform a deed of daring and trust."

However unlikely it might have seemed to Goff, Lew took the telegram, picked up his rifle, looked at his compass, filled a coat pocket with matches, and darted out the door into a stormy evening sky that was as dark as the thick fur coat of a black bear.

"Ten of us were left," wrote Goff, "before the alluring fire. But somehow, it seemed as if there was not a MAN among us all. All the manhood and manliness had gone out with Porter. All our talk seemed vacant and cheap, after the MAN went forth; as if, what of manliness there had been in the rest of us, dishonored in its habitation, had deserted our breasts, and gone forth with him, leaving us a sense of shame we could ill conceal.

"A spark of sympathy had been lighted in Porter's breast that was a light to his feet over the faint trail; that helped to sustain his already weary body over the steep paths, smooth the rough places and bear him safely through the mountain streams, as he sought the dying father's son."

Getting lost in the woods can be an unpleasant experience and sometimes pretty terrifying. Losing your way at night could be disastrous.

A week before Porter's nighttime venture into the wilds, a party from the Seventh Lake House had gone out near the south shore of Seventh Lake to gather balsam boughs. A fine balsam tree was found, cut down, and dragged to the shore of the lake. They had gathered a large sack of boughs, but to their dismay, they could not tell which way to return. They were all badly frightened and it was decided the group would stay together while one member of the company ventured out within calling distance and searched for a trail. The party's scout found a trail, which eventually brought them to a sandy road, where they were still at a loss as to which direction to go, until two guests from the Seventh Lake House came along and showed them the way back to the hotel.

Unlike the lucky balsam-gathering party, Lew was on his own in the dark of night. However, with years of guiding experience and familiarity with the expansive territory of the Moose River Plains, he made his way along the miles-long Delmarsh Trail that ended where he hoped he would find Abner Blakeman and John Sherman's son.

Goff's camp journal tells the rest of the story.

Abner Blakeman and his fishing client were "not found at either Upper or Lower Mitchell Ponds although Porter tramped the forest-bound shores of both, shooting and hallo-ing, and listening for an answering call.

"Disappointed, he rested…in the wilderness of forest, darkness and storm." The only sounds he heard were "a bear that crashed through the brush before him…and the calling of a hoot owl." There was an occasional distant flash of lightning from the storm clouds and one "horrible rending and crashing to the earth of a giant hemlock tree."

Weary and fagged, voices in Lew's head tempted him to either seek shelter or attempt to return to Inlet. According to Goff's account, one voice was "telling him of the soft bed under the home roof for his bruised limbs. Another, whispering of steaming hot coffee and food, awaiting him at home to relieve his hunger. He thinks of the waiting and perhaps worried wife and three sleeping children; and he ten miles from them back in the wilds.

"The tempters seemed to say, 'You have come to where the man was. He is not here. How can you hope to find him on such a night as this? Do you not hear the wind screaming like the gull? Do you not hear the trees clashing their branches like sabers? This is a wild night! Return, or at least rest where you are till morning.'"

Goff's description of Lew Porter's wandering search is overly dramatic, as only Isaac Channing Goff could write it. Perhaps because Goff was not a woodsman, his imagination got the best of him. The writer had never trod alone in the forest, never penetrated its dark. No doubt his particular style of writing was especially flamboyant. But it is obvious that Lew's bravery and generous offer of help left an impression on him.

"At such a time, amidst such surroundings, such entreaties would sound to most of us, not like the voice of a tempter, but like the voice of reason," continued Goff in his melodramatic way, "but not so with Lew Porter.

The head of navigation on Fourth Lake, Inlet, N.Y. *Courtesy Winfred Murdock*

"'I'll find John Sherman's son,' he had said. And find John Sherman's son he did.

"A certain woods sense guides these men-of-the-woods, and suggests many of the things they do. There was the Red River over yon mountain. Maybe the better fishing had lured the party there?"

"Lew did not turn toward Red River up the Delmarsh Trail high over Mitchell Ponds mountain.... He knew its rugged steepness, knew of the part that skirted dangerously along the rock precipice at the top.

"He knew, too, the tangle of alders at the bottom of the mountain beyond....

"Treacherous footing, on the brightest of days. Hopeless at night; and such a night as this!

"He knew of the river to ford, and the plains to cross before Red River could be reached. He was doing his best to perform a duty he had undertaken. He followed where that duty led, though it led farther into the wilderness, the tempest and the night.

"It was three o'clock in the morning, when bruised, wet and exhausted, Lew Porter handed the message to John Sherman's son.

"His best, and I am ashamed to say, almost his only reward was his consciousness of a duty well-performed."

Lew Porter was a woodsman, guide, carpenter, friend and a hero in Isaac Channing Goff's eyes.

His tale does not tell about the return the trio made, or the gratitude young Sherman surely felt. Goff chose instead to end the courageous saga with a poem that attempted to illustrate that you can never tell from someone's appearance who just might prove to be a hero.

> And boys I tell it hurts my heart,
>   When I see a man like Lew,
> Walking thru our city streets,
>   that you treat him as you do,
> Of course I know it's thoughtlessness-
>   Not 'cause you're bad at heart;
> For if you knew him as I do,
>   You would act a different part.
> Just because a fellow's awkward,
>   And gawks, and stops, and stares,
> And wears a hat and pantaloons,
>   That take you unawares,
> Don't sneer, and jeer, and call him "Rube,"
>   And be continually poking fun
> For he might prove a hero like Lew,
>   To you, and John Sherman's son.

Chapter Twenty-One

The Millers' Camps

WHEN I WAS BUSY SEARCHING for people to talk to about their connection with the Miller family's three camps (at Bear Pond, along Benedict Creek in the Moose River Plains, and on Seventh Lake), Leonard and Marg Harris, John S. Miller, D.M.D., Dr. L. Miller Harris, Tom Thibado, Gordon Rudd, and Norton "Bus" Bird saved the day. Each one had been there, Leonard and Marg Harris even provided two log books of Leon S. Miller's Seventh Lake camp. The records contained early family goings-on and statistics of the guides and workers employed. Gordon and Bus provided snapshots. Bus also offered personal material based on his years of guiding the Millers from 1925–1933. Without this evidence it would be hard to imagine the wilderness camps once existed where now brushy clearings of brambles and pioneering species of trees grow in a tight tangle that makes investigation of the ground difficult.

But there they were, the Millers' camps captured in black and white photos—sturdy buildings where sportsmen and women enjoyed the jingle of running brooks, the twilight, midnight, dawn, and sunlight, and the rain that pattered on hand-split cedar shingles. Surely some were satisfied to return home with empty game bags, content simply to have enjoyed being out of doors. There the businessman forgot his troubles. Bank balances, accounts payable and receivable, and the competition were forgotten. The Moose River country was such a world apart from the one they'd left behind that it was easy to leave their cares behind too.

At one time there were many large and small camps throughout the south branch of the Moose River country—"like buckshot pellets fired at a sheet" former Plains forest ranger Gary Lee once illustrated. But of all the camp sites I have investigated and made inquiries about, had it not

Lewis "Lew" Porter, Inlet, N.Y. 1913. *Courtesy Lewis H. Payne (The Payne Family Collection)*

been for those six people no history would have ever surfaced except for odds and ends of tableware, crockery, scattered cooking and eating utensils, and some old hand tools I found in rotting mounds of wood and inside the tilting, porcupine-chewed ice house in 1985—and now even that dilapidated building has been reclaimed by the earth.

According to the Miller Camp log book, Brayton Bela Miller's first Adirondack camp was built on the big island on Seventh Lake. Miller, a typical-1880s Fulton Chain sportsman hired local guides and workmen to construct a camp with little regard to ownership of the property where the building was sited.

In later years Brayton, known as "B.B.," relocated the island camp to the mainland and, wanting a frugal wilderness location for adventure afield, established a hunting and fishing camp in the Moose River Plains.

The Miller's family camp at Seventh Lake.
Photo from The Great Adirondack Wilderness: Souvenir of the Fulton Chain Section

"O" Camp Limberlost is taken from Leonard and Marg Harris's collection of B.B. Miller's Bear Pond Camp papers. The author and date are unknown. Bus Bird speculated it was crafted between 1920 and 1931, based on some

Twig art designed in the shape of fish decorate the front door of Mrs. Isaac Channing Goff's Camp Meenahga on Seventh Lake Island, sometimes called Goff Island. The inscriptions read: "Mr. LC. Goff, Seventh Lake, July 25, 1907, Ab Blakeman, 14 lbs., and 3 lbs. speckled trout, 19" long, H.L. Goff, August 10, 1908." *Courtesy Lewis H. Payne*

of the events he knew about. The attempt at lyrical artistry reads more like an informal history of those who hunted from the camp miles back in the woods. The poem leaves a lot of questions a century later, but it would probably have been hilarious to those who knew the people and situations it describes. Even without that advantage, it remains a biographical story-of-sorts, and with a little imagination on the reader's part it can be appreciated for its insight into life at the Millers' Bear Pond Camp. The last lines indicate that the writer left a radio at the camp for all to enjoy—probably the very people mentioned in the poem.

O' Camp Limberlost

In the Adirondack Region,
Not far from Seventh Lake,
Stands a camp owned by Leon Miller,
Of Lowville, New York State.
Surrounding this camp is a forest,
In the distance the great hills loom high,
And the shores of the famous Red River
Are dotted with deer that must die.
For the hunters, who visit this country
Are with the Vikings of old,
In the way they murder "pet" weasels
And play for each other's gold.
There is Harris, the "aim straight shooter,"
He is graceful running them down
With his leaps and bounds o'er the brush heaps,
And yelling till the echoes resound.
But when he gets two or three started,
And calls to the boys to "come down,"
He'll pause to reload his rifle,
And then will take aim "in the ground."

And then comes a deed quite historic,
Concerning our sharp shooter "Dine,"

Who hunts not for bear meat or venison,
Guess not, it's a much different line.
He will face any kind of weasels,
No matter how small, or how old,
For he never can see any danger
In facing an animal so bold.

It was near that old Red River
Only a few years ago,
That "Brad" thought he knew the country,
No matter where he would go;
So he wandered away from the party,
Not thinking no one was around;
He thought he sure would be lucky
And bring down a two-hundred pound;
But the party discovered his absence,
And oh! how the bullets did ring,
Brad listened, but paid no attention,
Didn't know they were firing for him.

Then there's "Joe," a Tug Hill veteran,
As faithful as one can be;
But one day he met with an accident
That sure was amusing to see.
He was driving through the streets of Lowville,
The weather was bright and fair,
Accompanied by "Peck," the sheriff,
Exercising a chestnut mare.
He drove down toward the Strife House,
Can you imagine the scene?
Of "Joe" turning to go round the "Dummy,"
And hitting it slick and clean;
Knocking the lamp to the pavement,
And shooting the flames in the air,

Escaping, "our Joe" and the sheriff,
But scorching the poor chestnut mare.

Then there is Ralph, another famed hunter,
Who can sure tell a doe from a buck,
When he saw one or two in the distance,
He cried, "There's a fawn, OH! What luck!"
So he paused for another moment
Till horns, "five points" came in sight,
Ralph fired—without hesitation,
And the boys ate venison that night.

But "Skip" hunts for game much different,
All he seeks is a souvenir
So he can mount and keep as a memory
For many and many a year;
For he aimed at a great big "husky,"
And the bullets flew straight as a rail,
But when he went to the spot for his game, boys,
All he could find was the tail!

There is "Parker," a regular hunter,
He gets them one at a time,
And this is the way he does it,
Try it, and see what you find:
You have notices he is always seeking
A place where he thinks deer will browse,
His judgement! Well—only "three" has he murdered,
And now 'tis a "slaughter house."

Let's pause for a moment and picture
The "Colonel" in his hunting attire,
With an old fashioned thirty-eight rifle,
As "light" as a ton of wire,

Chasing the wilds of the country
After a wounded, yes, "wounded deer,"
Thinking 'twas a "Pontiac Mary,"
And not having one bit of fear.

And o'er on a log sat another,
"The Boss" with his checkered hose,
Awaiting his chance for a "good one"
Not thinking of his "graceful pose,"
When suddenly in the distance,
The form of a deer caught his eye,
He rolled off the log, then fired,
And it sounded like the Fourth of July.
The boys were amazed at "his" shooting,
And rushed to the aid of "Our Boss,"
And there laid his "first real venison"
On a beautiful patch of moss.

But when night dawned on the party,
They all bunked in, hunter's style,
There came forth those dainty "pajamas,"
Which caused everyone to smile.
For "Gaber" always exhibits his ankles,
More than any fair dame in town,
So why cover them with "pajamas,"
Or a "lady-like" evening gown?

We wish you a Merry Christmas,
And a very Happy New Year,
And trust you'll enjoy this radio
In your camp, many miles from here.

—Poem provided by Leonard Harris

The land B.B. Miller called "O' Camp Limberlost" was in a remote location below the steep cliffs of Seventh Lake Mountain and at the southwest end of Bear Pond. It was a small-scale replica of countless similar old-style lumber camps found throughout the Adirondacks in locations that are barely known today.

The large-scale pergola built by Billy Gilchrist on Goff Island. *Courtesy Winfred Murdock*

Millers' camp was positioned between forested mountaintops beside a jeweled tiny lake; there are to this day rocks as large as trolley cars, little clearings and trackless forest, and without guideboards to mark one's way through brush and swamps it was, and still is, easy to get bogged down in muck and mire, brooks and brambles, with your boots full of water and skin scraped and clothing torn in many places, with your pack straps irritating your shoulders as experienced by B.B. when his .35-55 rifle felt like it weighed a ton. The virgin forest land of The Plains was once described by Irishman guide Archie Delmarsh as, "The forest where the hand of man never put foot." During the 1890s, it could be added "where the hand of man had never put an axe."

In 1891, a photograph of Millers' recreational island camp was included in *The Fulton Chain Adirondacks*, an attractively-designed souvenir booklet published by The James Bayne Company of Grand Rapids, Michigan, that promoted the Fulton Chain of Lakes. The photo shows a comfortable-looking two-story vertical spruce log structure with a wrap-around veranda. A cross-buck porch railing separated the porch dweller from the rocky yard. The design was typical of many of the private camp-like homes found along the Fulton Chain of Lakes in the day.

Miller's Bear Pond camp complex is shielded by trees. L.S. Miller's log quarters are on the right; the guides' building is on the left. *Courtesy Norton Bus Bird Collection*

A list of guides employed by Miller in 1892 and '93 tells the employer hired and relied on a large crew of local men. The guides and workforce included A.R.U. Church, Milo Bull, Abner Blakeman, Elmer E. Higby, Phil Christy, Perk Rivch [sic], Ira Parsons, William Weedmark, Vernie Gilbert, Frank Hughes and Dan Hess.

Sturdy and rugged, these men-of-the-woods, all early natives of the Fulton Chain of Lakes, lived a tough life. It was often austere, but it was a life that satisfied them.

For B.B., his locally-built camp meant fun—a diversion from his everyday work, the enjoyment that comes from the bond and camaraderie between guides and camp members, the merriment and pure joy and pleasure of living in the forest. I imagine great meals that included wild game were prepared and enjoyed, fishing and hunting tales retold, and simply taking a break from partridge hunting and chasing deer to wash clothes and shave in the outdoors is what B.B. might have felt camping was all about.

In October of 1986 I traveled to Lowville, New York to visit with John S. Miller, D.M.D., and to talk with Leonard Miller Harris about the old Miller hunting camp at Bear Pond and their small fishing camp along Benedict Creek. Both men said they had always had a keen interest in their genealogy and were itching to see the old pictures of Bear Pond Camp that Bus Bird and Gordon Rudd had given me.

Miller's main camp was designed and built to look, and function, like the old-time logging camps. *Courtesy Lewis H. Payne (The Payne Family Collection)*

According to family history, Brayton Bela Miller started a cheese business in Lowville. B.B. had two sons, Frank and Leon S. Frank became an evangelical preacher. Leon joined his father in the cheese business, and he and his father were both lovers of the woods and enjoyed outdoor pursuits. The team built a large cheese cold storage that became B.B. Miller and Son. Following B.B.'s death Leon continued to run the business until he joined it with that of another Lowvillean, R.J. Richardson, whose produce business was widely known. R.J. was renowned as a man of more than unusual business ability. For 17 years he served as the county's commissioner of agriculture and judged cheese at the state fair. Together, the businessmen built Miller Richardson Cheese Company, the largest cheese cold storage in the world at that time.

Standing between the two canvas wall tents at Bear Pond are (lt. to rt.) Milo Leach, guide and L.S. Miller. Circa 1917. *Photo by A.P. Ford, Courtesy Norton Bus Bird Collection*

About 1927, Miller and Richardson's firm merged into the Kraft Cheese Company of New York. Leon passed away in 1933.

Unidentified men with bucks. *Photo by A.P. Ford, Courtesy Norton Bus Bird Collection*

It was Dr. Miller's understanding it was Leon who improved the family's Seventh Lake camp following his father's death.

Miller said, "Ellen Parsons Miller, B.B.'s wife, lived with Leon and my father, Stanley, after B.B.'s death and she visited the Seventh Lake camp. My cousin Dr. Leon Miller Harris, who lived in Watertown, is the present owner of the Seventh Lake camp." [1986]

Leonard M. Harris, who provided the "O' Camp Limberlost" poem, also contributed his knowledge of Millers' Bear Pond Camp. In 1986, Leonard, the younger brother of Dr. L. Miller, was a dental laboratory technician and owned his own dental lab in Lowville.

Leonard began, "B.B. wanted a place to relax, hunt and fish." At that time The Fulton Chain of Lakes became the destination for well-heeled people in the Lowville area. His diary tells the route he traveled. "Left Lowville by horse and buggy to Utica. Train to Thendara. Boat to Wood Hotel." A guide would meet him with a carriage to transport passengers and gear to Sixth Lake, where another boat would take them to Seventh Lake.

"Later on, when cars came into use, B.B. and Leon would drive their motor car from Lowville to Port Leyden to McKeever to Thendara. B.B.'s diary mentions he always carried a large blanket in the car to be laid in front of the wheels to provide traction to climb up the sand hill to Moose River Station."

All in a day's hunt. Diane Thibado explained about the sports that hired her grandfather, Henry Thibado, and later her dad Charlie and his brother who made extra money in exchange for their guiding and hunting services in the fall: "Dad and Tip would, on the average, harvest at least twenty bucks (deer) each in the fall. Grandpa Henry, would then sell the deer to unsuccessful hunters, who would put their own tags on them. Grandpa sold the deer for ten dollars per point, so a spike horn would cost twenty dollars, a four-point buck would be forty dollars, and so on.

"The money they made helped take the entire family through the long winters. And, of course, they always had several deer 'hanging.' Back in those years the game wardens would look the other way if they knew the deer meat was there to feed a man's family.

"You really have to wonder how many of the hunters who came out of the woods with bragging rights really shot the bucks they took home. And how many of those deer were actually shot by the guides to save face for their clients.

"Dad said if Grandpa, Tip or he fired three rounds, they would return home with three kills (rabbits, birds, squirrels, deer).

"I expect that was likely true for most guides in the Inlet area. Guiding was an annual business, and a truly good guide would be sure his clients had a successful hunt (especially if he wanted to be hired again next season). And if one of the sportsmen bought his deer, I'll bet the story of how he got it probably got better every time he told it." *Courtesy Lewis H. Payne (The Payne Family Collection)*

Edwin R. Wallace's 1880 descriptive *Guide to the Adirondacks* tells the route from the "Forge" to Seventh Lake. Leonard read the account from The Head [Inlet today]. :

> "The Fifth to the Sixth Lakes are considerably noted as deer resorts. Their shores are generally marshy, and numerous pond lilies abound in their waters.
>
> Passing from the Sixth up the narrow and rapid inlet we enter the Seventh Lake, delighted with the panorama at this point unfolded to us. This lake has one island (White's) of some 50 acres, not far from its center, covered with rocks and pine timber. Near the island, off its S. shore, salmon trout have sometimes been caught, weighing from 15 to 20 lbs. in 100 feet depth of water. For speckled trout, visit the little stream that enters near this place, and (fish?) the inlet and outlet.

Inlet guide, Bill Payne, is shaving in front of the canvas wall tent. This picture was taken before Miller's log camp was built. Circa 1917. Photo by A.P. Ford. Courtesy Norton Bus Bird Collection

"Eligible camping places will be found near the foot, on W. shore; at a spot about ½ m. from the head, on the same side (Camp Comfort); opposite this, across the lake, at 'Pt. Pleasant' and near the inlet, by the 'silver beach,' (Camp Lookout.)

Six unidentified men at Miller's Bear Pond Camp. Circa 1917.
Photo by A.P. Ford, Courtesy Norton Bus Bird Collection

Fourteen years later Wallace's updated 1894 guidebook footnoted that the once-panoramic view between Sixth and Seventh Lake had changed.

"Later—The Sixth and the once lovely Seventh L. now present a scene of desolation. A dam has been placed at the foot of the former, and ghastly dead trees now skirt the once bright and verdant shores of these waters. The silver beach at the head of the Seventh, so long the boast of that locality, has disappeared.

Its inlet and outlet, from pleasant streams have become dismal swamps, divested of every charm; and thus some of its most attractive features are perhaps lost forever."

Leonard said the Millers arrived by train in Thendara in 1899 that their caretaker, Milo Leach, was there to pick them up with a wagon. It read, "Arrived at camp in small boat since the steamer was not working yet."

"Milo was a man of many and varied talents," said Leonard. "Both he and Walter Rossa worked endless hours at camp on Seventh Lake when the Millers were in residence. B.B. started out on the big island. B.B. referred to it as Glory Island and White's Island. It's known now as Goff Island. The Millers' island camp was referred to as Lake View Camp, but in 1910 the state survey team found they were squatting on state land so they purchased property on a point on Seventh Lake's main land known as Camp Comfort that was opposite the island.

Henry Thibado stands at the far left. *Photo by A.P. Ford, Courtesy Norton Bus Bird Collection*

"The Millers liked their out-of-doors retreat and especially enjoyed fishing, reading, playing cards, boating, and hiking. A perennial favorite was to boat to the portage between Seventh and Eighth lakes and then hike to Bug and Eagles Nest lakes to fish."

283

Wallace's 1894 guide describes the route. The lakes remain a popular destination for hikers today.

> "To reach Bug and Eagle Lakes, 2 little sheets lying alone in the forest, west of Eighth Lake, we follow the path north that starts from the east shore about 100 rods northwest of the mouth of the inlet of Seventh Lake. The route, part of the way (1½ mile) is a mere trail, followed by the aid of barked trees. Bug Lake is an uninteresting body of water, in shape similar to that of a boot. 'Boot Lake' would be a more appropriate name. It furnishes no fishing. When leaving this lake on the return trip, by turning sharply to the left and proceeding 80 or 100 rods we will reach Eagle Lake.[26] The shores of this little loch rise boldly, almost precipitously, from the water's edge. It was once famous for its numerous large speckled trout, and it still affords some fine catches.

Supplies bound for Miller's Bear Pond Camp are being loaded on Henry Thibado's horse-drawn jumper at Split Rocks. This rough horse trail and footpath roughly follows the Totten and Crossfield survey line, over Seventh Lake Mountain. The starting point was along Route 28 just past the Fynimore camp outside Inlet. The Seventh Lake lookout is on the opposite side of the road. *Courtesy Gordon Rudd*

Journal entries indicate hunting in the Adirondacks was unusually good. Deer were numerous and the woods were alive with partridges; the ponds and lakes in the remote regions offered wonderful attractions to the duck shooter as well.

L.S. Miller stands second from left; Milo Leach is third from left.; Henry Thibado (with the cigarette in his mouth) is on the right. Other guides and campers are unidentified.
Photo by A.P. Ford, Courtesy Norton Bus Bird Collection

B.B. had heard reports of the noted Indian guide Elijah Camp and Archie Delmarsh's stories of guiding clients in to the headwaters of the south branch of the Moose River, and he had read Raymond S. Spears's description of a trail leading to Col. Beecher's old camp along the south branch. Raving reports of wild game and a romantic notion of a hunting cabin tucked back in a rugged location undisturbed by the hand of man might have been his motivation to have Milo seek out a location for his own wilderness retreat from which he could hunt, fish and invite guests to accompany him.

A drawing of Bear Pond from the camp's journal. *Photo by A.P. Ford, Courtesy Norton Bus Bird Collection*

"I haven't found any explanation for B.B.'s decision to locate a camp at Bear Pond," said Leonard. "All I know is that sometime in the early years 1890s a rough horse trail and footpath was cut out that basically followed the Totten and Crossfield survey line, which cut up over Seventh Lake Mountain at the present Split Rocks just past the Fynimore camp before state land begins. There was no description given of the route in the camp record book. It is simply described in every trip recorded as this June 13, 1909 entry read: 'Went over the mountain to hunting camp.'

"One other route the party took was longer but physically easier. The Millers called it the High Rock Road Outlet. It's a portion of the old Uncas Road. It led to Bear Pond by first going to Mohegan Lake. The basic route can still be traced today. It begins across Route 28 from the entrance to the Seventh and Eighth lakes camp grounds.

"The hunting camp was located on a rise on the southwest side of Bear Pond near a marshy cove. The camp first consisted of large canvas wall tents. Sometime during the late teens B.B. contracted with many guides to construct two log buildings to replace the tents on Bear Pond as well as build a log structure for a fishing camp along Benedict Creek.

A page from Miller's daughter's diary. *Author's photo*

"I'm guessing, but according to the Miller camp log book the list of guides and workmen employed during the middle teens, all of these men must have had a hand in the construction of the buildings: Gerald Kenwell, Lewis Porter, Fred Trotter, Charles and Floyd Puffer, Sam Brakey, A.P. Ford, Matter Rosa and Abner Blakeman. The notation of 'cook' after William Patrick's name in 1917 indicates what his position was."

Margaret D. Miller was guided over the mountain in 1916 by Milo Leach and wrote the following in the camp journal after her arrival: "The trip took 2 hrs. and 25 min. There I found a dandy log camp. The main camp was 50 feet long, being a log structure; the kitchen and dining room was one large room and the other half was bedroom space. I had a dandy supper and bed."

Leonard continued. "There was also a guide's cabin off to the left of the main camp. The Millers' fishing camp, crafted from spruce logs, stood on a slight bluff overlooking Benedict Creek."

During my interview with Leonard and Marg Harris, the couple inquired about Bus Bird's health and asked me to extend a fond hello to him. They had not seen Bus for years, but retained precious memories of him taking them on scenic flights on Bird's Seaplane Service on Sixth Lake to fish at Bug Lake.

Late start for Lime Kiln.
Two minnow traps set on arrival.
Very few obtained. Three of party
trolled lake; heavy wind; no strikes.
In P.M. still-fishing by whole
party — no strikes. Suckers at dam for bait.
Home at six o'clock.

Whole party set out for Red River for a
two days sojourn. When we reached
the clearing we were overtaken by
a heavy shower, and found that
the camp we had expected to use
was occupied, so we took shelter

OPPOSITE AND ABOVE: **Diaries, journals, letters, scrap books and snapshots are valuable research materials.** *Journals from Leonard Harris's collection of Bear Pond memorabilia, Photo by the author*

"My name is Norton Bird," said Bus the day I told him about my meeting with the Harrises and returned the collection of Miller snapshots he had loaned me. "I want to set the record straight. The nickname was hung on me years ago and I haven't been able to shake it.

"I knew all of the guides in these photos," Bus recalled as he pointed out each person. A.P. Ford was my father-in-law, Milo Leach was Miller's caretaker and guide. Fred Trotter was owner of Trotter's Restaurant, now Scotts Inn (1986). Henry Thibado, Bill Payne, … the whole lot of them were all from Inlet.

"You'll note most of these pictures were taken in 1917. They were some that A.P. Ford had.

"I started to guide for the Millers in 1925 and went to 1933. This was the year that Leon Miller died. I don't believe the [Bear Pond and Benedict Creek] camps were used by the Millers after that. They were great people to work with. Every year the guides received an expensive present. One year each guide was given a Savage rifle. At Christmas everyone received a large cheese and a ten-pound block of chocolate candy.

"The last time I saw [Leon] Miller was 1933. He called to see if I had any fish, as he was coming up to camp with guests. I went out and caught him a lake trout and he gave me $20.00, which was a lot of money in those times. I told him it was too much and his reply was, 'When I give you money, take it because you may not get it anymore.' A week later he was dead."

After locating the remains of the Benedict Creek camp, I spoke to Tom Thibado in January 1987. Tom reported, "My grandfather Henry bought the property from Milo Leach, who had obtained it from the Miller estate, but he didn't know what year that was.[27]

"I looked through my father's [Alfred's] photos and could only find two pictures of the Benedict Creek camp, but I did find a picture of one of my grandfather's horse-dawn jumpers going into camp."

The outbound camps were used primarily for fishing Brook Trout in spring and hunting deer and bear in the fall. Land was simply squatted on, since logging companies owned it, although permission was often given if the companies were approached.

"It was infrequent that parties from the Miller camp ever tramped far beyond Bear Pond or the fishing camp," guessed Leonard, based on what he had read. "A party recorded they followed a foot trail 3½ miles from Millers' to Rousseau's Ponds. They wrote: '…fished and ate lunch. It was a long walk but pretty.'"

I wish now I had photocopied the pages from the Millers' log book. I remember I flipped through it looking for interesting adventures, but not finding any I ended up jotting down snippets and did not always include the date of the entry. What follows are a few of the odds and ends I did record.

"The Millers were dog lovers. They always owned English bull-dogs but never used dogs to hunt."

"October 1924: Lewis, Milo and Bert went over the Mt. with a load. Hunters were called in from the woods by troopers due to dry forest."

"Henry Thibado heads to Bear Pond over 7th Lake Mt. just before the lookout [on Seventh Lake]. There's a small stream on the right and Split Rocks."

"Bert Ford and Vernie Gilbert [are] going to Vernie's camp."

"Louise Porter Payne married, Tuesday 20 at noon [no year was recorded]. We went down to see her off. Her heel came off."

I'll never know why I didn't ask Louise the date of her marriage and about this incident the Millers recorded when I interviewed her. Louise had visited Bear Pond Camp with her father Lew Porter.

Louise recalled: "Oh what a trip it was to reach Millers' camp. It took 2½ hours on foot over a rough trail. I remember lightning struck very nearby. I also remember a rat in the ice house. It hit me on the leg on my way out. Leon Miller told me it made no difference what condensed milk I bought, that at his plant they produced milk for three major companies."

The Bear Pond and Benedict Creek land the Millers called "upper and lower camp country" is now a part of the historic Moose River Pains country. It is a microcosm of untold similar settings scarcely known today.

In addition to the workforce employed in their cheese business, Brayton Bela's and Leon Miller provided employment for many early Adirondack inhabitants—pioneers who first settled the Fulton Chain of Lakes region and who did more than build camps and move and support the Miller party into hunting and fishing camps. Those natives of the late 19th and early 20th centuries were tough, self-reliant Adirondack folks who stuck out their hardscrabble lives in the mountains despite a scarcity of jobs, the fierce winters and the black flies. When there was no work, they augmented their larders with game and wild foods. Their lifestyle was sustainable only because they depended on themselves and each other. They contributed to the growth and popularity of the Adirondacks but left scant records of their lives except for the few remembrances and snapshots that have survived.

The coming of the sporting crowd, city people like the Millers who built rustic escapes in the mountains, followed by the arrival of wealthy summer people who stayed at more luxurious camps and hotels and relied on the natives' knowledge offered new opportunities and economically improved lives for the natives. B.B. and Leon Miller and their Bear Pond and Benedict Creek camps were part of this progression. Those camps left no trace that is visible now, but they were important at the time for both city-worn guests and woods-savvy employees.

The only remaining memories that partially explain the references in "O' Camp Limberlost" that I have turned up are a few notes Bus Bird jotted in the margin of the copy of the poem I gave him and some assumptions Jonathan W. Miller offered.

"The reference to 'the famous Red River' and 'pet' weasels [in the first stanza] refers to the abundance of wildlife and a jab at 'sharpshooter Dine,'" said Bus. "Dine, while on watch for deer, shot a weasel and never lived it down."

Jonathan believes, "One of Leon's best friends was Louis Touissant (probably Toussaint?) of Lowville, who I believe was referred to as 'Dine' or 'Dyne.'"

"Harris," Bus pointed out, "was the father of the Millers you have talked to. The line 'he gets two or three started' refers to a bad case of Buck Fever, when he fired all his bullets in the ground and the deer went on."

Jonathan agreed adding that, "Russell Harris married Margaret Miller (Leon's daughter) and was the father of Leonard and Miller Harris."

The line in the fourth stanza: "That 'Brad' thought he knew the country," Bus said referred to a search and rescue party. "Brad took off by himself against the advice of the guides and became lost," Bus told me. "We had quite a time to find him as he wouldn't answer our shots."

Miller's lower camp, referred to as the fishing camp, was built on a rise above Benedict Stream. To this day [2020] bits of debris from the camp are visible.

Photo by A.P. Ford. Courtesy Norton Bus Bird Collection

 293

Bus speculated about Ralph and Skip in the sixth and seventh stanzas. "I would think he [Ralph] probably killed the doe and the buck got away. Parker always watched the same runway, which was really productive.

"Leon S. Miller is the Boss toward the end of the poem. Leon was squatted behind a log taking a crap when the deer came along. The 'venison' referred to was the crap he took."

Bus ended with a line drawing of Bear Pond Camp that showed the log building was laid out in a north-south direction. "The camp was divided as shown," he said. "The kitchen and dining room was one large room. A door led to the bunkroom."

"The O' Camp Limberlost poem is very interesting," said Jonathan W. Miller in an October 2016 email. I'm not sure what the timing of that poem is, but I would have thought pre-World War II and, more likely around the last 19-teens or early 1920s. …My own grandfather, Stanley Miller, was referred to throughout his life as 'Gaber.' He was quite a dapper dresser and thus I would guess that is the 'Gaber' who is referred to in the penultimate stanza of the poem. …I also think that the Peck who is referred to as the sheriff was Nelson Peck, who was the Lewis County sheriff in the late 19-teens."

Jonathan's father, John, was Leonard Harris's first cousin. The Seventh Lake camp was built by his great-great grandfather B.B. Miller. Jonathan, a recently retired lawyer from New York City, told me he has been spending "most of the last year in the North Country at an Adirondack camp we have over on Crystal Lake in Lewis County."

It seems clear that a 100% history of the Miller's efforts to enjoy the wildlife and wildlands around Seventh Lake and the Moose River Plains will never be completely unfolded, but what has surfaced amounts to great strides in entering an informal reckoning of B.B. and Leon Millers' Adirondack camps.

Chapter Twenty-Two

Louise Payne's Mountain Echoes

ON THE FIRST DAY I visited with Louise, she was knitting mittens. It had snowed a good deal and because our conversation wandered between her father's camp, the Moose River Plains and growing up in the mountains, her childhood's winter entertainment came up.

Louise and Richard Payne. *Courtesy Louis H. Payne (The Payne Family Collection)*

Gordon Rudd leans against the log side wall of Miller's camp, circa 1932.
Courtesy Gordon Rudd

I knew Louise as a modern grandmother with a notebook stuffed full of recipes she had swapped with friends and relatives and saved since she was first married. I found it remarkable she had saved the original baking powder biscuit recipe her dad whipped up at Camp Savage. It makes a good-tasting biscuit. Louise said it hasn't changed except for the substitution of shortening for lard. Over the years, she experimented with sugar, butter and buttermilk. Lou's Perfect Baking Powder Biscuits is a basic standard.

Talking with Louise was better than reading a history book. Her memory went back to the day when dirt roads were typical connections between Adirondack towns and villages. This picture shows Route 28 between Sixth and Seventh lakes. *Courtesy Leigh Portner*

Lou's Perfect Baking Powder Biscuits

Ingredients:

2 cups flour

3 teaspoons baking powder

1 teaspoon salt

1⁄4 cup shortening

3⁄4 cup milk

Directions: Mix flour, baking powder and salt together with a fork. Blend in ¼ cup shortening. Mix all with ¾ cup milk. Pat or roll out to about ½" thickness. Cut out with biscuit cutter or cut into squares with a knife. Place in ungreased 9 in. x 12 in. pan. Bake at 450°F. for 10 to 12 minutes.

Our conversation vacillated between present-day Adirondacks and the days gone by. In comparison to the McCauley ski slope in Old Forge and flooded skating rinks, Louise recalled the old hill, where the shiny, painted, store-bought sled was the exception. "I remember the jumpers, made by nailing an upright piece onto the barrel stave; a board nailed to that served as a seat," she said. "It took a little time to learn to balance this, but after the stave was worn smooth as glass, it would go like the wind and for a long distance after reaching the bottom of the hill." If a hill was icy, her mother's dishpan served as a sled. Another common sled was nothing other than a smooth waxed board on which to whiz down the hill. It was the spirit of youth and the invigorating air of the North Country that counted, rather than the vehicle used.

Louise Payne's experiences went back to the pioneer days. The road to Inlet, N.Y. in the 21st century is now a paved highway—the mountain ox-roads and by-roads have disappeared. In her mind, however, the dirt track known as The Kenwell Trail that led into the woods where her father's and horses' feet once made their imprints was as clear as the day she last went into Camp Savage. *A Seneca Ray Stoddard photo. Courtesy Maitland DeSormo Collection*

Close-up of the sturdy log construction of Miller's camp. *Courtesy Gordon Rudd*

Despite her enthusiasm for old-time sledding, Louise said she found it more fun now to watch Inlet's big snowplow clear the road outside her picture window than it had been to watch the neighbors of her youth make the roads passable with a sleigh and plow.

And what fun were the sleigh rides, when the children were taken for a ride on a sunny afternoon or a moonlit night! She remembered the jingling sleigh bells, the sweet-smelling hay on the bottom of the sleigh, and the abundance of blankets and robes. "We called them buffalo robes but they may have been old cowhides or sheepskins with the fleece still on them, or they may have been old bed quilts," Louise added.

Ice skating was another winter pastime that Louise and her friends enjoyed. Lacking skates, children could run and slide on Fourth Lake, which had frozen to a nice glare of ice. What fun they had until the kids were told to stop because they were wearing out good shoe leather.

299

The three following recipes brought memories of lunches she took to school—"We carried dinner pails." A two-quart pail with a cover was the kind most often used, but some pails were a square box. It was common for fathers to reuse their Prince Albert tobacco tins, which had a hinged cover. There were no thermos bottles in those days.

Sandwiches were not yet so popular. The dinner pails contained just good homemade biscuits, bread and butter, a wedge of pie, cake, and maybe a cookie. It was a happy day when the cake was frosted.

Those were some memories from Louise's good old days—days of simplicity that were nonetheless pleasant, and delightful for her to recall.

"The lure of the woods had a strong attraction for sports," said Louise. "They'd follow a guide for miles out into the forest or climb away up on a mountainside to a camp among the balsams." City slickers found the call of the blue jays and the chatter of squirrels a unique experience. They'd sleep on the ground and listen to owls hoot and smell a skunk's balm in the wee hours. Then they'd rise up at dawn and endure a cold scrub at the spring before a breakfast of coffee, venison steak and flapjacks.

This photo shows corduroy along a mucky section of Fawn Lake's shoreline. Louise remembered following her dad over this route into The Plains. *Courtesy Jane and "Red" Ritz*

Louise's Apple Sauce Cake

Louise said she had used this old-time recipe for years. I didn't find it much different from my grandmother's old-fashioned scratch cake recipe. Gram used a raisin-lemon sauce for a topping.

300

Ingredients:

1 cup apple sauce

1 teaspoon baking powder

1 cup brown sugar

½ cup butter

1 teaspoon salt

2 tablespoons cocoa

1 cup raisins (add some walnuts if you like)

1½ cups flour

Directions: Cream butter and sugar. Add remaining ingredients. Spoon into a greased 8" square pan and bake at 350°F. for 25–30 minutes or until it comes out clean.

Moose River Ginger Bread

Favorite scratch recipes that are passed down from one generation to another are not only tasty but carry memories. Louise's formula is classic gingerbread, perhaps just like she remembered it as a young girl. I consider myself a gingerbread aficionado. This is easy to whip up and a great-tasting treat.

Ingredients:

¼ cup shortening

1 cup sugar

1 egg

½ cup molasses

½ cup hot water

1¼ cups sifted flour,

¾ teaspoon baking soda,

½ teaspoon each of cinnamon, ginger and salt

¼ teaspoon cloves

Directions: Blend shortening (scant) and sugar. Add 1 beaten egg and mix well. Blend molasses with hot water. Sift together: sifted flour, baking soda, cinnamon, ginger and salt, and cloves. Add flour mixture and liquids alternately and mix until well-blended. Pour batter into 8-inch greased cake tin. Bake in moderate oven (350°F. to 375°F.) about 25 minutes.

Louise pointed to the man standing by the pack horse and said, "This is my father, Lew Porter back at Kenwell's on the Moose River Plains. I'd say this was about 1895."
Courtesy Louise Porter Payne

Ever since mountain pioneers managed to eke leafy greens and other vegetables from the soil, neighbors visited and swapped recipes. Kinfolks have testified to finding notebooks stuffed full of recipes relatives saved, sometimes since young women were first married. There were as many inventive salad dressings as there were whiskers on a hermit.

Salad dressing might not sound very "Adirondackish," but Louise testified her dressings were "Delicious!" The following formula is one that is easy to prepare and great as a dip for raw veggies.

Homemade Ranch Dressing

Ingredients:

½ cup mayonnaise

½ cup buttermilk

½ tsp. dried parsley flakes

¼ tsp garlic powder

¼ tsp. onion powder

¼ tsp salt

Dash each of pepper and paprika

302

Directions: Put all ingredients in a bowl and whisk together. Pour into glass jar or other small container and put in the refrigerator for a few hours to let the ingredients mellow. Shake or stir before using. *Note: To make this into spicy Southwest dressing, blend in ¼ cup of jarred salsa. Another good addition is grated parmesan cheese, about ¼ cup.*

Listening to Louise and other older Adirondack natives has been my favorite way to learn about the past. Their first person memories about the old days and old ways speak directly to what they saw and learned from even older folks. She had heard about Timothy L. Woodruff's magnificent summer home on Lake Kora and the many prominent politicians and State officials that were entertained in the days at Kamp Kill Kare when the ex-lieutenant governor was high in the councils of the Republican Party.

Louise found this scene of three youngsters rowing a guide-boat on Sixth Lake a typical activity, city sports who came to the mountains wrote volumes about the joy of being in the Adirondacks. *Courtesy John Chamberlain*

Her father, as guide and carpenter got around. When Woodruff purchased land from William West Durant for $12,000, the fabulous sum must have seemed like a small fortune to Adirondack folks and surely caused much speculation among the residents. The land was then nothing more than a vast virgin forest, but with the improvements Woodruff had made on the place—building roads, erecting costly buildings and furnishing them luxuriously; stocking the streams and lakes with bass, salmon, trout and pickerel, and the preserve with deer, bear and other animals—the camp had vastly increased in value, far beyond the original purchase price.

Guests are congregated around the ground level door at Kenwell's Sportsman's Home.
Courtesy Ora Kenwell

OPPOSITE: **"This is Norman D. Chapin. He came over from his brother's Camp Nit on Beaver Lake. Somehow he hurt his leg. Dad fixed him a crutch." —Louise Payne.**
Courtesy of Louise Porter Payne

Louise had heard the speculation about Woodruff during the administration of New York Governor Hughes. That was during the time the Woodruffs purchased the land. "It was the subject of investigation," she said. When Woodruff acquired the property, he was a member of the Land Purchasing Board. An effort was made by investigators to show that Woodruff got a much better bargain than he would have obtained if he had not been connected with the board. Reports in newspapers of the day said the state had tried to "buy the large tract of land, which included the property now called Kamp Kill Kare from Mr. Durant, who had offered It at $127,000. Mr. Durant would not consent to include Lake Kora, which was then known as Lake Sumner, and the offer was refused. The state later acquired the tract for $168,000, an excess of $41,000 over the original price, while Woodruff got Kamp Kill Kare, in the heart of the tract."

Camp Strategy (aka Savage). Vertical log construction was much faster than the traditional way. "I remember Lost Ponds was also known as Pine Grove Ponds at one time. The name easily could have come from the nearby Pine Grove Creek." —Louise Payne. *Courtesy Louise Porter Payne*

OPPOSITE: **Louise Payne.** *Courtesy Louis H. Payne (The Payne Family Collection)*

The Tuesday evening edition of *The Rome Daily Sentinel* summarized the findings in its column "T.F. Woodruff on Witness Stand." Woodruff explained to the satisfaction of the investigators that there was nothing out of the way in the purchase of the camp. Mr. Durant at first would not consent to sell Lake Sumner to the State, for the reason that it would then become public property and depreciate the value of his two adjoining preserves [Sagamore and Mohegan lakes] After having refused to sell to the State, Durant later offered it to any desirable private purchaser, and it was then that Woodruff acquired the property. The fact that Woodruff was a member of the Land Purchasing Board had nothing to do with the sale whatever.

Louise's father's Camp Savage [aka Camp Strategy], tucked back on a hillside deep in the Moose River Plains, wasn't a luxurious camp. Louie Porter might have lugged a pack basket loaded with beans, salt pork and potatoes dozens of miles up and down hills, across streams, and through valleys, leading sports through marshes, and over slippery rocks, to rest finally at a night's makeshift shelter where a smoldering campfire might have been somewhat sheltered clients from the rain of mosquitoes. Louie's and Louise's lives were simple compared to the meals and standard of living of the Adirondacks' wealthy campers, but it was because of Louise's everyday perspective that I gained much more knowledge about the old days and ways.

In the mid-1980s a portion of Bear Pond's "Refrigerator" building was still standing. Inside I found small hand tools, eating utensils, metal and china plates and cups.
Author's photo

Chapter Twenty-Three

A Sportsman's Memory of Adirondack Deer Hunting in 1921

F.E. BRIMMER was a newspaper reporter, an occasional writer for *Fur News* and *Outing* and he was an avid sportsman. Brimmer trapped, hunted, fished, and manufactured his own snowshoes. He also enjoyed rambling around the wilds surrounding Inlet throughout the teens and early 1920s. It's more than likely he came in contact with Louis Porter and Wellington Kenwell. During his earliest outings, Brimmer hired Gerald Kenwell to take him hunting on The Plains.

Eliza Jane Darling, the Hamilton Country historian says of Inlet:

> Inlet is the youngest child of Hamilton County. Its first settlers broached the region from the west, hunters and trapper who came from Herkimer County to ply their trade around the Fulton Chain of Lakes extending from Old Forge nearly to Raquette. It quickly grew into a resort community favored by Sports, and guiding became a popular occupation. By the turn of the 19th century, the Town of Morehouse was surprised to find a thriving community in its far northern reaches, and like Wells before it, attempted to incorporate this population into the official life of the town. And like Hope, Lake Pleasant and Benson before them, the people of Inlet found it more convenient to form their own government than to travel days to the town center to participate in municipal politics. Morehouse was unperturbed by the break, and by 1902, the last of Hamilton County's town had formed.
>
> Inlet prospered primarily around its picturesque lakes. A few years after the town's formation, it boasted several grand hotels,

including Hess Camp, Cedar Island House, Rocky Point Inn, Seventh Lake House, Hart's Cottages, and the Arrowhead, which in 1906 found infamy as the spot where Chester Gillette was apprehended after murdering Grace Brown at Big Moose Lake, the subject of Theodore Dreiser's *An American Tragedy*. This was one of several improbable tragedies to plague Inlet's earliest formal days. The following year, a gas explosion at Hess Camp took the life of its proprietor.

A hunting party from Miller's Bear Pond Camp arrived at Camp Strategy, circa 1917.
"Very few clothes were needed for the city sportsman," Frank Fayant wrote in his camping remembrances. "Long trousers were essential to keep legs from being exposed to stinging insects and briars. Then there were two or three bandana handkerchiefs, a pair of gloves, a felt hat (it was better than straw), heavy-soled, waterproofed leather shoes, heavy woolen socks, canvas leggings because they protected the trousers from getting caught in twigs or brambles and from getting wet by the early morning dew and wet grass, comfortable woolen or flannel shirts, wool sweater, fairly heavy underclothing and two sack suits of serviceable wool."
Fayant considered the list "requisites" in 1904. The older the camper's clothes were, the more comfortable he would feel, for without a doubt he would get wet and dirty many times if he sought adventure with either rod or gun. He also recommended that a "small pillow tick to be filled with balsam will add much to one's comfort at night."
Courtesy Louise Porter Payne

310

As roads improved access to nearby rail stations in both Eagle Bay and Raquette, Inlet thrived nonetheless. Hostelries, restaurants, shops and guides proliferated in service of the summer visitors, while schools, churches and a public park were established for the local population. Inlet remains a bustling resort community into the 21st century.

Limekiln Lake has been a popular and accessible Adirondack region south of Inlet for well over a century. Early vacationists and the sporting crowd found it offered good places to camp, to ramble around, and to hunt for those elusive bucks with a record-setting rack of horns.

Log camp on Limekiln Lake. *Photo from a post card, Courtesy Winfred Murdock*

The beautiful lake was Brimmer's chosen vacation ground. By the spring of 1921, he found Limekiln was "being opened up to automobile parties and vacationists." He considered the lake to be off the beaten track and found it strange that hotels had not been built much earlier simply because of the sand beaches and beautiful shoreline. He knew "camping parties had come here for years." Brimmer described the improved course he found under construction. "The road strikes off the new Seventh Lake road just beyond the bridge at Sixth Lake Dam. It is sandy and hilly, but the grades are easily negotiable and a deal of labor is being expended on the road. The woods are apparently untouched upon its shores, and the beach is very fine.

Entrance to Fawn Lake was over the shoreline of Limekiln Lake. Courtesy Winfred Murdock

"Mid the evergreens has been opened this year Limekiln Lake Hotel by Wallace J. Darling. It will impress anyone as being an ideally woodsy camp. The forest is heavy and tangled behind it… The unconventional woods life is to be had at its best. and home cooking will be found on the table. In spring and in the fall the place will be popular with fishermen and with hunters."

OPPOSITE: **Approaching Limekiln Lake over the new road.** Photo from a post card, Courtesy Winfred Murdock

proaching Lime Kiln Lake.

But as comfortable as camps and hotels were becoming in Inlet and around his favorite lake, the avid sportsman also enjoyed a rougher shelter of his own making of hemlock or spruce bark peeled fresh from the tree and supported by light cross pieces of saplings, or a ready-made deserted hunter's shack.

Darling Hotel, Limekiln Lake, from a post card. *Courtesy Charles E. Herr photo from a post card*

Whipping the streams and ponds with a fly road, profiting from the grand exercise shouldering a pack and "roaming through the woods," as he liked to say, as well as enjoying plain camp meals compared to food at a boarding house or hotel actually appealed to his "darn cheap" vacation plans, and it also gave him "a new lease on life."

An easily accessible Adirondack hunting grounds for deer and other game that Brimmer liked to tell about "is south of the Chain Lake Section, centering about Limekiln Lake." It was in this that adventurer-writer said he had hunted for "several years and here last season [1920] he shot" his best trophy buck, "a beautiful red fox, as well as many white rabbits and partridges, with a few ducks thrown in for good measure."

Brimmer writes of his sportsman's world in a 1921 article:

> The Limekiln Lake section is reached from New York over two railroads and two highway routes. By rail one may take the Delaware & Hudson to North Creek, then by auto stage go to Blue Mountain Lake village. From here the hunter will be transported with his baggage through the watered part of the route, a picturesque trip, by boat through Blue Mountain Lake, the Marion River, and then through Raquette Lake to Raquette Lake village. From here the railway takes him to Eagle Bay and from here an auto stage to Inlet. Inlet is three miles from Limekiln Lake.

Limekiln Lake, Inlet

Limekiln Lake's sandy beach. *Courtesy Lyons Falls History Association*

The other railway route will be over the New York Central by way of Utica. This road will take the hunter to Eagle Bay by a change at Carter. Or if he desires a part water trip, he may leave the train at Old Forge and take the Lake boat there for Inlet.

The better of the two automobile highways lies by way of Utica to Old Forge and around the north shore of Fourth Lake to Inlet and Limekiln. You can drive your car to the very lake and find good places to pitch a tent. A most picturesque auto trip is one by way of Saratoga Springs to North Creek, turning west and then going to Indian Lake on in to Blue Mountain, ferry your car through Blue Mountain, Marion River, and the Raquette, then over a dirt road to Eagle Bay and Limekiln Lake. Car ferry costs $8.00.

The quest of an Adirondack buck was the dream of numerous hunters who frequented The Plains. *Courtesy Margaret Wilcox (The Beaver Lake Collection)*

Good Guides Available

There are several good guides in this section, and the writer will recommend the following who may be reached by mail for arrangements: Jack Finch, Inlet, Limekiln Lake; Ab Blakeman,[28]

Travel by train was a typical way for tourists to travel in Brimmer's days in Inlet.
Courtesy Town of Webb Historical Association

Inlet; William Hemstead, Inlet, Limekiln Lake; Gerald Kenwell, Inlet, Sixth Lake; Mr. Parquette, postmaster at Inlet is a registered guide, as well as Mr. Williston, manager and owner of the Inlet Supply store. Other reliable guides may be reached by asking the Conservation Commission, Albany for their names and addresses.

There is no reason why any party cannot hunt this section without guides if this is preferred. Personally, I strongly recommend a guide for the initial trip at least. One guide will take care of your party of up to four or five. His wages will be $5.00 a day. Accommodations in camps and hotels may be had at Inlet and Limekiln Lake. At Limekiln Lake or Sixth Lake, there are several camps that may be rented furnished or unfurnished, and Mr. Williston will help about rent of camps at Limekiln, while Mr. Kenwell can do the same at Sixth Lake.

Likely the more popular way will be for you to go with your party and tent right in the hunting country. Mr. Kenwell will meet you at the train at Eagle Bay on arrangement and carry you into any country shown on the accompanying map with auto and horses, where you may make camp anywhere on State land that is everywhere available in this section.

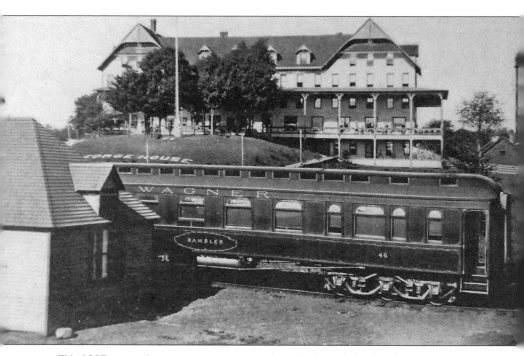

This 1897 scene shows a passenger car at the train depot below The Forge House.
Photo from The Great Adirondack Wilderness: Souvenir of the Fulton Chain Section

Interestingly Brimmer did not mention meeting Miss Ann Perkins, who was an interesting and unusual woman—a Limekiln Lake character since 1912. Nicknamed "Persistent Ann" by the natives, she was a well-known figure who lived at her lakeside cottage at Echo Bay, which was one-half mile from the end of the gravel road that ends at the north end of the white sand beach at Limekiln, from spring until November snow drove her out of the woods.

Perkins had a dream to develop a section of the shoreline at Limekiln Lake which was virgin, but people tried to discourage her. They told her no one could get to that remote spot; lumber and supplies would be hard to tote in. It was just a woman's fool notion, they told her.

But Ann was dogged about her notion, and natives who at first shook their heads at her eventually admired her for her persistence and her faith in that remote spot. By1932, Ann, doing much of the work herself, had completed an attractive boat house constructed of native rock, had built six cottages in a setting of virgin timber that are almost entirely hidden from the shore, had dug out a root cellar, had piped water from a spring she dammed up on the mountainside, had built a fireplace chimney of native stone on her central camp, and had in many ways rounded out her dream.

Brimmer identified a place across from Echo Bay and about a mile below Limekiln Creek as the location where he shot a buck on the second day of his 1921 hunting season. He continued his description of his vacation:

Good Hunting Grounds

This is reached by taking boats across Limekiln Lake to the outlet and following Limekiln Creek down two and one-half miles. An old lumber trail follows this stream. The deer feed in the raspberry bushes along Limekiln Creek bottom. [He suggested hunters] Put two to four watches on the lumber trail where deer runways cross and then drive the raspberry bushes.

Improved road conditions by 1921 made automobile travel more popular. *Courtesy Rene Elliot*

The trail does not begin right at the outlet, but half a mile to the east at Hedges' Camp, and anybody about the lake will tell you where this place is.

He pointed out another excellent deer hunting country was in the vicinity between Mount Tom and Bear Pond. He admitted he had never visited this section without seeing and shooting at deer. "I have seen as many as eleven in a day. To reach the section a plain lumber trail is followed from the beach to Limekiln Lake to the east, known as the Red River trail. It goes over a corduroy roadbed past Fawn Lake. You cannot get over this road with your car. It is only passable for man and horse."

In the Mountain Bad Lands

Way to the east end of Seventh Lake Mountain is the country where deer are always in evidence. Here there are regular 'bad lands,' with jutting parallel ridges extending north and south and almost at right angles to the main ridges of the mountain. Follow up any of these parallel 'hog's backs' overlooking the

A hunting party in Inlet, N.Y. *Image is from a post card*

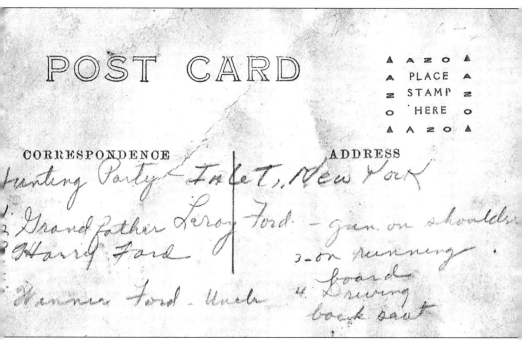

Hunting Party — Inlet, New York

Grandfather Leroy Ford – gun on shoulder
Harry Ford   3 – on running
                                      board
Hannum Ford – Uncle   4 Driving
                                      back seat

valley of the Red River to the east and you will surely get shots
at deer. The valleys between the parallel ridges seem to make
the deer feel that you can't get near them without warning, and
they race up the ridges, always toward the top of the mountain.
Frequently I have shot across three 'hog's backs' to get my buck
in this country.

All of this section was lumbered perhaps twenty years ago
and there are old trails everywhere in fan shapes that make still
hunting easy. It is an ideal section for snow hunting, and there
is little probability of becoming lost because you can at all
times see the big ridge at the top of the mountain running for
five miles east and west.

Everywhere about this section will be found signs of bear,
as well as deer. Every pin cherry ridge will have its ground torn,
trunks broken, and trees ripped out by the roots where bears
have gathered the cherries in summer. Also the mountain is one
big berry patch, and here the bears have wallowed.

321

Should the weather be warm, one can get accommodations to keep his deer in a cooler at the hotels at Inlet for several days if he so desires.

"Likely," he continued, "the very best hunting section in the entire territory south of Limekiln Lake is the Indian Clearing also known as The Plains. "No hunter should invade this section without a guide. The man who knows this section best will be Gerald Kenwell.

Toward Moose River

For the hunter who wants a good set of antlers, I will recommend The Plains section, because here one can 'Look 'em over' more than anywhere else and shoot only the one wanted. From a camp in this section also there is the region of Mitchell Ponds, and here is a log hunter's shack that belongs to anyone who occupies it in season. It will take a good guide to get your party into this region.

A fourth location where Brimmer vouched was "good hunting that will invariably bring game" is in the area where the Red River joins the south branch of the Moose River. This is still locally known as Rock Dam. He recommends the vicinity, "can best be reached by going over the Red River trail to the river and following the trail down this stream to the Moose River. There is a more direct route which cuts across three mountain ranges from Limekiln Lake southward to Rock Dam, but only a most experienced eye can follow it."

"If you go without a guide," he recommended the best and most easily accessible hunting regions to be Rock Dam or the backside of Mount Tom. If a hunter employed a guided hunt, his first choice was The Plains or else the region below Limekiln outlet.

"Game is carried from the Mount Tom-Bear Pond and The Plains by arrangement with Mr. Kenwell, who will send in a wagon over the log roads. There are also two [Gould Paper Company] lumbering operations on the upper and middle Red River and the supply teams make the trip to

Inlet once a day through the fall bringing winter supplies. The teamsters will bring out your buck for $2.00.

"There is only one way in to take out your game from the region… [below Limekiln] and that is on your back. The trail is fairly good and three or four men can manage a big buck, taking plenty of time."

The Inlet House, later renamed The Arrowhead, was a popular hotel for hunters who desired comfortable accommodations. *Photo from* The Great Adirondack Wilderness: Souvenir of the Fulton Chain Section

Almost a century has passed since Mr. Brimmer related his Moose River hunting experience. The areas he described have changed considerably, yet each fall with hunting in the air, sportsmen have their eyes on the Moose River Plains, and their spare time devoted to checking guns, clothing, and camping gear. To those who like it, hunting can be one of life's great adventures.

Chapter Twenty-Four

Summer Camp at Gamawakoosh

THE LOG OF THE WALKAHEAPS, the title page proclaimed, "As Transcribed from the Daily August 20–September 5, 1925 Entries, By the Camp Scribe." That scribe, Arthur W. North, added this subtitle to a privately-printed book about an Adirondack expedition he enjoyed with his family.

North was a California legislator and a trial lawyer. He was also the manager of the University of California track team, the first college squad to cross the continent in 1895. Known as a riveting speaker, North addressed a diversity of organizations, schools and clubs where he presented homemade movies and slide-picture shows based on extensive explorations in northwestern Mexico, remote sections of the Rocky Mountains, and the Canadian bush. Eventually he settled on property in Delaware County, N.Y. Now with a wife and children, North began sharing his outdoor interests by taking his young family on jaunts to remote regions around the globe, They visited South American republics of Colombia, Ecuador, Peru, Bolivia, Argentina, and Chile. The family traveled by dog team to Hudson Bay, by flat-bottom boat down the lower canyons of the Colorado River, on foot and by reindeer sledge through Lapland, far above the Arctic Circle. Closer to home, they led Union College winter adventure snowshoeing trips into remote sections of the Adirondacks. And these were just some of their travels.

Daughter Mary Remsen North Allen was there for her family's worldwide explorations and mountaineering in the Sierra Nevadas, hiking in the mountains of California and Japan, and trips in the Alps, but she remembered with most fondness trekking on snowshoes, with a pack on her back

OPPOSITE: **Irene North and her children Mary and Arthur. Mary's earliest memories of heading to the Adirondack Mountains never faded.** *Courtesy Rabbi Katy Z. Allen*

filled with provisions and blankets, as the family sought out remote sections of the Adirondack forest, spending nights in lean-tos they fashioned or bivouacking in the open, which was often the case. Always close by were Mary's little dog, Dan, and her brother Robert's huge St. Bernard, Viking, who hauled a toboggan laden with camp supplies in winter. The family's goat, Nell, tagged along on summertime outings.

Mary North and her goat on the summit of Mount Marcy, circa 1920s. Well into her ninth decade of life, Mary's outdoor experiences were forever in her heart.
Courtesy Rabbi Katy Z. Allen

Heading North

After such extensive travel as a child and as an adult, Mary never forgot how great it was to be at Gamawakoosh with her parents, Arthur and Irene Davenport North. It was "my favorite place in the whole world," 90-year-old Mary told daughter Rabbi Katy Z. Allen.

August 20, 1925, was prime time for the North family to leave their Walton, N.Y. home and head for Gamawakoosh, where they planned to continue the construction of a small, snug log cabin to use for future family camping they had begun two years before.

Gamawakoosh is a made-up name. It's unknown if it is a corruption of a prior name. If you try to find it on even the oldest 1898 and 1903 West Canada Lake Quads you won't see it, but you will see a symbol on the 1933 West Canada topographical map. The small black square near Sly Pond outlet indicates the location of the Norths' cabin on a mountainside in the Moose River Plains.

A panoramic view of the Cedar River Flow Headquarters. This was the entrance to the Moose River Plains that Arthur North and a friend took on their preliminary 1922 Adirondack tramp. *Courtesy Indian Lake Museum*

"The Gould Paper Company owned this particular mountainside, "Mary later wrote. "Father took Robert when he called on the paper company president. Father was a lawyer and he did things right. We carried a cross-cut saw and each year added a few logs to the walls. Finally came the summer to haul a half-roll of roofing paper and some nails up the mountain. We wanted only a tiny cabin, shelter in case of rain, where we could leave a few things like a little kettle. Next summer, we found the kettle's rim and handle have been chewed off by a porcupine."

Arthur North characterized himself as the scribe of the Log of the Walka-heaps, as well as the guide, pack mule, and photographer. He wrote in the preface of the journal how he and a companion identified only as George cherry-picked Little Moose Mountain as a family camping destination. "I haven't forgotten how we plugged along the twenty-fourth of June [1924] a year ago, traveling by the compass until from a tree top you espied the lake which Robert and I had discovered the preceding November. Nor have I forgotten how we plunged into that lake while our clothes dried before a fire, the crackling warmth of which that night served us in lieu of blankets. Man, our cabin is the phoenix sprung from that fire. And there is an interesting lot of hewing to be done about that cabin in 1925."

North described the family's auto trip from Indian Lake Village to Cedar River Flow: "Fifteen miles of dirt road…to a charmingly situated lumber camp, where we engaged a cottage for the night." Packed into one car with Irene were their six-year-old daughter Mary; four-month-old Nell, the kid goat; and family friend Galen Fisher and his eight-year-old son Ralph. Arthur drove a second car with ten-year-old Robert, and the Norths' ever-faithful collie, Argonne, along with Ebert (Ebe") and Mrs. "Totts" Butterworth. Hugh Moran, another member of the party drove separately.

Cedar River Headquarters, circa 1920. Photo by George Purdue, Courtesy Indian Lake Museum

Headquarters is the name given to the tiny lumber settlement that grew up around Cedar River Flow. It had long been a favorite destination for hunters long before Arthur North learned of it. *Courtesy Indian Lake Museum*

North's log of August 20–29, 1925, details the family's "roughing it" venture to Little Moose Mountain, where they began at Headquarters, a lumber company settlement clustered around the dam at Cedar River Flow. North said he selected the name "Walkaheaps" "as a most appropriate designation" during a preliminary 1922 Adirondack tramp. North didn't say how the term came about but based on the miles of footwork members of the party covered daily, it's assumed he meant "a heap of walking." Arthur enjoyed using this honorary title as a greeting when corresponding with those who had backpacked with him. For example, he wrote to "Dear Walkaheap

George" that "The outstanding part of the outing was the good fellowship," and would bestow the title to new members with this announcement. "We have accepted the Fishers, unhesitatingly, as Walkaheaps...."

The lumber company dam on the Cedar River created a great flow. *Courtesy Indian Lake Museum*

From the Walkheaps Log

"...After loading our possessions upon a stout wagon, we set forth at 9 a.m. on a deserted and deep rutted lumber road (marked out by White and Indian market hunters in 1867), which was presently blocked by a fallen maple, providing preliminary exercise for our pioneers. Meantime, more subtle than the restless wind, submarine workers had been diligently destroying the highway a couple of miles further on so that we found the road a small pond with a narrow winding mud pathway at the left. How we did have to labor with adz and hooked sticks ere we lowered the waterline by breaking the mud-and-stick dam which ever-industrious beaver had painstakingly constructed. After four hours of slow advance, the neglected road petered out, wagon progress became impossible, and inspirited by a hearty lunch we said goodbye to the wagon, team, teamster and all other human beings in general. We were alone, 'somewhere in the Adirondacks,' or, to be more definite, in Hamilton County, most sparsely settled section of the Empire state...."

"...Our outfit was as properly selected...[the] choice qualities of dehydrated vegetables making possible the carrying of a most ample supply of provisions. Provided the harness is rightly fitted and you carry the proper sort of stuff, there is a marvelous degree of independence and zest in entering a forest wilderness with shoulder packs. To begin with, you can proceed practically anywhere. In our case we were so well-supplied with provisions and incidentals—a total of some 260 pounds—that we felt at liberty to carry along a roll of cabin roofing. While this entailed an additional sixty-five pounds, the country was so attractive that there were always ready volunteers for double trips. Thus upon the departure of the wagon, Ebe, Hugh, and the Scribe proceeded ahead three or four miles to a pretty camping spot by a rushing brook.

John Mitchell's boat is loaded with lumber in this undated photo. The note on the back of this photo said the lumber is headed for Little Moose Lake. *Courtesy Indian Lake Museum*

331

"Emptying their packs here, the three turned back, meeting the main party, which was then led on by Hugh to the campground while Ebe, Galen and the Scribe returned to the road's end for a small balance of outfit. Ere darkness fell they were at the camp site, now most attractive with balsam-boughed beds and two pitched tents, with crackling fire and an appetizing supper.

No snapshot existed of the North's auto, but it is known the neglected road petered out beyond Headquarters, requiring them to transfer their duffel to "a stout wagon."
Indian Lake Museum

"Stretched out restfully with tired shoulders at ease, it was good to review the day's advance, to feel that now, in the primeval fragrant forest, coughs, colds and kindred irritants presently would abate, that fagged nerves would soon cease their nagging and wearied brains find clarity and rest. Through the tree tops twinkled the friendly stars that once had looked down on other bivouacking parties in this same forest for, hard by, our course had crossed the old Indian war trail which Hendrik, the Mohawk king, ere that bloody day by Lake George had disclosed to his friend William Johnson and over which in 1776 Sir Johnson, false-to-his-word Schuyler, had hurried his band of Tories and Iroquois, tugging away at the brass cannon which once guarded Johnson Hall. Thirty-odd years later and another war party passed along the trail, this time Colonel Jessup with his pioneer regiment en route to battlefields on the Canadian frontier. Shortly after that struggle, Jessup's military road was made into a state highway, connecting the towns of Wells and Russell, but the forest right quickly claims her own and by 1850 it was recorded that: 'the greater part of the road is now overgrown with trees.' Today, even to locate its course is difficult.

Road to Headquarters Camp

The Cedar River entrance road to the Moose River road went through several stages of development during the 1950s and '60s. The North party saw only a rough track with abysmal holes. The harshness of the landscape was made worse over the decades by rain and erosion that caused masses of rocks to come to the surface. Indian Lake Museum

"Rested by outdoor sleep, six in the morning found our four men again on the trail with packs, two in due time returning for residue of the party while others began the ascent of the mountain. (Heretofore, the course had been across a rolling country with much level travel.) At noon all reassembled by a small river which was hastily bridged with poles for cautious crossing. After hard climbing without trace of trail, luncheon was enjoyed at a charming spot part way up… [Even 8-year-old Ralph was carrying over 10 pounds.]

Thence, after passing a succession of water-falls and relaying the outfit, by 6:30 p.m., the party paused, exultant on the wooded shores of a small glistening lake set aloft on the shoulder of a huge spruce-clad mountain. With happy exclamations, Robert and Mary pointed out their log cabin, welcoming all to its shelter. Argonne, pausing on the rocky shore, lapped thirstily. After whiffing disapprovingly at a nearby weed, Nell folded with obvious content a large leaf between her small lips and chewed her cud with imperious unconcern....

"On the site of that June campfire...perhaps twenty feet above the lake shore, the foundation spruce logs of the cabin were set in place on Thursday, August 16, 1923.... Architectural blue prints called for an edifice containing a floor area to cover with carpet of 10 by 12.... Walls three feet in height were in place only after four days of diligent labor. Facing sleet and a bitter cold wind, November 6–8 of that same year plucky young Dr. S. and the Scribe completed the walls and made some headway with the gable ends. The work on these gables was finished the 26th and 27th of the ensuing August. At the same time a substantial ridge pole was set in place and the northwest corner of the structure raised half a foot....

A group picture with the teamster hired to take the North party back in.
Courtesy Rabbi Katy Z. Allen

Cedar River Flow's enchanted region. *Courtesy Rabbi Katy Z. Allen*

"Now, on our return, it was a satisfaction to find the little cabin unmolested and cached provisions undisturbed. For the first twenty-four hours we were quite willing to loiter, enjoying the sensation of unburdened shoulders. At night, out under the stars, we spread a wide bed over boughs and in the morning were refreshed and ready for work. First, Ebe and Galen sawed and carried in, shoulder-high, weighty spruce logs for Hugh and the Scribe to wedge, split and, finally to hew down the rough surfaces. Then, after Galen, the Architect, had nicely hewed and fitted the ends, the split halves were raised aloft and with bark sides down, set one end spiked against the ridge pole, the other projecting over the adjacent side wall. But, alas, the nail supply gave out—already the axe handle had split into fragments—and so, turning from carpentering, the Boss Architect and a few others sallied forth to find the summit of the dominant mountain. Two hours clambering brought success and fine scenic reward—partly won from wind-swayed treetops. Surrounded by scrubby growth, the summit was a rocky knob inset with two metal markers bearing these inscriptions:

'Verplanck Colvin, Supt. 1882, S.N.Y. Adirondack Survey' and 'N, Sta No 68, U.S.G.S 484. N.Y.' Above the markers a wooden scaffolding had been erected, but so long ago that the framework was a crumbling heap from which—had ever Swiss Family Robinson more opportune fortune?—we gathered dozens of rusted nails.

The Adirondack country had overpowering charm. *Courtesy Rabbi Katy Z. Allen*

"Thanks to this find, our cabin presently had in place overhead a dozen split logs and then the roll of roofing paper was spread and nailed over the split log roof. Though shy of completion by a single width of paper, the final result was most nifty and into the cabin we all moved, bag, bedding, and baggage. (N.S. Next time, take in an iron splitting wedge, a 3/4 inch auger, hand saw, 8a & 20s nails, a strip of roofing, an axe handle, a screwdriver and a folding stove.) This event we properly celebrated by a lineup and inspection followed by swimming baths. Ebe and the Camp Mother, with various medical concoctions, had charge of the inspection.

"The three youngsters made play on their own initiatives, too. The level white rock floor over which the lake waters found outlet was a constant inviting playground for them. Wading they enjoyed daily, and then what a boat of war with gun turrets and cannon they did construct! They were good children.

"In interest in culinary matters we were children, and all the higher mathematics acquired at Bryn Mawr [College] were requisite for the industrious 'Totts' to keep track of the endless succession of tin plates and cups ever demanding hot water, soap and the dish mop. Our appetites were satisfied merely to be whetted again. If the 26th was not Ebe's birthday, it should have been, for there was a real birthday cake forthcoming. For some of the party the cookery was nigh of as much delight as the eating. About the fire Hugh was an ever-increasing luminary, first appearing in the cuisine sky with an unbeatable oriental receipt [an "old-fashioned" spelling of recipe—Editor] of two cups of rice to nine cups of water. Soups, dehydrated apples and vegetables, biscuits, stewed fruits, hot cakes and maple syrup; all were prepared just as they should be. And will we forget terrapin—no, porcupine stew!

The Adirondack Mountains summer's grandeur was a long-held memory.
Courtesy Rabbi Katy Z. Allen

"This certainly was a most appreciative group of Walkaheaps, each one most generous in approval of his fellows and all truly appreciative of the blessings being received from the Supreme One who somehow seemed so near. And so at each repast thanks were expressed by one or another. Thus at supper one evening by Hugh:

Lord God of the forests and lakes, and mountain fastnesses, and of all the myriad hosts of heaven, we thank Thee for these days of peace and rest amidst the glorious beauty of Thy world. We thank Thee for friends and for the hours of companionship which we have had together, and we thank Thee yet more that in all this we can see Thy love and come in some small measure to know Thee. Wilt Thou bless these Thy gifts to our use, refresh us in body and spirit for the tasks that lie ahead, and accept the humble services that we would render unto our fellow men. In the name of Christ Jesus, our Lord. Amen.

The North party was witness to how bridges were built. *Courtesy Rabbi Katy Z. Allen*

"Early at camp, Galen's library came into its own and we listened eagerly, whether to experiences in an unexpected nobleman's home, or to the verses of long-forgotten poems. Personal reminiscences were related and enjoyed, of other camping experiences, of campus days, of Japan, China, Siberia, Mexico, Switzerland, Spain and the battlefields of the Great War. Mary's proposed visit to the cabin in late October for bear and deer was soberly discussed and an adventure into the Canadian wilds in 1926 was approved. Ebe regretfully could not see how the necessary time might be his. Galen and Hugh agreed they might make such a trip in midsummer or mid-winter, but not during the autumn. (Now, as the Scribe writes, this idea presents itself: possibly with George and Robert he might enter the northern wilderness in November, kill, freeze and cache the big game needed by the entire party, then meet the belated ones at the railroad, turning back with them to the chosen camp ground.)

Arthur and Irene used every opportunity to teach what they came onto. In this picture, curious members of the party learned how the lumber company constructed a bridge to span a stream. *Courtesy Rabbi Katy Z. Allen*

"The evening that Hugh, speaking on the 'Faith of Our Fathers,' held our deepest interest was a prelude to thoughtful discussions on religion, politics, philosophy, and mountaineering. One day we realized with surprise that coughs and colds had abated, fagged nerves had found repose and that wearied brains were quickening with wholesome vigor. Meantime, by night the stars twinkled down at us and by day rays of sun sparkled on Gamawakoosh, for the weather man spread out for us his rarest wares."

On the camping party's final evening Mrs. Butterworth, labeled the "Camp Poet" in the Walkaheaps register, read the following poem.

GAMAWAKOOSH

(By the Camp Poet)

Gamawakoosh, wood-nymphs' mirror,
Framed in birch and balsam glades,
Every hour though growest dearer,
With thy myriad moods and shades.

We must bid a year's good-byes,
Turn our feet to wonted ways;
When city dust and noises rise,
Again we'll live these haunting days.

Lisping lakes and soughing trees,
Solemn owls beneath the moon,
Distant thunder down the breeze –
All in memory's ear will croon.

Pillared shrines for reverent feet,
Sparkling glances of ruffled mere,
Skyey meads for cloudlets fleet –
Through the year our eyes will cheer.

The North party taking in the health-giving atmosphere of the mountains.
Courtesy Rabbi Katy Z. Allen

Arthur and Irene North. *Courtesy Rabbi Katy Z. Allen*

"If we could only have a month of this!" was the over-whelming sentiment of each member of the camping party the morning of the 29th of August, 1925. Their cabin-building time had fled, and it was time to don "greatly reduced" backpacks and begin retracing their steps.

"After two or three hours we met fishermen, the first people we had seen in a week. By midafternoon we arrived at the logging road where we regretfully bade farewell to the Butterworths.... Then, turning to the right along a side trail, we presently made camp by an old log cabin overlooking a charming mountain lake...."

The old-growth forest had served as the Norths' sheltering canopy, as did their hand-built cabin act as a woodland penthouse. That "home" suited them well. The feeling of belonging at Gamawakoosh persists throughout later camp logs. When they were there, they were free.

Mary North's later-day writings convey that the family instilled in their daughter a sense of respect—perhaps even reverence—for the ecosystem. Mary might have seen herself as a tiny speck on earth as she touched the trunks of trees, listened to the wind whish through branches, and splashed in the water of Sly Pond.

Gamawakoosh in 2014

In 2014 the site of the Gamawakoosh camp was finally found by Walter Hayes and Indian Lake historian Bill Zullo. Hayes said he accidently met Bill Zullo "in the woods on the Foxlair Estate where we were exploring independently to learn more about the place. We also explored the tannery on the West Branch of the Sacandaga River in Arietta and Foxy Brown's farm near Piseco."

The youngsters rest near Sly Pond outlet. *Courtesy Rabbi Katy Z. Allen*

Hayes had read Almy Coggeshall's 1933 record of camping with the Norths at the cabin they had started ten years earlier, and Zullo had found North's 1933 camping journal that included the stay at the cabin on Sly Pond. Walt told me, "Bill sent me a copy of the journal. Participants included the whole North family and various other young people of college and high school age." The men decided to make it their mission to locate the site of the camp.

Coggeshall's transcript indicates the Norths were still improving Sly Pond cabin in 1933. Hayes continued, "Almy, was a good friend of mine. He was a president of the Adirondack Mountain Club. I was a vice president and treasurer of the Club, so I rode to many meetings with him. Finding historic sites, such as old camps, in the Moose River Plains intrigues me."

In the years since the Norths' last visit, the mountainside has changed greatly. Between the Gould Paper Company's logging operation and devastating windstorms, the terrain is not easily navigable. A Moose River Recreation Area map and guide brochure indicates there is a blazed yellow marked trail to the pond. The starting point of the 5.4-mile trail veers off the main road between the Cedar River Flow and Limekiln Lake gates about halfway between Bradley Brook Loop and Lost Ponds. The 1998 Department of Environmental Conservation description reads: "This trail climbs a portion of Little Moose Mountain before descending to Sly Pond, one of the highest bodies of water in the Adirondacks. The pond is acidic and devoid of fish."

I knew of the camp through my Moose River Plains research, but had never found the site. Learning exactly where it was from Walt Hayes, I finally tracked it down. The forests around Sly Pond have not totally recovered since the logging, so the brush and low growth has not yet been shaded out. The camping around Sly Pond had to have been better in the Norths' day than now. The snapshots taken by the Norths and Coggeshall show it was a peaceful, untangled scene—just the opposite of today.

Sly Pond's crystal-clear water surrounded by soft green foliage. *Courtesy Rabbi Katy Z. Allen*

Scrutinizing the site of the camp, which is less than a shadow of its former self, I thought of what Walt shared with me about his friend: "Gamawakoosh was very significant to Almy Coggeshall. He was an only child. The campfire discussions at Gamawakoosh taught him to understand the give-and-take of opinion, where he was used to having his way at home. I am told Arthur [North] took him aside to explain how to take part in discussions without trying to dominate. Almy credits the North family with giving him the appreciation of camping in the Adirondacks."

As I gazed over the pond, I thought of those campers eighty-four years ago as I looked at copies of Almy's pictures I had loaded into my electronic notepad. No need for me to fashion a pole raft as they had, to float over the surface and fish from. I sat on a rock to eat a bite of food and gazed into the yellowy light. Then I turned and meandered back through the jungle of deadfalls and underbrush to my tent campsite along Silver Run.

Sly Pond's half-built cabin's side walls provided the perfect setting to record the progress of the Norths' construction project. *Courtesy Rabbi Katy Z. Allen*

On my way off the mountain I reflected on a passage I remembered woods-woman Anne LaBastille saying: "It's not important what one calls oneself:

344

ecologist, field geologist, natural historian, naturalist, environmental biologist [or whatever else]. What's important is that one has a close and fluid fascination with nature and life in its many forms. It all comes down to the Greek work for ecology, 'oikos,' which means 'home' or 'place to live.'"

A group gathering on what Arthur called a haunting, mystical kind of beauty.
Courtesy Rabbi Katy Z. Allen

I think the Norths and Almy Coggeshall felt close to the earth when they were at Gamawakoosh. It was a favorite place to live in a rough cabin in the forest by a beautiful lake in the Adirondack Park.

Walt's, Bill's, and my experience on our fact-finding trips provided a sense of satisfaction too.

In our own way we have been shown the steadiness of the forest in the next stage of regeneration and had the satisfaction of bushwhacking around a little-visited area of The Plains. Content and fulfilled by this finding, I turn to my informal history of the Moose River Plains Country to share the story about a camp very few knew existed.

Remembering Gamawakoosh

Even as a 90-year-old resident in a nursing home, Mary Remsen North Allen never forgot Gamawakoosh. Daughter Katy tells how she would steady Mary as they slowly strolled over the inviting garden paths on the grounds of her nursing home, and how mother and daughter would enjoy a picnic lunch among the mixed plantings of annual and perennial flowers and pretend they were back at Gamawakoosh. "It makes me cry," Katy said when she thought of the scene. Her mother's appreciation of camping in the Adirondacks was so significant in her life.

The completed cabin was a great success. *Courtesy Rabbi Katy Z. Allen*

Mary and her brother Robert were raised with an appreciation of investigating the world around them for the sake of widening personal horizons, savoring adventure, and surrounding themselves in the joy found in the natural world. Mary eloquently explained her vision in the preface of her

346

book, *Falling Light and Waters Turning: Adventures in Being Human* (see http://fallinglightwatersturning.com):

"For years I had been telling stories of my childhood to anyone who would listen. They started coming back, as stories often do, battered and bent. I should write them, I thought, so my children will know what really happened. The effort became the work of a lifetime."

The youngsters found the high mountain pond's cooling water delightful.
Courtesy Rabbi Katy Z. Allen

Mary said that her resulting book, "is the journey of one mind's eye, commenced in a childhood close to the earth, ordained by parents dedicated to living the good old virtues of their Puritan ancestors. Childhood leaves me with mysterious unease.

"Through one kind of adventure after another, the questing eye searches, vaguely aware of need for something, anything, that might clear the fog of bewilderment.

"I study biology, love every minute of it, delight that I am learning much, but some obstruction is standing in my way.

"I marry and have children. I know from biology that growth occurs from within, yet I'm feeling I ought to be 'growing' my children, like garden beans and peas.

Sly Pond, a lofty lake. Today one needs to weave their way around, over and through an array of obstacles to reach Sly Pond. *Courtesy Rabbi Katy Z. Allen*

"Unease turns into crisis. In desperate search for clarity I return to school, this time to study photography seriously.

"Photograph-as-Metaphor opens a channel. In light/shadow mutuality, mind's eye starts finding clues, goes probing into color interactions. The mystery remains.

"Passing age eighty, arriving in the dimension of old age, I become acutely aware of the significance of changes across time, changing relations within place, human history, planet, the entire world we call our own, changing requirements of what we call mind.

"The child, slowly emerging as person, survives into old age where the long view reconsiders all. What started as memoir becomes creative non-fiction. Is it ever possible to know what 'really happened'?

"The living of a human life might be the greatest Adventure of all."

—Mary North Allen, Madison, Wisconsin, Circa 2007

Postscript

The site of Camp Gamawakoosh would no doubt be nearly impossible to find today, but a sharp-eyed observer will certainly find remains of some old vehicles.

Donald C. Wardell of Verona, N.Y. shared with me what he found shortly after the last logging job had been completed.

348

"My son and I camped in 1968 at a small clearing just off the Sly Pond trail. At that time there was an old garage and a large bunkhouse which was mostly fallen down.

"At that time a small room which I believe was the office at the end of the bunkhouse was still good enough that we fixed it up with some boards and a plastic tarp for a deer season camp and used it for two years.

"In the fall of 1988 a friend and I hiked up there from the main road through The Plains. We had some trouble locating the spot but we finally did find it. The only visible telltale signs were an old Pontiac coupe that had been had abandoned along with some rusting oil-drum stoves. A lot of brush and trees had grown in twenty years."

That same fall I bushwhacked from the former site of Gerald Kenwell's Otter Brook Camp to Sly Pond. Not only did I find the old car, but I also came across other pieces of old iron I imagine had to have a connection to the logging. The most surprising find was a lovingly-designed mahogany wooden cross with an engraving of the name of the person whose ashes had been laid to rest beneath it. Attached to the cross was a note of explanation to anyone who happened to come across it. The note explained the cross marked the remains of a dear son who loved to deer hunt with his dad.

All sorts of memories are buried in The Plains, but this one was particularly touching.

The old cabin that overlooked a charming lake. *Courtesy Rabbi Katy Z. Allen*

Part Four

Adirondack Mountains

Moose River Plains

THE MYSTIQUE OF OTTER BROOK CAMP

Otter Brook. "Its waters are crystal clear. The forest screens its banks. It runs the gauntlet of temperament from placid smiling pools to rippling shoals and roaring falls. It is an unspoiled product of the wilderness. Born on the slopes of Little Moose Mountain, it wends its way through diminutive canyons and over rocky ledges, until at the end of its eight-mile journey it emerges on The Plains and mingles its waters with the Moose. —Edward A. Harmes, July 1944

Otter Brook Camp, winter 1943–44. *Courtesy Jack Tanck*

OPPOSITE: **Otter Brook trout for supper, 1944.** *Photo by Edward A. Harmes, Courtesy Jack Harmes*

"To the Bunch at Otter Brook Camp"

Cross the Moose on Gerald's cable,
Walk the grade if you are able.
Then before you almost totter,
Comes the camp upon the Otter.

There the wind sings through the spruces.
Wily deer fool you with ruses.
It's a spot to treat sore eyes,
There you'll find the swellest guys.

Gerald Kenwell's winter camp was smaller than his ranch-house style main camp.
Courtesy Town of Webb Historical Society

Take a look at Graybeard Hughie,
Just a pirate like French Louie,
Has one hung on every hill
Just can't seem to get his fill.

This must be his 20th year
That Hugie's come to get his deer.
Now he's getting kind of old,
A big black heart but full of gold.

Then there's Lou, the brave old fart,
And his lusty brother Art.
Like a snort before they eat,
Puts them back on aching feet.

Otto, when he's home sells auto parts,
Up at camp he snorts and farts.
Yes you bet he got his buck,
Damn good hunter not just luck.

Neil got his deer the first day in,
Now he leads a life of sin.
Says he's hunting for a bear,
Can't you smell a rat right there?

Frank's the guy who shines his plate,
Won't start hunting till it's late.
Cracking nuts or mending socks,
To hell with time or Big Ben clocks.

Shake the hand of husky Lysle,
He's the man to make you smile.
Just taste his biscuits, bread or pies,
When grub comes up he is the guy.

353

He totes the buck just like a cinch,
And he can count the turns by the inch.
A peanut magnate too by gad,
Now tell the folks he is the lad.

If you get a buck or the whiskey's low,
Get Wrangle Slim "Winnie" and his Pinto.
14 miles is a helluva long haul,
Winnie does it like nothing at all.

Young buck Girly is a handy lad,
Dumps the fires on the floor and makes Hughie mad.
Damn good kid not much on quickness,
Got a mighty bad case of sleeping sickness.

The three "G" men let out today,
Damn good riddance—hope they'll stay.
Lots of others come and go,
Everyone the best I know.
Last and best is the big camp boss,
Gerald Kenwell, the tough old hoss.
Been toting these trails since a barefoot boy,
The games best friend and the sportsman's joy.

You'll sure like him and you'll like his place,
You'll like his boys and you'll like his pace.
Otter Camp is the place for fun,
So pack your basket and shoulder your gun.

—Written by Vic Skieff on November 11, 1935

This poem was tacked to the
inside door of Otter Camp's outhouse.

Chapter Twenty-Five

Gerald Kenwell's Opinion to Alter the Forest Preserve

THROUGHOUT THE EARLY MONTHS OF 1952, the Conservation Department initiated a discussion of the Forest Preserve in the belief that such a discussion would eventually lead to better management of New York state's property. As part of the initiative, Department officials reached out to informed and interested leaders outside of the Department. It was their intention to highlight not only the Department's views but also those of contributors. Among the people the Department reached out to were Gustav A. Swanson, head of the Department of Conservation at Cornell University; Paul Schaefer, a director of the state Conservation Council; John E. Hammett, chairman, of the Committee for the Conservation of Forests and Wildlife; of the Campfire Club of America; William Person Tolley, chancellor of Syracuse University; and Gerald Kenwell, Adirondack woodsman and guide for 50 years.

Kenwell's open letter appeared in the February–March, 1952 New York State *Conservationist* magazine. The letter, which contained opinions that did not conform with those of the Department, appears here as it was printed.

I wish every youngster could have the wonderful experiences I was lucky enough to have as a boy growing up in the Adirondack wilderness. Over 60 years ago when I was only four years old my father took our family by team and wagon from Indian Lake to the now famous Moose River Plains, cutting his own rough wagon road down the South Branch of the Moose River. The spot where our log home (gone now) stood on the Plains is still marked Kenwells on the map, because the first surveyors stayed with us.

My folks catered to hunters, fishermen and outdoorsmen from all over, and many of them were famous people. I had a chance to roam around this big country and to know old French Louie of West Canada Lake, old man [Frank "Pop"] Baker and many others. What boy could ask for more?

Gerald Kenwell stands on the porch of his summer camp building as he takes in his beloved woodland domain. *Photo by Dante O. Tranquille, Courtesy Town of Webb Historical Association*

As time went on I built my own camp on Otter Brook and spent part of each year there. Now I'm back there, I hope for good. By now I suppose many of the young generation regard me as an old-timer.

It has been my privilege to show hundreds of men, women and youngsters how to hunt, fish, and enjoy the woods through more lenient laws. So I am glad to see this discussion about it and add my ideas to those of others.

Back in 1890, Gov. David B. Hill forwarded to the Legislature a special report urging the establishment of an Adirondack Park and the purchase of lands necessary to such purpose. He also made recommendations more lenient to public use than were adopted. One of which I thoroughly agree with. The one was to make the wilderness of the Park more accessible to more people for recreational purposes.

Taking in the Forest Preserve's natural beauty. *Courtesy Leigh Portner*

To date very little of that recommendation has been followed for there are vast areas that only the hardiest woodsmen could contact. The majority of people that helped buy and pay taxes on all this wild land have never had the pleasure of enjoying it, for reason it was inaccessible to them.

Therefore, I would personally recommend slightly revamping one section of our Conservation Constitution, on Article XIV (by referendum).

When I stand on one of these mountain tops looking out over this scene of panorama grandeur, I have a feeling of selfishness. Why should only I and a very few others have such a thrill and so many others be deprived of it? They were just as much a part of buying this beauty as myself. Why not make a few alterations in our Constitution and make it possible for others to enjoy this privilege?

In recommending this, I will suggest that we gear the law to privilege our Forestry Department, under strict and efficient management, to clear out many foot trails to the interior of our wild lands. Also provide for Ranger, Protector and traveler huts at intervals, back in remote sections. Say huts not to exceed 16' x 18' in size and equipped with overnight gear such as a few cooking utensils, small stove and a few camp blankets. Such camps would be a big advantage to our Foresters and Game Protectors as an outpost to run down forest and game violators, as well as an overnight haven to a tired and weary sight-seer and vacationer.

By having these overnight cabins (and I would advise not closer than five miles apart) equipped with the necessary camp gear, it would relieve the unaccustomed traveler of packing on his back anything but his food supplies, therefore enabling the less muscular fellow to enjoy some of this outdoor life and the beauties of our wild land in remote sections.

Another advantage to this program would be to open up the fire trails so if a lightning fire started in one of these inaccessible locations we could approach it from some direction to squelch the fire. Again I would like to recommend that these proposed trails be of a uniform design, say six feet wide. With that stipulation it would prevent these prosed trails from becoming a public vehicle right-of-way, yet be roomy enough to be a practical foot trail.

Some people say that this sort of thing can be done under the present Constitution. I am not a lawyer but I can read, and when I read the Constitution, where it says we cannot cut trees, I don't see how the things I recommend can be done.

Now it is my intent to recommend that we should all take up the spirit and further our forefathers' wisdom in behalf of the general public welfare. I solicit my many friends and fellowmen of this Empire State to scrutinize these proposals and lend a hand to our Conservation Department by writing in your recommendations and helping them draft a concrete plan to be presented to the general public for referendum, to further our public benefits.

The creation of the preserve did not end all problems it was intended to solve. To begin with, the $1,000,000 request for land requisition was not granted. Instead the Forest Commission received an appropriation of $15,000 to cover administrative expenses. The commission issued annual reports, and in 1886 it recommended granting itself the authority to lease state land for limited uses. The legislature refused permission in 1886 and again in 1887. The report for 1891 contained a map outlining the proposed park area in blue, hence the term, "blue-line."

In this period from 1886 to 1892, a new reason for a park was advanced—the recreation boom. The Sargent Committee had foreseen this development, but even they did not foresee the immediacy of its impact. Tourism was well on its way to becoming a big business in the North Country, and as visitors to the preserve increased each year, the idea of creating a park made more sense. The park owed its existence to worries concerning the protection of the watershed and the supply of lumber.

These concerns were not forgotten, but supporters of the park felt it would exist side by side with the preserve. Again, the fight was led by a downstate group, the Adirondack Park Association, organized by some of New York City's leading citizens. Their aim was "the preservation of the Adirondack forests, and by practical means the establishment of a state forest park therein." [Alfred L. Donaldson, *A History of the Adirondacks.* Vol. 2, p.183]. *Photo in the Author's collection*

Chapter Twenty-Six

Kenwell's Hunting and Fishing Camp

GERALD KENWELL, WEARING a dark tight-woven wool shirt with his signature well-worn matching wool-blend winter cap, vamped for talented photographer Dante Tranquille as the Utica newspaper reporter visited Kenwell's camp during the mid-winter season. The editor of the *Observer-Dispatch* wanted a photo feature, and he knew Tranquille was just the man to take pictures for the profile scheduled to run in the January 27, 1952, Sunday outdoor section. There was time only for the paper's star photographer to spend a day and a night in the Moose River Plains to capture the essence of the celebrated fame of the man many called the Mayor of Otter Brook.

Gerald Kenwell's uncle Ike Kenwell is wearing the black coat. *Courtesy Indian Lake Museum*

OPPOSITE: **Gerald Kenwell, the winter of 1952.** *Photo by Dante O. Tranquille.*
Courtesy Town of Webb Historical Association

Gerald Kenwell, "Mayor" of Otter Brook Country.
Photo by Dante O. Tranquille. Courtesy Town of Webb Historical Association

362

Kenwell stepped outside his woodshed, where he had been splitting stove wood, to pose when Tranquille arrived. His image was snapped while he looked wistfully skyward. Clean-shaven, thin and sinewy, or full-bearded and large of frame, Adirondack guides were known for their great physical endurance; versed in the woodcraft and hardships of the wilderness, they served their clients faithfully.

Otter Brook Camp before the second story addition. *Courtesy Ora Kenwell*

Gerald Kenwell was an Adirondack guide and woodsman who had followed his trade of distinction since he was a little boy growing up on The Plains in the 1890s. By 1952, he was considered among the talented oldsters of the mountains. Some would say he was among "the last of a breed," but The Mayor had said that about well-known characters such as Sam Dunakin and "French" Louie Seymour a generation earlier.

Gerald recollected that Dunakin was about the oldest guide on the Fulton Chain that he remembered meeting; that was when Kenwell was seven in 1890. "Sam was a big, rough, weather-beaten man," he said, "nearing the close of a notable career in the woods as a guide." Those were not the only noteworthy Adirondack characters he told Tranquille about the evening that they sat around Otter Brook Camp's warming stove as Dante took in the stories of Gerald's early life in the North Woods.

Had the photographer been assigned to write a book instead of producing a simple photojournalistic feature story, he might have filled the pages with trivia Gerald learned from Louie Seymour. Louie was a close Kenwell family friend and mentor to Gerald.

In 1947 the Gould Paper Company began developing a lumber road through the Moose River Plains in order to truck out hardwood logs. *Courtesy Town of Webb Historical Association*

Sam Dunakin, oldest guide on the Fulton Chain. Gerald Kenwell remembered seeing Sam many times when Gerald was a boy of 7 in 1890. Sam was then a big, rough, weather-beaten man, nearing the close of a notable career in the woods as a guide.

Courtesy Town of Webb Historical Association

 365

Gerald pointed out the direction of Louie's sugar bush, beyond Otter Brook Valley on the outlet of Falls Pond. Louie described the sap-collecting spot as "mor'na hundert trees." As a youngster, Gerald learned a thing or two about gathering and producing maple syrup from Louie, who built three small log buildings for his sugaring operation. One he used for storage, one for boiling down the maple sap, and one for living in while he produced a final product. Gerald showed Tranquille sap collection system, located behind his log summer camp where the sap was boiled down.

Then there was the story about treasure hunters who hired Louie to guide them in their quest to find a cannon reported to have been filled with gold and silver coins. In some old papers, the cache was said to have been buried in 1817 along the old military road in the vicinity of the beginning of Cedar Lakes. Nothing was ever found, but Louie told that while they followed portions the old road that still remained visible, the searchers did spot vague indications that they were on the right track when peculiar markings were found carved into large rocks.

There were stories about Gerald's Uncle Isaac "Ike" Kenwell and Louie's logging connection with "Ike." Gerald remembered his uncle saying Louie was like a "lone wolf." Similar to many old-time lumberjacks, Louie was a spendthrift with the wages he earned, spending them for booze and enjoying one hell of a good time all by himself, but never causing harm to anyone. Ike once asked Louie something along the lines of, "Why do you act the way you do? You waste hundreds of hard-earned dollars and get nothing out of the spending spree but empty pockets, and cavorting around town sometimes in your bare feet howling like a wolf."

Louie answered, "Meester Kenwell, ah do sam ting lak white man do." Louie was satisfied to reason himself an Indian.

That evening other stories of legendary lumbermen Sol, Abe and Irv Carnahan, guides Giles Becraft, Dick Burch, Frank Baker, and Johnny Leaf and

OPPOSITE: **Woodsman-hermit-guide Alvah Dunning. "Alvah was well-liked by some sportsmen. Admiring sports he served referred to him as 'Uncle Alvah.' But Dunning also had his share of distractors, and among the Fulton Chain guides he was, for some reason, an unpopular man-in-the-woods."** *S.R. Stoddard photo, Courtesy Maitland C. DeSormo*

loners like Kettle Jones and Atwell Martin were told. Hotelmen Trume Haskell and Amazia Dutton Barber all came up to feed Tranquille's imagination of earlier times.

"Time oh time, where did you go?" Might have been on Dante Tranquille's mind as he developed his photojournalistic story, but it is not what his "Mayor of Otter Brook" story covered. Instead he offered the newspaper's readers an overview of his journey into The Plains that began under a picture captioned: "Start of long trek into forest, to the 'mayor's mansion' on Otter brook, was by means of a 'covered-jeep' which was driven over the old Limekiln Lake lumber road. When the road 'ran out,' this delegation of visitors took to snowshoes and trekked the remaining distance through wild forestland."

The private old logging haul road he talked about was used by the Gould Paper Company to haul logs from the forest. The road was the only means of reaching Kenwell's log ranch house, which was nestled deep in the mountainous country on the Moose River Plains.

"Like father, like son," wrote Tranquille about Gerald. "That's how it is in 'Mayor' Kenwell's family, for his father, Wellington Kenwell, also was an Adirondack guide. Except for two years spent farming at Mexico, N.Y., Gerald Kenwell had been part of the Adirondack wonderland."

In one picture, Gerald is standing over a grand cast-iron wood-fired kitchen range stirring several kettles of homemade food for his guests. The photographer labeled the scene: "The pot's always on, filled with substantial and tasty food at Mayor Kenwell's house. Although he always has lived alone, he welcomes the unexpected visit of friends."

This was not the only time the Utica photographer had visited Otter Brook Camp. Tranquille proclaimed The Mayor was "always a perfect host who insists his friends have second helpings" at every meal.

Dante Tranquille labeled Gerald Kenwell as a master Adirondack storyteller, having chronicled everything from his parents' pioneer days on The Plains to operating two successful businesses at Sixth Lake Dam in Inlet, N.Y., and at Otter Brook, to becoming a renowned and widely-recognized wildlife expert. Truth has a way of being more interesting than some of the mythologizing that has whirled around some real old-timers Gerald knew

"Adirondack French" Louie Seymour, right. *Courtesy Edward Blankman (The Lloyd Blankman Collection)*

369

of, such as Louie Seymour and Alvah Dunning—men whose lives ultimately influenced youthful Gerald.

I consider Gerald Kenwell to be the greatest woodsman of the central Adirondacks. *The Moose River Plains Vol. 2* explores Kenwell and his camp in depth. Volume 1 takes only a brief look at Gerald Kenwell.

Mart Allen fondly remembers meeting the legendary Gerald Kenwell: "I was barely old enough to trek by foot with my Uncle Stan Narewski into the Moose River Plains on my first fishing trip. We were about halfway into the head of The Plains in the spring of 1940 when we met Gerald on his way out to Inlet. He looked tall, angularly rugged and impressive to a kid of 12 as he visited with Uncle Stan. He was the quintessential woodsman in his woods clothes, woven pack basket and slouch hat." *Courtesy M. Lisa Monroe*

Chapter Twenty-Seven

Olive Wertz's Moss Lake Girls Camp's Adventure

"I WAS AN EARLY MOSS LAKE CAMPER," Olive Wertz told me during a 1984 Adirondack Discovery "Walk Back in History" evening lecture program. The following day I was leading interested members of the talk to the site of Gerald Kenwell's former Otter Brook Camp, and Olive's statement definitely intrigued me. I asked her if I might record some of her memories, and when she said yes, I pulled out the hand-held tape recorder I nearly always carry with me.

Olive Wertz in 1926. *Courtesy Town of Webb Historical Association*

Moss Lake Camp was one of a number of George H. Longstaff's exclusive private children's camps. Longstaff owned and operated Moss Lake from 1923 until 1972. The beautiful small lake is three miles from Eagle Bay, along the Big Moose Road, and is between the communities of Inlet and Old Forge.

Today, the lake is part of the state Forest Preserve and is a popular area that offers paddling, birding, hiking, fishing and primitive camping.

Olive was an energetic older woman who was bubbling with excitement as she rode with me over the former Gould Paper Company access road that entered the Moose River Recreation Area through the Limekiln Lake gate. She told me her first glimpse of the Moose River Plains country was during the summer of 1926.

A Moss Lake wilderness party on the Big Plains. *Courtesy Olive Wertz*

Olive shared a history lesson about the founder of her camp: "Dr. Long-staff's Moss Lake Camp began in 1923. He had spent the majority of his life as he was growing up learning and working in the hotel trade in the Central Adirondacks. His parents owned and operated exclusive seasonal hotels. After graduating with a university degree in dentistry, and with the support of his parents, he started a string of highly successful summer camps for boys and girls and later a private school in Florida for the socially elite from around the western hemisphere.

"Throughout the 1940s and '50s he owned three lakes in the Big Moose area that were comparable to those (at the) Great camps held by the Morgans

Olive only had photocopies of her original photos. *Courtesy Olive Wertz*

at Mohegan Lake, the Woodruffs' Kamp Kill Kare at Lake Kora and the Vanderbilts' Sagamore Lodge.

"Moss Lake Camp's name for the horseback trail ride into the interior of The Plains was 'The Wilderness.' Back then the Gould Paper Company had a vast land holding where there were no roads, development, nothing. The softwood had largely been lumbered off. There was evidence of old dams built along the streams. I clearly recall seeing remains of a former lumber camp along the upper Red River not far from where the lumber company had built a dam. That reservoir of water, we were told, was used to float logs all the way down the river and into the Moose. There were logging clearings that were filling in with brambles. We were constantly watching for black bears eating berries in those areas. We had been told horses had a fear of bears. No one wanted to be bucked off if their mount was startled at the sight of one of those big beasts."

At Otter Brook Camp. *Courtesy Olive Wertz*

Olive recalled that in 1926, the third year of Moss Lake Camp's existence, Longstaff and his team hatched plans expanding the camp's outdoor activities to include a backcountry horseback trip to The Plains. Charles Chapin offered his camp as a destination, while Gerald Kenwell rented his Otter Brook hunting camp to be used as an endpoint for Moss Lake's riders' overnight stays. Chapin was a successful Rochester, New York, businessman and the owner of a large comfortable lodge at Beaver Lake deep in the Moose River Plains whose daughter Emily was a Moss Lake camper.

Kenwell's camp served as a backdrop for numerous snapshots. *Courtesy Olive Wertz*

"I attended Moss Lake for its first four years," Olive said. There were not that many girls—22 girls and 9 counselors, two bungalows with four bedrooms in each one that looked over Moss Lake. We were required to wear very neat uniforms. Our blouses were white and grey. Our culottes were navy blue.

"I recall the camp's dining room was in an old hunter's cabin the Longstaffs had. There was a living room in it too, and rooms upstairs for the counselors. Then the following year the attendance and rooms doubled and they had 36 or 54 or whatever.

"The first year there were very few rules aside from being careful. Of course, Babe Longstaff [George Longstaff's sister Caroline's nickname] and I were kids together. I enjoyed the rather relaxed but formal-style resort hotel feeling of the camp. It was typical for steaks and chops to appear on the breakfast menu. The table setting included linen napkins and tablecloths. New wide-range activities were added each year. All were athletic in nature and included horseback riding, tennis, archery, water sports, high-caliber swimming instruction, canoeing, dance, and fencing. By the fourth year the camp rules were too rigid for me. I'd had enough. I never returned."

Olive continued describing the trail ride. "The wilderness trip was a horse-back trip of many miles from Moss Lake. I recall the old Kenwell path that went along the edge of Fawn Lake. It was very wet in spots. There was corduroy that spanned the muddy sections, but it was quite old. There were places in those sections where lots of black muck oozed in between the joints of the logs. It was scary because the horses would slip and we'd have to keep their head up with the reins to keep them from falling. In fact, some of the rotting corduroy was under water and it was impossible to see it.

"When we reached the Great Plains that the counselors told us was also known as the Indian Clearing, I remember the beautiful, beautiful trees. They were black spruce. The blue-joint grass grew high, right up to our hips. Because we rode horseback we could see over the tall grass a long ways. It was all so interesting—all those old deep-rutted wagon trails and such.

"Once we passed over The Plains and forded the Moose River, the trail was only slight. Along with our party was a man named Joel or Joe. He was the teamster in charge of the horses. Then there was a local guide and our counselors.

"After crossing The Plains the trail wandered along Otter Brook through a forest of beautiful towering trees. At our destination, Gerald Kenwell's Otter Brook hunting and fishing camp, we slept on a long row of log bunks that was raised two and a half feet off the floor. We used bedrolls.

"Well, we slept overnight and the next day we took a trip over to Beaver Lake. It was beautiful, like our Moss Lake Camp. The caretaker was there. He told us to call him 'Pop.' He talked a lot. I don't think he got outside the woods too often. He handed us a pair of field glasses and we looked out across the lake from the open porch. I counted 17 deer feeding on water lilies that grew in the shallow water.

"Pop told us a story about a woman in the olden days. The woman was a pioneer who worked in a logging camp. She shot wolves and distinguished herself by working with the men. She was a powerful person. She used a pikepole, waded streams and even broke up log jams.

OPPOSITE: **Olive and a camp mate pose along a footpath.** *Courtesy Olive Wertz*

"We shared with him the activities the camp offered us: swimming, riflery, athletic and cultural things.

"When it came time to return to Otter Brook to spend another night, we first stopped along the south branch of the Moose River to fish. The counselors cooked the trout we caught in frypans right by the water's edge."

At the time I presented the Discovery program, I was focused on Olive's horseback riding experience through The Plains to Gerald Kenwell's camp. In retrospect, I wish I had asked her more questions. However, I turned the hand-held recording device off shortly after she said, "I'll have to tell you a funny story." What is related below is Olive's most memorable event of her entire Moss Lake Camp wilderness trip.

The Moss Lake wilderness party poses on Kenwell's roof. *Courtesy Olive Wertz*

"By the time our wilderness stay was over and it was time to begin the return trip to Moss Lake, our horses had not been fed the oats they were used to. I was convinced my horse's stomach had become much narrower because it had only grazed in the pastures. When I tried to cinch the saddle

378

it was not tight. I mean, there wasn't another hole to pull it tight, so the whole saddle was loose. I was concerned that as we moved along, the saddle strap would loosen and slip sideways. It seemed very precarious, so I brought the concern to one of the counselors. I told her I was not going to ride this horse. I couldn't make the cinch any tighter. She told me it was nonsense: "The saddle will not side off.'

"Well, I became upset when the counselor told me I was just being fussy and that I was not going to be allowed to walk and lead the horse. So I challenged her.

"She mounted the horse, trotted the horse around Kenwell's corral and said, 'See, there's no problem.' Then just as quickly as she had finished scolding me, the saddle did slip. As it slipped sideways, knocking her off, it ended up under the horse, hitting its vital male part. The horse didn't like it. He kicked back and bucked up. Well, she had flown off into the bushes. We nearly died laughing as the horse went bucking with feet flailing in the air as it went through the fence and began heading down the hill.

"We all ran behind anything to protect us to avoid the kicking horse, but the scene was terribly funny. After catching the horse and calming it down, we walked it back into the camp's yard.

"There were two packhorses with all our food and gear. One I recall was named Felix. When we started out from Moss Lake we drew lots to see what horse we'd get to ride. I got a horse that seemed to always want to keep its neck down.

"We went two nights and three days. When we got back to Moss Lake we were just in time for dinner.

"There were a lot of buildings at Otter Brook. On one canoe trip we took down the south branch of the Moose River, we feasted on veal cutlets—lots and lots of them. But somehow the counselors had forgotten the dishes, and so we had to use big leaves to eat off. That was a lot of fun.

"The wilderness horseback trip and the canoe trips were some of the happiest parts of my camp memories."

Later that summer, Joan Payne, Discovery's originator, introduced me to Dr. Longstaff when he attended a slide show I presented about early sporting camps in The Plains.

Longstaff's introduction to The Plains was a brief deer hunting trip led by Henry Froehlic. He said Froehlic was a "skilled German chef" who often worked at George's mother's hotel, The Mohawk on Fourth Lake. George's mother arranged to have Henry, whose real love was the deep woods, guide George on a deer hunting adventure and instruct him on how to use a gun. George remembered the first and last time he hunted in his book, *From Heyday to Mayday* (1983).

> I must have been twelve or thirteen when my mother, knowing that Henry would be a skillful and careful mentor, approved my first hunt. Since I had no skill with firearms. Henry suggested a shotgun, and we started off through this territory. The first two days I enjoyed immensely—Henry's cooking in the

Group photo before departing Otter Brook. *Courtesy Olive Wertz*

380

woods seemed even better than when he used the hotel stoves, but then on a quite rainy morning I found my first deer within range and shot it. It dropped in its tracks with only a startled look. There was no thought of romance, only some meat to pack out a dozen miles. I have not hunted since.

Apparently Longstaff found the idea of being an Adirondack youth camp owner far preferable to being a deerslayer, and Olive Wertz's camp memories are an indication that his choice was a good one that provided many girls with summers filled with camaraderie, an appreciation of the magnificence of the Moose River Plains country, and outdoor skills they would carry with them throughout their lives.

Postscript

Olive Wertz attended Moss Lake Girls Camp in those bygone years of recreation when there were none of the enticements offered to today's youngsters. There were no TVs, Internet, or cell phones; radio was in its infancy and there were no other electronic gadgets to entertain children—or adults.

Gladys Yost (See: *Moose River Plains: Land of the Deer Vol. 2*) was another summer camper at Longstaff's Moss Lake Camp who I interviewed about her early forms of recreation both at the girls' camp and at home.

Consider a typical family celebration in their day that might include music provided by a Victrola windup phonograph with quarter-inch thick recordings—the wonder of the age. Or when relatives gathered for a picnic dinner. They ate cold fried chicken, homemade potato chips and salad, pickles, bread and cheese, hard-boiled eggs, cakes and pies and cookies, until they were near to bursting. Cold tea and fresh squeezed lemons cooled with chipped ice were favorite drinks.

For their ladyship generation, horseback riding and wilderness trips were two of their favorite activities in the Adirondack camp. There, if a young rider won a ribbon, her pride lasted a year.

Yost reflected on those days in Longstaff's book, *From Heyday to Mayday*. Here follows a sampling of how hard she feels it is for a younger generation to understand an older generation's lifestyle.

No one now over twenty-five can comprehend a world wherein all societies can communicate—but in which few can understand each other. It is not so much a matter of language barriers as of emotional barriers. Nor can anyone over twenty-five truly grasp the meaning of life run by machines. Nor can anyone over twenty-five accurately sense a world which can be ended by a bomb. We can intellectually accept these changes, but we cannot *feel* them.

On the other side of the coin, those under twenty-five cannot possibly understand any other world than the frightening one into which they have been born. They can study the past, but they cannot *feel* it—a 'small' world of common communications, wherein man and not machine was master.

I think Yost's sentients might be one of the reasons Olive Wertz and she enjoyed sharing stories of wilderness trips in the Moose River Plains, although when they brought up trail riding, Dr. Longstaff, then into his nineties, insisted Olive and Gladys had to be mistaken about riding horseback in spite of both girls insisting they did and had snapshots to prove it.

I promised Dr. Longstaff I would include his rebuttal, so his reasoning that contradicted the girls' memories went on record—both suggesting he had simply forgotten that exceptions were made.

"I fear you will be disappointed in the substance of this letter [09.26.1991] for we [Moss Lake Camp] never staged a riding trip to either Gerald Kenwell's camp or to Beaver Lake. The girls you interviewed are younger than I, but logic so clearly supports my memory that I must substitute my recollection for theirs. We always sent a pack horse with the heavier supplies, but our riding string was made of horses that seldom had traversed anything rougher than a bridle path and I would have been unwilling to risk either their legs or the necks of my girls on such a trip. Incidentally, I reviewed several reels of Moss Lake film and one included a shot of girls with their packs going along Limekiln beach on foot with their personal gear.

"The usual Wilderness Party consisted of 8 to 12 girls (selected for their maturity and camping skills), a nurse, a counselor, and a cook-guide. On one or two of our earliest trips the guide was Henry Froelich, who for many years worked for Gerald as camp cook and spent his summers as chef in Rocky Point, the Mohawk and perhaps some other hotels. I recall one group we sent without Henry, and as the substitute was unfamiliar with the Otter Brook area I decided to visit the party on the second day. I did take a mount from the stable, but she was an especially placid and surefooted mare. My trip was uneventful except for a brief sector. Shortly after crossing the Red River we passed within a few feet of a bear intent on berry picking. A hundred yards or so farther on, a small buck crossed our path and my mare seemed quite nervous. Within minutes a partridge flushed near her feet and I nearly lost her."

Today a quarter-mile trail leads from the parking area off the Big Moose Road to Moss Lake's sandy beach. There is little evidence of the private camp complex that once occupied the location. The lake is a small jewel. It's very scenic and makes a wonderful easy-to-reach body of water for a leisurely paddle. Nesting ospreys and loons and a variety of other wildlife are often seen.

Adirondack Discovery was based at Inlet, New York. It was an educational outreach of the Adirondack Park Visitor Interpretive Centers, partially funded by the Adirondack Park Institute. Its programs opened people's eyes to aspects of the region's heritage they might otherwise never have been exposed to. One older gentleman told founder and director Joan Payne, "I've been coming to camp for 40 years and never had any idea there was so much to learn about this place!"

I enjoyed presenting programs for Discovery for 17 years. I found participants returned year after year, excited about the caliber of the learning experience, the camaraderie of others eager to learn, and the warmth of the settings as true experts shared their passion for some facet of the Adirondack experience. Since I had already begun gathering personal stories for my research, I was grateful for the connection I made with Olive and with many others during the nearly two decades I participated.

383

Chapter Twenty-Eight

The Lions of West Canada 'Crick:'
An Adirondack Capture

TWO OF THE MOST LOCALLY famous historical figures in Adirondack history, "French" Louie Seymour and Johnny Leaf, were subjects in Harvey L. Dunham's Adirondack French Louie *(1953) and Roy E. Reehil and William J. O'Hern's* Adirondack Adventures: Bob Gillespie & Harvey Dunham on French Louie's Trail *(2012). In this story, outdoors writer Eldridge Spears casts a fresh look at the flesh-and-blood men behind Gerald Kenwell's true stories of two woodsmen, genuine heroes to him who survived their entire lives as loggers, woodsmen, guides, hunters, fishermen, and poachers, protecting themselves against wild beasts and the natural world of the headwaters of the West Canada Creek and south branch of the Moose River. Here men, women, and children now find appealing recreational opportunities because the land was set aside, protected and designated as Wild Forest and Wilderness as part of New York State's Adirondack Forest Preserve.*

Before the turn of the 20th century, hunters traveling "around the rim of the Adirondack Mountains used to speak of a mysterious man who lived along somewhere in the West Canada Lake country," wrote Eldridge A. "Elgie" Spears.

Eldridge, a native of Northwood, a little village now wiped out by Hinckley Reservoir, explored the West Canada Lake country. He recalled the many hunting and trapping camps, and of meeting "a man, a bit stooped, grizzled and gray…and with arms and hands that seemed to reach gorilla-like almost to his knees. Rather old, yet plainly a man of great strength. Yes, it was French Louie."[29] Louis "French Louie"[30] Seymour was 77 when Elgie wrote of him

OPPOSITE: **French Louie, standing in the back door of his camp on West Canada Creek. The woodsman took great pride in the vegetable garden. When this picture was taken by Francis Harper, in 1910, Lewey said he "was about 78."** *Courtesy Maitland C. DeSormo Collection*

385

and his two-story West Canada Lake log cabin with a combined living room and dining room where big-wig "city sports" hung out when they came up to hunt or to fish on the 5,000 acres owned by the Union Bag and Paper lumber company they worked for. The old woodsman-guide was still a strapping fellow even then.

There have been all kinds of true tales and amazing stories told about Louie, but there have been few recorded examples of Louie's outlaw ways.

After spending 40 years in the woods, working to make a living and often getting by with spending less cash annually than did Henry David Thoreau at Walden Pond—some $39.00—you might imagine Louie had his share of run-ins with the game protector.

Elgie claimed Louie not only had "the swellest of any trapper's camp in the whole Adirondack region," but also 15 additional trapline camps and 35 boats stashed from Moose River to Lake Pleasant. All of those shelters needed to be well-stocked with supplies, although by Louie's seventh decade he admitted he wasn't much on toting heavy packs. However, Gerald Kenwell remembers Louie, at age 74, was still capable of carrying 50 pounds of Moose River maple sugar on his back from his Falls Mountain sugar bush back to Big West.

Kenwell laughed with amusement at his good friend's ability, telling how Louie might have been old but he still had it in him at 74 to pull a good-sized kitchen stove Louie described as "light. It don't weigh more than 200 pounds," Louie told Spears. That winter Louie pulled the stove over to a camp in the Moose River country.

George W. Andrews was another admirer of Louie. Louie was George's guide over many years. Andrews wrote about a number stories of crusting and floating for deer and hunting trips throughout Louie's stalking grounds "that contained four lakes, as beautifully arranged as one could wish," he said. Andrews said Louie had "a well-known cry of victory" whenever a deer was taken either with hounds, by floating or by rifle.

There were other times Louie was characterized not only by his hollers, but as a wiry little fellow who knew his way around and was perfectly at home anywhere in the back country, but also as a bit of an outlaw. Those behaviors do not often surface. However, tucked in a February 23, 1895,

Forest and Stream newspaper is an account of the capture of Louie and another scofflaw for killing deer illegally. It follows just as it was penned by someone identified only as "S."

NYS Game Protector Maynard Phelps on duty at Twin Ponds, 1926. The primary mission of federal and state game laws is to protect and enhance fish, wildlife and their habitats for the continuing benefit of the people. New York State laws govern hunting and fishing within the state. The state is trustee of the peoples' fish and game, so fish and game belong to the state in its sovereign capacity as representative and for the benefit of all its people in common ownership with the owner of the land. Therefore, any right to fish or hunt that is granted by a property owner may be regulated by the state.
Courtesy Lyons Falls History Association

An Adirondack Capture

For several months past rumors have been afloat relative to the depredations of a couple desperate characters who have been slaughtering deer in the remote portion of the Adirondack wilderness about the head waters of West Canada Creek. These parties, one whom is a Frenchman known as "French Louis" and the other an Indian renegade from the St. Regis reservation, have been in the habit of killing large numbers of deer in

387

and out of season. It is said that the Indian has averaged a deer a day for several months past. The other has killed since the 1st of September last, no less than 27 deer. Most of the deer killed have been disposed of at the various lumbering camps in the vicinity of the slaughter, and such as they have been unable to dispose of are left to rot or be devoured by beast and birds. During the months of December and January the protectors succeeded in getting sufficient evidence and Protector Kenwell and Special Officer Lobdell went in after the pair.

The front of Louie's cabin at West Canada Lake.
Courtesy Edward Blankman (The Lloyd Blankman Collection)

OPPOSITE: **"Johnny Leaf would kill a deer for a pint of whiskey." —Harvey L. Dunham.**
Courtesy Edward Blankman (The Lloyd Blankman Collection)

After a long and tedious drive over very bad roads they reached a lumber camp in the town of Wilmurt late in the night of Jan. 28, the camp named being located about 20 miles from that of Lief[31] [Johnny Leaf]. Wishing to surprise the Indian in his camp, the officers remained here until the afternoon of the following day, and then proceeded on snow-shoes and by the aid of a lantern reached Lief's camp about daylight on the 30th, and found it without an occupant, but found plenty of evidence of illegal deer killing. Lief was tracked to the camp of the Canadian, Louis, about six miles further in the woods, and there these two worthies were found.

Under pretense of desiring to purchase furs, the officers endeavored to get sufficient information to convict the Canadian, but made only a partial success of it. Louis' case is one of 'I killed the dog but you must prove it,' and while there is little doubt of his having killed large numbers of deer illegally, the officers thought best to secure the Indian as the greater offender of the two and the stronger case for conviction. Lief accompanied the officers back to his own camp, for the purpose of selling them his furs, and was there put under arrest, after having shown Messrs. H.[sic] and L. a carcass of fresh venison meat which had been discovered by them during their first visit. He also brought to light the heads of three bucks that had not been killed earlier than the latter part of Dec. last. Louis, who seems to have mistrusted that all was not quite right, followed the party back to Lief's camp, and appeared very much frightened when he found the Indian a prisoner. He denied having killed any game out of season, or otherwise illegally, but it is safe to say that there will be sufficient evidence forthcoming

Eldridge A. Spears said of Lewey: "Lewey once had a dog which he said he fed in the wintertime by shooting cross-bills and 'summer canaries'—goldfinches. He sprinkled salt along a board, which cross-bills like. When a lot of them got on the board, Lewey sighted a shotgun the length of it and mowed 'em down." The Frenchman sold about 30 deer skins a year "left at his camps by parties," Spears reported, "and got $1.25 each. He got $15 to $20 for a bear skin." *Courtesy Edward Blankman (The Lloyd Blankman Collection)*

in the near future to convict him on several counts unless he
shall in the meantime leave the country.

Jonny Leaf's camp at Mud Lake dam. *Courtesy Edward Blankman (The Lloyd Blankman Collection)*

Lief was brought out to Sageville with the intention of taking
him to Fulton county for trial, but at Sageville he offered
to plead, and was permitted to do so, when he very obligingly
confessed to a killing, on which he could not have been con-
victed on any evidence in the possession of the officers and was
sentenced to 40 days' imprisonment in the Hamilton County
Jail. There are at least four or five other clear cases against him
that ought to keep him sent up for several months, after which

he will be sued for the penalties in the several cases, and if he does not flee the country, the chances are that he will be kept out of mischief for some time to come.

A few years ago Lief turned up as a witness in a rash of illegal deer killing, tried in Herkimer County, and by very stout swearing succeeded in prevailing a conviction where the people had a very strong case against one of his pals. He is a thoroughly bad egg, and it is to be hoped that both he and the Canadian, Louis, may be finally driven out of the woods.

Both have been in the habit of selling large quantities of deer skins to parties in Fulton and Hamilton counties and have no doubt been engaged in slaughtering deer for the hides also when they could not dispose of the venison. It is, however, difficult to convict on any evidence other than fresh skins, for the old story, "these skins were taken from deer killed by the several [guided hunting] parties who we guided during the season," will always be given as an excuse for having any large number of skins on hand. Lief is a half breed renegade from the St. Regis reservation, who has followed hunting and trapping in the Canada Lakes country for the past four years, and the Canadian, "French Louis," has followed the same vocations in that vicinity for a somewhat longer period.

Considering the information in this article, it's fairly easy to see how "French Louie" was able to live in the woods with so little in the way of actual financial resources. Barter was common when Louie was busy poaching deer, and it's likely he traded his illegal venison to the lumber camps for items the woods could not provide, such as coffee, flour, sugar, and beans. How many deer carcasses must he have hauled around the woods—for this article reports only one instance where he was unlucky enough to get caught and it was surely not a first offense? While the number of deer will never be known, the activity apparently helped keep him fit, so that hauling a 200-pound stove to camp through the woods was not a particularly arduous task for him.

Chapter Twenty-Nine

Louie's Little Trapper

LOUIE SEYMOUR, it is believed, was born in 1832, fifty-five years before Gerald Kenwell, and yet Gerald grew in spirit and was influenced all his life by his boyhood model.

Because of Louie's camp's location, his sugar bush on the western slope of Falls Mountain to the Kenwell's Sportsman's Home along the south branch of the Moose River and Gerald's father, Wellington, and his Uncle Ike's connection with Louie, it isn't hard to imagine that all helped to shape Gerald's life. Gerald's earliest memories of Louie are of the infrequent occasions when his parents let him cross the Indian Clearing from the Sportsman's Home to visit with the oldster if he was gathering maple sap. At his young age he might not have realized then what a treasure he had in "Louie"—a truly outstanding character who possessed all the woodcraft, grit and trapping skills that it took to survive in the backwoods. But all that boyhood interest in Louie crystallized later in "Louie's little trapper's" life.

There are three facts about French Louie I would never have known about, had it not been for Gerald's remembrances. I don't believe they were ever documented in Harvey Dunham's book, *Adirondack French Louie: Early Life in the North Woods.*

The one time French-Canadian born Louie returned to his old home near Quebec; the memory of his tartar-like stepmother so saddened him that standing in a nearby grove, unheard and unseen by his family members, he watched them come and go.

When Louie went hunting, his dog, Old Cape, at his master's bidding, would jump out of the canoe, swim to shore, run up a mountainside, and drive the prey down to the edge of the lake where Louie would have an easy shot.

Once he constructed a big map of the mountains around his cabin and his trap line trails. It was about four feet square, and probably the most

394

accurate ever made of the region with the exception of a U.S. Geological Survey map. The drawing survived after his passing, but it is believed some clerk who did not appreciate the significance of the map, destroyed it.

Inlet native Howard Burkhart, a partner in Burkhart Evans Insurance, at Otter Brook Camp helps himself to a stack of Gerald's flapjacks. *Courtesy Town of Webb Historical Association*

West Canada and Pillsbury lakes are beautiful bodies of water and the forest is a charming feature of a wild-feeling, lovely section of the Adirondacks. Louie made a good choice when he decided to build his cabin there on one of the highest lakes in that mountainous territory.

Gerald recalled a visit he made to Louie's place six years before he began the construction of Otter Brook Camp. "The winter of 1908 I made a trip on snowshoes to West Canada in the latter part of February with a fellow who was curious to see Louie. When we arrived at Louie's camp, there was a big beef paunch under the same stairway where I had previously seen a live fisher. I said 'Louie what in the world are you doing with that in here?' His answer was: 'I want him to get ripe so fox smell him long way; too cold outdoors to get ripe.' I guess it was getting ripe. It was quite evident at the time."

Louie "had not seen any company since early fall before; neither had he washed a dish or cleaned the camp, which had a bad effect on my companion, for he was very sensitive and spleeny, therefore he didn't eat enough in the two days we were visiting Louie to keep a sparrow alive. But I was familiar with Louie's housekeeping so I didn't pay much attention. I simply went ahead and cleaned up the end of the table we wanted to use, and washed and scalded the dishes we needed and we had our own supplies. I knew what we had to eat was clean, so why be fussy about anything else? But during the cleanup operation I started on the table dishes Louie had been using, for both the plate and cup he had in use had a rim of black and mold around the edges three-quarters of an inch wide by a quarter inch thick. Louie saw me start to clean his gear and yelled at me: 'Gerald, don't touch him. He's got the flavor right on him just like I like him.'

"After the clean-up job, Louie said: 'Gerald, what kind of meat you fellows want, some venison or fish?'

"'Well,' I said, 'Louie, I believe fish would be preferable for I haven't had any since last summer.' So he says, 'Go out in ice house and pick out fish you want.' So I went out to the ice house, and such a sight I never saw. This

OPPOSITE: **Gerald Kenwell prepares a batch of pancakes circa 1944.** *Courtesy Ora Kenwell*

 397

ice house I would say was around 12 feet square, with one layer of ice left in it, and that whole surface was one solid sheet of trout. Both brook and lake trout. So I picked out two 1-½ lb. speckled trout and took them back into the camp and said to Louie: 'For Heaven's sake, what do you do with so many fish?' His reply was: 'He's the best bait for trap line there is, for fisher, martin and mink.'

"'Well,' I said, 'how much fish do you use to the cubby?'[32] He said: 'Sometimes whole fish, sometimes half fish.' Just imagine. Some of those lake trout I would judge ran up to ten pounds or better, and in that case he used a half fish for one cubby. But when you think of it, why not? There wasn't another man within 30 miles of there to catch the fish and that amount didn't make much impression on that large area."

A Visit With Gerald Kenwell

Richard F. Dumas wrote a weekly column called "Naturally" in the *Oswego Valley News*. In his March 1975 column he remembered Kenwell's Otter Brook Camp and its owner.

"We spent one week at the cabin of one of the last remaining guides, deep in the woods, and about ten miles [sic, it is more accurately 17 miles] from the highway on an old logging road. Gerald Kenwell used to have wild critters as acquaintances, but these would come only when they wanted, which was fine, since Mr. Kenwell kept the old stump near the porch furnished with scraps for their pleasure. That stump was typically where Gerald placed leftover flapjacks. The variety he prepared were hearty. 'They stick to your ribs especially when you've a hard day's work ahead,' he claimed. Uninvited but welcome were the deer, who found Gerald to be their friend. When camp activity quieted down, the animals paid a call to the feeding stump to help themselves to 'leftovers,' which in many cases were buckwheat cakes with a dash of maple syrup." Gerald officially came out of the woods three times annually for the sole purpose of getting supplies from the Village of Inlet.

There are many similarities between French Louie's and Gerald's lives. According to Gerald, "Louie went out to civilization twice a year for supplies." His destination was usually Speculator. "Supplies consisted of flour, beans, salt pork, salt and tea. The rest he got in the woods. He had his own fish and meat, raised his own vegetables, such as he wanted. He made his own sugar form the maples and he bought very few clothes. I have seen him with as many as six or seven patches thick on his pants and the patch material ran all the way from pieces of underwear to socks, and occasionally a piece of deer skin."

Left to right: Howard Burkhart, Steve Gidley, Hans Holl, Gerald Kenwell, F. Felician, Len Harwood owner of Hot Top Camp, and Lansing Tiffany on Len's right. Gerald Kenwell is serving this group of Inlet natives in January 1952. *Courtesy Jack Tanck*

As the numbers of Adirondack League Club (ALC) members who made their way to Louie's doorstep continued to grow throughout the 1890s, so too did the word go out far and wide about "Mayor" Kenwell's Otter Brook place. No visitor had a second thought of turning back onto the old lumber road when it "ran out," and delegations of visitors were required to take to snowshoes to finish their trek over the remaining distance through the wooded wilds, where there was always a pot on the stove filled with substantial and tasty food.

Jack Tanck holds one of French Louie's muskrat traps Gerald gave him. Later on, Gerald guided Jack to the site of Louie's old sod-built overnight trapline a short distance upstream from Kenwell's camp. After I took this picture, Jack presented me with the trap. *Author's photo*

400

"Time meant very little to Louie," Gerald learned from Frank Baker, who was often a loner. Baker served as caretaker of Charles Chapin's Camp Nit on Beaver Lake. Camp Nit was about 20 miles away from Louie's place. "When he went into Baker's camp," wrote Kenwell, "he asked Baker if it was Sunday. Baker told him no, it was Thursday. Then Louie asked what month it was, and Baker told him it was March.

Gerald accompanied assistant biologist Jack Tanck on numerous snowshoe trips during the winter of 1943. Gerald rented his camp to Conservation Department personnel during the years they did deer studies in the Moose River Plains. *Courtesy Jack Tanck*

"'Well,' Louie said, 'I thought it must be getting along towards spring, for I struck my ax into a maple and the sap ran out.' That was one of Louie's ways of keeping track of what time of year it was."

Gerald didn't use folk methods to keep track of time. There was a windup Baby Ben alarm clock and a yearly calendar hanging in his camp that he marked to note when parties planned to come in.

Hal Boyce, a friend of the Kenwell family, reported in a 1949 newspaper column, "There isn't a better woodman in all the central Adirondack

401

Mountains than Gerald Kenwell." He knows "every deer in the hills by its stomp. Kenwell is a cat-footed man with the posture of an Indian and eyes as fresh as Eden." At sixty-three years of age, Gerald "can still sling a fresh-killed buck deer over his shoulder and tote it fourteen miles to the hunting camp he has run for thirty-two years. The camp is in the center of a 50+ mile stretch of virgin wilderness.

Old time guides: Left to Right: Mose Leonard, Reuben Mick, Gerald Kenwell. The photo was taken the year Kenwell was hired as a caretaker of Camp Uncas, J.P. Morgan's Adirondack Great Camp on Mohegan Lake. *Courtesy Ora Kenwell*

"Many city-bred people picture a hunting guide as a brush-faced, tobacco-chewing illiterate who never has the common sense to come to town. Kenwell doesn't fit into that portrait at all. He is a courteous, well-bred, widely-read man who stayed in the woods by choice. And he has his own opinions of people who crowd their lives out in stone cities and never wake up to the smell of balsam.

"'Nature put you on earth to keep busy,' he said, and 'you'll keep busy—or pay the penalty.'

"Gerald doesn't have much respect for modern-day guides who go to the forest in automobiles. He likes to yarn about the real old-timers and their endless resourcefulness.

"Two of his heroes were Fred Hess—taken away in the prime of his youth—and 'French Louie,' who schooled Kenwell himself in the lore of the woods.

"Hess could carry out two bucks on his broad back and use any tool and once skinned a wolf with a safety pin."

Gerald recalled this true story about Hess. "Fred was what you would call a determined man. Never would give up. Never would back down from a bear either. Used to go right into their caves after them.

"One time Fred caught a bear making a bed of spruce boughs in the deep snow. Fred was on snowshoes and didn't have a gun but he said, 'I want that bear!'

"So he tied his hatchet to a long pole and swung it at the bear trying to bash in his skull. The bear just grabbed the hatchet and sat on it.

"Then Fred tied his knife to another pole and crept up and tried to stab the bear to death. The bear finally grabbed that pole too, and I don't know who was the madder—him or Fred. Then the bear tried to grab Fred but couldn't catch him in the deep snow.

"Finally, Fred snowshoed back to his cabin, grabbed up a gun, went back and got his bear."

Such went the life of the man who came to be the Mayor of Otter Brook. There are many more facts and stories told about the renowned guide, but they are better left to a book about the Kenwells of Inlet.

In the meantime, sharing the Mayor's philosophy is a good way to end:

> "I have always had the sense of being firmly rooted in a sure world that was always full of the promise of life, even in the midst of dissolution, if only a man would but look."

Chapter Thirty

Trapping with Gerald Kenwell and "French Louie"

WHEN GERALD KENWELL WAS 65, he liked to reminisce, or in his words "yarn, about old times, the real old timers and their endless resourcefulness, as he did when he penned "French Louie" for the August–September, 1952 issue of *The New York State Conservationist* magazine.

Kenwell was heralded by many sportsmen and sportswomen as the best woodsman in the central Adirondacks (in his time) and newspaper columnists Dick Long and Hal Boyce called him "the last of the great Adirondack guides."

Kenwell didn't get hopped up over how others perceived him. The one thing that did stick in his craw and what he cussed over was the "real cute-looking beavers," he told Hal Boyce, that were viewed in an exhibition during the 1904 St. Louis Fair. Once almost trapped to extinction—*Castor canadensis*—North America's largest rodent—was subsequently reintroduced into the Adirondack Mountains. Kenwell continued, "Some of our guides went out in the St. Louis Fair. They saw some beaver on exhibition... so they brought a pair back and turned them loose; then somebody put out some more."

Understand the old woodsman spoke in generalities. The reintroduction had a history and a purpose.

Harry Radford, a noted outdoor writer of the day, wrote in the 1906 *Annual Report of the New York Forest, Fish and Game Commission* (the forerunner of today's Department of Environmental Conservation) that "until

OPPOSITE: **Louis Seymour (1832–1915) lived deep in the West Canada Lakes country for over 40 years. Louis is holding a prized snake. He said snakes were part of his garden's army of farm hands. Gerald Kenwell helped Louie capture snakes on the Big Plains.**
    Louie warned everyone not to harm his camp snakes. The two largest ones were named Darby and Joan. Once, Louie placed Joan in his flour barrel in order to rid the flour of little white worms. *Courtesy Edward Blankman (The Lloyd Blankman Collection)*

404

three or four years ago . . . hardly one in ten of the guides, hunters, trappers and lumbermen who spend a large part of their lives in the woods of the Adirondacks knew that there were any wild beavers remaining."

French Louie and Trume Haskell standing in front of Louie's camp at Big West. Lloyd wrote on the back of the picture: "Taken about 1900. Given to me by Trume Haskell. One of my best and rarest pictures."
    When thirty-six-year-old Louie arrived in Indian Lake Village in the Fall of 1868 one of the first people he met was Gerald's uncle, Isaac "Ike" Kenwell. *Courtesy Edward Blankman (The Lloyd Blankman Collection)*

Two large landowners who tried to reintroduce beavers on their private estates in Kenwell's neck-of-the-woods were Edward Litchfield, owner of Litchfield Park between the villages of Long Lake and Tupper Lake, who tried in 1901, and Timothy L. Woodruff,[33] who brought some to Kamp Kill Kare, his private preserve at Lake Kora, in 1902.

John Warren reported in his Wednesday, April 8, 2009, online column, "Extinction: A Short History of Adirondack Beaver":

406

In all, about 20 beaver from Ontario were reintroduced between 1901 and 1906; of these, seven were purchased from the Canadians at the St. Louis *Louisiana Purchase Exposition* in 1904 by the state and brought to Old Forge for release in the South Fork of the Moose River.[34] The state later brought fourteen more light-colored "yellow beaver" (same species, their color varies) taken from Yellowstone National Park; these were scattered around the Adirondack region.[35]

Gerald liked to tell stories about his good friend Louie, who he often spent time with both at Louie's camp and on the Big Indian Clearing. Louie kept a sugarbush camp near Otter Brook. Louie showed Gerald a metal-lined box in which Harry Radford, publisher of the magazine *Woods and Waters*, brought beaver into the woods and released them.
Courtesy Edward Blankman (The Lloyd Blankman Collection)

The reintroduction worked amazingly well, and by 1915 it was estimated that there were 15,000 beaver in the state. Six thousand were taken in the first two special trapping seasons (in 1924 and 1925); regular trapping seasons began in 1928.

The opinion that the beaver reintroduction "worked amazingly well" was one expressed by John Warren almost a century after the reintroduction of the beaver into Adirondack waters.

Lyon DeCamp, a Thendara/Old Forge businessman and large landowner of Adirondack Mountain property felt differently, as evidenced in a letter he responded to dated June 6, 1917. DeCamp was replying to a Mr. Agar's inquiry if DeCamp, "knew of other locations outside his own property on which beaver had caused damage… "

DeCamp responded by alluding to that the beaver reintroduction program was visibly in full swing. He cited, "Mr. Kenwell of Inlet, Herkimer [County], a woodsman who lives on Sixth Lake of the Fulton Chain," was familiar with the damage the lately reestablished beavers had caused to State land in Township 4 of the Moose River Tract, Hamilton County. "Two ponds known as the Mitchell Ponds, lying between the south branch of the Moose River and the Red River, had been dammed and flooded…also upon their outlet, three miles from the mouth of Red River, a dam has caused the flooding of about ten acres. Another, farther down, floods about 50 acres. Another dam, on the outlet of a pond known as Fall Pond… flooded about 10 acres. Also, a lake in that same locality known as has been raised about two feet, with consequent destruction of the virgin timber about the shores. Also, a lake known as Hell Diver Pond has been flooded. Also, a stream running into Seventh Lake of the Fulton Chain has had about 20 acres flooded, with the consequent destruction of timber."

The letter continued to cite numerous other instances as well as reporting all the acres of timber killed along the banks as a direct result of "…the damming of creeks and streams, and the flooding of the lands on which this

OPPOSITE: **When Louie had one person in camp, Slim said Louie generally was talkative— to a point. If there were two or more people in camp, Louie would go about his business quietly.** *Courtesy Edward Blankman (The Lloyd Blankman Collection)*

408

409

character of timber stand…" He suggested that if Mr. Agar climbed to the summit of Bald Mountain, "the condition" caused by damming Third Lake Creek where it enters into Third Lake could be viewed. It would look like a "strip of land that has been fire swept."

Gerald Kenwell holds Midnight, his camp companion. Gerald's gait was much like Louie's stride. Both men moved through the woods with a strong jog of about three miles an hour. *Courtesy of Ora Kenwell*

This was a time of a new wave in the Adirondacks. There were writers telling that today *there are places where the muskrat, the beaver and the otter frolic about the entire day, seeking food, constructing dens, or following their own natural desires; and with no fear of molestation by man.*

While some flowery-tongued reporters in the press touted the successful resurgence of the beaver, public opinion began to condemn the millions of dollars' worth of forests and other property reported destroyed annually. The beaver were becoming too plentiful. Another faction would suggest that perhaps it was not the beaver but the wanton waste and greed of man that was taking away the great woods.

In 1926, noted trapper E.J. Dailey wrote: "At one time, the future of the beaver seemed doubtful, and less than twenty-five years ago, were all but extinct. Careful supervision by the State and a comparatively long closed season worked wonders for the beaver, and within recent years there has been a number of legal trapping periods, netting the trappers many thousand dollars. It does not take a moment's thought to note the abundant justification of closing the season for any animal if the trappers insist on taking the last of the species."

Protected for years by a closed hunting season and with few natural enemies to catch them, the beaver thrived like rabbits. In 1949, Gerald Kenwell told his friend, outdoor columnist Hal Boyce, "they've got nature out of balance."

Most important to Kenwell was that Adirondackers could make a living in the mountains; this was his link with a glorious Adirondack past. Looking back on his years as a lifetime resident of the Central Adirondacks, Gerald said, "I believe French Louie[36] was the greatest character of all whom I had the privilege to meet and come to know very well. In fact, we became the best of friends."

Besides the history Gerald and Louie shared, there were also parallels between their lives. The majority of Louie's annual income came from his success along his trap lines. Gerald's main source of revenue came from paying customers who came to fish and hunt, but he did trap fur-bearers. Both men made their living from the land.

Memories of nights spent in camp with Louie lingered fondly with Gerald Kenwell. He enjoyed recalling morning plans the pair made while at

Louie's cabin, as smoke from the stove pipe rolled away in rings, and the fire in the box stove cracked in a cheery warming way. Louie would talk of rushing out of a rough trap line shelter at daybreak to scour the grounds, stopping only long enough to grab a doughy flap-jack or two that he carried in his pocket, then rushing on until darkness forced him back into another uncomfortable tumble-down camp for the night.

Gerald remembered, "Louie had many outpost trapping camps arranged all through the woods at intervals of six or eight miles apart, just small overnight camps. Louie was the most expert otter trapper I ever ran across. So good in fact that I could never find an otter track within 15 miles of his domain. Louie was an extravagant trapper as far as game was concerned. I was snowshoeing across country on one of my trips to Canada Lake the latter part of December and crossed a small pond with a rocky island in the center, and in the crevices of rocks I discovered five deer carcasses piled up in one spot. When I reached Louie's camp I asked him about it and he acknowledged he did it, and that lots of bait attracted lots of foxes so he could catch them. But of course it didn't matter much in those days, for there was no one traveling that country but Louie and occasionally someone like myself just passing through there."

It's a well-known fact that "French Louie" found much pleasure in being kind to children. He genuinely enjoyed them. Gerald said Louie, "had a regular habit of leaving a kind word with each child he met. Children looked forward to his visits to town," when they would flock around him to hear his stories and get their pennies or candy." I imagine Gerald found great joy in paying him a tribute in his *Conservationist* article.

Hal Boyce said he was always in paradise when Gerald shared French Louie remembrances at Kenwell's wooded outpost. Located on a level niche between a tumbling stream and a steep rocky ledge, Otter Brook Camp was the perfect name for the place. As a youngster, Gerald said he had decided to call it that because when he first entered the territory, tracks of otter were in evidence.

Both Kenwell's and French Louie's camps were located in trappers' country. It was not out of the ordinary for Gerald to be following along Otter Brook and just by luck come across something that had once belonged to

Louie. During a short investigative bushwhack, as Shawn Hansen and I took down a drainage beyond Gerald's spring hole where there are the remains of three hit-and-miss generators Gerald used to draw water to his camp, I thought of Louie trapping along Otter Brook. Jack Tanck, a wildlife biologist, gave me one of Louie's traps. Tanck and Kenwell were good friends. Jack said Gerald had given him the trap in 1943 as a keepsake, and felt passing it on to me would help keep alive some of his memories of Gerald—and Louie's, for that matter.

Gerald Kenwell (Rt.) and an unidentified man shovel snow, winter 1943. *Courtesy Jack Tanck*

Gerald related French Louie stories not only to Jack but also to many other people over the years.

Hal Boyce always had an ear for stories. He also enjoyed being out and about in the territory of the Moose River. Once he asked Gerald if they might cover a stretch of the nomadic trapper's territory northeast of Otter Brook Camp. Boyce was hoping to spot some remains of one of Louie's rough trap line abodes he had established near the headwaters of Otter Brook. Gerald guaranteed nothing. He had no idea if they might uncover anything. Hal's

413

hope was there might still be an old stretching board or two resting against a moss-covered log wall that the "quill pigs" (porcupines) had failed to reach. He didn't expect to find a shelter with a roof intact, but perhaps some parts of the walls that kept the chill winds away might be spotted.

As the men gulped a scanty noon-day bite to eat, Gerald related that while Louie was a skillful trapper, that didn't mean he was entirely bullet-proof when it came to avoiding accidents. This tale tells of Louie's peril while on a trip to Gerald's place. Gerald begins:

> "In all the years Louie was around water he never learned to swim, and he was telling me a story one time of making a trip in late March from West Canada over to the Otter Brook. On his course he came across Brook Trout Lake, and on his way back later that afternoon he got out within 50 feet of a big rock in Brook Trout and broke through the ice into about eight feet of water. He said: 'I swim to the bottom just like stone, but I keep eyes open and walk on bottom to this rock and climb up rock to surface. I believe you see my fingernail marks on rock yet.'"

Those stories and places are the kinds of things that will keep Shawn Hansen and me returning to The Plains just for the fun of revisiting history in what others who don't know anything about what it was like back in the days would consider simply a vast forest.

Shawn makes his living as highway superintendent for the Town of Inlet. Neither he nor I live the way Gerald and Louie did, but it is enjoyable to hear how an earlier generation got along in their lives.

Far back in the once unbroken Moose River Plains lived, and still does, the voracious fisher, known to trappers and hunters as the "Black Cat" because it is about the size of a large house cat. Adirondacks they knew well. Louie taught him about using a thin sheet of paraffin (waxed) paper placed over the trap and held with the aid of a bough. Snow was brushed over the set; various scents or lures were used with trail and water sets. Then there was trail-bait. An old-time fisher trapper would take the tail of a beaver, smear it with beaver castor and oil from the oil sacs, and drag that from one set to another. Louie vouched for the fact that it paid dividends. Gerald's nephew, Winfred Murdock, said he knew for a fact Gerald had dragged such scented bait for almost uncountable miles, and the result was he trapped more fishers. The following story Gerald launched into has to do with Mr. Fisher, with his needle-like teeth.

"Louie was the one man that showed me how to capture a fisher alive," Gerald said. "One time I went to his camp for a visit and under his stairway that went up into the loft he had a live fisher wired in. I said: 'Louie, how in God's heavens did you ever get that thing here alive and what have you got him here for?' The first answer was 'Oh, he easy to get. You just chase him in hole in ledge or hollow log, then you set trap, then you pull him out. Fisher he's just like bulldog, he grab onto anything that smells like man and hangs on. So I take off my overalls and tie on stick, he grab it. I pick him up and shove in bag and bring him home.'" Louie planned to keep the animal until the fisher's pelt was prime.

On one 1949 morning snowshoe when the forest was robed in a fleecy blanket of white, Hal Boyce pressed Gerald about the beaver, since in his last fall travels he found evidence of families of those busybodies living almost everywhere around The Plains.

"The beaver is the death of the woods," he said. "They've dammed up the streams and flooded the natural winter quarters for the deer, leaving the deer nothing to eat.

"And they're destroying the trout too. The trout can't get past the dams to spawn, and the water in the ponds heats up in the sun, and the trout can't stand that either."

Mayor Kenwell held that the otter was also increasing rapidly and was an equal threat to the anglers' fun.

"An otter catches and eats about two pounds of fish a day and 50 of them will get rid of a lot of fine trout."

The old guide put much of the blame on "The cussed conservation rules." The state then [1949] had a two-week open season on beaver and otter. But Kenwell thought it ought to pay a bounty for trapping the pests and a bounty on bobcats too.

"There's more of them around now," he said. "And for bears—why there's 30 times as many now as there were 40 years ago. The old bear hunters are gone, and the bears have their way."

He pointed to a bear that had raided his hunting camp the summer of '48, smashing through during the winter and eating everything that wasn't in cans.

"The thing to protect is the thing that has value," said Kenwell, "not the thing that causes damage.

"I figure for every deer shot in the hills, hunters spend $200. So it's the deer that have value—not the beavers, otter and bobcats.

"They say there's more deer now than there ever was. And that's true. But where are the deer? Down in some farmer's pasture mixing with his cows and looking for food. They're not in the woods. Some of 'em even go right into the city, they're so hungry.

"The farmer wants to get rid of them. They're a nuisance. And he doesn't want hunters climbing his barbed wire fences to shoot at deer in his pasture. It's too hard on his cows.

"And the hunters don't like it either—it isn't sporting."

Kenwell figured the deer would return to the woods if "the conservation fellows" would spend about $65,000 a year to stock their winter quarters with feed—a fraction of the amount sportsmen spend for hunting licenses alone.

"It would also help the deer and trout both," the old woodsman added, "if they turned every cussed beaver into a hat."

The last time I paddled the south branch of the Moose River below the site of Kenwell's Sportsman's Home, I saw evidence of both bank and lodge beaver all the way to the remains of the old Wheelock dam. They have continued to flourish, leaving me, a non-trapper, to assume there are good prospects of beaver trapping today.

The one animal that seemed to leave evidence and tracks on both sides of the Moose River that Gerald never saw was the moose. They are protected today, but perhaps sometime in the future, if disease doesn't become a factor, their numbers will increase to the point that hunting moose in the Adirondacks will be as common as white-tail deer hunting is today.

Chapter Thirty-One

A Voice for The Plains

*My older friend Winfred Murdock spent many years of his life
living and working with his Uncle Gerald Kenwell in the Fulton
Chain of Lakes and in the Moose River Plains. Winfred, who
went by the handle "Winnie" back in the 1920s, but who I and
other people call "Slim" because he was once tall and lanky, was
Otter Brook's long-time packer. Slim made numerous cassette
recording tapes for me from 1986 through 1990. All the voice
recordings document his memories and Adirondack work experi-*
ences. The Moose River Plains Vol. 2 *contains many of his
stories.* "A Voice for The Plains" *is excerpted from his March 5,
1986, recording. His oral history humbly represents one person's
way of documenting personal history.*

"YOU KNOW I would put Gerald ahead of high school students today," Slim
said. "He was a smart man—self-taught in many ways. He learned to scale
timber on his own. He had bookkeeping skills you wouldn't believe. You
figure all the boats he had, and he had a gas pump on the dock, a hotel and
sporting camp, an ice cream parlor, a taxi service, his truck that he hauled
things in for hire, and he had the horses—with the cost of the upkeep, vets'
services, the hay and everything—just his taxes alone were a mathematician's
nightmare, but he handled it all right here [Slim pointed to his head]. He
used to joke, 'That damn Underwood typewriter of mine spells terrible.'

"Wellington and Gerald were very well read. They could start a conversation on most any subject. When I lived with Gerald, we subscribed to 23
different magazines and it was to our advantage to be 'world wise' with our
different patrons that came to Otter Brook Camp. Gerald had many wealthy
people in camp and seemed to hold his own in conversations with them.

418

"I remember Wellington telling of Governor Black, while in office, bringing parties to his place along the south branch of the Moose River. Lieutenant-governor Timothy Woodruff was Black's aide. Black was a man of the people. A story that circulated then was when an orderly at the state capitol saw Governor Black coming along the corridor he sprang to open the door to the executive chamber but before he could grab hold of the handle the governor had reached over him and pulled the door open with the remark: 'You need not open the door for me. I am just as able as ever to open doors for myself. There is no reason why you should. I am no better than ordinary mortals because of being elected governor.'

"From what I've heard, Black distanced himself from ceremonial frills and formalities usually regarded as part of the honors that belong to high official positions.

"Governor Black enjoyed outdoor activities. I imagine that because Wellington was such an outstanding woodsman and trapper and because Gerald followed in his father's footsteps with those qualities, and because they were so well-rounded, many prominent people enjoyed listening to them tell about their youths and their knowledge about deer conditions.

"The stories are true about how Wellington spent some of his spare time reading the classics and looking up any word he didn't know in a huge dictionary that came into his Plains boarding house with a wagon-load of supplies from the railroad depot at North Creek.

"It's also said of him that if you gave him a passage from the Bible, he'd tell you the chapter and verse; if you read the first line of 'Thanatopsis,' he'd recite the rest from memory; if you mentioned an Adirondack lake, he'd tell you who surveyed it first and when. He was an ascetic pioneer who neither chewed nor smoked tobacco, nor drank.

OPPOSITE: **Slim absorbed stories about the early, older guides like Frank "Pop" Baker, Giles Becraft and Eddie Robertson from Wellington and Gerald Kenwell. Baker, Giles and Robertson were topnotch guides at Amazia Dutton Barber's Forest Lodge at Jock's Lake, renamed Honnedaga when the Adirondack League Club acquired the property in 1892. As time passed, League members learned of Louie Seymour and wanted to meet him. Harvey L. Dunham wrote in** *Adirondack French Louie: Early Life in the North Woods,* **that Louie took "pride in being an owner of a place that attracted the honest and unpretentious people. It was character and decency that Louie recognized and respected, and he could quickly distinguish that from any affectation based on money alone."** *Courtesy of Winfred Murdock*

"Wellington's wife Eliza had her own skills. She was apparently a nurse and doctor by intuition. She once fixed an injured guest with two broken ribs and a fractured collar bone so effectively that when he finally arrived at an Albany hospital, doctors didn't even have to reset the bones.

Group at "Dut" Barber's Forest Lodge on Jock's Lake: Mrs. Barber on the porch. Left to right: Andy Carmen, Frank Baker, the Carmen sisters, Eddie Robertson, Giles Becraft, and A. Dutton Barber. Baker was once the head guide at Forest Lodge.
Courtesy of Edward Blankman (The Lloyd Blankman Collection)

"Camp guests enjoyed hearing about The Plains in the early days. Gerald would tell how his father hunted with dogs during the meat market days. Wellington claimed a good dog could bring down a deer in five minutes but that practice had been discontinued by the time he was operating his sportsman's home business. Gerald never hunted with dogs. He shot his first buck when he was eight years old.

"Gerald's Otter Brook Camp patrons were free to enjoy hunting, if they wished, from what he called a 'camp-hunt,' meaning hunters were free to come and go without regard to hours for meals.

"Always of interest was the discovery of a cannon while walking along the Totten Crossfield Line, and not far from it was a wooden marker carved with 'Old Cuss died here.'

Frank Baker. There were three woodsmen whose lives were as much a part of the West Canada and Moose River country as the very ponds, rocks and trees—Louie Seymour, Johnny Leaf and Frank Baker. In 1905, on the recommendation of Wellington Kenwell, Charles Chapin hired Baker to be the caretaker-guide of Camp Nit on Beaver Lake. It was at Camp Nit that he gained the nickname of "Pop." Each year during his long employment he received $350 in crisp new five-dollar bills. *Courtesy of Edward Blankman (The Lloyd Blankman Collection)*

"It's been years since I worked back on The Plains, but each year as sap starts to run I think back. Ice break-up varied from year to year. Some years when I snowshoed in to Otter Brook Camp I'd cross the streams and rivers on ice, other times I waded. I often forded the Moose at Chapin's Crossing just past Wellington's old place," Slim continued. "Gerald had a wagon road all the way to the Otter. I always took pack horses or a wagon but still carried things on my back. There was always something more to take in. Very rarely I ever went in without a pack basket. You know there were some things we wouldn't put in a wagon. For instance, what would you do with eggs?

The east end of the Indian Clearing, circa 1890s. *Courtesy of Edward Blankman*
(The Lloyd Blankman Collection)

"..now back at Kenwell's Crossing [Slim frequently interchanged that reference with Chapin's Crossing when talking about the same ford across the south branch of the Moose River] I used to grab ahold of Pinto's [his favorite horse] tail on the downwind side and let him pull me across when the water was high. That river could come up six-or eight feet in a matter of a few hours. It was real swift one.

OPPOSITE: **A party of sportsmen from Barber's on Jock's Lake, led by Eddie Robinson, are on their way to the West Canada country and Louie Seymour's camp.** *Courtesy of Edward Blankman*
(The Lloyd Blankman Collection)

"Geraldine, Gerald's daughter, named Pinto because of his markings—his white feet and white flash on his forehead. Sometimes I'd call him Dynamite because there were a few times he damn near killed me. I loved that horse. He was like a part of the family. There were a lot of times and places you couldn't ride because of the trees back there. It wasn't open like it is now.

Giles Becraft, one of the more famous of the Adirondack guides (second from left). The Adirondack League Club kept a roster of fifteen to twenty guides on call, and Giles was one of the best of them. This quiet and unassuming man died suddenly of a heart attack on the Piseco Lake road in 1893 at the age of 43. Chapter 30. "Grandpa Giles and Grandma Maggie Becraft's Mountain Home" in *Adirondack Camp Stories* by William J. O'Hern (In the Adirondacks, 2017) tells about Becraft's life. *Courtesy of Edward Blankman (The Lloyd Blankman Collection)*

"… I brought a lot of loads into Beaver Lake for Chapin's camp too. A normal load for our horse was about 150 pounds. We loaded old Army canvas packs.

424

"Gerald maintained a six-week program: two weeks cutting wood for fall, two weeks trapping and two weeks for making maple syrup. Weather decided the order of the plans. Sometime the sap run would be before and sometimes after the beaver trapping season.

"When Gerald was growing up on The Plains there was plenty of work for man and child. Gardening took a lot of time and hard work as the tools were crude and often needed repair. Hay for the livestock was not plentiful and had to be gathered from many places. The Kenwell homestead had a barn for the cattle, horses and sheep. It's also where they stored the hay. There were guided fishing parties in spring and summer and hunters in fall. I remember complaints about a three-month hunting season.

"My duties for Gerald varied. Animal care, building repairs, clearing the tote trail, maintenance of harnesses, wagons, jumpers and so forth took lots of time.

"During my time, there was an unwritten 'law' of the woods that cabin doors were never locked. A vacant camp was used by anyone for emergencies or overnight stops. It was the custom to 'lay a fire when leaving, and bedding was to be hung back up, clean used dishes cleaned and if there was spare food to leave some, as well as replenish the firewood supply. Coming into a vacant camp in cold weather it was nice to be able to just light a match and start a fire in the stove. There were a number of people who used Gerald's Red River Halfway Camp (see *The Adirondacks' Moose River Plains, Volumes 2* and *3*) in that way. I remember when Gerald sold the place to the 'Hart Gang.' They were known as the Red River Hunting Club. I knew some of the Hart family from Solvey. The original members were okay, but others came in afterwards and gave the place a bad name.

"Here's something I just remembered. There was a so-called post office back on The Plains. It was really a forked pine tree that was used for mail in my time, located just before Wellington's old place. Letters were left there for Camp Nit at Beaver Lake, Joe Broker's camp on Squaw Lake, Otter Brook and Dick Chambers camp. (Dick later became quite an outlaw and was run out of the country.)

"Being Gerald's packer who went back and forth between Otter Brook Camp and Inlet, I would pick up mail from that tree going out to Inlet and leave mail there coming in. Sometimes letters and packages came to Beaver Lake by plane to go to Otter Brook Camp and they were left at the tree for me to pick up.

Wellington Kenwell stands on the ruins of the Gould Paper Company's upper Red River dam. One story that came out of the last spring log drive on the Red had to do with dynamite used to blow the ice on the river to start the logs downstream. The incident is recorded in *Calked Shoes: Life in Adirondack Lumber Camps* by Barbara K. Bird (Prospect Books, 1952). "April 8th—Bill's little dog mistook some dynamite for what he supposed to be a stick thrown out on the ice for him to retrieve. He ran with it toward his frantic master. The dog was blown to pieces and Bill was stunned by the explosion." *Courtesy of Ora Kenwell*

"Sometime, but not often, mail was also left at another tree located by the forks where the Kenwell Road split by Governor's Brook for Mitchell Ponds and camps down the Red River. Of course all that has changed now. There used to be a lot of camps along that route: Tin Cup Creek, Governor's Brook, several down Red River, Balsam Lodge Valley, Bear Brook, Sumner, Big Plains, and many others that I delivered mail and supplies to.

"Tote roads were tough on jumpers, wagons and horse shoes. I often had to set shoes on the pack horses and at different times Gerald had drivers

OPPOSITE: **"French" Louie Seymour. "Hard as Laurentian granite and tough as Adirondack spruce." —Harvey L. Dunham.** *Courtesy of Edward Blankman (The Lloyd Blankman Collection)*

that couldn't set a shoe and I would come by and find them stalled along the trail and have to set it for them. Sometimes a wagon wheel would break or a part of the wagon bed. Those situations called for a bit of ingenuity to get the wagon to the end of the trip.

"Charles Chapin [owner of Beaver Lake] used Wellington and Gerald as guides—in fact there wasn't much he could do without them. Businessman Chapin, away from his office, was helpless in the woods. He needed a nursemaid continuously. In my time, Chapin had fishing parties in spring, family parties in the summer and hunters in the fall use Camp Nit.

"One time Wellington said when he came into Camp Nit he heard some awful screaming and hollering back of the camp. When he went to investigate, he said all the noise was coming from Chapin teaching a couple of his nephews how to still hunt!"

Wellington Kenwell, in addition to being an outstanding woodsman, was well-rounded educationally. *Courtesy of Ora Kenwell*

"Here's something that really burns me today. Why do you suppose hams and bacon were smoked? This was the way of preserving meat. They're not smoked today. The first thing you read today is smoke flavor and water added, keep refrigerated. That proves it's not the real thing. Years ago my family had their own smokehouse, did their own butchering. Where the hell can you get real smoke-cured ham nowadays? We didn't have any refrigeration up at Otter—just natural cold storage.

Gerald Kenwell loading a deer. Over the years, Louie Seymour packed hundreds of hides to Newton Corners (Speculator today). They were traded or sold at hotels, stores or fur buyers. After a period of time deer became so hard to come by around Newton Corners that natives traveled as far as the Indian Clearing to get deer meat for their personal needs. *Courtesy of Ora Kenwell*

"...Ike Blair used to get a lot of bobcats in his traps back there. He and Bob West were big bobcat trappers. Blair trapped mostly along the Red River down to Rock Dam. I knew Ike well. I liked him. He was a good rifle shot. Jim Meneilly's father had a camp down there too. There were three boys and a girl. Ann Meneilly was a beautiful girl. Harry drowned in Fifth Lake, and then there was Jimmy and another boy—I don't recall his name right now. The family was always good to me...."

429

Slim sketched a diagram of the layout of Otter Brook camp site and talked about the various positions of things. "This is where the water pump was," he pointed out, "and directly back from it, up on the top of the bank is where the root cellar was located." Both areas are still visible today. "Now let's say this is the kitchen part of the camp, the cook shack. It was right on the edge of the hill…and right here was the second story. This is the original part built in 1914. The stove was right here. Then there was a small table here where he kept cookies and bread, where we ate.

Winfred "Slim" Murdock and Pinto, his favorite pack horse. *Courtesy of Winfred Murdock*

OPPOSITE: **Winfred C. "Slim" Murdock shows the author Billy Buckshot's snowshoes he kept as a memory of the Inlet guide's life and tragic death. Slim absorbed stories about the early, older guides like Frank "Pop" Baker, Giles Becraft and Eddie Robertson from Wellington and Gerald Kenwell. Baker, Giles and Robertson were topnotch guides at Amazia Dutton Barber's Forest Lodge at Jock's Lake, renamed Honnedaga when the Adirondack League Club acquired the property in 1892. As time passed, League members learned of Louie Seymour and wanted to meet him. Harvey L. Dunham wrote in *Adirondack French Louie: Early Life in the North Woods*, that Louie took "pride in being an owner of a place that attracted the honest and unpretentious people. It was character and decency that Louie recognized and respected, and he could quickly distinguish that from any affectation based on money alone."** *Author's photo*

431

"Right over the door there were two boxes labeled incoming and outgoing mail. That was where anybody who wanted to send anything out would put it. You know if somebody wanted mail to go out or needed me to buy them booze, it was also my message box. Sometimes I wouldn't get in there 'til 10 or 11 o'clock at night. Everybody would be in bed. If I'd read there was a buck to pick up at Squaw Lake early the next morning because a hunter wanted it taken out to Thendara the next afternoon to catch the train, then okay, I knew what I had to do…. There was a breezeway between the two camps and here is where we had bunks, a table and a radio…then there was the chunk stove and a bigger table where we played poker…."

Slim continued explaining in minute detail the horse barn, nearby lean-to, the privy, and Gerald's sap evaporator. Beyond that he drew the location of another two-story building. That was built later. "A trail climbed up the ridge behind the new camp and worked its way down to the Moose River. Then about four to five hundred feet from the camp was a garden in a large clearing above the main camp. Old Billy Williams, he lived on the island at Sixth Lake. He was probably all of eighty years old, he used to walk in, then spend the rest of the day working in the garden for Gerald. Then beyond the garden we had another trail that went over to Wolf Lake. It was just a footpath but marked real well…."

Slim's explanations of the layout continued, but I think the illustration provided offers a clear representation of the camp complex for the curious who choose to hike to Kenwells' just to see the site.

There was no chronological organization when I interviewed Slim. His taped reminiscences range from the time he was a young boy to Sunday, November 25, 1950, when he and his son were caught in the woods during the devastating hurricane. The temperature dropped down to zero that night…. I was with my son heading to Otter Brook. We managed to get to the Moose River and I knew we weren't going to go any farther. I began stuffing the inside of my shirt with as much birch bark as I could peel off.

"My son questioned, 'you must be thinking of building an awfully big fire.' I told him I ain't going to tell you, you just got to wait and see. There's so much woodcraft you can't tell a guy, you got to show 'em. So the spot I was looking for was a big gravel bar that had a good-size boulder by the bank right along the Moose River. Well, we built ourselves a fire and that was the night I taught him how important is was to keep warm using the reflective heat from the fire and a big beached drift log we muscled in to create a shelter no bigger than the length of a coffin. Well, we had warm ground and sides. It became very clear to my son that night how important it was to be resourceful, to stay warm and to always keep one's back warm because that's where your kidneys are and they are most sensitive to heat and cold. An old-time hillbilly trick said always sleep with your back to the fire so this is what we did...."

A party of campers on Camp Nit's observation deck. Charles Chapin, is the fourth from the left. *Courtesy of Margaret Wilcox (The Camp Nit Collection)*

Slim said, "Otter Brook Camp wasn't damaged at all" by the great storm, "but over at Beaver Lake was another story. Beaver Lake was more or less open; Gerald's place was in a deep, protected valley. There are big ledges —well anyway... let me tell you about some bodies I carried out of the woods..." and before Slim could take a breath he was off on another tangent. "Now Gerald had a great joke, well to me it was a joke. First-time

433

hunters that came in would ask, 'Where are all your guides?' He'd say, 'We don't have any guides, it takes too much trouble to hunt them up at night. All right, now here is an example. Here are these three ridges...''

Slim would illustrate Gerald's methods of insisting his hunter know how to read a map and compass, then be able to follow Gerald's instructions to go out from camp four or five miles along a well-defined foot trail or wagon road, and only then begin to hunt back toward camp. "Then they wouldn't get so doggone tired."

After the removal of Camp Nit's observation deck, Charles Chapin hired the Kenwells to build this sunroom. In volume 2, Slim Murdock tells the story of the injury Gerald Kenwell sustained when he was contracted by the camp owner to relocate this addition to the east side of the camp. *Courtesy of Tom Gates*

Slim questioned immediately offered what one well-heeled long-time client who regularly hired Gerald to guide him in Canada and Alaska did when he came to camp. "Well, how in hell can anyone with any common sense get lost? he'd begged. Well, Johnny Bates, who owned a Packard dealership who came for years out of Pennsylvania, what he'd do is cut just the center section out of West Canada map and glue it onto a piece of cardboard covered with plastic and carry it in his breast pocket. Bates wouldn't live without it. Now he wasn't a woodsman, but he had sense enough to know where the streams flowed and the Otter Brook went into the Moose, and he'd either have to go across the Chapin Crossing or come back across the Otter Brook Crossing…he wasn't an outdoorsman but he had the reasoning… Gerald never really took people out. Only once in a while to get them started…."

Hours of voice recordings provide interesting listening but do not always result in substantial material. Slim was a man who had a far-reaching wealth of information. He could tell you about what makes the best scotch whiskey; his depth of knowledge on types and function of firearms was encyclopedic; the man was a fearless ironworker ("You never look past the beam you're walking on."); he did a bit of rodeoing and trick shooting; and through Gerald's careful training he became an expert in explosives.

Slim illustrated: "One of the tests Uncle Gerald gave me was right at the end of Sixth Lake Dam. There used to be a place right there called the station house. Well, right near there was a large flat rock as big as an easy chair—it wasn't more than 50 to 75 feet away from the house. He says, 'I got to go down to Old Forge. While I'm gone see what you can do with that rock. The dynamite is over there inside the garage.' Well, by the time he got back that rock was gone and Gerald was pleased that the blast didn't even crack the windows in the dam house."

Slim was talented in countless other ways, but his stories that focused on The Plains were what most interested me. My ears would perk up when Slim said something like, "You take Dick Chambers, he was one of two cases of thievery I know of back in the woods. He was an outlaw who had a camp along the lower portion of Otter Brook down closer to the Moose." His remembrances zapped social history into the otherwise obvious forest and mountains and bodies of water.

"Chambers had a place right after you pass The Plains and cross the Otter where there is a draw. He kept a back trail from there to Squaw Lake. He'd kill a deer and just take enough for a meal. He'd also bust into camps in the spring, and during the winter when he knew nobody was occupying their place. He'd take whatever he wanted and move on. Leave the camp door open so porcupine could get in and everything else.

"Well, we finally run him out of the country. The day he left, Joe Jenkins was the game warden down in Thendara. Gerald and I planned to meet Jenkins at Beaver Lake when packing in supplies and groceries for Allen Wilcox. Well, unknowingly we must have really been hot on Chambers's heels. To show you how close we were, Chambers had just broken into Camp Nit, the door had been left flung open and his gun and pack had been left behind in his haste to get out of Dodge. We figured he shot off toward the lumber camps over by the Indian [River]. He had broken into camps all the way from Rock Dam, Delmarsh's camp, up to Otter Brook, Beaver Lake, and all over hell and we came that close to catching him in the act.

Slim Murdock holds one of Gerald Kenwell's deer rifles. Slim's memories, like those of so many other contributors, have helped to preserve the informal history of the Moose River Plains. *Author's photo*

"And another party of Syrians, they operated a packing house in Utica, they used to camp at Governor Brook where the bridge is now. Well, the original trail crossed and continued through the woods and then dipped down to the Red River. Well, right at that corner, on that little flat past Governor Brook, they used to tent right there—about three tents in a row. They all owned shotguns and shot at everything that moved, rabbits, squirrels, birds, everything. They'd hunt with pack baskets and anything they shot was tossed into the packs.

"Now up at the Halfway Camp, right across the Red [River], Roy Perkins couldn't get his partner to come with him one year so he got his wife to come along. The Perkinses were camped back there not all that far from the Syrians' camp. Well Roy was hunting downriver when he shot at a deer and wounded the animal. So he and his wife were tracking it and just about where the Gould's old dam was, they came up on the buck along with the gang of Syrians all armed with shotguns around the animal. "That's our deer," they snarled. What's Roy and his wife going to do in that situation? Well they went back to camp and they passed the word around to me, when I was going into camp, and they told a few other parties and about twenty armed hunters got together and paid those Syrians a visit. Well, those people were smart enough to know to get when the going was good. They vacated camp leaving pretty much everything they owned. What was left we burned. All they had was their guns, their own hides and the fear of a mob.

"Now Gerald and I, we never saw any reason to take illegal deer out of season unless we really needed it—and then we never wasted a bit, but then there was this gang that took over the Halfway Camp;[37] we believed some of those guys made a business of it. They would invite friends in there and make sure each one went home with a deer. In fact, they'd guarantee them a deer because they already had the deer hanging up…"

The remembrances of Slim and oodles of other old-timers do not constitute a formal history of The Plains. On the other hand, their remembrances provide factual information that helps shape a societal record of times gone by.

Numerous accounts of Slim's memories are found in *The Moose River Plains, Vol. 2.*

Chapter Thirty-Two

A Modern-day Visit to Otter Brook Camp

THE LOW MOUNTAINS are quiet in winter. Black bears are in their winter dens, most birds have migrated southward, and during one time I snowshoed along Otter Brook, I thought how quiet and peaceful it must have seemed to Gerald to be living alone so far back from the hamlet of Inlet, N.Y.

A gathering of curious hunters at the site of Otter Brook Camp, November 2018. Left to Right: Don Townsend, Shawn Hansen, and John Townsend. *Author's photo*

I know winter was not a lean time because Gerald always cached a ready stock of food in a root cellar below the kitchen floor. Vestiges of the earthen storage room can still be seen once one identifies the sections of laid-up perimeter stone walls.

It was there, in 1917, that Gerald built his hunting camp complex, known as Otter Brook Camp. He lived alone most of his life at this camp, 17 miles from the nearest highway. From the camp he guided hunting and fishing parties from as far away as Ohio, Pennsylvania, New Jersey and New York City.

Kenwells' is clearly marked as such with three squares on my 1954 West Canada Lake Quadrangle just below the 2,065-foot benchmark in a boulder along an unmarked tractor trail Gerald Kenwell and Len Hardwood used for years. That trail served as a link between the men's camps and as a clearly-marked pathway hunters from their camps struck off on. I found it was once a short cut to Sly Pond. Today I would call it nothing less than a demanding bushwhack.

I've led a number of people back to Gerald's former digs. There's not much to see today. It's not difficult to travel over the unmarked footpath. I've often wondered why the Department of Environmental Conservation doesn't establish marked trails and post historic markers at designated places that were once part of the history of the area.

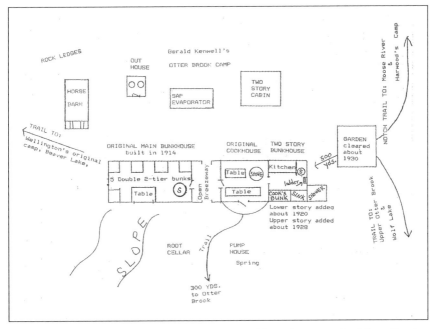

A general location map shows the placement of buildings that comprised Otter Brook Camp. *Drawing by the author based on Slim Murdock's knowledge*

As one enters Kenwell's clearing, the barn would have been on the left. Slim said after long hours of packing in supplies, he would usually catch a whiff of brewed coffee at the barn. *Courtesy Jack Tanck*

Today's Moose River Plains campers use their vacation in a wide variety of ways. The following pictures offer images of what once existed in Kenwells' clearing to make clearer what was there, for each year the remains become harder to find. For those who are interested in seeking out Kenwells', there are enough rusting relics of the past to keep one occupied for a good hour or more as they think about the Mayor of Otter Brook and others who once occupied these mountains.

The ranch house looking east. *Courtesy of Jack Tanck*

OPPOSITE: **The author holds what is left of the evaporator in 1987. Gerald used the same trough technique "French" Louie used to bring maple sap down to camp from the sugar bush on the ridge above Otter Brook Camp.** *Author's photo*

440

The front of the barn. "The horses knew when they were approaching camp," said Slim. *Courtesy of Winfred Murdock*

The stand-alone winter bunkhouse was the last building on the left. This was one of the last additions to Kenwell's complex. *Courtesy of Winfred Murdock*

The sap evaporator was between the outhouse and the winter camp. *Courtesy Winfred Murdock*

443

Gerald Kewell's only contact with the outside world.
Photo by Dante O. Tranquille. Courtesy of Town of Webb Historical Association

The main ranch house looking west. Courtesy of Winfred Murdock

Gerald's cold storage. The rock walls of the cold storage are still visible. The storage pit filled in when the camp was burned following Gerald's death. *Photo by Dante O. Tranquille.* Courtesy Town of Webb Historical Association

In later years Gerald used a small caterpillar in place of pack horses to transport things in and out of camp. Ora sits in the driver's seat. *Courtesy of Ora Kenwell*

Gerald Kenwell's back is to the camera. Slim Murdock said, "Gerald had some special places he would place his special customers. One area a hunter was always assured to see deer was at a place he called The Kindergarten. Another special spot was the stillwater where the Sumner dumped into the Moose [River]. All that swampy area is alder. Well, out in that alder you'll see a little spruce tree poking up. You walk out there and that's where the old wise bucks would hang out. Gerald knew that so if he had a special customer who wanted to go home with deer meat, that's where he'd take him in to get one." Otter Brook valley hold so many more untold stories. *Photo by Dante O. Tranquille.*
Courtesy Town of Webb Historical Association

Woodshed. *Courtesy of Winfred Murdock*

Part Five

Adirondack Mountains

Moose River Plains

CAMP NIT, BEAVER LAKE

The Wilcox's Beaver Lake camp. Harold Scott's float plane is moored at the dock.
Courtesy Margaret Wilcox (The Camp Nit Collection)

447

Charles T. Chapin, original owner of Beaver Lake property. *Courtesy Margaret Wilcox*
(The Camp Nit Collection)

Chapter Thirty-Three

Legalities Surrounded Camp Nit

A LETTER written by an unidentified state agent from Raquette Lake to W.F. Fox at the Forest, Fish, and Game Commission on June 8, 1905 is the first red flag that raised questions about the legality of Charles T. Chapin's ownership claim of his Beaver Lake property. It reads in part:

Dear Sir:

Mr. Wellington Kenwell is putting up a building on Beaver Lake on Lot 81 Township 4 for Mr. Chapin and Senator Lewis. The building is about 80 feet by 40 feet and there are three other small buildings: an ice house, barn, and men's camp all built out of logs. I wrote to Mr. Pond the latter part of March about it and Mr. Pond said that they [New York state] owned Lot 80 and that they claimed the map was not right. Mr. Pond said there would be a survey made. They have cut a lot of timber since and are cutting more right along. The building is about in the middle of Lot 81…

The following response was found among Charles T. Chapin's correspondence:

Rochester, N.Y.
Dec. 11th, 1906

Hon. James S. Whipple, Forest, Fish, & Game Commissioner, Albany, N.Y.

449

My Dear Sir:-

Some time ago, I received a letter from Mr. John K. Ward, attorney, representing your department, in which he called my attention to an alleged trespass and unlawful cutting of timber on State Lands.

I have since been in correspondence with Mr. Ward, and so far, no action has been commenced.

I feel that I should furnish you with a complete statement of the situation, so far as it is within my knowledge, and of my position in order that you may be fully advised of all the facts in the matter.

During the construction period of Camp Nit, Chapin had Wellington Kenwell set up canvas tents for the owner's many camping parties. Guides were provided to cook as well as accompany interested campers on various outings.
Courtesy Margaret Wilcox (The Camp Nit Collection)

In January 1904, or thereabouts, Mr. Geo. N. Ostrander, of Albany, offered to sell to me lot 80, Moose River Tract, Hamilton Co., and named a price therefor. I regarded his price as excessive, and some months elapsed, during which negotiations were continued. In July 1904, we agreed upon a price for the lot.

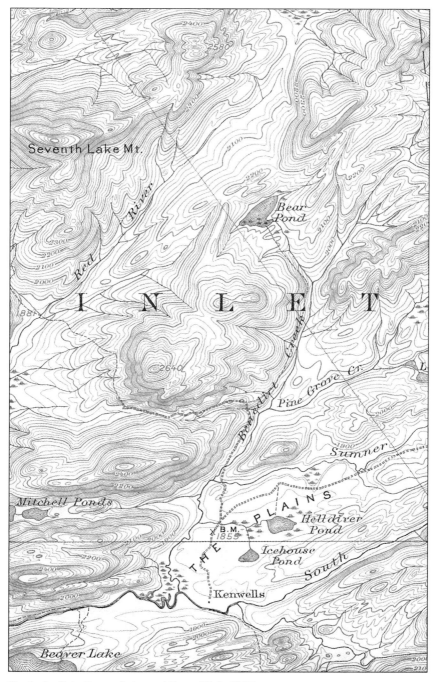

The footpath to Beaver Lake and Camp Nit in 1937. *Courtesy Margaret Wilcox (The Camp Nit Collection)*

451

Roughing it did not mean giving up creature comforts, as this scene of cheerful diners shows. *Courtesy Indian Lake Museum*

Thereafter, acting under the advice of my attorney, and as a precautionary measure, I employed Mr. Theodore C. Remonda, a Civil Engineer, living at Morehouseville, N.Y., and who I understood had done considerable work for the State, and was therefore well-qualified, to make a survey for me of the lot. He made such a survey in the fall of 1904, and on the 14th, day of October, 1904, he wrote me a letter, of which a copy is attached hereto, and forwarded a map, of which I attach a blueprint. Later, in response to some inquiries I made, he wrote me another letter, of which I attach copy.

On the ninth of January, 1905, after the title to the lot had been carefully examined, I paid Mr. Ostranger for the lot, and took his warranty deed thereof. Thereafter I entered upon the land and built my camp thereon, and have since occupied it as a summer camp.

I never had the slightest idea that I was trespassing or encroaching upon State Land, until I received Mr. Ward's letter.

I have spent several thousand dollars in improvements, and every dollar was spent under the supposition that I was the absolute owner of all the land, as shown by the map.

I understand that your department has had a survey made, which shows the lines of the lot differently than it appears on my map, and that I am encroaching.

I do not know what your purpose is in the matter, but I am advised that in similar cases, the differences have been adjusted by agreement. The plan adopted in those cases was, as I understand, for your department to commence an action in trespass; the defendant served an answer, denying the allegations of the complaint; and an agreement was thereafter reached, by which the defendant conveyed land to the State, equivalent in acreage, or value, and a judgment subsequently entered in the action, decreeing the title to the lands described in the complaint to be the defendant's. The decree established the title, as effectively, as would a deed itself.

Family size canvas wall tent at Beaver Lake. Circa 1900. *Courtesy Margaret Wilcox (The Camp Nit Collection)*

Chapin had a mixture of smaller A-style tents and larger family-style size tents.
Courtesy Margaret Wilcox (The Camp Nit Collection)

If you are of the opinion that my map is wrong, and that I am a trespasser, I am willing, for the sake of avoiding expense and trouble, to adopt that course.

I could convey to the State all that part of lot 80, not shown on my map, as you claim, and the decree of the Court could establish my title to all that part of lot 80, as shown on my map, which the department disputes.

In view of the great precautions, which I took before paying my money for the lot, and the unquestionable good faith, with which you must credit me, I feel that the suggestions, which I have made as a way out of the difficulty, are proper, and should be accepted.

I do not want a litigation, and I do not want to be put to the trouble and expense of tearing down my buildings and erecting them somewhere else. I do not know that the land in dispute is any more valuable that the land which I could convey, and an arrangement, such as I have suggested, would, I feel sure, be equitable all-around.

May I ask you to kindly give me your views on the subject, at your early convenience, and greatly oblige.

Yours very truly,
Charles T. Chapin

Since it is known that Chapin did not relocate any of his buildings, we can probably rightly assume that the State of New York accepted his proposal. Margaret and Allen Wilcox provided additional details about this conflict with the State in Chapter 28 "The Story of Beaver Lake."

Charles T. Chapin. Chapin was taken with the solitude and natural beauty of Beaver Lake during his vacations at Kenwell's Sportsman's Home. *Courtesy Margaret Wilcox (The Camp Nit Collection)*

Chapter Thirty-Four

Charles T. Chapin, a Devotee of Out-of-Door Sports

ON A DARK SUNDAY predawn morning on August 2, 1909, Charles T. Chapin,[38] Mr. and Mrs. E.G. Lapham, and Jessie M. Johnson had every reason to relish hiking the Kenwell Trail through the Moose River Plains. The area was a land of deer Chapin had grown to love from his first retreat in the mid-1890s at Kenwell's Sportsman's Home on The Plains. There Chapin wandered the blue-joint and wild-flowered Indian Clearing. He glassed deer in concentrated numbers living less disturbed than in certain localities where butchers hounded them outside of the eyes of the game protector. From Wellington Kenwell, the master of operations of the sporting inn, Chapin learned hunters who still-hunt had less chance to kill a deer than during the days when hounding was legal, but enjoyed the sport of hunting much more as well as gained valuable skills. Kenwell had seen a time when hounders watched every lake, pond, and stream and every deer started by hounds was killed. He quickly grew to be disgusted at the sport of hounding deer.

By July 26, 1905, four years following the closing of Kenwell's business on The Plains, it was Chapin's turn to begin to enjoy a camp life of leisure and recreation in the heart of the Moose River Plains, a few miles distant from the Little Plains where he once had spent many enjoyable vacations. Chapin listed Frank Baker and Wellington Kenwell as his guides who accompanied him to his newly completed camp on Beaver Lake.

Now, four years following his first camping experience, Chapin continued to frequent his wilderness camp most often in the company of a congress of friends and always supported by Kenwell.

Chapin's camp diary described his 1909 itinerary:

The Chapin Party left Rochester, N.Y on "Sunday, August 2 at 3:33 AM. Breakfast at Utica. Boarded train at 7:35 AM. (Arrived at) Fulton Chain to Old Forge. Boat to Inlet. Driver (conveyed us) to Wood's Inn at 1:30 PM. Supper, lodging and breakfast. Wagon to Kenwells at 6th Lake. Arrived at 8 AM. Left 6th Lake 8:30 AM. 11:30 AM lunch at Governor's Brook. Canoe down Moose River from 'Coonville' arriving at Camp at 3 PM. P.S. Saw 1 deer at 'Coonville' and 'Reception Committee' at Beaver Lake consisted of 10 deer, 1 flock ducks, 1 sea gull, 2 loons, 1 hawk and later 1 hoot owl. Guide—Wm Thompson."

Chapin's scenic snapshots of Beaver Lake capture the wild peaceful setting that captured his interest in the land of the deer. Courtesy Margaret Wilcox (The Camp Nit Collection)

June 13, 1916, was the last day Chapin relied on the train to reach camp. By August 10, 1916 the underlined word in his camp entry describes his new means of transportation. The route described continued with very little variation for years.

"Left Rochester Thursday morning at 7 o'clock by <u>automobile</u>. Victor, Clifton Springs, Phelps, Geneva, Waterloo, Auburn, Syracuse, Utica, Fulton Chain, Old Forge to Woods Hotel, Inlet; arrived 5:30 PM. Supper, lodging (Mr. Trotter's) and breakfast; auto to Lime Kiln Lake. 2 horses to pack and 1 horse to ride. Left Lime Kiln Lake at 9:20 AM. Arrived at Camp 4:20 PM. Clear, warm day. 1 deer and 2 loons in lake. 4 rabbits and 'flock' of coons (2 old/7 young) at camp."

Camping in the Adirondacks was a tranquil break from Chapin's business life. He was always accompanied by a guide. The duffle was put on pack horses or loaded into a wagon and carried over the 12 miles. Each person had something to carry in pack baskets appropriate to their size and strength.

Members of the party were met by a man who knew how to cook good things for hungry arrivals. One specialty enjoyed by all consisted of bread and butter with cooked venison between the slices and fried cakes, all of which were warmed and toasted over a large wood-burning kitchen range.

The *Mohegan* steamer, formally named the *Fulton* after 1901. Chapin's camp scrapbook records many aspects of camp life. This steamer was one of many he would have taken from Old Forge to Inlet up until he began driving a motorcar. Unfortunately, most photos lack captions that would have added to the history of Chapin's camp ownership.
Courtesy Tom Gates (The Camp Nit Collection)

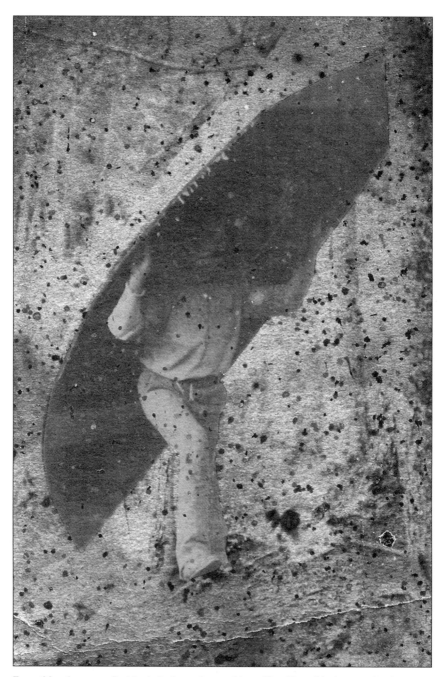

Everything from small objects to large heavy things like this guide boat arrived at Camp Nit by horse or was carried by guides. *Courtesy Margaret Wilcox (The Camp Nit Collection)*

Leaving camp to return home was never easy for the owner and guests who left parting words in two Camp Nit journals that spanned 34 years.

I love the fish. I love the deer but oh your "pan-cakes." —Anna Clarke Benson July 19, 1909

"We think our host gets his pleasure out of life by making others happy." —Unknown writer

Horseback party at Chapin's Crossing at the south branch of the Moose River. The blazed trail that served as a canoe portage which passed Kenwell's Sportsman's Home and led to Chapin's Crossing is no longer maintained by the Department of Environmental Conservation. *Courtesy Margaret Wilcox (The Camp Nit Collection)*

"The outing OH! The outing in the woods to our friend Chapin's camp called '<u>Nit</u>' was one that did the whole being good. Such complete <u>rest</u> and every day a day of pleasure. Fishing, canoeing, walking, and the beautiful table—oh! Your <u>Brook Trout</u> and <u>Fish Balls</u> and the sight of the Deer each day on Beaver Lake made a picture that our memory will look back for all time as one of the <u>best</u> 8 days of <u>rest</u> and pleasure, and our wish is that Charlie may live long to enjoy his camp and give his friends a new lease of life filled with the Balsam air, which seems to be one of his aims in life—long may Charlie live, so say we all of us." —Matt Reilly, Edgar Lewis, Chris Brown June 4 to 11, 1911

"Fine time. Good fishing. Some flies but not as many as usual. Newspaper and letter received from Gerald Kenwell." —C.T.C.

"We are eating like a horse, Sleeping like a top.
Having such a Jolly Time We hate to have it stop."
—Wm. S. Riley and Chars. J. Brown, June 9 to 20, 1912

Outfitted in the accepted hunting attire of the day, four want-to-be deer hunters show the photographer what they'll do when they spot a prize buck. *Courtesy Tom Gates (The Camp Nit Collection)*

OPPOSITE: **Camp Nit had its own collection of rifles for arrivals who didn't bring their own.** *Courtesy Tom Gates (The Camp Nit Collection)*

"To Our Host Chas. T. Chapin: If we could pour out the nectar that Chapin can, we would fill our glasses to the brim and wish best success to that Chapin man and Camp Nit which is run as best he can with all the Jokes that was told and the Laughs that was laughed. We would fill up our glasses of joy again and all told a story new and tan at the fireside in the cabin of Camp Nit. And when he invited us all to return next year, we all accepted with one '<u>good big round cheer</u>.' For we lived <u>free from care and harmony</u> all the time at Camp Nit in the good old summer time." —Wm Riley, Charles Owen, Chas. Brown, E.S. Osborne, Friday, June 27, 1913

Beaver Lake offered a variety of recreation activities. *Courtesy Tom Gates (The Camp Nit Collection)*

"Just a few words, to thank you for the past eight days so pleasantly spent at Camp Nit. And also for the many favors extended by you and Frank Baker. My greatest wish is that you may continue to enjoy your future as well as I have the past eight days." —J.A. Sheehan Nov.16, 1916.

"Camp Nit, whose windows frame a million dollar picture of 'God's Country. In appreciation" —Mr. and Mrs. Frederic Dewey and Dana Blackman, Dog "Eukra" Sept. 17, 1919

☆ ☆ ☆

Of all the sporting activities Charley enjoyed 'roughing it' Chapin-fashion in the Adirondacks as one of his favorites.

Empties made the ideal target for further enjoyment. *Courtesy Tom Gates (The Camp Nit Collection)*

Refined and connected socially as he was, Charley enjoyed a good meal. French snails—escargots de Bourgogne—and red head duck were not beyond his palate, but when at Camp Nit at Beaver Lake he dined on ruffed grouse, trout, and venison, all legally-taken and prepared by his caretaker-cook, Frank Baker.

There were many differences between camp owner and camp caretaker. The latter was a life-time woodsman. Baker would not hesitate to get a piece of deer meat in April. Natives didn't go around advertising it, however, but slipped the meat into an ice house, or salted it down and consumed it when no one was around to tell the game constable.

Chapin took no spring deer, nor did he approve of seeking wild meat illegally (and unsportsmans-like) by floating, hounding, or jack-lighting[39] deer. He learned all about annihilating the game from his host, Wellington Kenwell, during the years Chapin stayed at Kenwell's sporting camp. Kenwell told stories about "murdering city hawks," a local expression that stood for sports who would come into the Adirondacks to senselessly bang away at wildlife, and tell tales about how beautifully their dogs worked at decimating the game. Neither did Chapin shoot chickadees, like Kenwell and Baker's old friend, French Louie. Instead he enjoyed a solitary woods life that included legal hunting and fishing, drinking whiskey, smoking cigars, playing cards, and reading his favorite sportsman's papers.

Caretaker Frank Baker is giving some final advice to first-time anglers.
Courtesy Tom Gates (The Camp Nit Collection)

Chapin maintained, "roughing it in the mountains is an ideal vacation," and he enjoyed playing host at his Camp Nit in the Adirondacks.

☆ ☆ ☆

Beaver Lake is one of my favorite camp sites. From the shore of the lake I have bushwhacked in every direction, investigating locations I first learned about by reading entries in the Camp Nit journal. I have scouted the property, finding small dumps of flattened #10 cans, and broken rum and beer bottles. Air bubbles in the glass and the thickness of the bottles put them from plus or minus 1920 to the late 1800s. I never tire of paddling the lake and following the outlet to where it enters the Indian River,

nor of thinking back to the time when the log camp Chapin hired Wellington to build was a congenial camp that played host to so many family
members and visitors. It has been my great fortune to acquire a large box
of Chapin family photos and Camp Nit's journal and guest register.

**Fishing the deep holes at Squaw Lake. Gerald Kenwell blazed a trail that connected
Beaver Lake to Squaw Lake, where a simple dock and boats were stored. In the 1980s
the author still found traces of the path.** *Courtesy Tom Gates (The Camp Nit Collection*

The following description comes from a 1924 article that appeared in
the *Rochester Democrat and Chronicle* for which Chapin supplied photos
and material that tells why he felt camping was a real pleasure.

"Camp life is what you make it," stated Charles T. Chapin.
"There is no running around camp unless everyone is congenial
and willing to follow the crowd in whatever is on tap for the
particular time."

Chapin had no doubt about his style of camp life. Charley owned a large preserve in the Adirondacks with a good-sized lake in the center. He said, "My camp has been visited by men well-known in public life: County Court Judge Willis K. Gillette, District Attorney William F. Love, Park Commissioner William S. Riley, Mayor Van Zandt and others have visited the camp nearly every year for some time."

Camp Nit, as he named the sprawling lakeside lodge, was a typical log-built Adirondack camp complete with a sleeping porch and observation deck that was built on piles out over the lakeshore. It contained a large living room and several small bedrooms. The kitchen, caretaker's room and guides' quarters were attached with an open breezeway typical of the lumber camps of the day. In back of the guides' quarters were the wood shed and a storage room.

The log dock was one of the first improvements built since camp life centered around the lake. The dock served as a mooring for boats that were carried in from Limekiln Lake, and for swimming and fishing. Numerous snapshots indicate the dock was used daily for camping vacations. *Courtesy Tom Gates (The Camp Nit Collection)*

Frank Baker, Camp Nit's guide and caretaker, was a typical Adirondack character. Frank lived at the camp year-round. He carried his provisions in during the fall months and during the winter spent his time making necessary repairs and building additions. His main occupation, however, was chopping wood. The large wood pile Charley always saw at the rear

468

of the camp each spring when he descended the slope to the lake was the result of Frank's winter efforts.

Chapin's Camp Nit photo album. *Courtesy Tom Gates (The Camp Nit Collection)*

Camp Nit was about twelve miles from a passable automobile road that ended at Limekiln Lake outside of Inlet, N.Y. Provisions had to be carried in by pack horse or light wagon. The best time that can be made by horse and wagon is two miles an hour. Chapin said, "The camp is reached quicker by walking. Mrs. Chapin visits the camp every year, and I swear 99% of the time she walked the entire distance while some of the camp's visitors rode in on horses. Only a breath of the clear air in the Adirondacks is needed to give anyone strength to hike to camp."

There were a number of private camps in the Fulton Chain of the central Adirondack wilderness when he commissioned Wellington Kenwell to organize and begin construction of the camp. Chapin did not want a beautiful vacation retreat. He only wanted to be back from the main roads. "The camps on main routes of travel are fine," Chapin claimed, "but the ideal camp is where one can eat dinner without dressing in dinner clothes." His many guests heartily agreed with him on that.

1916 marked the year Charles Chapin began to drive to Inlet. "Left Rochester on Tuesday morning June 13, 1916 at 9 AM. Lunch at Utica train. Fulton Chain to Old Forge. Boat to Inlet arriving at 6 PM. Wood's Hotel supper, lodging and breakfast. Auto from Woods to Lime Kiln Lake. Two horses to ride and two horses to pack. Left Lime Kiln at 8:20 AM and arrived at camp at 2:20 PM. Wednesday, June 14th, Flag Day. Warm day. 3 loons and 1 deer in lake. Trail to Moose River full of wind fall. Very few flies. Saw deer on Big Plains, 2 jack rabbits and two coons at camp, [illegible] hawks and 1 flying squirrel."
—W.W. Hizzard, C.T. Chapin, Wm. S. Riley, Willis K. Gillette. *Courtesy Tom Gates (The Camp Nit Collection)*

Lloyd Culver, one of Chapin's good friends who owned several small camps near Fourth Lake, reported snow at his camp during Memorial Day 1924. This was unusual for the Adirondacks, although Chapin remembered driving through snow drifts and over ice on the roads in Tupper Lake in the middle of May in 1917! He claimed this is one reason why the Adirondacks became so popular. The mountains are cool in summer, when the cities are unbearable. Blankets are always comfortable in the extreme parts of the central Adirondacks. The more southern points are not quite so cool in the evening, but they are indeed comfortable. One never suffers any discomfort from a campfire in the evening.

Frank Baker, caretaker-guide stands by Camp Nit. *Courtesy Margaret Wilcox (The Camp Nit Collection)*

For the uninitiated Camp Nit guest, one of the great surprises waiting the visitors was their first campfire. Chapin said, "The evening campfire is the social event of the mountain camp. In the main camp's living room is the massive stone fireplace, but there are also outdoor campfires by the lake. Sitting around a roaring campfire, the tales of the day's hunting and fishing trips were told and the story contests were held. The stories were usually 'The Big One That Got Away,' or 'I would have had that buck if that tree had not been in the way before he turned.'

The campfire was the gathering place of true friends and companions, where song and story entertained until eyelids started to droop, which is usually in the mountain country after a hard day of hunting or fishing. There is no rest like a night's sleep in the chill clear air of the Adirondacks, and I find that as true today as in the days when Charles T. Chapin was a devotee of outdoor life.

Chapin identified this stand-alone cabin as "The guides camp built in 1900."
Courtesy Tom Gates (The Camp Nit Collection)

472

**Wellington Kenwell's cabin was built under towering pines east of Camp Nit.
It commanded a scenic view of Beaver Lake.** *Courtesy Tom Gates (The Camp Nit Collection)*

Empty liquor bottles were saved for target practice. *Courtesy Tom Gates (The Camp Nit Collection)*

Chapter Thirty-Five

Chapin 'Roughed It' in the Mountains

BACK IN 1892, and even by 1898 when Charles Chapin was vacationing at Kenwells on The Plains, "camping out" for many outers consisted of challenging recreation. The roads into the mountains were bad. Provisions were kept to a minimum to cut down on weight, and food was basic: slap-jacks flipped on a hot cast-iron griddle, bacon, saleratus[40] bread, milk-less tea, and wild game. Fried trout and boiled and fried venison were staples. The backwoods offered limited possibilities, for ablutions and shelters were often rudimentary camps, most often quickly-built, three-sided, open-faced lean-tos fashioned from poles, brush, and hemlock bark, entirely open in front, and about two feet high in the rear. The floors were of fresh hemlock boughs, which served as a bed. Pillow ticking stuffed with moss served as a cushioned headrest.

Charles Chapin might have felt that all well and fine for youthful, vigorous sportsmen and women with unimpaired digestion, but from a city-bred sportsman's point-of-view, he preferred a more comfy, pleasing outdoor life style.

At Kenwells, guests avoided the formality of Mr. and Mrs. as well as the familiarity of each other's Christian names. Thus, it was there that Chapin's handle—"Chapes" originated.

Arriving with his fishing and hunting outfits, Chapin enjoyed Eliza Kenwell's sumptuous dinners. Few hosts cooked meals as well. Corned venison, rice, and hot rolls are only examples of the items she prepared. Over the years, Wellington Kenwell developed a close friendship with Chapin.

OPPOSITE: **Two members of a party bound for Beaver Lake pose for a picture along the trail that crossed the Indian Clearing.** *Courtesy Tom Gates (The Camp Nit Collection)*

This undated faded letter to Chapin reports about a trip the writer and a companion took to Chapin's camp. It reads in part: "Fourteen miles is easy to talk it, but damn hard for a greenhorn to walk it. The devil had measured with his tail. It took us 10 hours to walk over that trail. Bill Sandford …(illegible) found it a pleasant grind…. So Frank Baker, in his talk describes the distance as 'only a few miles….' Well Pop Gibson sent you some Booze. Please make of it good use. If the Cookoo does call, take a drink for us all but none for that English vassal." Reference to the "Cookoo" has to do with Chapin's Swiss windup coocoo clock that often malfunctioned. *Courtesy Tom Gates* (The Camp Nit Collection)

Over evening smudge fires to keep mosquitoes away, Chapin took in life stories Wellington shared with guests. Everyday accounts helped Chapin gain insight into an earlier era when the Kenwells' brother, Isaac, first met woodsman "French" Louie Seymour at Indian Lake and when Eliza and Wellington Kenwell worked at Raquette Lake and at Little Moose Lake.

Charles Chapin is seated fourth from the left in the first row. Camp Nit's log book tells Chapin was generous to his many friends. Guests had permission to use his camp even when he wasn't there. *Courtesy Margaret Wilcox (The Camp Nit Collection)*

Wolves were still present in the 1880s. Wellington predicted if they kept on increasing, the state should offer sufficient bounty to insure their extinction, as wolves killed more game than the sportsmen. He also related that during certain winters hawks, owls, and foxes were very destructive of partridges. Chapin also learned about the death-dealing deerslayers' unethical practices of crusting, hounding, and floating deer, and how from the late 1880s on how what had remained of the last moose were exterminated by the same methods used by unscrupulous hunters.

With the cooperation of those Adirondack League Club guides Kenwell knew, he secured a visitors' card that allowed Chapin to legally enter League property below Rock Dam, located south of Kenwell's place.

One summer Gerald Kenwell caught a young squirrel which he soon tamed and kept around camp to the delight of visitors. Even before the age of 12, it was Gerald's custom to guide guests on short walks to observe deer, which were readily seen by daylight anywhere in that section.

The caption that accompanied this picture read: "Original Camp Nit, winter 1901." This shows the back of Camp Nit that served as the caretaker's quarters and kitchen. Since Camp Nit's log book began in 1905, its assumed construction continued to 1904. *Courtesy Tom Gates (The Camp Nit Collection)*

And in the West Canada Lake Country, where Louie Seymour lived, Chapin learned that Pillsbury Lake was named after a true sportsman, a warden of Blackwell's Island.

OPPOSITE: **Before the Big Blow of November 1950, the last few miles of trail to Beaver Lake was under beautiful virgin pine trees.** *Courtesy Tom Gates (The Camp Nit Collection)*

Seeped in knowledge of the vast country, and having traveled to the Fulton Chain for several years, Charles Chapin was appreciative of Wellington's help in learning about Beaver Lake. Following Chapin's purchase of the lake and surrounding acreage, he commissioned Wellington to oversee the construction of a log lodge on the shore of Beaver Lake.

A roof over the side porch provide shade and shelter. If you look closely, you'll see the beginning of a raised boardwalk in the background. *Courtesy Tom Gates (The Camp Nit Collection)*

By July 1905, the year he began to occupy Camp Nit, his new log cabin lodge, rough-and-ready camping was not what Chapin would have seen along the Fulton Chain's eight lakes. Fourth Lake was perhaps the most popular among those who longed for a private camp with urban-like conveniences.

Chapin's trip to the central Adirondack Lake Country would have also been interesting from the time he ate breakfast at the Bagg Hotel, then boarded the train at Utica's station. The countryside was boldly diversified. On the journey north, he passed over the coffee-colored waters of Trenton Falls, saw vast logging operations, and traveled through impressive stands of forest. At Old Forge he would board a lake steamer that would take him to the navigation dock at the end of Fourth Lake.

OPPOSITE: **Frank Lapham leans on one of the many beautiful pines along the route to Beaver Lake. Chapin's logbook entry for February 17–22, 1907 winter trip to camp describes they were guided by Gerald Kenwell over an interesting route. It reads: "Left 6th Lake dam at 8:30 AM via 6th and 7th lakes. Uncas Road and Caruahan [sic] Camp at Russu Ponds [Lost Ponds today] to Sumner and Bear Brook and Coonville. Mild day Snowing. Sleigh and team rode all the way.** *Courtesy Tom Gates (The Camp Nit Collection)*

N. Hudson Moore was a travel reporter for *The Four-Track News.* His 1904 description of plying the waters between Old Forge and the head of Fourth Lake paints a scene of tranquility:

> ...through creeks and waterways, and past shores wooded by evergreen and forest trees down to the water's edge. These shores are dotted with camps in every direction, from the retreat of the millionaire consisting of many small log houses with piazzas, and landing-stages where every variety of little craft is moored, to the tent or even open shack of he who comes there to rough it by preference.
>
> When once you have experienced the charm of life in such a spot, the rest, the sense of leisure, the communion with nature and, best of all, the ease with which the necessary "human nature's daily food" can be obtained, you go there year after year.

Camp Nit's centerpiece was a large elevated deck. A boardwalk connected the camp to the scenic lookout built around a tall pine tree. In later years, the deck was replaced with an elevated sunroom constructed of logs. *Courtesy Tom Gates (The Camp Nit Collection)*

Nit's elevated deck served as an observation platform and as a well-used and enjoyed gathering place. *Courtesy Margaret Wilcox (The Camp Nit Collection)*

No clamorous milkman wakes you at an unearthly hour, but when the morning is well-aired, say between eight and nine o'clock, you hear a shrill little whistle, and a bustling little boat sweeps past your dock; a milk pail is deposited and a comfortable market-basket stands beside it, taking the place of the empty cans and basket which had previously been left there.

Have you a fancy for rare roast beef? You'll find a roast in the basket. Does your peace of mind depend on peaches in their season? Well, friend, you may have those too, and they will all come by this same busy little boat, which also brings your mail twice a day, and your laundry.

With ready supplies at Chapin's command, his real wilderness retreat at Beaver Lake became a beacon for friends and family. The setup didn't mirror the luxury and social pleasures of the hotels along the Fulton Chain, but the path to Beaver Lake over time became beaten by men, women, and children who, at Arrowhead (where they would walk across from Fourth to Fifth Lake) would find the growing little settlement of woodsmen and their families that came to be known as Inlet.

Unquestionably, camp life was totally different from Chapin's days at Kenwells'. Camp Nit's journal indicates the Rochester, N.Y., businessman spent as little as a few days to not much more than a few weeks at a time in camp. There were no large-scale social gaieties such as he frequented in those in the city. Parties and receptions, golf, tennis, horse-racing, and baseball were left behind—replaced by a variety of simple forms of relaxation such as short hikes, fishing, rowing on the lake, meals served on the open piazza, and a wide variety of bountiful dishes prepared by Frank Baker.

Camp Nit deck parties were as popular over a hundred years ago as tailgate parties at sporting events are today. *Courtesy Tom Gates (The Camp Nit Collection)*

Having practically nothing to do must have seemed a joy for the active entrepreneur and civic-minded camp owner.

Mail, newspapers, magazines, and supplies were carried in by guides who procured them from the lake steamers. Hired hands preformed basic services around camp. The names Frank Baker, Wellington Kenwell, Jake Haiuer, Ben Snyder, George Burdick, Sam Breakey, C.L. Tiffany, Frank Murdock, Fred Trotter, Bert McCormick, and Gerald Kenwell appear frequently as the principal guides and workmen.

Gerald and Wellington Kenwell laid out and cleared, a mile-long fishing trail from the top of the hill overlooking Camp Nit to the shore of the south branch of the Moose River. The route formed a gentle arc to a rude dock where boats were stored for fishing and travel. The blazed footpath provided Chapin a connection to the lower stillwater created by an artificial dam built years earlier by Lumber-Jobber William D. Wakeley[41] to facilitate logging operations. The lower stillwater is located about a meandering one mile below the upper stillwater, which is opposite of the Indian Clearing. In 1873, Joseph W. Shurter pronounced this section of the south branch of the Moose River as, "the most beautiful stretch of running water in the Adirondacks."

The construction process of the log cabin dubbed Camp Nit was not documented. Cabin-building—like the sod houses built by homesteaders on the Great Plains—was born of necessity and expediency. Both were products of the builders' ingenuity and skills in utilizing native materials available.

Camp Nit on Beaver Lake. The camp's raised deck overlooking the lake was a popular gathering place. Slim delivered many supplies to Camp Nit.
Courtesy of Margaret Wilcox (The Camp Nit Collection)

Wellington and Gerald Kenwell developed a mile-long trail from Beaver Lake to the remains of Wakeley's Dam on the south branch of the Moose River. There is still evidence of the dam in 2021, but no trace of the once well-used blazed connection trail exists. *Courtesy Margaret Wilcox (The Camp Nit Collection)*

486

It's possible, based on knowledge of how similar camps were built, to speculate on how Camp Nit came to be. Once the site for the cabin was selected, Wellington and his crew pitched large canvas tents for temporary shelter and quickly built a small camp that would serve as quarters for workmen brought in for future projects.

Margaret Wilcox said the elevated sunroom was her favorite place at Beaver Lake.
Courtesy Tom Gates (The Camp Nit Collection)

The next job was to get something "growin' in a hurry." The undergrowth and small trees were cleared from the site. It's possible some large trees outside the patch of ground designated for the cabin might have been girdled as the first stage in opening an area for a future patch of ground for a small garden plot: a notch was cut, through the bark and into the sapwood, entirely around the trunk, to admit more sunshine once the tree died.

The workmen would go to work cutting trees and logs as straight and uniform in size as possible, in the lengths required for the sides, ends, and gables of the cabin. Spruce, tamarack and cedar are particularly desirable because they naturally grow straight and hold their diameter well up to the proper length.

For tools the following would have been customary parts of a carpenter's box of trade: a good double-bit axe or axes, a cross-cut saw, a hand saw, a broad axe and an adze—for hewing— and a chalk line, plane, hammer, level, spikes and nails, door hinges and door hasps with staples.

The laborious efforts of many hands working together helped to skid, roll, and raise the logs into place after a rectangular foundation of four big logs had been laid in place. Each time a wall log was rolled to a pair of axemen stationed at the corners, they would notch and mortise the undersides of each end so that it fit snugly upon the ends of the cross logs and, if possible, left little or no space between itself and the one beneath it.

An unidentified logger standing by a mass of logs felled for the construction of Camp Nit. Once trees were dropped and limbed, the painstaking job of peeling the bark began. *Courtesy Tom Gates (The Camp Nit Collection)*

Wellington's cabin-building method was to have the logs peeled by splitting the bark from one end to the other, then forcing it off, much the same as a trapper would skin an animal. This prevented wood-borers from hatching out under the bark. Besides being destructive, borers are rather noisy when chewing on the wood. Peeling the bark from logs a few weeks before the cabin was to be built also allowed the logs to season much quicker, and make them lighter to handle. Flooring and roof lumber in the backwoods was hewed out of pine or cedar, which was first split about the desired thickness, then hewed level and planed smooth.

Ordinarily, after the walls were up and the ridge-pole and rafters, or longitudinal roof poles, had been added, it was the up to Kenwells' carpenters to finish the interior. They would have had to roof it with shingles made

488

by hand right there; cut openings for the door, fireplace, and windows; and chink the walls with splints of wood held in place by clay, moss, or lime mortar. The wide stone and masonry fireplace, for heating, was surely built by one of few expert masons who lived in the Inlet area.

The construction of Camp Nit and numerous stand-alone outbuildings required hundreds of different-sized logs. *Courtesy Tom Gates (The Camp Nit Collection)*

489

Inside there was a stove for heating and a kitchen range for cooking, a table, camp stools, and beds.

The log cabin is the standard of the Adirondacks when it comes to choosing a camp for a warm, convenient, and secure dwelling. Wellington had come to realize long ago that a real woodsman always sought comfort in preference to everything else, and that a well-built log cabin would give its owner more satisfactory service than any other camp.

It would have been interesting to learn about the construction of Camp Nit—for instance, who was in the crew? How long did it take? Were there any accidents? But no record existed. The only documentation was various snapshots Margaret Wilcox said were fly-specked and tacked on the log wall and an album Tom Gates purchased at an auction. *Courtesy Tom Gates (The Camp Nit Collection)*

Camp Nit's log walls' sheltering protection immediately began to serve as a pleasant refuge for owner and friends after the construction was completed. Loggists entered comments that filled the 168 pages of Nit's 1905–1919 log-book. They told of the temperature and weather, of animal encounters, and of the tremendous number of frogs, fish and deer caught. It's amazing how many experiences, how much praise for Frank Baker, and how much pleasure is recorded in the log-book, in the accounts of big and small vacations made possible by the owner, Charles Chapin T. "Chapes" Chapin. I shall wake some of them again:

> "...I have spent 8 days at Camp Nit, the best I ever had without a doubt. The only fault I find is the name of the camp. IT should spell CAMP IT real large..." (Illegible signature)

It's a guess at best, but it's assumed Chapin probably took snapshots to document the progress of construction during his annual camping vacation at the lake. The brief caption that accompanied this picture reads: "Various stages of construction of Camp Nit, 1900–1901." The photos are among many scenes of camp guests and activities found in Camp Nit's photo album. *Courtesy Tom Gates (The Camp Nit Collection)*

Camp Nit was constructed with only hand tools that required skilled labor. Notches needed to be secure, horizontal joints were made air-tight, windows and doors had to work smoothly, wooden shingles had to first be hand split before being applied to the roof and chimneys needed flashing to prevent leaks. *Courtesy Tom Gates (The Camp Nit Collection)*

"…I am sorry to go out in the cold snow; it sure makes me fret but that I must forget after the good time at Camp Nit." —Peter Van

"…From Schroon Lake via Jessup River by canoe to Pillsbury, Whitney, West Canada, Brook Trout, Fall's Pond….
What a long way to come but it was worth it all to get here."
—Hamilton Gibson

"Good time, good weather, few flies." —Unknown loggist

"…after ten days of Frank Baker's cooking, we are all unanimously of the opinion that home was never like this." —D.F. Fraser

"Greatest vacation ever and no other host on earth could be half as hospitable as Mr. Chapin. Great weather. Fine time. All well." —Unknown loggist

"...before coming again I will learn to walk a log without slipping." —A.R. Tuthill

From the decades of enjoyment Camp Nit provided, I would venture to guess he would have agreed that the best type of backcountry camp was a comfortable log cabin habitation for the Beaver Lake's cold winter region.

To Our Host Chapin, Friday June 27, 1913:
If we could pour out the nectar that Chapin can
We would fill our glasses to the brim
And wish best success to that Chapin man
And Camp Nit which is run as best he can
With his smiles as we drink to him now and then
With all the jokes that were told
And the laughs that were laughed
We would fill up our glasses of joy again
And all told a story now and then
At the fireside in the cabin at Camp Nit
And when he invited us all to return next year
We all accepted with one good big round cheer
For we lived free from care and harmony all the time
At Camp Nit in the good old summer time.
        —Wm. Riley, Chares S. Owen, Char. J. Brown,
        H.E. Hau (illegible) and E.S. Osborne
Courtesy Tom Gates (The Camp Nit Collection)

Chapter Thirty-Six

Rest and Relaxation at Beaver Lake

Guests found any number of reasons to blow Nit's bugle beyond the traditional "We have arrived" blast. *Courtesy Margaret Wilcox (The Camp Nit Collection)*

Charles T. Chapin crossing the Big Plains. *Courtesy Tom Gates (The Camp Nit Collection)*

Horse and rider crossing the Big Plains. *Courtesy Tom Gates (The Camp Nit Collection)*

Camp Nit was truly a recreational camp. It embraced men, women and children. Competitive card games was one example of the camp activities. *Courtesy Tom Gates (The Camp Nit Collection)*

Arrival by air to Camp Nit. *Courtesy Margaret Wilcox (The Beaver Lake Collection)*

Beaver Lake is large enough to paddle from head to foot and feel as if you had a good workout. One of Chapin's guest invented a watersport called "Duck Day." The main objective was to see who could paddle up to a brood of ducklings as they swam behind their parents and ever so carefully scoop and lift a baby duckling up on a paddle.
Courtesy Tom Gates (The Camp Nit Collection)

Outdoor fall life included white-tail deer hunting. Chapin established camp all rules that included no swearing, no wearing hats at the table, all gun were unloaded and left in the appropriate room and all hunters had to document their kill in the camp log **book.** *Courtesy Tom Gates (The Camp Nit Collection)*

Numerous snapshots show campers wearing Rochester sweaters, Chapin's home town.
Courtesy Tom Gates (The Camp Nit Collection)

Over a period of a few years Camp Nit continued to have add-ons with precision joinery.
Courtesy Tom Gates (The Camp Nit Collection)

Thee guests are wearing the accepted swimsuits of the day. A goal for the bravest was to swim across the lake as the swimmer was followed closely by a canoe for safety. Interesting Chapin must have favored canoes over guide boats. *Courtesy Tom Gates (The Camp Nit Collection)*

Riders bound for distant Camp Nit stand by their horses on Limekiln Lake road. *Courtesy Tom Gates (The Camp Nit Collection)*

According to the tally of fish recorded in Nit's logbook, fishing was successful from the dock as well as from a boat. *Courtesy Tom Gates (The Camp Nit Collection)*

Deer were among the common wildlife campers enjoyed watching. This picture was taken from the "spring water sign" that was posted near the beach at the head of the lake. *Courtesy Tom Gates (The Camp Nit Collection)*

Holding rifles and standing by fishing gear at their feet, these gals are wearing the fashion of the times. *Courtesy Tom Gates (The Camp Nit Collection)*

Two of the many caretaker duties were to always have enough firewood on hand and fill the icehouse in winter. Eventually Frank Baker grew too old to perform many of the labor-intensive responsibilities. *Courtesy Tom Gates (The Camp Nit Collection)*

This canoeist posted his adventure in Camp Nit's log book. "Monday, September 6, 1909. Left Schroon Lake, via Jessup River in canoe to Pillsbury, Whitney, West Canada [illegible]. Trout, Falls Pond [followed by a drawing of a canoe being portaged over the canoeist's head]. We had a long way to come. Visit was well worth it all to get here." —Hamilton Gibson. *Courtesy Tom Gates (The Camp Nit Collection)*

To keep in touch with the outside world, Charles Chapin hired Gerald Kenwell to bring letters and newspapers to Camp Nit during the time it was occupied. "June 9 to 20, 1912: Our Vacation time: We have eaten like a horse. Slept like a top. Having such a Jolly Time. We hate to have it stop. Good bye Camp Nit." —Wm. S. Riley and Charles J. Brown. *Courtesy Tom Gates (The Camp Nit Collection)*

A page from one of two known Camp Nit's photo albums. This group of four week-long campers recorded their arrival: "Left Rochester at 9:30 Saturday morning, June 3, 1911. Dinner at Utica, via Clearwater [steamer] to Eagle Bay. Wagon to Inlet. Woods Hotel for supper, lodging and breakfast. Wagon to Sixth Lake, Sunday, June 4th. Left 6th Lake 10:10 A.M. Arrived at Camp Nit 3:40 P.M. Team packing and Riley on horseback. Horseback across Sumner and Moose River. 3 deer in lake and loon nest on arrival. Weather clear-fine." *Courtesy Tom Gates (The Camp Nit Collection)*

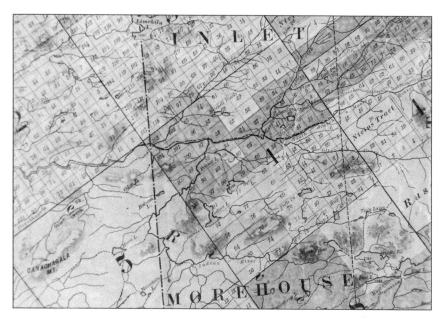

Township 4 Moose River Tract includes Beaver Lake, Mitchell Ponds, The Indian Clearing and the Little Plains, site of Kenwell's Sportsman's Home. *State of New York, The Forest, Fish and Game Commission's 1900 set of Adirondack Maps.*

The Beecher Camp. *Courtesy Town of Webb Historical Association (The Adam's Collection)*

504

Chapter Thirty-Seven

The Story of Beaver Lake

By Allen and Margaret C. Wilcox

ABOUT THE TURN OF THE CENTURY, a guide named Wellington Kenwell moved from Indian Lake and the Cedar River region across the Moose River Plains and built a house on the South Branch of the Moose River near the confluence of the Otter Brook, Summer Stream and the Indian River. This was an area especially known for its hunting and fishing. Mr. Kenwell guided and knew a great many notable men. Theodore Roosevelt hunted with him and Kenwell lived about two miles upstream from the camp of Henry Ward Beecher, father of Harriet Beecher Stowe, who wrote the famous book *Uncle Tom's Cabin*.

Allen Wilcox took this picture of some deer hunting buddies at Governor Brook camp. I've always regretted not learning the camp's location and history. *Courtesy Margaret Wilcox (The Beaver Lake Collection)*

The remains of the Beecher camp's fireplace and chimney mark the site today.
Author's photo

Among the men who hunted that region with Mr. Kenwell was Charles Chapin, a wealthy manufacturer of railroad car wheels from Rochester, NY. He fell in love with the area so much that he bought Great Lots 1 and 2 of the Moose River Plains area. These lots included Beaver Lake. Mr. Chapin had Wellington Kenwell built a log hunting lodge on the shore of Beaver Lake, whereupon the New York State Conservation Department immediately sued Mr. Chapin, claiming that they owned Lot 2, and that he had trespassed by cutting trees and building a camp which was partly on Lot 2. The former owner of a huge tract of land which included the Beaver Lake property was a Mr. Shedd, who had died without leaving a will, but had 32 heirs. Mr. Chapin stood his ground, and hired a very competent lawyer, who spent six months in a horse and buggy or horse and sleigh, hunting up the Shedd descendants. He was successful in getting a clear title from two thirds of the descendants. The fight finally ended with Mr. Chapin owning two-thirds undivided interest of Lot 2 and a clear title to Lot 1. Therefore, for each tree that was cut, Mr. Chapin had committed only one-third of a "trespass" and Mr. C. had a clear title to an undivided two-thirds of that lot. The state of New York withdrew their claim, and there the matter stood, until the following owner [the Wilcox's] took possession in 1938.

Mr. Chapin enjoyed a great many summers in his hunting camp and was guided by Wellington Kenwell. Mr. K employed the caretakers for the camp when Mr. Chapin was not using it. When the Chapin party would arrive in camp, they would come in Kenwell's wagon, pulled by two sturdy Belgian horses. Mrs. Chapin was enthroned in a rocking chair in the front part of the wagon, and although the road was very rough, Mrs. Chapin loved Beaver Lake so much that she came whenever possible.

Frank "Pop" Baker and a Chapin party. *Courtesy Margaret Wilcox (The Camp Nit Collection)*

The Beaver Lake camp was about three and a half miles from where Wellington Kenwell lived on the shore of the Moose River. Many happy years were spent in the Beaver and Moose River area. Sadly for Mr. Kenwell, when Timothy Woodruff became Lieutenant-Governor of New York State, he had Mr. Kenwell dispossessed as a squatter. The Rev. Beecher had passed away, leaving Beaver Lake Camp as the only inhabited place within an area taking in Sumner Lake, West Canada Lake, many small ponds including Deep Lake, Wolf Lake, Falls Pond, and Little Indian Lake. This made a private hunting preserve for the Chapins of many thousands of acres.

During those years, a son had been born to Charles Chapin, Sr. and was named for his father. Charles Chapin, Jr. showed no great liking for the woods or the life of an outdoors man.

The caretaker and guide at that time was Frank "Pop" Baker. Pop lived at Beaver Lake year round—walking out the 23 miles to Inlet sporadically for a visit. He would get lonely in camp and many local people were having excellent hunting and fishing trips paid for by a few quarts of liquor brought in to Pop.

In Pop's older years, he was not able to walk around a great deal or do much hunting or fishing, but he kept himself well supplied with trout by pulling a small net behind his canoe. The local game warden had tried for years to catch Pop doing this, but was not successful. One night about midnight in weather well below zero, the game warden staggered into camp and asked for some food and shelter. Pop took a can of soup off the shelf and said, "Here be God is your dinner and breakfast, too." The warden told Pop he wanted a place to sleep. Pop took him into the main camp that had no heat, unfolded an army cot and threw a fish net over it and said, "There, be God, this will strain off the coarsest of the cold."

As you can realize, human companionship was very scarce in that area. One day a young raccoon came round and Pop threw him a slice of bread. Soon the coon and Pop were fast friends. Outside the kitchen door, Pop put a small board with a wire on one end leading up to the ceiling and attached a little sheep bell to the wire, and when the coon would get hungry, he'd ring the bell and Pop would let him in and share his dinner with him.

After Pop was discharged as caretaker, he was succeeded by Billy "Buck-shot" Saunders, an Adirondack native with a penchant for broad-brimmed western hats. He was coming home from Inlet one late night in the fall of the year before the ice on the stillwater had frozen very hard. He was found under the ice with his hat on the top of his head, but there was a sheet of ice and a lot of water between them.

508

Billy was succeeded by Bert Brown, who wasn't addicted to walking too much, so he invited the local pilots to hunt and fish at Beaver whenever they wished. Bert's main pastime was reading western pulp magazines. Bert was using a considerable amount of canned goods, and one or two hams a week—too much for one man to consume—so Charles Chapin, Jr. figured things didn't add up and decided to sell the property to us.

The Chapins' children at the Mohawk Hotel. *Courtesy Tom Gates (The Camp Nit Collection)*

Buying Beaver Lake turned out to be one of the wisest things I have ever done both for business and pleasure. Before a hard summer at the Mohawk Hotel, a fishing and canoeing trip at Beaver put us in excellent condition to face the difficult coming season. During the season we would occasionally invite close friends to spend the night over in the woods and all of them felt that it was one of the happiest experiences they had ever had.

In April, during the beaver-trapping season only Allen spent two or three weeks at Beaver trapping. The reason for this was not only the pleasure of being in camp, but to reduce the beaver population, as they were building too many dams and killing too many acres of fine timber.

While we are hearing about acid rainfall,[42] we firmly believe that these industrious little animals have created a lot of acid for the scientists to find. They will take certain streams and start building dams, moving upstream with one or two dams every year. There are usually flat lands bordering these mountain streams and timbered with balsam, spruce and occasionally poplar, which the beavers love to feed on. Damming these flat lands kills the soft woods that eventually fall over and rot, including the bark which produces tannic acid, as well as other acids which are deadly to the fish occupying these lakes that the streams lead into.

Allen Wilcox's business card. *Courtesy Margaret Wilcox (The Camp Nit Collection)*

Beaver Lake suffered from a great deal of beaver damage, which greatly reduced its generation of brook trout; other so-called rough fish such as perch and others will continue to survive in water that trout cannot tolerate. However, at Beaver Lake there were three streams of fresh water that the beavers couldn't dam, and we soon learned the "spring holes" where we could always find a trout.

51097 Camp Mohawk, Fourth Lake, Adirondack Mts., N. Y.

The Mohawk is a Complete Summer Resort. *Courtesy Tom Gates (The Camp Nit Collection)*

Beaver being an isolated lake made a wonderful spot for Blue Canadian Geese to rest over on their flights north and south. There were almost always deer in sight on the opposite shore, many times large herds of them. Often, when we were in a canoe the otter would come alongside. They would jump and swim and play, much like the dolphins you see in the marine lands in a warm climate.

When we took over from Bert Brown, who was the last caretaker that Charles Chapin, Jr. employed to stay at Camp Nit, we opened a hunting and fishing camp. This worked out very well until the game began to be depleted, particularly the deer, because of the Conservation Department licensing the killing of does. This enraged many local people, but the policy is still followed although the game has become very scarce.

The Gould Paper Company created the road that goes to Beaver Lake today.
Courtesy Jack Swancott

As the game began to decline in number, and many species went almost extinct, we decided to turn the almost square mile of land and the 100-acre lake into a game preserve. Of course there was some poaching in the summer when we were busy at the resort. However, the local airplane pilots, friends of ours, made a habit of checking Beaver Lake as they took

Fred Waldhauer and Norm Bullen stand next to one of the many enormous pines along the trail to Beaver Lake. Fred said it took four men with arms outstretched to encircle this tree. *Courtesy Margaret Wilcox (The Camp Nit Collection)*

 513

sight-seeing trips over the lake. This was a very satisfactory arrangement and gave us protection which we could have hardly afforded.

The site of Wilcox's Beaver Lake camp following the fire. *Author's collection*

OPPOSITE: **The Wilcoxes had a horse barn, a tractor shed and a sawmill in the clearing above Camp Nit.** *Courtesy Margaret Wilcox (The Camp Nit Collection)*

515

Beaver Lake's barn was located beside a large shed in the present-day clearing atop the rise above Camp Nit. *Courtesy Margaret Wilcox (The Beaver Lake Collection)*

Perhaps the turning point in our concept of Beaver Lake and what should be done with it came on Thanksgiving Day, November 25, 1950. There was a terrific hurricane [known as The Big Blow] which leveled many of the tall old pines and destroyed more than 50 percent of the virgin timber. In order to save the lumber it was decided to put in a small "Pecker-Wood" sawmill. We built an addition on the small guides' cabin and carried an average crew of five men. The harvest of lumber gave us enough to build a number of new cottages along our 1,400 feet of shoreline on Fourth Lake.

The Gould Paper Company owned many thousands of acres of timberland in the Beaver Lake–Moose River areas. It was necessary for them to harvest all the timber on their holdings. This made the construction of a road very necessary from Limekiln Lake to the Moose River Plains, to the boundaries of their holdings. In the course of a few years all of the timber of any value was harvested. The soft wood for the paper mills in Lyons Falls and the hardwood was sold on the stump to a Vermont company which was manufacturing plywood. Beaver Lake was the only privately-owned lake and property in that vast region, running from the Little Moose Lake in Old Forge to the Little Moose Lake which is the source of the south branch of the Moose River systems.

When the timbering was finished, the Gould Paper Company holdings were sold to New York State and became part of the Forest Preserve. The roads built to take the logs out attracted so many hunters, fishermen, backpackers, and sightseers that it became impractical for us to own the Beaver Lake property. We felt it would be wiser to sell the property and the state was, of course, very anxious to acquire the last little bit of private property in the whole region.

So, in the latter month of 1962, a deal was completed which transferred the property to New York State.

When we left Beaver Lake, our hearts were heavy—so heavy that we left them at Beaver Lake and vowed never to return so as not to spoil the memory and vision of our happy days at the lake.

A short time after we left Beaver and the State took possession of the property, our beautiful, comfortable Adirondack camp in the woods was burned by vandals. The culprits have never been apprehended.

Gerald Kenwell stored his "cat" in the Wilcox's shed at the top of the hill above Beaver Lake. *Courtesy Margaret Wilcox The Beaver Lake Collection)*

Chapter Thirty-Eight

Margaret Wilcox's
Remembrances of Beaver Lake

HIGH ABOVE THE BEAUTIFUL sheet of placid water of Fourth Lake, 82-year-old Margaret Wilcox and I looked out through the window of her Mohawk Lodge home as she talked of earlier days, answered my questions and pointed out snapshots of herself and her late husband, Allen H., and the lonely trails that snaked through the mountains on the first day they visited Beaver Lake together.

Margaret had a commanding view of Fourth Lake from her home and hotel.
Courtesy Tom Gates (The Wilcox Collection)

518

A rare photograph of Allen and Margaret Wilcox at the Mohawk Hotel in 1933.
Courtesy Margaret Wilcox (The Camp Nit Collection)

I visited with Margaret whenever she had time to meet with me in 1986 and 1987. Allen had passed away and the Mohawk Hotel the couple had owned had been sold to a Catholic foundation for the deaf who renamed it Mark Seven at the Mohawk Hotel in September 1981. Margaret was still occupied managing a number of rental camps on Fourth Lake and other business interests I never asked about. She graciously managed to find time to talk with me and I gathered information about Beaver Lake.

Allen Wilcox in one of his cross-country skiing upsets that Margaret called "Oh Nos!"
Courtesy Margaret Wilcox (The Camp Nit Collection)

Margaret told me, "Early in 1938, Gerald Kenwell took Allen to Beaver Lake. He was the storyteller and entertainer. He knew it was to be sold and thought Allen could make something of it. At that time, Gerald told Allen that he was responsible for Mr. Chapin buying the Beaver Lake property, as he had brought Mr. Chapin there when Gerald was a young boy.

"Al and I talked about purchasing the property. I knew if we bought Beaver Lake, my stays would not be as frequent or as long as Al's. We were operating the Mohawk Hotel, and with guests and employees, someone had to be on the hotel's premises all the time.

"I knew nothing in particular of the family of Charles Chapin Sr. or Jr.," she said, "except that they lived in Rochester, New York. Allen probably knew more about them."

"As we understood the story from Gerald, Charles Chapin, Jr. inherited Camp Nit [the property on Beaver Lake] from his father and did not have the interest in life in the woods, whether for recreation, hunting or fishing, that his father did. All I know is a combination of a lack of interest, the taxes, and the expense of keeping a caretaker and paying for his food all combined were an unnecessary expense for young Chapin as he did not get any pleasure out of Camp Nit and the surrounding woodland. It was also a long trip for the couple to make from New York City to reach the lake. He was glad to sell it and shift the responsibility to someone else. Al and I traveled to New York City to finish the deal for the sale of Beaver Lake. We met in their apartment and had dinner. To my knowledge, Chapin did not come to Beaver Lake any time after that. Our conversation that evening was cordial but businesslike. Chapin's caretaker, Bert Brown, was mentioned. We know his food was part of his income, but we didn't make any inquiry such as to what amount of money Bert was paid.

Allen Wilcox approaching Beaver Lake after the couple's unanticipated bivouac.
Courtesy Tom Gates (The Camp Nit Collection)

"I remember I was exhausted by the time we came to the bank of the Moose River at nightfall. We had left Limekiln Lake by a corduroy road along the edge of Fawn Lake early in the morning. From there we went up Fawn Lake

Mountain, along Governor Brook to the Red River. At the Halfway Camp we stopped for a sandwich, then started around Mt. Tom, then crossed Bear Brook, Benedict Creek and Sumner Stream, crossed the Moose River Plains by the stand-up pipe of [Wellington] Kenwell's pump that is the only remaining sign of their Sportsman's Hostelry, and forded the Moose River.

"It was April 1938. There was still snow on the shady parts of the trail. I used cross-country skis and Allen wore snowshoes, which we put on and took off depending on the terrain. We climbed over logs of fallen trees and waded streams. I had never been in the woods and was very much a 'greenhorn.' I remember thinking 'What a way to spend a wedding anniversary!'"

Early April 1938 at 9 A.M. arrival. "Beaver Lake was spectacular." —Margaret Wilcox.
Courtesy Margaret Wilcox (The Camp Nit Collection)

When the Wilcoxes went in to take possession of the property, Margaret said Allen carried a pack. "It was in April and the weather was beginning to warm up. As the day went on the melting snow flowed into the streams, filling them to capacity. By the time we reached the south branch of the Moose River it had grown dark enough that Allen said it was unsafe to risk crossing on the piled-up shell ice. We went back from the river to a little

Margaret and Allen found many snapshots of unidentified visitors pinned to the kitchen wall. *Courtesy Margaret Wilcox (The Camp Nit Collection)*

point of dry land and started a fire on the leeward side. It began to sprinkle rain so we quickly improvised a lean-to with a tarp Allen carried. It wasn't set up well. Before long our roof drooped in the center because of the weight of rain water that had filled the tarp. We had no dinner. We hadn't anticipated bivouacking, but we managed to brew a spot of tea in a tin can of smoking tobacco. I'm not going to describe the primitive sleeping conditions other than to say we were uncomfortable, yet somehow we soon fell asleep from exhaustion. The next morning we walked along the shoreline of the river until we found a safe bridge of shell ice to cross. Once on the opposite side of the river, we followed the narrow foot trail that led to Beaver Lake.

"Along the way from the Moose, we spotted something hanging from a tree. From a distance it looked like grey flannel until we drew closer for an inspection. It turned out to be a bear hide that had been hanging there probably several years.

"We arrived at Beaver Lake about 9 A.M. Bert Brown, the caretaker, was astonished that we could leave Inlet and get there so early in the morning. We never told him that we had spent the night a few miles from camp!

"Beaver Lake that morning was spectacular. The beautiful pine trees, sparkling lake and many deer in the yard, the beauty of it all washed away everything I had gone through the previous day and night. The emotional uplift made me feel a lot better.

The sunroom was Margaret Wilcox's favorite room. *Courtesy Margaret Wilcox (The Camp Nit Collection)*

"Several deer were in the yard—one sad-looking doe's ears were hanging down. We later learned Bert had named her Matilda. She was very tame, and deaf. Bert said it was not unusual to see 40 or more deer gather in the yard next to the camp. Their movements were as precise as a chorus line.

OPPOSITE: **"There were so many unlabeled pictures. It was impossible not to wonder who they were and think about their time at the lake." —Margaret Wilcox.** *Courtesy Margaret Wilcox (The Camp Nit Collection)*

When you whistled, their ears would go up, then their tails would go up like white flags all in unison and the herd would sprint up the hill, only to return in a few minutes.

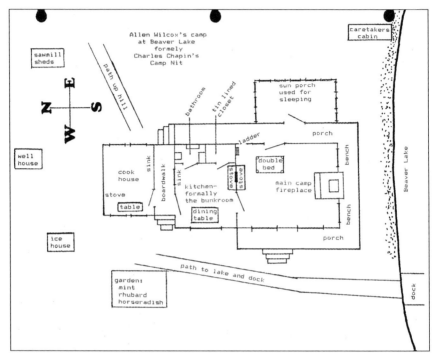

Interior layout of Camp Nit. *Author's drawing*

"As you would imagine, there were introductions when we met Bert. The sale of the property was not a complete surprise to him. Bert prepared breakfast. There were many fly-speckled and faded pictures of people in canoes and guides playing cards. There were many of Frank 'Pop' Baker—he was a big man, a well-known guide and the Chapin's first caretaker—and scenes of Beaver Lake and of people who had obviously been Camp Nit visitors over the years because the background was definitely Beaver Lake.

"Following breakfast, Bert showed us around. As I remember the main camp building, it was like any woods camp that has been closed for some time. It needed a good cleaning. The moss chinks between the logs in the walls were disintegrating. The fireplace needed repairs. Spiders and dust had made the windows opaque, and there were signs of squirrel occupancy.

"Bert Brown had been the last caretaker to have lived in the cook cabin. It was very dark, walls and ceiling stained with grease and soot. An iron stove on the south side was an old-fashioned cooking stove and burned wood. Also a flat iron sink with pails of water from the lake. The kitchen table was covered with an oilcloth. Kitchen chairs were worn. Lamps and lantern were run on kerosene.

"Bert was talkative. I think anyone who has been living alone in an isolated place like Beaver Lake without another human being to talk to is apt to talk a great deal when he has someone to listen.

The fireplace was a Wilcox addition to the Beaver Lake camp. *Courtesy Margaret Wilcox (The Camp Nit Collection)*

On the day we met Bert, he was dressed in a wool shirt and black leather britches which required no laundry! He wore the same clothes the following day also. In fact, I only saw Bert Brown a couple of times. He left the camp soon after we took possession of the property. I do not know where he went. We knew very little about Bert. We had learned it was Bert's custom to always buy a ham or two at Inlet's Red & White store when he went outside of Beaver Lake. He charged them to Chapin's food bill. I understand it was a commodity that he could exchange for a bottle or two when visitors or hunters came to Camp Nit, but the local grapevine also had it that Bert enjoyed eating ham.

"Bert told us about Matilda. She was his pet deer. He talked to her, but she could not hear a word he said. On our first trip to Beaver Lake Camp, we had taken a pound of butter to Bert. Matilda got into the kitchen before we were awake in the morning, and the butter was well-licked by that time. She also loved potato peelings and knew where Bert kept them for her.

"That evening we slept in the sleeping quarters on the sun porch. It was off the open porch on the same level. No stairs were needed. Cots were used. There was a small, old-fashioned wood-burning stove in the center of the room—a metal stove pipe went through the roof above.

Mrs. Chapin's wicker chair that arrived with her sitting in it.
Courtesy Margaret Wilcox (The Camp Nit Collection)

Allen Wilcox (Lt.) converted the former cookhouse into a combination food preparation-kitchen-drying room. *Courtesy Margaret Wilcox (The Camp Nit Collection)*

"Allen told me about an accident Gerald Kenwell had as a young man at the camp. Chapin Sr. had hired Gerald to move the sleeping porch, which jutted out over the lake from the front of the main building, Chapin hired Gerald to move it to the east side of the camp building. Gerald said it was quite an operation with no machinery. During the reconstruction, he cut his leg with an axe. The injury required him to be laid up all winter at Beaver Lake.

"Before we left the camp, Bert provided a bit of the history of some of the contents of the camp. There were a few pieces of decorative plates that Mrs. Chapin had prized, and her wicker rocking chair. The story is when on one trip into Beaver Lake the chair was tied to a wagon so she could conceivably ride all the way in over the rough trail. There were some of Wellington Kenwell's sheep bells, which he tied around the animals' necks. They rang as the sheep free-ranged far afield. Later Pop Baker rigged up a contraption for one bell he used to teach his pet raccoon to ring when he wanted to be fed. I gave that bell to the Old Forge Historical Association and kept the dinner bell that was used in Charles Chapin's time. Oh, and there were a few items Allen later on found at the old Beecher camp down the Moose that were added to Beaver Lake Lodge's bygone artifacts. Later we found stacks of western pulp magazines in the attic of the camp.

Beaver Lake's well house. Remans of it are still visible. *Courtesy Margaret Wilcox* *(The Camp Nit Collection)*

"In the early years of our ownership, Allen and I made most of our trips to Beaver Lake on foot—usually in the fall when the rivers were lower and easier to cross and we could walk the stream beds. Sometimes we were able to cross on stones, but that was rare. We wore pack baskets with the supplies we needed. Once we got to the Moose, we felt we were almost home. One trip we took in on a horse-pulled sleigh in winter.

"We never called Beaver Lake Camp—Camp Nit. It hardly fitted that beautiful place.

"Allen and I began improvements the year we took possession. In the cook house, we put a shelf around three sides of the room about a foot below the ceiling to hold canned goods and so on. A weasel moved in soon after and took care of the mice and squirrels. Flour, cereals, cornmeal, beans and so forth were stored in a big bread box—the kind that was used on trucks to carry supplies of bread. There was no refrigeration. Perishables were placed in glass bottles submerged in the lake. Later on, they were stored in an ice house.

"Furnishings were scanty—a few old kitchen chairs, well-worn easy chairs. There were good kerosene lamps with wicks. We brought in Aladdin lamps with mantles, which gave better light. The entire fireplace in the main room needed rebuilding. When we made the original bunk house into a kitchen, we purchased a new wood-burning kitchen range. The old cook house was cleaned out and used for storage.

"Besides repairing the fireplace in the living room of the main house, we installed a new oil-burning furnace—the space-saving type that was made for indoor living—and it shared the chimney with the kitchen stove.

"There was a ladder of sorts at one end of the main room and a trap door above. The floor of the attic above was also the ceiling of the living room. The attic space was only used for storage. It was not suitable for sleeping quarters.

The icehouse at Beaver Lake was a short distance from the well house.
Courtesy Margaret Wilcox (The Camp Nit Collection)

"A large wool rug from the Mohawk made the living room more comfortable on cold days, and we also brought over a few comfortable chairs from the hotel.

Harold "Scotty" Scott's plane as it leaves Beaver Lake Lodge's dock after delivering hunters at camp. *Courtesy Margaret Wilcox (The Camp Nit Collection)*

"The following year we asked our employee, Freddie Kroput, a former Polish lumberjack, to build an ice house and well house out of field stone and cement. He was in our employ when we had horses, and he went to Beaver Lake to cut wood for the stoves and fireplace. We used the well for several years until a passerby left the door unlatched and a deer got in and fell into the well. The carcass was removed when it was discovered after several months. The well was never used again in spite of attempts we made to purify the water. From then on we carried water from the lake.

"There was a very good spring toward the sand beach at the east end of the lake. It used to be marked with a sign and a blue enamel cup hanging from the post. I wouldn't be surprised if it might still be there.

"Our Polish worker also built a double bed from small trees and twigs and that was in one corner of the room. Bedding for the cots and bed came from our supplies at the Mohawk. Freddie also designed and built a small table from a burl of a tree, and split log benches.

"A small so-called caretaker's cabin stood about 200 feet from the main building toward the beach. Gerald Kenwell said his father, Wellington, built that to stay in while he and the hired carpenters built Camp Nit. We used it for the workmen we hired. I was never in it, but I imagine it was set up like all woods camps, with a wood-burning stove for heat, and for cooking and drying wet clothing.

"I did not spend much time at Beaver except in the fall when the Mohawk was closed. It was really a men's camp and Allen's venture. He loved the woods, and all the hardships were a challenge to him. Someone had to be at the home base and I did not relish the long hike over rough trails. The last few years we flew in, first with Harold Scott and later with Bus [Norton] Bird in his open cockpit plane. I remember the updraft over the south branch of the Moose River was very strong and gave the plane a jolt, which was anything but pleasant!

"Harold 'Scotty' Scott operated his seaplane out of Inlet [New York] for many years. He was one of the pioneers in air transportation in the mountains, and during one season toted supplies for the Gould Paper Company from White Lake to Indian Lake and Squall Lake camps in The Plains. On October 19, 1945. he was about to make a landing on Beaver Lake to discharge deer hunters Bob Harwood, and Francis and John Breakey, who were bound for Beaver Lake Lodge, when the plane crashed in the tree tops.[43] The three occupants were badly injured.

"Bus told us that if you were going to fly in the Adirondacks you had to know what you were doing. The mountains can go out of sight real easy and you've got to know where you are whether you see any mountains or not. If you don't you're in trouble. You can't just fly by radio and any of that; you have to be able to fly by the seat of your pants. He talked about step-turn take offs on Beaver Lake. What that means is the plane goes around the lake near the edge. The plane is in a skid as one float is out of the water—it's a funny feeling because you can't use the aileron like you can in the air to bank your airplane until just before you lift off, so it feels funnier than the dickens.

Camp "Nit,"

owned by,

Chas F. Chapin,

Rochester, N.Y,

1905,

Welcome,

to all,

who register here,

Chapter Thirty-Nine

Margaret Wilcox's Chapin's Camp Nit Log Books

"CHAPIN'S CAMP NIT log books are noteworthy to thumb through. I found it interesting to read the Decoration Day, May 30, 1906 entry when ex lieutenant-governor Timothy L. Woodruff and his wife Isabel, along with a woman identified only as 'Sunburnt' Mary spent the night at the camp.

Woodruff's entry read:

> We have greatly enjoyed and are very thankful for the hospitality extended to us in the absence of the 'lord of the manor' from whom we hope for a reciprocal visit at Kamp Kill Kare this summer. Then we will tell him how we came to drift in here at nightfall and secured a night's lodging where we had never been before , but what found to be one of the most comfortable of the many Adirondack camps we have visited. In Frank Baker we found an old friend who did everything possible in our comfort and enjoyment.

The party had hiked down along the Sumner stream from Woodruff's Kamp Kill Kare and gave praise to Frank Baker for his hospitality. Baker was a well-known guide and the camp's first caretaker. Woodruff held a leadership role in the Association for the Protection of the Adirondacks. Woodruff recorded that his guides on that trip were Harry Symmes and Thomas T. Somerville.

OPPOSITE: **The title page to years of memories, game caught, travel time and weather observations.** *Courtesy Margaret Wilcox (The Camp Nit Collection)*

"Allen used to hire Gerald Kenwell's excursion boat, the *Osprey*, and take Mohawk guests on cookouts at Sixth and Seventh lakes. Trips to our Beaver Lake Camp were almost always float plane flights. I had taken over the Mohawk's kitchen by that time. I packed food for them, but my work kept me too busy to go on the trips.

"Allen kept horses at Beaver Lake temporarily when they were used to bring supplies into camp. We had stables and grooms at the Mohawk on Fourth Lake, as we had a riding stable there for many years. Up the hill back of Beaver Lake Camp was a lean-to where the horses were kept.

"Bob Lee was one of the horses kept at Beaver. Allen was a loyal Southerner and an admirer of General Robert E. Lee.

Bette and Kerry O'Hern sit lakeside where Camp Nit stood in 1985. Had the logbooks and photo album not survived, no one would know much more than that a camp once occupied this opening in the forest. *Courtesy Margaret Wilcox (The Camp Nit Collection)*

The *Osprey* returns from an excursion-dinner party at the head of Seventh Lake.
Courtesy Winfred Murdock

"The trail rides that Allen took into Beaver Lake were for Mohawk guests only. They usually made a stopover for lunch at the camp on Red River, and made many side trips from Beaver Lake into the surrounding countryside. One time they climbed Kitty Cobble on horseback. They were the first riders ever to attempt that feat."

On my first visit with Margaret she told me about reading the book *Woodswoman* by Anne LaBastille, in which Anne writes about building a cabin. Ann did not reveal where she built her cabin and gave fictitious names to the lakes, but Margaret, like most nearby natives, knew Anne lived at Twitchell Lake beyond Big Moose. Margaret said, "She was trying to protect her privacy. I've thought about her, a single, divorced woman out there in the woods. It's made me reflect on old Bert Brown living alone back at isolated Beaver Lake without another human being to talk to. And maybe Anne's isolation in the frigid Adirondack weather led her to become the writer she turned out to be."

Before I left that day, Margaret handed me a February 27, 1987, clipping from the *Adirondack Echo*. The headline read, "A Moose River Plains Wedding." The bride and groom had planned the "T" at Moose River Plains as the setting for their marriage. It read in part: "Snowmobilers passing by stopped to wish the new bride and groom luck and happiness. Even the deer popped out of the woods to see what was going on."

Bob Lee, Allen Wilcox's favorite horse. *Courtesy Margaret Wilcox (The Camp Nit Collection)*

I think Margaret had a twinge of nostalgia as she talked about the group who enjoyed the traditional champagne and a somewhat frozen wedding cake. I guessed it might have brought back memories of her own April wedding anniversary trip past that very spot forty-nine years earlier.

One serious plan that would have forever altered Margaret and Allen's land purchase was the Higley and Panther mountain dam proposals in the mid-1940s. Margaret told me she would have been more than regretful had that initiative by the Black River Regulating District had ever succeeded.

Margaret said, "The Higley Mountain area is fascinating backcountry," and she knew some of its history. "Right across an 800-foot wide arm of the proposed Higley Reservoir," she told me, was one of the state's famous old survey lines. This one was laid out in 1772 by a determined surveyor, Archibald Campbell, and by a task force of less-determined Indians who, when the whiskey gave out, quit cold, leaving the V-shaped 110-mile trail of blazes dangling in the wilderness."

I had read about those blazes. They had served as a coat hanger of sorts for draping later surveys.

Margaret handed me a story about the survey she said was written by David Beetle, a friend and newspaper reporter who worked for the Utica *Observer-Dispatch*. Beetle interviewed the Wilcoxes in 1946 to learn how their Beaver Lake property would be threatened by the proposed dam.

The "T." A familiar junction near the foot of the Big Plains. *Author's photo*

Beetle's telling about Campbell's line was part of a longer story titled "Kilroy Was NOT Here." It first appeared in the Utica *Observer-Dispatch* and later was reprinted in the spring 1947 issue of *North Country Life* magazine. Beetle's story presented a description and something of the historical background of the Adirondack wilderness site of the Higley and Panther mountain dams over the construction of which was a tug-of-war that raged in the New York State Legislature during the time the article was first published. Beetle tells the rest of the story.

Called the Totten-Crossfield Line, it puts on today's maps the names of a couple of obscure Manhattan ship's carpenters who served as a front for land speculators seeking to buy the Adirondacks from the Indians. To press the venture, they started Campbell & Co. out from Sir William Johnson's hunting lodge on the Sacandaga with instructions to proceed bee-line through the wilderness 30-degrees west of north until he came to a point which he calculated was due west of a curiously shaped boulder on Lake Champlain. Somewhere near a big pine on the South Branch of the Moose River, he decided he had reached that point, drove in a copper spike, and turned east. Thirty-five miles from Champlain came the sit-down strike.

Probably Campbell and the Indians didn't look around much, but if they had they would have found a rock cut at a point where today's river regulators hope to put in the two-million-dollar, 100-foot-high, 800-foot-long Higley Dam. Beyond that (and slated to be flooded out) are three little lakes, currently known as Ice House, Hell-Diver, and Beaver [Lake]. On one side of the river for about a mile rise the Moose River cliffs. And opposite them are the Moose River Plains—a wide stretch covered with foot-high blueberry bushes and flanked by what the sportsmen call "virgin forest," although there's more than gossip to indicate that a century after Campbell left, a lumberman by the name of Rousseau moved in, cut down some whopping big pines, and sent them floating down the Moose [River] to the Black [River].

"Allen and I came in to Beaver Lake camp," Margaret recalled, "after we had returned from a vacation and found that the state engineers had marked the flow line on most of the big trees on our property. We could judge from these markings that the water would come up the hill in back of the camp.

"Al talked to a friend, a lawyer, who had hunted many times at Beaver and he agreed to take our case against the state.

This scene of Beaver Lake taken from the shore would have been underwater had Higley or Panther dams been built. A full discussion of the ten-year battle against the proposed dams is covered in *The Adirondacks' Moose River Plains, Vol.2: The Land of the Deer*. *Photo by Paul Schaefer*

"It took a long time, I recall two years, to get the case before a judge, but the decision was in our favor and the whole thing was dropped.

"Paul Schaefer stayed at the Mohawk and at Beaver Lake Camp when he and his Moose River Committee were working with Allen and me to lobby Albany against the Higley Dam project. He invited us down to Albany to see a film that had been produced about The Plains in the 1940s.

You should talk to Schaefer. He should have all sorts of information about these dam threats."

Left to Right: Gerald Kenwell and Allen Wilcox. Wilcox relied on Gerald for all camp-related needs. *Courtesy Margaret Wilcox (The Camp Nit Collection)*

When it came time for me to leave, Margaret told me how pleasant our visit had been and invited me back anytime. Before I left she said, "Several years ago, before Allen passed, he helped me make up a scrapbook on the history, as we knew it, of Beaver Lake. There are a couple of photos of The Plains as well as pictures of the camp, people, and the surrounding country. I would be glad to loan you the scrapbook if you would care to see it."

Not only was I eager to see the scrapbook, I also found interesting the hand-drawn map she handed me. I knew of today's route to Beaver Lake which was the approach she and Allen had first followed. Margaret and Allen's illustrative map and simply written directions revealed there were two routes. She said they used both. It all depended on the weather and water levels. She said Allen learned the unconventional route from Gerald Kenwell. She said she felt a bit like "your best hunting hound" when following that track. "Gerald called it the 'Sheep Trail.'"

Margaret loved how peaceful winter's snow and deer looked from inside her cozy sunroom. The site of the Wilcox's camp was part of the Conservation Department's experimental deer feeding program. *Courtesy Margaret Wilcox (The Camp Nit Collection)*

The directions read:

The 1938 Trails to Beaver Lake
1. Limekiln Lake to Beaver Lake is approximately 17 miles.
2. Limekiln to edge of Fawn Lake, and across Fawn Lake Mountain. Walk along Governor Brook, follow to Red River

Halfway Camp. From the Halfway Camp there were two routes if on foot.

A. Cross Moose River Mountain from the Lower Dam on Red River by way of Mitchell Ponds. Cross the Moose at the lower end of the upper Stillwater. A short mile along the trail to Beaver Lake. This was known locally as the 'Sheep Trail' because Wellington Kenwells's sheep occasionally wandered down the river. Pop Baker's little bell that his pet raccoon rang originally hung around the neck of Wellington Kenwell's bellwether, his lead sheep.

B. The other trail from the Red River Camp was on somewhat lower land that crossed the lower part of Mt. Tom, then Bear Brook, Sumner Stream, and the Moose River below the confluence of Otter Brook where Bear Brook, Sumner Stream and the Indian River flowed into the Moose. From there about 3.5 miles to Beaver Lake.

Margaret and Allen Wilcox's story was a treasure—the story of Beaver Lake Lodge continues in the couples' own words.

Gerald Kenwell's Red River Halfway Camp and barn, 1930. Very little visible evidence of this camp exists today. It was located a short distance from the Gould Paper Company's upper Red River logging camp. *Courtesy Winfred Murdock*

544

Chapter Forty

Beaver Lake Hunting Club

WHEN I FIRST MET MARGARET WILCOX, I felt immediately embraced by her warmth, her charisma, and her generosity (something for which I will forever be grateful). From that initial meeting grew a number of others, all at her magnificent Adirondack home. She was fond of reminiscing about her husband, Allen, and their ownership of Beaver Lake Lodge in the Moose River Plains and of the Mohawk Inn on Fourth Lake.

Margaret was a true businesswoman of the hotel boom in the Eagle Bay area of the beautiful lake country in the central Adirondacks. She was also a notable cook and renowned culinary expert.

Deep-rooted connections to the Beaver Lake country served Margaret's memories in all aspects of her outdoor life—and what an active business life!

Clara V. O'Brien remembered Margaret in her book, *God's Country: Eagle Bay, Fourth Lake in the Heart of the Adirondacks*. In it, she explained that:

> From 1933 to 1975, under the Wilcox management, The Mohawk Inn grew and developed many firsts in the Adirondacks in sports and recreation (horseback riding, water skiing, children's program, putting green), as well as outstanding food and service. The cornerstone of this most successful operation was based on the certainty that each meal would be excellent. The food service was developed by Margaret Wilcox. It was recognized by a number of colleges and universities as one of the best training grounds for students. The consistently outstanding good food was the chief reason the guests continued to return each year. The lovely pine-paneled dining rooms decorated with Adirondack ferns, and with picture windows overlooking the lake and a rock garden, were a delightful setting and atmosphere for the delicious food.

I know from talking to Nancy Best, who worked under Margaret, that all those who knew her felt blessed that they had been able to share a portion of her working life at the Mohawk.

Allen and Margaret Wilcox knew the purchase of the Beaver Lake property would widen their customer base. *Courtesy Margaret Wilcox (The Camp Nit Collection)*

I brought Margaret a homemade pie that we shared during our interview. I can well remember her quizzing me on the varieties of apples and spices I'd used and my recipe for pie crust during our first of several visits. At the time I didn't know of her outstanding reputation for cooking. I remember being thrilled when she presented me with a box of old snapshots and her large handmade scrapbook titled in cursive, "Beaver Lake 1905–1962."

Nancy says this wonderfully successful Adirondack businesswoman will be remembered through a cook book. Nancy plans to relive her memories of employment at the Mohawk with stories connected with some of the Mohawk's best recipes. I will always remember Margaret for her kindness. Without her thoughtfulness a gaping hole would forever remain in the history of Camp Nit, the original camp the Wilcoxes purchased and then referred to as Beaver Lake Lodge.

☆ ☆ ☆

Margaret and I always sat at a table by a huge picture window that looked out over the lake. As she cut two slices of my pie during our meeting in the late fall of 1987, she was talking, and mostly I was just listening, an arrangement that was quite common in my method of interviewing. She always had a lot to say.

From the dock at Beaver Lake, Allen Wilcox is pointing out some land features to a client. *Courtesy Margaret Wilcox (The Camp Nit Collection)*

A cottage built before 1893 originally occupied the site of the Wilcox's hotel. A fire destroyed the large cottage shortly after Caroline M. Longstaff purchased the property from William Seward and Eliza Osgood Webb. To replace the building, Caroline and her husband, Dr. G.H. Longstaff, built a small hotel that they christened Camp Mohawk. In 1909 the Longstaffs built an enlarged building then known as The Mohawk, which they opened in 1910. It was one of the most modern area hotels of its day. Carrie ran it until she retired in 1933, when the Longstaffs leased the Mohawk to the Wilcoxes. Then in 1944, the Wilcoxes purchased the property from the Longstaffs.

The dining room at the Mohawk Hotel. Some guests, especially hunters, chose rustic Beaver Lake Lodge over the comforts found at the Mohawk. *Courtesy Tom Gates (The Camp Nit Collection)*

OPPOSITE: **Unlike the outdoorsmen of Charles Chapin's era, Allen Wilcox's clients dressed down and didn't always require a guide.** *Courtesy Margaret Wilcox (The Camp Nit Collection)*

Allen Wilcox (top row, right). Often Allen would fly summer guests at the Mohawk Hotel to Beaver Lake for the day. *Courtesy Margaret Wilcox (The Camp Nit Collection)*

I recall Margaret saying that if she had learned anything in her years of cooking, it was that new recipes will always come along and replace established ones posted in current magazines and in the vast array of cookbooks, and that no matter how diverse recipes become, there will always be a place for traditional recipes.

At the time, I took her comment to mean there are immeasurable kinds of soups, salads, casseroles, stews, pastries and so forth under the cooking umbrella, but that my conventional apple pie would have been as popular a hundred years ago as it would be a hundred years in the future.

My original interest wasn't in cooking, however. I was focused on the history of Camp Nit, a purchase the Wilcoxes had made in 1937. Camp Nit was a log lodge built by Inlet pioneer Wellington Kenwell for Charles T. Chapin, the president of the National Car Wheel Company. Dana Blackman described the camp in her September 17, 1919, entry in the camp's register as *Camp Nit* "whose windows frame a million-dollar picture of God's Country in Appreciation."

It was clear Allen spent far more time at Camp Nit than Margaret did. Her domain was the efficient management of the hotel. Allen used Camp Nit as a wilderness retreat and managed the camp and property as a sportsmen's lodge popularized by the plentiful fish, wild game and scenery passionate sports and nature lovers found alluring about the Moose River Plains.

Along with stories of Camp Nit's first caretaker, Frank "Pop" Baker, and his pet raccoon that rang a bell each time it arrived in camp, Margaret talked of substitute caretaker Billy "Buckshot" Sanders's live fox and the camp's last custodian, Bert Brown. Chapin claimed he spent so much money on canned goods for Bert Brown that he decided to sell the property to the Wilcoxes!

Back row, standing, Allen Wilcox. Allen stands with a group of hunters at Beaver Lake, circa 1940s. *Courtesy Margaret Wilcox (The Camp Nit Collection)*

552

"I have only heard stories about Baker," Margaret said when I asked what the nickname "Pop" might have referred to. "The way I understand," she replied, "it had nothing to do with his age. It was in reference to his status among his peers when he worked at Amaziah [Dutton] Barber's Forest Lodge back in the late 1880s. Frank was the senior guide and looked up to by all— hence the term 'Pop,' in reverence. The name just stuck.

While Margaret didn't know "Pop" Baker, she evidently thought enough of Bert Brown that she preserved three of the recipes Bert followed when cooking for the Chapin family and their many guests.

Allen Wilcox (3rd from left) accompanies a group of hunters who returned to camp year after year. *Courtesy Margaret Wilcox (The Camp Nit Collection)*

Margaret's contribution of a big box of old snapshots and the loan of Camp Nit and Beaver Lake Lodge's journals took away what otherwise would have been like an eye patch over the camp's history, for it no longer exists today.

OPPOSITE: **Left to Right: Elmer Olsen, unknown, Allen Wilcox. Fishing was a popular sport at the Mohawk Hotel on Fourth Lake. Circa 1930s.** *Courtesy Margaret Wilcox (The Camp Nit Collection)*

"Beaver Lake Lodge was another part of Allen," Margaret told me. This chapter might be viewed as a sort of early reality series in still pictures from the vast collection Margaret provided documenting common, everyday activities such as fishing, hunting, paddling, and socializing at the lodge.

Left to Right: Whitey Masters and Allen Wilcox return to Beaver Lake dock from a deer hunt. *Courtesy Margaret Wilcox (The Camp Nit Collection)*

The captions are short stories condensed from Margaret and my conversations—each scene capturing the essence of Camp Nit's daily life. Like apple cider captures the bouquet of October to be savored over and over, these images parade across the pages, honoring a vanished life, yet making it look as if it has lasted forever in the Beaver Lake country where the Chapins and Wilcoxes built and sojourned so long ago.

Chapter Forty-One

Bert Brown For Who
No Dog Will Bark

HE LIVED ISOLATED among forests of maples, birch and other deciduous trees as well as plentiful stands of scattered pine, balsam and spruce that gave off a health-giving scent that filled the mountain air. All that natural beauty might sound idyllic to an occasional camper, but Bert's occupation was full-time caretaker at Beaver Lake Camp, owned by the Chapins.

Brown lived somewhat like a solitary trapper, but he didn't need to ramble in the mountains and forests to eke out a living. He lived off a well-stocked larder the Chapins provided. He did do a bit of trapping and hunted the deer, but his greatest outdoor enjoyment was fishing. Bert didn't want much. The thing Bert Brown craved most was company.

Brown had been through the war. He'd tell he learned by degrees that the whole world had got mixed up in World War I, and it seemed that everybody was more interested in guns and food. (Than what? He never said.) After his war experience, he decided to live in remote solitude in exchange for food, shelter and a small sum he could deposit in a bank account each year.

It was because he was employed by a wealthy, respected businessman and was richly rewarded that his day-to-day living was not difficult. He faced no hardships or suffering, but he would be the first to confess that when a passerby or sportsman came to camp, he'd welcome them with a hearty handshake.

Bert would elaborate about the terrible circumstances he had seen during his war years and talk endlessly about his younger days of trapping. Bert was also knowledgeable about an era of yesterday in The Plains that few people could imagine today.

"For which no dog will ever bark," was a favorite saying with which he often concluded a story.

This man is believed to be Bert Brown. Photo taken at Otter Brook Camp.
Courtesy Ora Kenwell

Archie and Eri Delmarsh were husky, fun-loving woodsmen. Back in the 1890s they were hired as guides. They became famous. Packed all the provisions, trudged into the woods for miles to stay for weeks. The deer they shot were often brought out by pack horses. Their patrons would be lost without them boys. Their customers were so proud of their guides they'd write up their experiences in magazines of the day. Arch Delmarsh later managed the Cedar Island Hotel for Joseph Porter. After Arch bought Rocky Point, brother Eri ran the Cedar Island Hotel until it was sold to Otto Berg. Then Eri went to Limekiln Lake and ran Limekiln Lake Inn. Marvelous men who made a mark on the area's history and *for which no dog will ever bark.*

Brown's expression was often used when he referred to people like Arch, Eri and others who he felt were taken for granted and would never get proper credit for their accomplishments.

Brown was more than happy to satisfy his guests' hunger in many ways. He took them to the best fishing and hunting spots, entertained them with stories from his vault of tales and was known for being a superb cook. Here are five examples of Bert's accomplished recipes that Margaret Wilcox found in the Beaver Lake Camp journal when she and her husband Allen, bought the camp from the Chapins.

Beaver Lake Spider Corn Cakes
"Favorite with the hunters"—Bert Brown
Ingredients:
1½ cups of corn meal
⅓ cup flour
1 cup sour milk
1 teaspoon soda (scant)
1½ tablespoons butter
2 eggs
2 cups sweet milk

¼ cup sugar

½ teaspoon salt

Directions: Mix and sift corn meal and flour, and add sour milk mixed with soda, well-beaten eggs, one-half of the sweet milk, sugar, and salt. Heat an iron frying pan, add butter, and, when melted, turn in mixture. Pour remaining milk over and bake in a moderate oven fifty minutes. Cut into pie-shaped pieces for serving. [The "spider" in the title is an old-fashioned term for a cast iron frying pan.]

Hunter's Venison Barbecue

Beef can be substituted for venison.—Bert Brown

Ingredients:

1 lb. ground beef or venison

¼ chopped green peppers

¼ cup chopped onions

¼ cup chopped celery

¼ cup ketchup

8-ounce can tomato sauce

1 tablespoon wine vinegar

1½ teaspoons Worcestershire sauce

1 teaspoon salt

⅛ teaspoon pepper

mustard to taste

Directions: Brown meat, drain, add remaining ingredients. Simmer 20 minutes. Makes enough for about 12 rolls.

"Bert knew how to cook up a mess of trout, too, whether it was for a shore lunch or back at camp for tired anglers." —Margaret Wilcox

OPPOSITE: **An unknown and well-dressed woodswoman, photo found among Bert Brown's things.** *Courtesy Margaret Wilcox (The Camp Nit Collection)*

558

Bert's Fancy Trout Recipe

Prepare trout by gutting and beheading. Pour canned tomatoes in a skillet. Lay fish on top. Sprinkle on cut-up black olives and parmesan cheese with a little pepper. Simmer until fish flakes.

☆ ☆ ☆

Among Camp Nit's possessions were numerous rifles, shotguns, fishing poles, tackle boxes and scores of hooks, sinkers, spinners, bobbers, lures, and some articles of interest taken from the Beecher Camp. For the Chapin family of Rochester, N.Y. and their many guests, hunting and fishing were the whole point of an Adirondack camp. Fishing was a rite of childhood for the many junior anglers who passed through the cabin's door.

When it came to fishing, Bert didn't mess around either. He was fond of fishing—spending hours out on the water in a guide boat with a bottle of his favorite hooch lying sideways between the boat's ribs, and never without a good cigar during black fly season.

Ben Bradley, the wildlife researcher who boarded with Bert during the winter of 1935, knew all about the price of groceries and other items that were affected by the depression. The men were acutely aware money was tight and often talked about it, along with how fortunate Bert was to have a wealthy employer.

Old Bert, a short, pudgy older gentleman—hat tilted at a smart angle—always took a jaunty stand when it came to commenting about the times he followed carefully on the camp's battery-powered radio. A broad smile would crinkle his weathered face, and there would be a shrewd twinkle in his eye. Left hand on hip, right fingers delicately grasping an imaginary cigar by the middle and holding it level before him, he'd tell Ben: *What the world needs is a good five-cent cigar.*

Ben got Bert's drift. Beyond all the philosophizing and chitchat about world affairs, Ben remembered Bert's cooking and those days he'd open the door to the Beaver Lake camp after snowshoeing for hours to hear Old Bert yell: "C'mon! Git it, Ben! This meal will thaw you out." This is the sort of meal Ben looked forward to as he tramped through the cold all day.

Camp Nit Meat Patties
Ingredients:
2 cups soft bread crumbs
¼ cup chopped onion
1 teaspoon salt
⅛ teaspoon thyme
½ cup water
1 pound ground venison or beef
1 cup sliced onion
¼ cup brown sugar
1 tablespoon flour
¼ cup vinegar
2 tablespoons water
2 teaspoons prepared mustard

Directions: Combine crumbs, chopped onion, seasonings, and ½ cup water. Let stand 5 minutes. Mix in meat. Shape into patties; brown in a small amount hot fat. Cover with sliced onion. Combine brown sugar, flour, vinegar, 2 tablespoons water, and mustard. Pour over meat. Cover and simmer 35 minutes. Makes 4 to 5 servings.

☆ ☆ ☆

When Chapin's Camp Nit's ownership passed from the Chapin family to Allen and Margaret Wilcox, Margaret saw to it that Bert's deer meat marinade was documented in her handwritten history of the camp they renamed Beaver Lake Lodge.

Marinade for Venison —Margaret Wilcox
Note: Venison improves with freezing, both flavor & texture.

Chop finely:
1 lb. raw carrots
1 lb. yellow onion
½ lb. celery, tops included
Cook them gently in 4 tablespoons lard without letting them take on color.

When soft, moisten vegetables with:
2 qts. vinegar
1 qt. red wine
Season with:
1 T. chopped parsley
3 crumbled bay leaves and as much thyme
1 T crushed peppercorn
1 T whole allspice
1 t salt
Boil for ½ hr. and set aside to cool. When cold, marinate meat 3 days.

Bert Brown became Camp Nit's final caretaker following the death of William "Billy Buckshot" Sanders. The body of 69-year-old Sanders was found by Bob West after a three-day search. He was clinging to an overturned canoe and frozen solid in a thick layer of ice.

A portion of the Lowville *Journal Republican*'s December 1932 column that reads: "Guide's Body Found In Ice Under Canoe" follows:

> Robert West ... [of Inlet] and a trapper at Mitchell Pond, found Sanders missing from his home on Beaver Lake Monday morning, as the latter was employed as a caretaker on the C.P. Chapin estate. West notified G.A. Kenwell...who supervises the Chapin property, and search was instituted.
>
> Thursday morning a hat and an overturned canoe found frozen in the ice led to the discovery of the body. It is believed that Sanders broke through the ice as he was returning from an overnight stay as the guest of West on Mitchell Lake nearly a week ago. Tracks in the snow indicated that he was pushing the canoe until the ice broke, plunging him into the [south branch of the Moose] river, where he either drowned immediately or clung to the canoe until overcome by cold.
>
> R.J. Lewis and Winfred C. Murdock...[of Inlet], assisted Mr. Kenwell in recovering the body. It was left in the woods and was to have been taken out on a toboggan Friday. Reuben Mick,

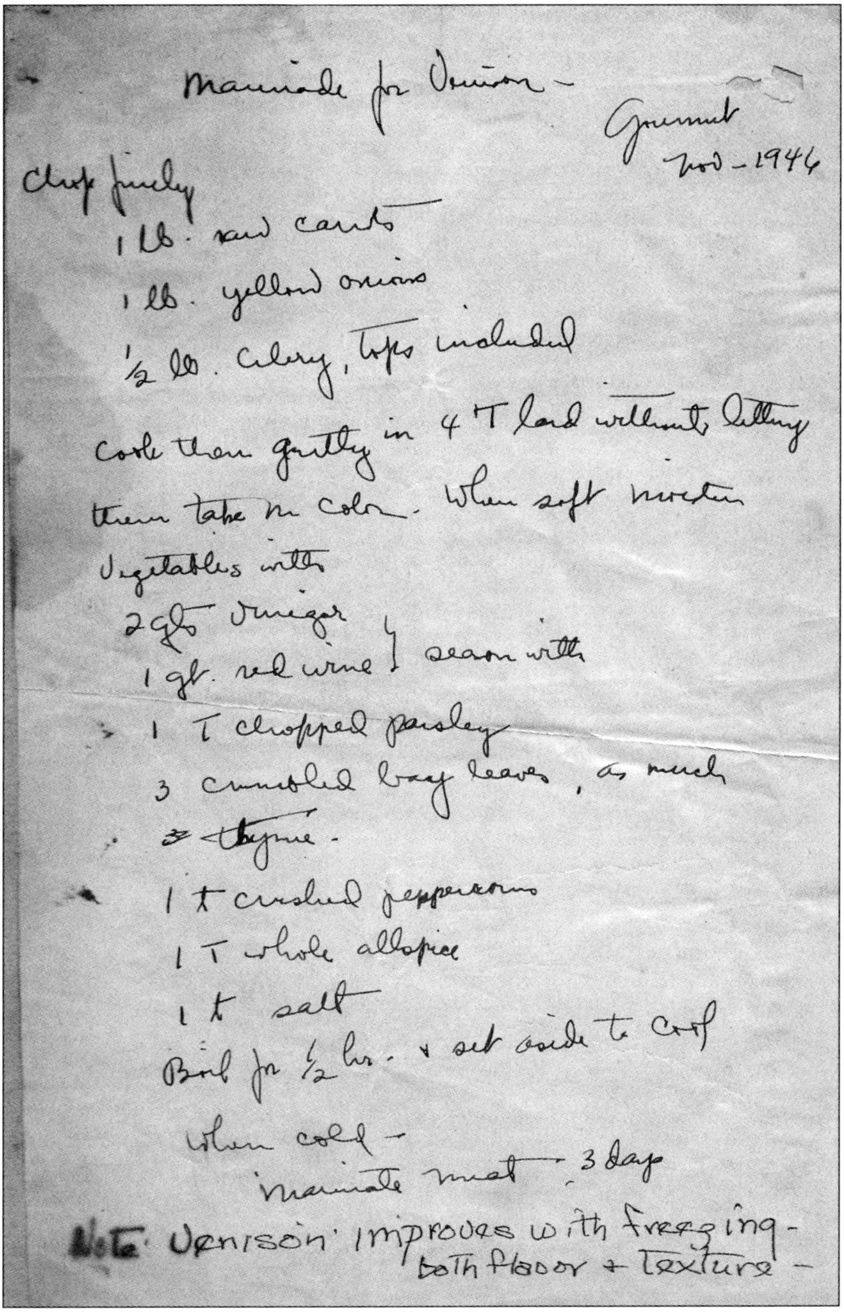

Marinade for Venison -

Gourmet
Nov - 1944

Chop finely

1 lb. raw carrots
1 lb. yellow onions
½ lb. Celery, tops included

Cook them gently in 4 T lard without letting
them take on color. When soft moisten
vegetables with

2 qts vinegar
1 qt. red wine } season with

1 T chopped parsley
3 crumbled bay leaves, as much
3 thyme.

1 t crushed peppercorns
1 T whole allspice
1 t salt

Boil for ½ hr. + set aside to cool

When cold -
marinate meat - 3 days

Note: Venison improves with freezing -
both flavor + texture -

Bert Brown's hand-written recipe which Margaret Wilcox saved. *Courtesy Margaret Wilcox*
(The Camp Nit Collection)

Raquette Lake, Hamilton County coroner, has been called.

Sanders was born in Schroon, Warren County, in 1863, and spent his early childhood in Stony Creek, later moving to Horicon with his parents. He spent the greater part of his life as a guide at Indian Lake. He leaves a brother, Harry B. Sanders, Albany, who will come to Inlet to take charge of the body. Interment will be at Warrensburg.

Bert undoubtedly knew William Sanders, and he surely added the tale of his death to his collection. After extolling the guiding expertise of "Billy Buckshot," the perfect addition was "for which no dog will ever bark."

Margaret Wilcox used this picture of Allen and another man testing the depth of ice on Beaver Lake on the cover of her hand-made Beaver Lake scrapbook. *Courtesy Margaret Wilcox (The Camp Nit Collection)*

Chapter Forty-Two

Beaver Lake's Caretakers: Frank "Pop" Baker, Billy "Buckshot" Saunders, and Bert "Warneke" Brown

"RICH IN FOLKLORE of the natural man, seasoned with salt-of-the-earth behavior, and so often admired by the people they served" seems a fitting description of Beaver Lake's three caretakers. While each man was unique, all knew the grand territory, its wildlife, and how to enjoy themselves despite the isolation of living deep in the Moose River Plains.

Margaret and Allen Wilcox knew about Frank "Pop" Baker from a distance. Charles Chapin Sr. knew him personally. For years, Chapin had swapped stories and yarns with the Wilcoxes about this Adirondack guide of distinction. In Baker's heydays, Amazia Dutton ("Dut" or "A.D.") Barber had elevated the skilled woodsman to be his head guide in charge of fifteen to twenty guides at his sportsmen's clubhouse on Jock's (later renamed Honnedaga) Lake. Baker had an outstanding reputation for his hunting, fishing and cooking skills and, in addition, his handling of a black bear that had been brought to Barber's as a cub by teamster Billy Hughes.

Harvey Dunham reported in *Adirondack French Louie* that Baker "would rather play and wrestle with the bear than eat." That might have been true of his daring back in the 1880s when Baker would fill the grown bear's belly first with a bottle of beer followed by a milk punch that consisted of a quart of milk and a pint of whiskey. It was all in good fun and provided entertainment for Barber's patrons to watch the bear cup the glass bottles with his front paws and slug the potent liquid down. Today people would consider the behavior cruel and inhumane. But, this was a typical early Adirondack merriment. Baker would lead the bear around wobbling, stumbling, and reeling on the floor until the animal began to sober up, showing the ugly side of how the alcohol affected its physiology.

During the construction of Chapin camp on Beaver Lake, Frank was living in the abandoned Beecher camp. It seemed stories about Baker were legendary except to Louie Seymour. "French" Louie and Baker never saw things eye-to-eye. Louie knew Baker could repair anything from a broken guide boat to a broken waterline and build just about anything with basic hand tools. Perhaps because it was claimed no one could land a bigger trout or drop a bigger buck than Baker, Louie might have been a bit green with envy.

"To Louie," Dunham explained, "Baker was the kind that would eat and drink everything in sight, but when it came to washing dishes or getting a pail of water would expect others to do it." For those reasons, the two celebrated characters didn't get along. Louie knew how to push Frank's buttons, too. Armed with the knowledge that Frank didn't like snakes, Louie took every opportunity to slip a snake somewhere Frank was sure to find it.

Frank "Pop" Baker stands at the far left with a group of campers by big pines on the east side of Beaver Lake not far from the spring. *Courtesy Margaret Wilcox (The Camp Nit Collection)*

Deer hunters seldom returned home from Beaver Lake without a deer.
Courtesy Margaret Wilcox (The Camp Nit Collection)

In 1904, a year before Baker's friend Wellington Kenwell completed building Camp Nit and subsequently recommended Baker to Chapin for the position of caretaker, noted New York City surgeon and Raquette Lake camper Arpad Geyza Gerster determined he wanted to meet the famous guide who was then living in the old Beecher camp,

A photocopy of a handwritten note passed on to me by Margaret Wilcox was among Camp Nit's papers. Margaret said it more than likely was one the first camp entries by a visitor. In it Gerster describes a trip to meet Baker at Beecher camp, built by a son of Henry Ward Beecher, the famed Brooklyn clergyman, and the nephew of author Harriet Beecher Stowe, who wrote the famous book *Uncle Tom's Cabin*. Following the exit of the original keeper of the south branch of the Moose River log cabin, the

Honorable D.F. Wilber, a New York State Congressman from Oneonta, N.Y. took possession. Following his connection, a number of itinerant individuals occupied the premises for short periods of time, including one skillful taxidermist who earned the nickname The Beecher Camp Hermit.

Frank "Pop" Baker, left, stands with an unidentified couple on Camp Nit's observation deck.
Courtesy Margaret Wilcox (The Camp Nit Collection)

The Wilcoxes had "great admiration for Wellington Kenwell," Margaret expressed in her camp journal, *The Story of Beaver Lake*. "About the turn of the century, Kenwell moved from Indian Lake and the Cedar River region across the Moose River Plains, and built a house on the South Branch of the Moose River near the confluence of the Otter Brook, Sumner Stream and the Indian River. This was an area especially known for its hunting and fishing. Mr. Kenwell guided and knew a great many notable men. Theodore

Roosevelt hunted with him—Kenwell lived about two miles upstream from the Beecher camp." Unfortunately, a rocking chair, a grindstone, a wire frame for jerking venison and a few other Beecher artifacts Kenwell saved from the camp before it was razed by the game protectors have been lost to the four winds.

Gerster's penmanship does not make easy reading. On Friday, May 27, 1904, guided by Wellington Kenwell, he left Sixth Lake dam at 11:20 A.M. on horseback. Gerster described his mount as "a sturdy, short and thickset Canadian pony belonging to Duprey at Fourth Lake." The men's route took them along the Limekiln Lake road. The dirt track already had a bad reputation, but a recent heavy downpour had added to the disrepair and distress. According to Gerster, when they reached the crossing at Fawn Lake's inlet, then ascended and descended on a spur of Seventh Lake Mountain, the effort was successful only "by the sagacity and surefootedness" and sheer strength of the Canadian pony. At 5:10 P.M. the men reached the south branch of the Moose River and the former Kenwell camp, described as "now occupied by one [Frank] Gray, an alcoholic."

Wellington Kenwell sold the former Kenwell place to Timothy L. Woodruff just prior to the Spanish-American War. Woodruff was a former lieutenant-governor and ambassador to Spain. David Beetle learned these details from Kenwell and subsequently reported in *Up Old Forge Way* that after a few years Woodruff "found the property too much of a burden." Shortly after, a nomadic farmer-woodman by the name of G. Frank Gray moved in. Word throughout the community was that Gray claimed to have been given permission to use the empty buildings that lay deserted. Wellington questioned Gray's claim to the property. The woodsman had a checkered reputation. He was a drinker and known to hunt out of season. He wasn't one to pay attention to the law, and he also wasn't known to have any means of a steady income.

Further evidence that Gray was occupying Woodruff's buildings illegally is offered in this official report to J.W. Pond:

By April 17, 1903, shortly after Woodruff vacated the old Kenwell place, Game Protectors R.B. Nichols and Winslow reported to J.W. Pond, Chief Protector of the Forest, Fish and Game Commission, that they'd had "just

 569

returned from Moose River and we carried out your instructions as far as possible. We destroyed the building [a barn] in the Indian Clearing and the main house at the Kenwell Place and one barn and two other small buildings, but we found a man by the name of Gray there and he had six cattle and 5 or 6 tons of hay in one barn and the cows were heavy with calf and he could not get them out now as there is some snow yet—so we left that barn and one cottage and told him we would be back there in about a month to tear them down; he forbid us of tearing any of the buildings down as he had been given an exemption…"

By May of 1904, all Kenwell's buildings had been removed but the shanty where Gray resided. Wellington Kenwell had no way of knowing Woodruff had given Gray permission to live in the building Woodruff used as a supply camp. Woodruff's Superintendent McSweeney had strung a wire for communication between Kenwell's camp and Kamp Kill Kare. That connection also provided a means of contact at each of Woodruff's three boathouses that were spaced along Sumner Stream.

The telephone line proved an important means of broadcasting the news in August 1907 that William P. Edwards, who had become lost in the woods for nine days while looking for Sol Caranahan's lumber camp, had been found.

After finding Gray in residence at the camp Wellington Kenwell had sold to Woodruff, Kenwell and Gerster climbed into a guide boat and traveled "about a mile down the Moose River Stillwater to Beaver Lake carry." Gerster continued that they "then hiked on a good, well-marked footpath southwest to the Indian River." After a tramp of about two miles downstream they reached "Baker's camp at sunset." Baker met the men as they forded the south branch. Gerster declared guide and client were "fed pretty well. Baker is a cheerful, clever, and honest fellow, in high favor with Wellington."

The following day the men "left Baker's at 7 A.M. in fine weather," retraced their previous day's track to Chapin's, "made a careful inspection of Beaver Lake [and Kenwell's building project], "and started from Gray's at 10 A.M." Five hours and fifty-five minutes later they arrived back at Sixth Lake dam, where Charley Jones was waiting for Gerster, who embarked at once over Seventh Lake on his way to Raquette Lake.

Margaret Wilcox said she had heard "Pop" Baker was very kind to Chapin's children, who did not show any "great liking for the woods. Pop lived at Beaver Lake year round—walking 23 miles out to Inlet occasionally for a visit. He would get lonely in camp and many local people were having excellent hunting and fishing trips paid for by a few quarts of liquor brought in to Pop.

Winter near Beaver Lake's outlet. *Courtesy Margaret Wilcox (The Camp Nit Collection)*

"In Pop's older years, he had not been able to walk around a great deal and not able to do much hunting or fishing, but he kept himself well supplied with trout by pulling a small net back of his canoe. The local game warden had tried for years to catch Pop doing this, but was not successful. One night about midnight in weather well below zero the game warden staggered into camp and asked for some food and shelter. Pop took a can of soup off the shelf and said, 'Here by God is your dinner and breakfast, too.' The warden told Pop he wanted a place to sleep. Pop took him into the main camp that had no heat, unfolded an army cot and threw a fish net over it and said, 'There, by God, this will strain off the coarsest of the cold.'"

Pop was employed as caretaker at Camp Nit for twenty-one years. His employer paid him in clean, new five-dollar bills. It's said he liked the feel

of the crisp, unfolded currency so much that it was the only kind of money he wouldn't spend. Instead the bills were kept in a black leather bag under his bunk. It's reported he had amassed several thousand dollars by the time of his departure in 1926. Chapin had encouraged him to deposit the money in a bank, but he would have no part of trusting his savings to an institution, even though he had little need to spend his earnings.

Chapin willingly provided him with anything he ever wanted, including twelve Baby Ben windup clocks. As the story goes, at the start of one cold winter Baker sent word to Chapin that he needed the timepieces. His employer might have wondered—even questioned the odd request—but nevertheless made sure they reached him quickly.

Once the clocks arrived, he lined them in a row on a shelf by his bunk that stood near a large-chunk-wood-burning stove.

"What's the idea of all the alarm clocks, Baker?" asked a fellow trapper, who had stopped in.

Pop replied, "Well, it gets a little nippy here in the woods sometimes, so I set the clocks before I go to bed. One alarm is set for seven o'clock, the next for eight o'clock and so on through the night. In that way the ringing wakes me up every hour. Without even having to get out of bed, I just reach over to the woodpile, grab a stick of wood and pop it into the stove—that way the fire don't go out. That was then, though. Fact is I've gotten so used to hearin' the alarms I don't really wake up any more. I just automatic-like stick the wood in the stove and roll back into the bed snug as a bug in a rug. Them clocks worked real good in solving that problem."

"As you can realize, human companionship was very scarce so far back in The Plains," Margaret told me. She knew that from firsthand experience, too. It was natural to find things to do that broke the monotony. One day a young raccoon came around. Pop spotted the critter, threw him a slice of bread, and soon the animal and Pop were fast friends. Outside the kitchen door, Pop placed a slanted board with a window wire for traction. Then he nailed on a little sheep bell, attaching a string to the ringer that hung

OPPOSITE: **Frank Baker never missed a chance to relax lakeside and share a drink in celebration of a day's work at Camp Nit.** *Courtesy Margaret Wilcox (The Camp Nit Collection)*

down close to the top of the board. It wasn't long before the raccoon learned when it was hungry that all it had to do to get a handout was reach and pull the string to let Pop know it was time to share his meal.

As legendary as North Woods characters French Louie, Johnny Leaf, and Pop Baker were, others began to surface as the sands of time moved on. When Pop passed on to the Great Beyond, he was succeeded by Billy "Buckshot" Saunders, an Adirondack native with a penchant for broad-brimmed western hats and clothing.

Buckshot's handle originated from his fondness for the shotguns he owned and his accuracy in securing partridges for the table. Buckshot was a skilled woodsman who made sure there was an active salt stump concealed but easily accessible to the camp. This was a common characteristic of old backwoods camps—and it was illegal. There were hunters who chose to believe those who made up the regulations were being too restrictive and perhaps felt their liberty was being stepped on. Others picked and chose what they cared to obey. Luring deer to salt licks or jacklighting deer are not the way a true sportsperson would hunt today. But back in the days many a hunter just got to thinking that either they were really doing no wrong, or that they could break the law and get away with it mostly because nobody would be checking up on them.

Buckshot, returning to his duties as caretaker at Beaver Lake camp from Inlet one late fall day, stopped at trapper West's cabin at Mitchell Ponds, then hightailed it over the Sheep Trail, coming down on the south branch of the Moose River's Stillwater. Buckshot broke through the ice and became trapped under the surface. His body was found the next day under a sheet of ice. He was still wearing his broad-brimmed hat.

Billy was succeeded by Bert "Warneke"[44] Brown, a man whose reputation included his passion for chewing tobacco and being so lonely at times he threatened to hold the occasional passerby hostage at the point of a gun just to have someone to talk with. Brown acknowledged that kind of gossip was pure poppycock, geared for grapevine entertainment.

Bert's main pastimes beyond hunting and fishing, were reading western pulp magazines and cooking. Bert's fish balls could easily claim blue ribbon fame. A November 10, 1935, Beaver Lake camp journal entry illustrates camp guests' fondness for Brown: "We have just finished several days of one of the most successful & most enjoyable hunting trips ever made in Mr. Chapin's Beaver Lake Camp. It has been altogether a hundred per cent part of harmony, pleasure, laughter, and every man has his deer…"

When the Chapins' son inherited Beaver Lake, the new owner found the camp's attic practically filled with pulp books. "Although the stories were just alike," Margaret reported, "that didn't seem to bother Bert any."

One fact about him that was God's honest truth was his confession that he was not addicted to walking too much. After 1929, when Al Brussel and Harold Van Auken began to operate seaplanes in the central Adirondacks, Brown hatched a landmark opportunity that benefited him. He called it "Smart Guy ingenuity." Brown knew Beaver Lake camp's location was far back from the edge of civilization. Why not invite the local bush pilots to hunt and fish at Beaver whenever they wished? In trade, pilots like Merrill Phoenix, Harold Scott and Red Panella provided him company beyond his trusty radio as well as free transportation in and out of The Plains. Sure, he might have been a wiseacre fattening on his employer's apathy, but who cared? He didn't see it as breaking any laws and he got away with it mostly because nobody was bothering to check up on him—besides there was no out-of-pocket cost to Brown for the little extra food he provided his guests. The new owner soon realized, related Margaret, that "Bert was using a considerable amount of canned goods, and one or two hams a week—too much for one man to consume—so Charles Chapin, Jr. decided to sell the property to us."

So many stories of Beaver Lake's caretakers exist they could fill a book of their own. My friend, Slim Murdock could reel them off one after another. I heard so many that each time one of their names is mentioned, I feel like I'm hearing about an old pal.

When Slim was in his eighties, he made up his mind I would accompany him on one final trip back to see the remains of his Uncle Gerald Kenwell's camp. Throughout the day, Slim relived various experiences and adventures he'd had packing throughout the 1920s and 1930s. I'll end this chapter with the following story Slim said he learned from his uncle, who heard it from Pop Baker, who fancied himself a good cook in his own right.

One day Old Pop drew a group of women who were all on a diet. He made his famous flapjacks, flipping them in the approved fashion, and served platefuls piping hot. He sat and watched the women barely nibbling and became highly insulted watching them make such a fuss over them. Deciding something drastic had to be done, he grabbed his rifle and pointed it square at the women. Looking them straight in the eyes, he demanded they eat every damn crumb of them damn paneecakes or he'd blow their brains out. Needless to say, the women were terrified and dove into the towering stacks of 'cakes.

It was customary for camp owners in The Plains to help each other out. Slim and Pop got together whenever Slim packed supplies into Beaver Lake on his way to his uncle Gerald Kenwell's place.

When Charles Chapin, Jr. sold Camp Nit to Allen and Margaret Wilcox, a former camp guest of Chapin's continued to visit the Inlet–Eagle Bay area and told Margaret with a smile, "You haven't eaten until you've tasted Pop's biscuits."

According to Margaret, the woman was referring to an incident that had happened at Camp Nit years earlier. During an evening meal, someone had remarked how unique his biscuits were. Thinking the enquirer would like to learn his secret, Pop began to reveal it was heavy cream, when the woman interrupted, remarking, "Pop, that was a stroke of inspiration to use caraway seeds."

"My God!" Pop shot back in shock. He dashed to the kitchen, lifted the lid of the flour barrel and shouted in disgust, "Just as I suspected! Those damn mice have been at that flour again." After that, he took up French Louie's suggestion and began keeping a "pet" snake in the flour barrel in spite of his inclination to fear the slithery critters.

And that IS the truth, both Slim and Margaret confirmed.

Chapter Forty-Three

Slim Murdock on His
Beaver Lake Caretaker Appointment
and Other Wanderings

"I LIVED IN THE BACK END OF CAMP NIT at Beaver Lake in the 'help portion' of the cabin." So began Slim Murdock as he began talking about his temporary caretaker job. "Uncle Gerald was the Chapin family's overseer of the place. He hired me after the passing of Buckshot. I looked after the place from late December 1930 'til the spring breakup of 1931.

The original Kenwell trail turned here. By carefully following what remains of the route you'll pass an old deer exclosure on the right. Next, sharp eyes will see the remains of the Kenwell's well. The old trail continues to the Moose River and Chapin's Crossing. During Forest Ranger Gary Lee's tenure site 80 was a blazed trail and served as the portage to the upper stillwater. Al "Carp" Carpenter took pride in mowing this trail for paddlers to roll their boats to the river. He'd be heart-broken to see how the Department of Environmental Conservation has allowed the portage to fall into disuse. *Photo by the author*

"I lived all winter alone. Old Bill 'Buckshot' Saunders had gone got drunk, fallen off a porch over at Schroon Lake, somehow made it back to Inlet, and then hoofed it back into The Plains, but he never made it back into Beaver Lake.

Winfred "Slim" Murdock at Chapin's Crossing, south branch of the Moose River. Slim used the large boulder to judge the depth of the water. If the flow was over the top he dismounted before entering the water, grabbed hold of the horse's tail and let the horse pull him across the river. Slim said horses were good swimmers. Circa 1920s.
Courtesy Winfred Murdock

"I knew Buckshot pretty well. Uncle Gerald and I were cleaning articles out of the Twin Lakes lumber camps, and this one time we were taking out the window panes that Gerald wanted to bring back to Otter Brook. Bob West was along helping us. About halfway to camp Bob said he just couldn't carry all his anymore. I thought that was a bunch of horseshit. Bob was known to be quite a walker. I've seen him carry a deer out of The Plains for a client,

OPPOSITE: **Slim Murdock, circa 1920s. "This picture was taken at Otter Brook Camp when I was truly slim." —Winfred "Slim" Murdock.** *Courtesy Winfred Murdock*

for as little as two dollars, and he never stopped—not once. Gerald told him to hold on and hurried ahead, dropped off his load and returned to pick up what Bob was carrying.

Slim holds one of his Uncle Gerald's rifles he used on deer hunts. "Gerald almost always invited friends and family to Otter Brook Camp. Sometimes there'd be several dozen guests," Slim said. His pack horses carried new potatoes and rice, a variety of dried beans, fresh ears of corn, tools, sacks of fresh apples, skillets, grain, tools and so many other things. There'd always be enough grub left that guests could stay long. *Author's photo*

"Well anyways, as caretaker I didn't just sit on my thumbs. There were various duties to perform throughout the winter. I had to cut the ice for the icehouse, and all the wood for the coming year had to be cut, split, and stacked to dry. Old Chapin kept 50 chickens back there so when he came in he could have his fresh eggs. Once in a while one would land in my stew

580

pot, but that was all right, it took care of itself because we had eggs in the spring and we raised chickens.

"Chapin's party would come into Beaver about three times a year—spring, summer and fall. Old man Wellington Kenwell told him about Beaver Lake when staying with him at his lodge [on The Plains]. Chapin couldn't have lived without Wellington. Wellington built Camp Nit. However, he never stayed in the caretaker's portion of the place. He built a separate cabin down along the side of the lake. After fording the river [south branch of the Moose] at Chapin's Crossing, the original Beaver Lake trail came in through the woods, then wound its way down to the beach, then followed along the shoreline for about a quarter of a mile to the big camp. Well, about 500 feet before you got to Camp Nit there was another small log cabin. That was Kenwell's own place when he was in to Beaver Lake working for Chapin. The Wilcoxes later used it as a guide-lumberjack shack. All this was after Wellington had moved from his lodge on The Plains and had established a store and hotel on Sixth Lake.

Slim often looked at Camp Nit's sunroom and thought about the monumental challenge his Uncle Gerald undertook to move the sunroom from the front of Camp Nit to the east side, all single-handedly! *Courtesy Margaret Wilcox (The Camp Nit Collection)*

"In my opinion, Chapin was absolutely helpless. He needed someone to wait on him hand and foot. Wellington would go out there and stay to guide for the Chapin family and their guests after his wife had died.

"One of Wellington Kenwell's pet stories about old man Chapin revolved around the time Wellington came into his guide camp at Beaver Lake. He'd just settled down to rest in a chair on the open porch, just getting ready to read, when he heard the most doggone screaming and hollering going on in the woods behind Camp Nit. Not being able to distinguish the reason for the strange noise, he decided to investigate to satisfy his own curiosity. When he climbed the ridge behind the camp there he found Charles Chapin with two of his nephews along the trail that led to the dam on the south branch. 'What's all the hollering?' he shouted out. Chapin replied, 'It's all right. I'm teaching my nephews to still hunt.'

"Another of Wellington's pet stories was that Chapin wasn't getting the kind of deer he once used to because *Wellington's* eyesight wasn't as good as it used to be!

"Chapin had to have his tea just so, pancakes 'round and brown,' and he occasionally dressed formally for dinner that was served in front of the fireplace. You couldn't wear your hunting clothes to the dinner table. Chapin hardly had nothing to do. There was an alleyway between the two parts of Camp Nit. Chapin kept to the big part of the camp and hardly ever came into the caretaker/guide's quarters unless he had some orders. That section of the building was two stories. Behind the kitchen stove there was like a cell in there and that was the caretaker's quarters. A set of stairs led up to where any visiting guides slept. No hired help ever used or slept in the front part of the camp. They had their own portion for living or they stayed in the stand-alone guide shanty down the lake. Guides did their own cooking.

"Chapin felt he and his party were upper crust and drew a line between them and his help.

OPPOSITE: **Slim Murdock at the Bear's Bathtub on Otter Brook. On Slim and the author's last visit to the Moose River Plains, they sat beside Otter Brook hour after hour as Slim shared story-after-story of the days back on The Plains and memorable sightings such as when the fruit ripened in the clearings, Slim said, "there would be a race with the bears to harvest the berries."** *Author's photo*

583

Harvey Nelson was a big insurance man in New Jersey, one of Chapin's best friends. Three different fellas I know who came in there owned banks. One of the fellas I could of damn near killed on the trip into Beaver [Lake]. On the 12-mile trip in to Beaver from Limekiln [Lake] this one fella had been fooling around with a pistol. He had had a few snorts, like a lot of men did on the way in. He owned a 6.5 Australian cavalry piece—they were just under an 18-inch barrel and were considered illegal, and back in those days a gun like that cost a hundred dollars. Somehow he busted the front sight on it on the way in. He asked me once I left and went back out to Inlet to send a telegram right away to the distributor and as soon as a new replacement arrived to bring it into Beaver Lake.

"The sight cost twelve dollars and I wanted to charge him another ten dollars for bringing it back in. Hell, that was about a 24-mile round trip for me. The damn SOB said that was too much and he would not pay me a cent. I grabbed him by the throat and had him on the floor beating the living hell out of him until some of the other guys that were around pulled me off of him. I brought that sight 24 miles, paid for the telegraph, and checked at the Inlet post office and yet $10 wasn't worth it for him, yet I'd seen that same man lose $1,200 at the turn of a card in a poker game back at Beaver Lake!

"Oh I had so much good times back there. Good memories that have lasted a life time. I could go on and on telling you all kinds of stories."

And Slim did just that. Slim was born in Glendale in Lewis County, N.Y. His family moved to Carthage in 1913, where he attended high school. His father and grandfather had lived in Inlet. Both Murdocks had operated steamboats on the Fulton Chain of Lakes. Gerald Kenwell married Slim's aunt, Ina. Gerald and Ina had one daughter named Geraldine. Slim left Carthage and moved to Inlet in 1917. "That's when I moved in with the Kenwells on Sixth Lake," said Slim. "Uncle Gerald was the gatekeeper of the dam. We were known as the 'Dam Family' in the 'Dam House.'

OPPOSITE: **Slim peppered his popular hunter training classes with stories from his experiences. He is shown here pointing in the direction of "The Kindergarten,"
Gerald Kenwell's term to a location he told first-time deer hunters to try.** *Author's photo*

Slim Murdock teaches hunters common sense

By KATHLEEN COOK

THE METHOD Slim Murdock teaches for finding direction in the woods is tried and true.

"Point your (watch's) hour hand to the sun," he says, lifting his wrist and squinting at his listener to see if she's catching on. "Halfway between that and 12 (o'clock) is south."

Slim's uncle, a government scout and rancher in the West in the late 1800s, shared the trick with him almost 70 years ago.

Slim was just a kid then, but it wasn't lost on him. Neither were his many experiences in the woods or his decades of hunting and trapping. Slim weaves them all into the hunting safety training course he's been teaching for 35 years.

W.C. Murdock, 77, of Liverpool, nicknamed Slim because that's how he used to be, is one of about 65 people in the county who are certified to teach the course, which is required for a new hunting license.

As one of what he calls the "old-timers," Slim has taught more than 2,600 students.

Originally from Carthage, Slim moved to the Adirondacks to live with his aunt and uncle shortly after World War I. They owned one of the largest hunting camps in the area and took care of lodges for people who'd come up to hunt.

Every spring was the same. Slim and some other fellows spent two weeks chopping and storing ice for "the summer people" who would come to the Adirondacks to vacation. That was followed by two weeks of trapping and two weeks of making maple syrup. One year in the 1920s he stayed six months in an isolated lodge — the whole time seeing only one other man, and that was just for a day.

During his years working in the woods, he carried 11 bodies out of the camp on horseback — men who had gotten lost and died of exposure, drowned or were shot by fellow hunters.

That bitter chore made a mark on his life. It's the reason why each year since 1953 he's gotten out his firearms, brushed up on new rules and volunteered to teach hunter safety.

"If I've saved one life," he said, "it's satisfied all the time I've given up."

Saving lives is the goal that's led the state Department of Environmental Conservation to do the same. The length of the hunting safety course went from four to six hours in 1976, and to 10 hours in 1986.

The courses are aimed primarily at preventing hunting accidents. But don't say the word "accident" to Slim. In his mind, there's no such thing.

"That word is awful hard for me to swallow," he said with a shake of his head. "Carelessness, lack of

"That's how I came to learn so much about the Kenwells, The Plains and Inlet in the olden days. Uncle Gerald taught me how to use dynamite. We blew up a hell of a lot of stumps and rocks. We were hired to clear pastures and roads and of course you already know I packed for Gerald and worked at his Otter Brook Camp.

Light Tilling   Snow Blowing
      Light Gas & Arc Welding

W. C. SLIM MURDOCK
🦌 DYNAMITE LICENSE 🦌
Stumps - Rocks - Ice Jams

7110 Buckley Rd.
Liverpool, N.Y. 13088   (315) 451-2015

Slim's business card. *Courtesy Winfred Murdock*

"Wellington was a smart man—good with mathematics and pretty much self-taught at everything. He was a sharp businessman. Gerald took after him. He could scale timber, did all the bookkeeping for the boats he operated, took care of the gas tanks on the dock, the hotel books, ran the ice cream parlor, had a taxi and trucking business, cared for horses. I remember Uncle Gerald had an old Underwood typewriter which had to be pounded on, yet Gerald could put typists to shame the way he would knock out letters quickly in the old hunt-and-peck system as he produced letters to businesses and customers who were inquiring about his rates, hunting and fishing trips, the *Osprey's*[45] schedules and such.

OPPOSITE: **Over the years Slim was the subject of numerous newspaper articles related to the Adirondacks and his volunteer work for local fish and game clubs. Slim was a walking encyclopedia regarding people, events and places in the Moose River Plains. His knowledge was extremely helpful. *The Adirondacks' Moose River Plains, Vol. 2: The Land of the Deer* contains more historical material he provided.** *Courtesy Winfred Murdock*

Gerald, Geraldine and Ina Kenwell. Slim lived with his uncle and aunt at Sixth Lake dam for many years. Slim emphasized those years of living and working in the mountains were some of the best years in his life. A favorite memory he talked about making pancakes for Geraldine when she stayed at Gerald's Red River Halfway camp.
Courtesy Town of Webb Historical Association

"The Kenwells made sure Gerald and his sister Laura got a good education back on The Plains. Wellington provided a tutor for the kids. He lived back there with them. After moving to Inlet they continued their education in the schoolhouse, although Wellington felt Gerald picked up a lot naturally from his work experience. He was very responsible.

"I enjoyed all of Wellington's remembrances of his early days. Once I tried to locate an old plow blade that he had found at the head of the Big Plains. I always wondered who in hell ever tried to come in so early and attempted to make a living by farming. That was back in the days when he moved from Indian Lake onto The Plains. No one gave a damn who was in there until Woodruff's[46] appearance.

"Besides my helping with the boat business on Sixth and Seventh lakes, Gerald taught me to handle packhorses. I became real interested in horses. I started out with one that first year. Each succeeding year the business seemed to demand more horses.

We had fishing parties in the spring and hunting in the fall [at Otter Brook camp]. Gerald didn't figure it paid to keep any guide boats on any bodies of water; he took his guests to fish differently. It was much simpler to tie a few logs together—double layered 'em and made a raft that could be staked to the bank with a rope. It also eliminated the extra expense and upkeep.

"Gerald's Uncle Ike [Isaac] was the sole representative for the Union Bag and Paper Company on the East Coast. The lumber company owned the property Gerald's Otter Brook Camp was on. The company eventually moved west without ever conducting much of a dent at any logging operation around Gerald's camp. Gerald once traveled out west in his teens. He never stayed there because of his family, and their holdings in Inlet required him to return and help out. He said Oregon was his favorite state.

"I learned to be alert along the trail. In some places there were ledges. Uncle Gerald taught me to always be on the lookout for natural crooks in trees as we hunted to make new runners that we replaced with wooden pins on the jumpers the horses pulled. I fashioned my first hockey stick from a crook. I learned to make handles for axes and so forth from maple and ash. Gerald showed me how to identify branches that could be used for a left- and right-handed handle for broad axes.

April 4, 1987.

Howdy:

Just received your large envelope containing some very good reading. I find that an awful lot has been left out in the book. Fred Hess was supposed to have come from Maine. Wellington owned that hotel before Philo Wood, (_____) Philo's grand daughter lives in Solvay (or did last I knew) Mrs. Hugh Birmingham. Charles O'Hara, father of prominent Syracuse lawyer Alton O'Hara, owned the Arrowhead Hotel and the Aroho (O'Hara backwards) that later became Hess Inn. If you could talk to Alton O'Hara you might learn a lot more of Inlet history. Also you might talk to Arch Delmarsh of Rocky Point Inn, whose great grandfather ran the Hotel on Cedar Island. My mother was a waitress there in 1904 (have picture of her). My dad was supposed to be the youngest licensed pilot-engineer on steam boats in N.Y. State, licensed in 1904 on the Fulton Chain. My Grandfather Allen Murdock had steam boats on both 7th & 8th Lake in the 1890's. Allen Murdock and Frank Murdock were among the first voters in Inlet. E. VanArnam, also a first voter was a relative on my mother's side. Henry Froelich, a widely known chef, was at Cedar Island when Mother was there in 1904. He also worked at Rocky Point Inn and the hotel at Theudara. VanArnams Tavern. He cooked in California and Florida, He also cooked several years at Jenwells Otter Brook Camps. The Osprey operated by Byrd as the biggest launch on the lakes, was built by Jenwells at Sixth Lake. They fed with the shore dinner parties for years. Cooking for as many as 300 people a day at 7-8th Lake Carry. The Osprey is now the Pirate ship at Enchanted Forest in Old Forge.

Slim's hours of voice recordings and numerous handwritten letters were an invaluable resource to the author, who is grateful for his help and friendship. *Courtesy Winfred Murdock*

"Oh boy, do I remember the awful loads I took in and out of Otter Brook—even carried things on my back."

Slim also remembered a whole lot of other things that I could not store in just one book. The many recording tapes I made of our conversations are full of his experiences. For instance, Slim remembered the day Harold "Scotty" Scott moved to Fourth Lake. "When Scotty first came to Inlet he didn't even make hardly enough to pay for the gas in his [float] plane. He used to keep his plane under the bridge in Inlet. Scotty and his partner, Chet Lawood lived over Panella's garage next to the Red and White store in Inlet. Early in their partnership they were coming into a dock over at Big Moose Lake, and whatever happened, a switch could have gotten turned back or something, but Chet was on the pontoon reaching out for a post on the dock when the motor turned over one more time and the propeller took his arm off. That ended that partnership."

Slim flew with Scotty many times. Once they were heading to Beaver Lake in a fog. Slim wondered how they would ever land. Another time when they approached Beaver Lake, Slim said, "The motor quit. The pontoons were hitting the treetops. Scotty was a man of guts. He'd come out with two canoes lashed to each of his pontoons and two deer in the cockpit of his plane."

Slim Murdock always felt his days spent in the woods were the best years of his life. During the Great Depression years he saw many wealthy people who used to travel to Europe decide instead to come to the Adirondacks. Slim recalled, "There was a predominance of women, though. They used the hotels and had camps to use to get away from the city."

If my research has taught me one thing, it's if you want to learn about something, just ask an old-timer. Slim was one of those people whose rich memories of decades ago routinely echoed through his mind throughout his lifetime.

The Beaver Lake camp Slim talked about has long passed into history. However, if one searches through the bushes to the west of where it once stood, they will still find remains of the well house and the cobblestone ice house where Slim used to haul blocks of ice he cut from the lake to store for the Chapins' next season at their Camp Nit.

Chapter Forty-Four

Pop Baker's Guardian Snake

WINFRED "WINNIE" MURDOCK has talked at great length about his connections with the old-timers he knew who were connected to the Moose River Plains.

The following remembrance came from Winnie, who observed it on a day he stopped at Beaver Lake to drop off supplies before continuing to his Uncle Gerald Kenwell's camp farther beyond along Otter Brook.

Frank Baker with a bear at Barber's at Jock's Lake when he was head guide for Amazia Dutton Barber. *Courtesy Edward Blankman (The Lloyd Blankman Connection)*

OPPOSITE: **Frank "Pop" Baker in Camp Nit's kitchen.** *Courtesy Joan Payne (The Bob West Collection)*

Frank "Pop" Baker had been a noted guide for Amaziah Dutton "Dut" Barber's Club on Jock's Lake (Honnedaga) and the Adirondack League Club. For many years Pop was the caretaker of Camp Nit, a lodge on the shore of Beaver Lake. Gerald's father, Wellington had built the log lodge at the turn of the 20th century for a Rochester, N.Y. car-wheel tycoon named Charles T. "Chapes" Chapin.

Memories of Camp Nit were fond ones. *Courtesy Tom Gates (The Camp Nit Collection)*

"Pop fancied himself a good cook in his own right," Winnie said with authority. I knew Murdock himself was an excellent cook. He wouldn't bestow laurels on anyone if he didn't know it was so.

"Pop had a flair of old-time guide-like flamboyance when preparing food; he could be a bit cranky if his food wasn't eaten with appreciation," said Winnie.

Louie taking a walk. Word had it at Barber's that Frank Baker and "French" Louie Seymour had an on-going rivalry. In *Adirondack French Louie* by Harvey L. Dunham wrote: "They liked Louie at Barber's and looked out for him. When he left after a visit, Dut usually had one or two of his guides trail him the next day as far as Jones or Poor Lakes or to the second stillwater to see that he got through all right. It would probably be Eddie Robertson and Any Carmen who followed him; anyone but Baker, for in an argument Louie had threatened to shoot him." *Courtesy Edward Blankman (The Lloyd Blankman Connection)*

"One summer day, Uncle Gerald asked me to stop by Beaver Lake to deliver some dry goods—rice, flour, sugar, corn meal, and other items. As I entered the kitchen Pop had drawn a group of women who were sitting at a table by the kitchen range. Pop was preparing his prized flapjacks, a recipe he was known for making. A large stack already set on a large platter on the warmer as he flipped the final "pan-e-cakes" high, catching each one with the deftness of an acrobat.

"As the piled-high platter was placed on the table, one of the ladies made a comment about a few of them being on a diet.

"Hearing the comment, Pop removed a shotgun that hung over the door, pointed the rifle at the women and growled, 'You'll eat every last one right down to the final crumb.'

"Needless to say, they all dove into that stack of cakes, never saying another word."

In the 1930s Allen and Margaret Wilcox were operating The Mohawk Inn on Fourth Lake in Eagle Bay, New York. During a conversation I had with Margaret in the 1980s, she shared this true tale about Pop.

"A former camp guest of Chapin's continued to visit the Inlet–Eagle Bay area. She vacationed at The Mohawk yearly. One day as I mentioned to her that Allen and I had recently purchased Chapin's Beaver Lake property she said to me with a smile that indicated she had an incredible story to tell. 'Oh, Pop! You haven't eaten until you've tasted Baker's biscuits.'"

According to Margaret, the woman related an incident that had happened at Camp Nit years earlier. During an evening meal, someone had remarked how unique Pop's biscuits were compared to any they had eaten. Thinking the enquirer would like to learn his secret, Pop had begun to reveal it was heavy cream, when the woman interrupted, remarking,

"Pop, that was a stroke of inspiration to use caraway seeds."

"My God!" Pop shot back in shocked horror. He dashed to the kitchen, lifted the lid of the flour barrel and shouted in disgust, "Just as I suspected! Those damn mice have been at that flour again." After that, he kept a pet snake in the flour barrel.

Chapter Forty-Five

Caroline Nelson and Emily Chapin's Beaver Lake Visit

IN THE ADIRONDACKS, swarms of stinging, biting, crawling and flying insects abound from spring into late summer. Natives throughout the Adirondack Park have a multitude of stories about the insects, about the concoctions they brewed up as repellents, and about the unsuspecting vacationers.

One old-time fly-dope mixture called for three parts pine tar, two parts castor oil, and one part pennyroyal oil. It was to be mixed and heated slowly to blend.

Caroline Nelson had strong camping ties to the central Adirondacks. Her family had owned a camp in Eagle Bay for over a generation. Caroline told me, "I have great camp memories," as she mentioned briefly a few details about her grandfather, who was a guide, before turning the conversation to her own outdoor experiences.

Like so many others who had close ties to the Old Forge-to-Inlet area, Caroline grew up at her family's camp on Fourth Lake. It's the largest of the eight lakes that comprise the Fulton Chain of Lakes—so named after Robert Fulton, of steamboat fame, who made a survey of the lakes under the waterway investigation ordered by the State of New York in 1811. The vast forest country surrounding the chain was a paradise for anglers, hunters and recreationists.

"You have stirred my memory," she exclaimed when I asked her to speak about her horseback trips in to Beaver Lake during the 1920s. "It was before sleeping bags," she began, "so I was taught how to use a poncho and blanket to make a bed roll, which included a change of underwear, socks, and personal items.

"On my 1926 trip I rode with an Eagle Bay girlfriend and Emily Chapin. Emily was camping at Dr. Longstaff's Moss Lake Girls' Camp.

"We began our ride into the Big Indian Clearing on pack horses from Limekiln Lake. Emily called it 'The Wilderness' because that's what she had learned at Moss Lake Camp, but she knew about the area because her grandfather, Charles Chapin, owned Camp Nit on Beaver Lake. He gave Dr. Longstaff's girls permission to use the family's comfortable log cabin."

Caroline found the old pictures of Camp Nit I showed her interesting. She remarked, "That's just the way I remember the place." I had amassed a large number of vintage sepia-tone snapshots connected with the Chapin family and their camp.

"We followed the Kenwell Trail," she said. "As I recall, it wound through a vast stretch of forest known as the Gould Lumber territory. While crossing The Plains we collected wildflowers and studied them in a book we found at Camp Nit.

"The entire trip was long but enjoyable. The log bridge was out when we reached the south branch of the Moose River, so we had to carefully descend a steep bank going down one side, wade the shallow river, and scramble up again over the bank to the Chapin Trail on the opposite side.

"The forest around Beaver Lake was delightful because it was so wild," she recalled. "If I remember correctly, we saw a moose swimming toward the center of the lake, a first for us."

On beaver-tail-shaped mile-long Beaver Lake, deep in the heart of the Moose River Plains, Caroline and the girls met Frank "Pop" Baker.

Baker, the caretaker at Camp Nit, had been a notable guide in his younger years. "Everyone called him Pop," she said. In Pop's younger years he had worked as a conductor on the Mohawk & Malone Railroad, later the Adirondack Division of the New York Central, but quickly shifted his attention to guiding—something he was good at.

In Pop's old age, Wellington Kenwell recommend him to Charles Chapin to be Camp Nit's caretaker. During Pop's years of guiding, he had rubbed

OPPOSITE: **Pop Baker early in his caretaker's career at Beaver Lake.** *Courtesy Joan Payne (The Bob West Collection)*

599

elbows with other noted guides and knew "French" Louie Seymour well. In his later years at Chapin's camp, he developed a reputation as an excellent cook and amusing host among the visitors who made their way to the lake by hiking or on horseback. Caroline said Pop told her some came by "to fish or just pay a neighborly visit to the old-timer."

1907 Camp Nit snapshots taken at Beaver Lake show some women dressed in white dresses, shirtwaists, low shoes and drop-stitch stockings. This must have made biting a cinch for the black flies, punkies and mosquitoes, compared to attacking the women who dressed in knickerbockers, leather leggings, flannel shirtwaists and felt hats.

Caroline recalled, "Fishing equipment was at the cottage, so we spent time out in the water, sitting on rocks, fishing. Somehow, I had found hip-boots. I put them on over my footwear and in the course of moving from rock to rock I fell into the lake. The rubber boots filled with water and the suction was so great the boots couldn't be pulled off, so I was held by Pop and my friends in a headstand while the water drained out, releasing the suction and me from the boots."

As the first faint shadows of twilight began to fall across the lake, the girls were seated with Pop on the high deck, which was constructed so the viewing platform extended out over the lake.

"We were rehashing the day's activity," said Carolyn. "Fishing and swimming, tracking some animals, helping prepare meals made the hours go too fast."

"I remember Pop served us warm apple muffins and tea," she recalled. "At a point in our conversation he interrupted to point out some activity, handing us binoculars to pass around. Across the lake, a black bear cub was busily scooping ants from a rotted log split open by its mother. In the bay, nearly covered with lily pads, two deer were extracting roots and succulent grasses. All was serenely quiet; only the gentle lapping of water kicked up by a mild breeze broke the silence."

As the group sat taking in the wild setting, Pop cautioned that with night would come mosquitoes. The girls had been on many wilderness trips. They were aware of mosquitoes. They didn't consider the insects something to be too concerned with other than the buzzing annoyance and bites. They had, however, been forewarned about bears, and all knew the dangers that could accompany a horse's fear of bears if the animal was frightened.

Pop agreed with them. An injury could happen if a frightened horse bucked in even a not-too-spirited way. That put aside, he warned that earlier in the week the insects had been acting up, tormenting the deer until they drove them crazy. The girls just laughed and told Pop they would not be put off by a few mosquitoes.

Horseback riding and care of the animals at Moss Lake were popular activities.
Courtesy Town of Webb Historical Association

Pop said a visitor had told him the same thing just last week. Pop, looking very serious, told them the man had sat unconcerned, right where they were sitting, until they heard an ominous drone of startling magnitude. The buzz emanated from the stagnant swamp water on the opposite side of camp. Looking up, the man saw a rapidly approaching dark object that quickly became recognizable as a formation of two titan mosquitoes descending toward him.

As fast as was humanly possible, Pop turned toward the camp door at a dead run. He knew he needed to get inside quickly before he was spotted. His guest, unfortunately, was too late; the mosquitoes had seen him. His only chance, however slim, was to leap as if his life depended on it into the lake.

Mr. Guest hurdled the railing hardly a whisker ahead of the blood-thirsty insects. But before he was able to drop like a cannon ball into the depths, he was lifted straight up in the air and carried out over the water by the pair of mosquitoes.

In his totally aghast state, he thought he could hear his two captors arguing over his elimination. "Want to eat him on the opposite bank or in the backwater?" he heard one ask the other. The reply was, "Are you crazy? We had better take him deeper into the woods before the big ones come along and take him away from us."

Terrified and thinking he was close to death, the man flailed out at the mosquitoes with his arms and furiously kicked his legs until they lost their grip and dropped him into Beaver Lake. The waves carried him toward shore, where he was pulled out by Pop. The camp guest left the Moose River Plains the next morning, swearing never to return for another vacation in the Adirondacks.

As for the girls, they escaped the sad fate of Pop's earlier visitor. Their wilderness trips to Beaver Lake and Pop's knack for storytelling were a happy part of their camping remembrances.

Carolyn ended her remembrance on a high note. "Everything was new and exciting then—the wildness of the whole area. No modern touches—not even radios. It was great. I wish the pictures I took were here [in St. Petersburg, Florida]. They are stored in my daughter's attic in Virginia."

☆ ☆ ☆

On September 4, 1926, following the girls' visit with Pop, who lived in virtual isolation and knew almost nothing of the events and the progress going on outside Beaver Lake, Utica realtor A.W. Rizika was announcing his initial step toward developing a new hostel on the site of the historic Forge House that had been destroyed by fire on July 3, 1924.

Rizika's contract for the burned-out structure, along with 22 building lots and an eight-room cottage, was for more than $50,000.

Decades earlier, Baker had known the area as a supply depot and hostelry for trappers, hunters, and woodsmen. The hotel gradually developed until before its destruction it had grown to be a famous landmark where many famous musicians gave concerts. Among its guests several presidents of the United States were numbered, and especially President Harrison, for whom the Central Adirondacks was a favorite stomping ground. But by that time Baker had been living in the woods and guiding sportspeople for decades.

Pop Baker would probably have also found it amusing to read a Saturday, September 4, 1926 article in an unidentified newspaper headlined "Indians, As of Old, Invade The Adirondacks." Baker, a long-time friend of the Kenwell family, might have found pause reading about Gerald Kenwell described as "Big Chief Helmsman Gerald Kenwell." Early Saturday, Gerald had been hired to erect tents and tepees on the shore of Eighth Lake, where he prepared a "large watch fire" and set up tables and benches where food would be served for a big wedding feast, described in language that would not be considered appropriate today: "prepared by the squaws, and spread under the low-hanging balsam trees at high noon."

Gerald was to guide the bride, Miss Margaret Webber, groom Eugene Cameron and the wedding party in a flotilla of boats through the Fulton Chain of Lakes to the shore of Eighth Lake, where "Big Bear Charlie Wright of Thendara" and Robert Crosdell of Eagle Bay Hotel, as "Medicine Man (or priest)…dressed in the shawls, beads, bracelets and carrying the jewels of a high Indian priest, many of which have been handed down through many generations, and have been actually used in the enactment of many wedding ceremonies…would faithfully conduct…" an outdoor Indian marriage ceremony.

Following a big wedding feast "…the modern sports pitched horseshoes, participated in races, bathing, and dancing [which] contributed to the enjoyment. The Gaiety Theater and Eagle Bay Hotel orchestra combined in the rendition of appropriate music for the ceremony and for dancing…."

Pop, who had taken men and women on genuine camping and hunting trips with only the duffle and necessaries of life that could be provided in an Adirondack pack basket, might have found himself smiling widely when he learned of the fanfare of Gerald's guided trip compared it to Pop's recollection of his first guided trip to the North Woods. Pop had been known to mutter that the most important function of the modern school of Adirondack guides was "picking lilies" and conveying guests in a guide boat around a body of water, then bringing them safely back to the hotel.

By 1926, 'guiding' was not what it used to be!

Chapter Forty-Six

What Happened
to Old "Pop" Baker?

BURIED ON PAGE FOURTEEN in the July 1, 1926, issue of the *Boonville Herald and Adirondack Tourist* is a sketch of Frank "Pop" Baker, once a renowned guide and accomplished woodsman who was still living—just barely—in the central Adirondack region. The reporter, who is identified only as the newspaper's Tourist reporter, interviewed Baker at the New Neodak Hotel[47] near Inlet, where Royal "Roy" Rogers was caring for him until other arrangement for his care could be made.

In that summer of 1926, the *Tourist* reporter characterized Pop Baker as "a bewhiskered old pioneer who had the instinct of an Indian and who could tell whopping stories of ancient game trails which led him hundreds of miles through mountain solitudes," and that was true. There were few oldsters of his caliber living by that time. The *Tourist* said, "One by one they have taken the long, long trail which winds its way throughout eternity, where there are no carries and where packs are light. If you had been with the writer of this article a few days ago and had seen and talked with one of those old fellows who literally had hewn his way into this greatest vacation land of the state, you would have seen the woods as they originally were."

The article, titled "Old Timers of the Adirondacks: Pop Baker, the Hermit of Beaver Lake" follows in its entirety.

> Feeble and bowed by his more than three score years and ten,
> he sits thinking of the days when as a boy he left his home in
> Boonville to answer the call of the great woods and of the
> many days and years he spent at the heart of nature learning

OPPOSITE: **One of the last pictures taken of Pop Baker before he left Beaver Lake.**
Courtesy Joan Payne (The Bob West Collection)

604

her secrets, her pleasures and her hardships, and incidentally earning his livelihood as woodsman, guide and trapper. The name of this old timer is Frank Baker, and for a great many years known to all as "Pop." For the past 21 years he had been stationed at Beaver Lake as caretaker. Last fall his employers considered him too old to continue in useful service and he was asked to vacate. Troopers helped him to the outside world, for it was hard for him to leave the place he called home. This friendly old-timer had hunted with Alvah Dunning,[48] Sam Dunakin and such people as those whose names are still by-words in this country.

Pop caught snoozing in the shade. *Courtesy Margaret Wilcox (The Camp Nit Collection)*

He was sitting on the dock of the New Neodak Hotel, where he had been stopping for a few days until he could find some place to live. His meager store of funds is nearly exhausted, and he has no friend or relative to whom he can turn. He is feeble and bowed with the years of labor, of carrying the Adirondack pack and guide boat through woodland trails, for the pleasure of sportsmen who could hire a vacation.

At Beaver Lake he lived as a hermit, and for 13 years he was never out of sight of the spot where he dwelt. As he sat on the dock of the New Neodak looking across the water to where the thriving village of Inlet now stands, there was a look of bewilderment in his eyes. He did not know the village where he had passed through years ago when there was only one shanty there. He could hardly believe his eyes that the old Hess Camp, which was the only place at the head of the lake 50 years ago, had given way to a lively little village.

Roy Rogers, manager of the New Neodak, took Pop to a barber shop while he was at the hotel, to get the necessary tonsorial work done to make him a little more presentable to the guests. When he was in the barber chair, he said it was the first work he had done by a barber for 14 years. He had cut his own hair and shaven himself for that time.

At Beaver Lake, although a long way to travel, he had many visitors. He had a faculty of getting the confidence of all of the animals and birds which abounded around his cabin. His tame coons were a wonder to all who saw them, and the timid deer used to come to the camp to get their rations at the call from the man of the woods. Birds would swoop out of the trees and pick crumbs from his hand.

He has lived his life, so to speak, a life of service to others, and as the old-timer sat looking over the waters of Fourth Lake, he seemed to look over the tops of balsams and spruce and through the eternal blue to the great throng that surround the bright campfire in the beyond, where the Head Guide who has been over the trails of life and knows how rough and stony the path, is telling the old, old-timers true stories of times that were from the beginning.

And now what is to become of our old-timer, "Pop," until he shall cross the "Great Divide"? There are institutions for the penniless and the friendless, but they are not along blue waterways and green shaded trails, and we wager a guess if "Pop" had his way, like Hiawatha, he would rather drift into the land of Golden Sunset, "The land of the hereafter."

Frank "Pop" Baker was a tough woodsman, as those of his generation of Adirondackers had to be. His courage, skill, and mastery of the conditions of his chosen life were absolute or he would not have survived as he had. Nor would he have chosen a woods life if he had not responded to the beauty and advantages of the Adirondacks and found in a mountain way of life something precious beyond personal safety, financial gain, and rugged comfort.

Pop was known to talk about the most interesting times at Beaver Lake as being the loneliness of an Adirondack mid-winter where snow was often six feet deep and foxes, fishers, mink, ermines, northern hares, porcupines, partridges, red squirrels, blue jays, and deer were his only company. Beaver Lake was a wild, lonesome place miles from the nearest village in the depths of the Moose River forest, but it was home.

Slim Murdock reported the last he knew: "Pop left Inlet and drifted off to some unknown place in the Forestport area where Josh Clayton had given him a horse." It is hard to speculate on what became of the impoverished old woodsman, so much admired in his prime, and forced to leave his beloved wilderness for what must have seemed a busy, modern and confusing place. One can only hope that "Pop" Baker's story ended well, and that his trail home was one that brought a smile of recognition.

OPPOSITE: **Pop was often the photographic subject of many people who wished to capture a memory of their Beaver Lake holiday.** *Courtesy Joan Payne (The Bob West Collection)*

Chapter Forty-Seven

Moose River Bushwhacks

"ON MY OWN and with the help and guidance of people like LeRoy Short, Ted Harwood, Bob Daws, Slim Murdock, and others, I've spent years searching for the locations of the sites of former lumber and sporting camps throughout the expansive Moose River Plains country. I have also been enlightened by old timers' experiences as well as absorbed stories of camp life shared by native and non-native families' remembrances of their connection with The Plains. The camp stories recorded in *The Adirondacks' Moose River Plains, Vol. 1* are only "the tip of the iceberg" as an old expression goes. I've collected the histories and stories about many other former camps, and look forward to sharing this further research, my adventures, and the finds I've made.

When I look at the snapshots I clicked of Lone Pine Camp near Bear Pond, I always remember how welcoming the cabin looked as I approached it just before dusk, having snowshoed Seventh Lake Mountain. My adopted frontier-like outpost was a miles-long vigorous trek. My weekend prowls took me winding through forests and thickets of snowcapped cripple bush in the upper Red River Valley, and then a drop down a precipitous open rock face led me to the frozen surface of Bear Pond. The path to my destination might have resembled that of a coyote wandering through the thickly-wooded base of Mount Tom. The last time I visited the spot in the summer, its burned-out remains had taken on that special look that whispers *I-belong-here* among the tight growth of brambles.

OPPOSITE: **Years of bushwhacking throughout the Moose River Plains, discovering evidence of human activity, and talking to old-timers, kickstarted the author's desire to document and share the informal history of the Moose River Plains.** *Author's photo*

Lone Pine Camp gave me a comfortable base to go out from and a warm, cozy end to a day of exploring. At night, lying awake in a bunk watching faint flickers of flame through the cracks in the cast iron wood-stove gave me pause to think of the work it took John Ferris and his campmates to raise the building. Again, the cabin spoke: *You shoulda been there then!*

John Ferris gave me permission to use Lone Pine Camp near Bear Pond for my winter exploring. The former camp led to my drinking Jack Rabbit Brew, a concoction I would have never anticipated I'd actually enjoy. This is how the story unfolded.

During the closing years of the 1980s, John Ferris offered the key to use Lone Pine Camp, his Mount Tom Hunting Club's somewhat derelict hunting shanty located a short distance northwest of Bear Pond outlet. The building gave me a comfortable base to explore the vast Moose River territory. In return for John's generosity, I packed out possessions he wanted. John knew he was not physically able to trek back for them.

Author's photo

I have not returned to the former site. The mountains, streams, pond, and tufts of grass that poked above the snow are clear in my mind. I occasionally think of making a return reconnaissance just to snoop around, but the frenetic outdoor activity of my younger days is largely over, although I believe I could still hold up to the physical requirement. No, I like the memories John Ferris related to me, and I also enjoy relishing my own. Besides, there are many other places throughout this big chunk of land that touch me in other ways.

A few of my other Plains rambles are relived in this ending.

I met LeRoy Short when he was 94 years old. LeRoy hammered out a trap line camp from the remains of Gould Paper Company's old granary at Camp 5, at the confluence of Wolf Creek and Indian River. That was back in the late 1940s. I had made two attempts to locate old Camp 5. Over time, a colony of beaver had created a flow that had obliterated any sign of an approach.

LeRoy promised to guide me to it after I failed to find it. "Give me three weeks to practice walking on the golf course, Jay. I'll take you right to it," he said confidently.

LeRoy had only two requirements. I was to meet him at 4:30 in the morning at Muskrat Creek in the Moose River Plains, and I needed to have a 12-cup pot of coffee ready to drink. "At exactly sunrise," he told me, "I'll be ready to start off. The coffee will be gone by then."

LeRoy downed cup after cup and rehashed his years of trapping from Wolf Creek to Little Indian Lake.

Every twenty minutes LeRoy stopped for a breather. By noon he had led me to the exact spot where I had given up—a beaver-created flow. Pointing, LeRoy announced, "It's about a two-minute walk after we wade through the water." All I had needed to do weeks earlier was push my way through the murky quagmire the beaver had created. I had been within a long stone's toss from the old camp!

The trip turned extra-exciting for LeRoy when he spotted the old outhouse, still somewhat standing forty years after he had spent his final night in the granary he'd converted into a rough trapper's hut.

☆ ☆ ☆

I carried a day pack on a damp mid-October day, when I accompanied then, eighty-five-year-old Ted Harwood and his brother Bob, who was ninety-one. They wanted to revisit the site of E.J. Turner's first camp, where their father had served as caretaker. The search for Bear Paw Camp was a family

Following an arduous Friday evening snowshoe over Seventh Lake Mountain to reach the isolated camp, my partner and I arrived well after dark. Once we had fired up the box stove, warmed the interior and settled in, I took on the job of camp snow scooper. The task was simple: Quickly dash out in the pitch dark into deep, cold snow, clad in only long johns and rubber bottom boots. Scoop snow, packing it into a large metal percolator. Then hightail it back into the cabin before I began to chill down. My natural inclination was to move at high speed in the freezing temperature. The drill preserved any noticeable loss of heat.

"Tea soon," I told my buddy as I plunked the pot onto the hot surface of the stove, watching the snow on the outside of the container immediately melt, fizzle and bounce on the hot cast iron top. We agreed the aroma of black tea infused the camp with a guacamole-like scent and commented that the brew had a taste never before experienced. *Author's Photo*

affair. The men brought along a few nieces and nephews. We bushwhacked from the site of their father's Hot Top Camp, located in a very low, wet, brushy section of the Moose River Plains. The Harwoods' parents spent a portion of their honeymoon there in 1931.

As we bushwhacked, my tape recorder picked up a colorful variety of comments as we sought out the former camp's location. Some remarks requested confirmation such as, "Which way do we go now, Bob?" Others quizzed: "I thought you said it was only a mile farther. It's already been over two!" One niece offered a heartfelt opinion: "Holy smoke! This is not my idea of a place to go to the bathroom." Then there were the feigned complaints: "Come on, guys. You're taking us through another swamp!"

Hours later, at the site of a huge boulder, the brothers led us to the former Bear Paw site. It had been fifty years since they had been there. They found it without consulting a map.

☆ ☆ ☆

Bill Apagar led me directly to the spot of his former Red River Camp the same way LeRoy and the Harwood brothers had found their way through the woods—without map and compass. Bill's choice of footwear to traipse through the cripple brush was cowboy boots.

He had set up camp in the headwaters of the Red River. He said he received the camp as a gift from an Indian who had lived in the Inlet–Raquette Lake area. On our return, we took several side trips to visit the ruins of Floyd Puffer's Red River Camp, the Miller Camp near Bear Pond, and Gerald Kenwell's timeworn Halfway Camp. All the sites still held reminders of their former occupants.

☆ ☆ ☆

My reaction at first light: "I reckon we're still alive." My rather droopy eyes opened wide as I unzipped the tent and guardedly stepped outside. Dawn was not quiet and the Indian River was not shy. The dripping leaves, pools of water, and the lightning-struck toppled tree that lay close to my aluminum canoe were all morning-after reminders of a fierce all-night thunder and lightning storm.

Two days earlier, Paul Sirtoli and I had launched into the south branch of the Moose River at Rock Dam and paddled upstream before beaching. Bushwhacking would be the only way, with any luck, to spot anything that might remain of a former camp. Later that day I added another black dot to my map. It indicated the location of remains of the Beecher Camp found about a mile upstream from Rock Dam.

Our success buoyed us for the next part of the expedition. Ed Maunton, an old trapper and retired employee of the state Conservation Department who joked that his job title had been Conservation Aide in Fur Resources, had filled my head with a French Louie find. Ed's professional trapping days had connected us. Our mutual interest was the far-back Moose River Plains country. I guessed Ed's curiosity, outstanding woodsmanship and luck helped him locate what he claimed were the remains of Louie's trap line camp near Stink Lake. He also claimed to have come across a hoard of rusty traps. Paul and I had no delusions about actually finding the camp.

Let no one ever tell you bushwhacking along the Indian River or anywhere in Stink Lake Mountain country is a "cake walk." The best way to describe it is an arduous beating of the bushes. Armed with a copy of Scudder Todd's "1930 Map of Adirondack League Club Preserve" that identified Gould Paper Company's log roads and camps, we did locate the site of a lumber company camp on the western end of Stink Lake Mountain and what we think was the site of "Johnson's Camp." It was smack dab between Stink Lake and Balsam Lake on the route Gould's secondary log road took between Canachagala Stillwater and the Indian River. By the time we had reconnoitered through Stink Mountain Pass and made it back to camp at the outlet of the Indian River, I avowed my historic curiosity was satisfied by that trip.

But, it wasn't just the expedition that has stuck with me all these years. It was a combination of my physical effort, the all-night storm with intense rain, wind, and seemingly endless thunder and lightning bolts, concerned that at any moment we might be killed if a strike grounded in the tree roots below our tent.

I saw a similar fear in the eyes of a lost hunter a partner and I had accidentally come across the previous year during deer-hunting season. He had gotten disoriented within fifteen minutes after leaving his Squall Lake campsite at

9 A.M. By 2 P.M. he ended up almost down to the flats on the first still-water on the Indian River. Luckily for him, that day we had been following the outlet of Little Indian Lake in hopes of finding what might have been the location of Al "Carp" Carpenter's camp somewhere along that flow. I'll save that tale for a later time.

Lone Pine Camp kitchen. Come morning, in the full light of a clear sky that lit the interior, we discovered, much to our surprise, a solid mass of soggy rabbit droppings on the bottom of the pot. The sighting raised our eyebrows in surprise and made us wonder if we would have food poisoning, but the eye-catching sight was also good for several laughs and served as fodder for some amusing names for our concoction: "Pink Eye of Rabbit," "Colon Grog," and "Graceful Bowels" were considered, but in the end we settled on "Jack Rabbit Brew," which perfectly described the drink and the camping story we have retold over the years. And, as for any ill effects—we lived through the experience without one bit of suffering.

Was it the boiling that saved us from getting sick or perhaps the bottle of Southern Comfort we laced the tea with, or a combination of both that protected us? In any event the experience added a new true tale of another memorable winter time in the Moose River Plains. *Author's photo*

Retired Colonel LeRoy Short stands on a section of corduroy road minutes from his old Camp 5. He leased vacant lumber camps from the Gould Paper Company from 1945 until 1964. The Wolf Creek area was his favorite deer hunting grounds. *Author's Photo*

My last trek to the former Little Moose Lake Clubhouse site included Hamilton County historian Bill Zullo and Piseco Lake historian, Bryan Rudes. There are no marked trails to follow, but the walking is easy over slightly grown-in log roads. It's necessary to refer often to a topographical map, or one could easily be misled and wander in the wrong direction. We found that out on our return trip. Instead of returning to Cedar River Flow, we inadvertently took a wrong turn that steered us to Silver Run and The Plains road from the Indian Clearing to Cedar River Flow. That unexpected additional distance cost us an extra five miles of hiking.

Little Moose Lake is one of my favorite places. I'm drawn back by the setting—quiet, peaceful, relatively remote. It's not a place where you would expect to find anyone else. I've thought about carrying an ultralight pack boat to investigate the lake and to fish. I have a marketing brochure David E. Farrington, the successor to Elijah Camp, printed. The Little Moose Lake business flyer announced in large letters that the lake had *"Excellent* TROUT *Fishing!"* Carrying a full backpack and a boat would be difficult at best for me, but I would like to at least flirt with the notion to attempt it sometime.

☆ ☆ ☆

Two almost century-old former camp sites I'd like to visit because of the remoteness and relative inaccessibility are an old Sumner Stillwater boat house and Camp English. Camp English was built for Lt. Gov. Woodruff of Kamp Kill Kare. No portion of the structure is standing today. There are visible portions of the old boat house camp. Both require a challenging bushwhack in backcountry where evidence of moose have been seen. I've attempted it twice. Both times a fly-in-the-ointment got in the way of the goals. The upside was a discovery of camp remains in the headwaters of Bradley Brook.

The fun is really more in the chase than in finally reaching the destination. Bob Moore, an old Raquette Laker who worked as George Vanderbilt's "Man Friday," told me about Camp English and two other outlaw camps. The first outlaw camp was near the headwaters of Bradley Brook, while the other was near Silver Run. Bob and George used to stay overnight in the Silver Run outlaw camp. There is still visible evidence of the Bradley Brook camp. It makes for an interesting one-day bushwhack.

Roy Wires, a friend from Florida who vacations at Singing Waters in Thendara from June to October each year, and I have enjoyed several reconnaissance trips that have taken us beyond the Bradley Brook camping loop. The terrain is challenging. Roy knows all about the rugged territory. His family lived at Kamp Kill Kare from October 1964 until May 1965 while his father, Edwin B. Wires, served as superintendent. Roy's book, *Kamp Kill Kare: Memories of Life in an Adirondack Great Camp*, is an interesting story of a grand camp complex located on the edge of the Moose River Plains.

☆ ☆ ☆

Chronicles of Moose River camp life and tales endure. It has often given me great pleasure to come upon a slight clearing, seemingly in the middle of nowhere, and find something that points to someone having been there before me. I've always done my best to find out who or what had been there. It's long been part of my Moose River Plains chase.

It has been so with the characters I've talked with in gathering my research. The tellers are spinners—weavers of yarns who thread their looms with measured phrases that step to a lumberjack's fiddle. "Honest liars" is a term I've heard to describe some of the storytellers I've talked to. It sounds somewhat flamboyant to talk about the people I've known who have shared their past outdoor lives with me. Their remembrances are stories not only of a vanished life, but also of a vanished Adirondack world. The background of woods and waters and log clearings, of ancient white pines and abundant trouty water has about disappeared and is in some places as irrecoverable as if it had never been.

☆ ☆ ☆

No matter the description, the chronicler of camp life is a purveyor of mountain folklore—stories that can slip down as slick as snake oil. Bob West is an example. He moved into a deserted logging camp near Mitchell Ponds after World War I. One story that has stuck about Bob is the time he was hired to guide three scientists. They described Bob's place back in the Moose River Plains as "way the hell and gone in high shrubbery."

After leading the scientists to his cabin, Bob went off to collect some firewood and left the men to poke around, as scientists are prone to do. It didn't take long before they noticed his wood stove was set on a platform about a yard off the floor. They gathered around, mulled it over and theorized.

Robert "Bob" West's Mitchell Ponds camp. Author David H. Beetle reported in *Up Old Forge Way/ West Canada Creek* (North Country Books, 1984) West toted "350 boards three at a time three miles," were he converted an abandoned lumber camp into an "ambitious lodge." *The Adirondacks' Moose River Plains Vol. 2* tells about West. *Courtesy Joan Payne*

"I think it's for conduction," said the first, and he went into a lengthy explanation, even drawing a diagram to illustrate his reasoning. The second scientist wasn't buying a word of it. "I think it's convection," he maintained.

The third was even less impressed. "Nope, you're both wrong," he said, maintaining that the stove was up on the platform for "radiation."

As they were discussing the possibilities, Bob came in and the scientists fell upon him with their theories.

"You know, I wish I'd thought of those—they're darn good ideas," Bob allowed after considering it all. "I wish I'd had the brains to think of them."

Now the scientists knew enough to know when you get into it with one of the old-timers, you're going to get it.

They bit anyway.

"So how come the stove is sitting three feet off the floor if not for one of those reasons?" they challenged Bob.

"Well," Bob said, "I'll tell you. I ran out of stove pipe."

I learned that story from Winfred "Slim" Murdock. He told me his Uncle Gerald Kenwell shared it with him.

Slim and I took several trips in the Moose River Plains. I plan to include in Vol. 2 more memories about his work-related adventures and remembrances about the Moose River Plains.

The Indian Clearing and surrounding acres of woodland is not a virgin wilderness today. The clearing that the Piseco pioneer farmer once thought would sustain livestock, a family, and their vegetable garden has grown in. Kenwell's boarding house, which devoted customers heaped with praise, is but a flicker in history, its guest register lost to time. The only remaining evidence is the iron shaft of the camp's well point hidden among a tangle of witchhopple and brambles alongside a derelict canoe portage that once was Charles Chapin's track to Chapin's Crossing, the shallow ford over the south branch of the Moose River and to his Beaver Lake camp beyond.

Time has brought some changes to the Indian Clearing country. The interior is not a primitive isolated destination any longer. People reach it by motor vehicle, not by buckboard, horse or by foot, today. There is no more logging but camping, hunting, and fishing are as popular now as in the past. But, the Land of the Deer hasn't really changed in any dramatic way. It is simply too big and too wild an area to be much affected by human activity, and all the pleasurable and familiar sights, sounds, smells and vistas are reassuringly as I remember from fifty-five years ago.

OPPOSITE: **Bob West's first camp was an abandoned cabin on Sumner Brook he learned about from Frank "Pop" Baker. West rented the camp to sportspeople.** *Courtesy Joan Payne*

Whenever I leave The Plains, it is with the knowledge I will return. Moreover, when I do return, it is always with the knowledge that it will look very much as it was when I left—baring messes some careless campers leave behind.

☆ ☆ ☆

While I might feel a wild urge deep within to load up my expedition Lowe backpack and head out for a distant spot in the heart of the Moose River Plains country, the opportunity to see again an old "French" Louie haunt like Poor Lake, paddle my rubber raft over Monument Lake's water, one of my favorite deep-country lakes, or revisit Yale Falls again, doesn't come easily anymore. Shouldering a heavy pack isn't as easy as it used to be!

At my age, bushwhacking countless miles through The Plains' expansive trackless forest is mostly a dream.

Memories of the deep woodland smell of balsam and the sites I once explored are strong. I still enjoy hiking the old Gould Paper Company logging track that traces past the base of Ice Cave Mountain eventually winding into Horn Lake at the western edge of the Moose River Plains Recreation Area. I've spotted deer and black bear feeding and am surprised an old 55-gallon oil drum I rolled from an old Gould dumpsite, placing it in the middle of a small meadow, is still there. It was my marker to turn slightly left as well as a reminder to be more cautious of black bears. Years earlier, a bear spooked me as I clambered through tight underbrush.

Wild areas are like that. I like to believe there's a bit of primal instinct dormant within me—a carryover from a distant ancestor's past, one who might have found a sense of adventure in their daily effort to survive.

Walt McLaughlin suspects that too. He is the author of several books, including *Arguing with the Wind*, a memoir about his two-week solo immersion in the Alaskan wilderness. McLaughlin has said in writing about a 2013 backpack he took through The Plains that lead into the West Canada Lake Wilderness, "After all, our bodies are made of the same elements found in the wildest, most remote places. The earth and our humanity are inexorably entwined." That is why wild-like places are important. I share McLaughlin's belief that in wilderness areas, "it's easy to sense our link to the world."

I leave you with a taste of the history, memories, and adventures that *The Adirondacks' Moose River Plains, Vol. 2: The Land of Deer* has in store.

Paul Schaefer is one such man who shouldered a pack that you will learn about in Vol. 2. If it had not been for his spearheading a deadly serious movement in 1945, there would be little to see in the Moose River Plains today. In fact, it would be mostly impossible to camp from cars, explore the deep woods, observe the diversity of ferns and wild flowers that the many marshes and wetlands reveal, nor traverse the major corridor that links Inlet with Cedar River Flow and Indian Lake beyond.

It used to be accepted practice to drink from bodies of water in The Plains. Within a five-minute walk upstream along the Indian River from where this picture was taken by my partner, Paul Sirtoli, we found a dead deer in the river. That sight brought a halt to drinking water without first treating it. *Author's Photo*

Before explaining what Schaefer did, a little background. From time to time, I travel over the former Gould Paper Company road through heavily logged forests toward Mitchell Ponds. Gould was one of the first companies to use heavy mechanized logging equipment to build roads and haul logs from the forest to pulp and sawmills

My target is a large boulder opposite a clearing which I determined decades ago, to be near the vicinity of Bob West's former camp. The rock is my starting point. I set the compass to due south and begin to bushwhack. The cliffs are steep and the ones that rise above the Moose River on Mitchell Ponds Mountain rise even higher.

My destination is a mile-long, mostly narrow rock-face open ledge that provides lookouts enjoyed only by robust climbers. Looking out beyond the south branch of the Moose River, directly below, affords a superb panoramic view of a sweeping landscape. A scene that had it been flooded it would not be visible today had it not been for a hard-fought 10-year legal battle that ended in what Paul Schaefer called a "Victory on the Moose River."

Schaefer recaps the long political battle:

> On November 8, 1955 the people of New York State decisively defeated the proposed amendment to Article XIV of the State Constitution which would have permitted construction of Panther Mountain dam on the South Branch of the Moose River. The vote was 1,622,196 to 613,927.
>
> Thus, has ended one of the longest and most costly conservation battles in history. It has also been the most productive for its effect on many other issues concerning the State Forest Preserve.
>
> The lovely valley of the Moose River near the heart of the Adirondack Park begins at Little Moose Lake and stretches westerly to McKeever about thirty miles distant. Because of this vote, this valley shall not become a vast mill pond fluctuating at the will of downstream power interests, nor shall its abundant wildlife be lost or its forests and plains become dreary mudflats, or its lovely lakes destroyed. And now that the proposed Higley

OPPOSITE: **Al Carpenter (without shirt) and Art "Pa" Lucas, circa 1930, were inseparable partners despite their difference in age. Pa Lucas was like a father to Al. The men rambled throughout The Plains during the early years. Art said his camp was a "good long walk" especially with a loaded pack basket. Al tells of the time he forgot some essentials and had to walk back to Rudd's grocery in Inlet and then return to camp. He admitted, "That taught me to plan my trip more thoroughly." Al and Art are profiled in The Adirondacks' Moose River Plains, Vol. 2.** Courtesy Vivian Carpenter Griepenburg

OPPOSITE: **Bill Apgar shows the author a drinking cup he left hanging on a branch beside a spring three decades earlier. Bill said he found the upper Red River territory very much as he remembered. Apgar's camp story appears in** *The Adirondacks' Moose River Plains, Vol. 2.* Author's Photo

Mt. impoundment has also become victim of an aroused public, the splendid natural conditions of this unique region shall continue to flourish as they have for so many ages past. And youth, in distant tomorrows, will be able to backpack the trail past Fawn Lake, down the Red River to the Moose River Plains and beyond to the virgin Beaver Lake and Indian River country. There they will find, as we have, the remoteness, the solitude and all the riches inherent in wilderness.

Len Harwood's Hot Top Camp near Bear Paw Creek. Hot Top's history is covered in *The Adirondacks' Moose River Plains, Vol. 2.* Courtesy Ted Harwood

The Panther-Higley dam battles took on a new life on September 25, 1945. On that day a brochure entitled "The Impending Tragedy of the Moose River Region" was mailed from Schenectady to newspapers statewide and to the relatively few conservationists we were acquainted with at that time. Up to then the issue, although planned for decades, had not caught the public attention. Those most intimately involved in the issue had all but given up hope to block the impoundments proposed by the Black River Regulating District Board and approved state agencies.

Ed Richard of Fort Plain and Alan Wilcox of Fourth Lake first supplied us with basic information about the proposals. They arranged a flight for me over the region with the renowned bush pilot, Scotty, of Inlet. We took off one cold, brilliant September morning in his open cockpit amphibian plane.

The author sits on the edge of the celebrated Moose River cliffs. *Author's Photo*

Climbing steadily for about a mile into the cloudless sky, we reached the apex he had headed for. He leaned over the cockpit and shouted to me, "The next time you look down, you'll see it all". And I did!

OPPOSITE: **Bushwhacking to the top of the Moose River cliffs and then carefully picking you way along the mile-long crest is worth the scramble.** *Author's Photo*

Forests unlimited, dotted with the crowns of giant white pines. Crystal lakes sparkling in the sunshine. The Moose River threading like quick-silver through the open plains and into the deep woods westerly. Trials twisting along tributary streams down towards the river. And in the distance, to all points of the compass, range on range of mountains, fading into far horizons. Unspoiled wilderness everywhere!

The author's canoe being hauled through a tight growth of shrubbery that clogs Sumner Stream. "I made it my quest to float on almost every body of water in the Plains." —"Jay" O'Hern. *Author's Photo*

Paul Sirtoli and the author's camp near the outlet of the Indian River. *Author's Photo*

I could hardly wait to reach the earth to tell the world what I saw and to plan trips down those tantalizing trails so visible from the air.

The very thought that all this marvelous country would be devastated was the catalyst that moved us all down that long road which ended the other day—November 8th—ten years and 14 days later.

The final order approving the Higley impoundment upstream from Panther had been signed and heavy equipment was being mobilized to start construction.

One of the definitions of the word impoundment describes it as "to seize and retain legal custody." The power interests would take *our* Forest Preserve, *our* lakes and streams, *our* wildlife haven—for *their* commercial purposes?

The battle started. It began as isolated skirmishes, gradually increasing in tempo as the public became aware of the issues. As newspapers took up the question, more and more people became involved. An Adirondack Moose River Committee was formed, mobilizing the best fighting abilities of the New York State Conservation Council, the Izaak Walton League, The Association for the Protection of the Adirondacks, the Adirondack Mountain Club, the Forest Preserve Association and many more. Service clubs, garden clubs, labor groups and churches all joined hands. The Wilderness Society, Parks Association and the Emergency Conservation Committee. All these and more.

Who can count the men, the women and the youth who contributed their time and talents to the fight since that fateful day in 1945?

Ed Richard was a dynamo. Herman Forster, Karl Frederick, Lee Keator, Martha Benedict, John Apperson, Don Tobey, Bob Thompson, Mike Petruska, Bob Young, Ira Gabrielson, Howard Zahniser—one after the other, they joined the fray, adding resources unprecedented. Assembly Speaker Oswald Heck, Lt. Gov. Frank Moore, Assemblymen Leo Lawrence, Justin Morgan, John Ostrander, Senators Francis Mahoney, Chauncey Hammond, Walter Stokes—one after the other became allies. And of major importance was our public relations chief Fred Smith of New York.

Legal action began early with Milo Kniffen and Judge Walter Bliss, the forerunners of a score of brilliant lawyers who pooled their expertise. Timothy Cohan, Assistant Attorney General, Sanford Stockton of the Adirondack League Club, Curtis Frank, mayor of Yonkers, were among them. Thousands of pages of briefs were submitted to the Supreme Courts and the Court of Appeals.

Travelling became a way of life, with business responsibilities for many put in the background. New York City, Buffalo, Rochester, Syracuse, Utica, Binghamton, Kingston, Morrisville, Brownville, Broadalbin, Cobleskill, Albany, Jamestown, Waverly.

634

The author studies the vast area that would have been flooded if the dam proposals had not been stopped. *Author's Photo*

And hundreds more. Movies and slides to overflow audiences. Billboards on highways. Doug's Roughriders—youth on horseback delivering pamphlets to remote rural areas. TV spots. Newspaper ads. And, on the last day, sportsmen in outdoor wear at hundreds of voting booths, at legal distances, urging the negative vote. A vote that became positive overnight and the rallying cry to save the Adirondacks from commercial exploitation!

After many legislative failures and numerous court injunctions to hold the line, the Stokes Act of 1950 banned dams on the Moose River. In 1953 the Ostrander constitutional amendment banned all dams "to regulate the flow of streams" in the Adirondacks if they involved the Forest Preserve.

It seems incredible that even with all this help, we were able to pull back from the brink of disaster that marvelous Moose River country. Midway through the fight that lasted a decade, it was said: "A citizen may not have title to his home, but he does have an undivided deed to this Adirondack land of solitude and peace and tranquility...To him the South Branch of the Moose River is a river of opportunity, for he has come to regard it as the front line of defense against commercial exploitation of *his* Forest Preserve."

We have been on the defensive too long. It is time to gather our forces and accomplish things that heretofore have been but dreams.

No amount of wandering throughout the Moose River Plains country today can ever connect you to what once existed, but learning what these folks saw of their favorite wilderness might enhance an armchair adventure or perhaps motivate you to take a wander back in time, as it has prompted my many exploratory trips that promised to take me to a particular spot just to say "Now right about here is where Slim Murdock helped pull Billy Buckshot's frozen body from the Moose River."

For me, all the sweat and effort for this little exploratory adventure in the Moose River Plains provides enough satisfaction to make me promise that the next time I visit The Plains that I will not leave until I satisfy myself with another pleasant outing.

The closing segment of this book contains an overview of what is included in *The Adirondacks' Moose River Plains, Vol. 2: The Land of the Deer.*

OPPOSITE: **The author snakes through a pass near Mitchell Ponds to reach Billy's Bald Spot. The location affords a splendid view of the Red River basin.** *Author's Photo*

The author lining his canoe through a mile-long section of rocks on the south branch of the Moose River below Wakeley's old dam. Had a dam been built on the south branch a huge area of The Plains would have been flooded.

"The south branch of the Moose River valley will always remain in the minds of conservationists as a battleground of profound significance in the continuing effort to preserve the integrity of the Forest Preserve in the Adirondacks.... Words and ideas, photographs and philosophies were the weapons used by the aggressors as well as by the defenders of the woods, waters and wildlife of the region. Let us remember that we shall maintain the victory over Higley and Panther Mountain reservoirs only by eternal vigilance." From Ten Critical Years in the History of the Adirondacks: 1945–1955 published by the Friends of the Forest Preserve

Moose River Plains Echoes

THE ADIRONDACKS' MOOSE RIVER PLAINS, Volume 1, concludes with an offering to the Indian Clearing's nostalgic past about the vast south branch of the Moose River country.

Life as it was in the Land of the Deer is no more. Kenwell's Sportsman's Home is gone, and the smaller sport and recreational camps built along the river and scattered throughout the woodland have been destroyed or have tumbled down. Surviving records, anecdotes, and snapshots of sweet remembrances of things past rest as dreamless dust to be looked at, enjoyed, and discussed by a younger generation.

The Moose River Plains' evocative historical story continues in Volumes 2 and 3.

Looking back over my almost half-a-century of exploring the backcountry, I feel that it has been a good journey. Learning about, and sharing the story of the Indian Clearing, in itself has been a rewarding adventure of research. Its story reveals what this present wild-like territory was like in its former glory days and underlines its present-day splendor.

Every year the trout lie sleeping in still cold pools, waiting for the Adirondack winter to gradually lift its icy mantle. Then it is not only the trout who greet the welcome warmth of summer. With each cycle, new people drive over 23 miles of The Plains' main road from the Limekiln gate to the Cedar River Flow gate, probably without a thought that had it not been for the work of ardent conservationists and concerned citizens the majority of the roadway would be at the bottom of a vast reservoir today. Campers continue to pitch their tents and level travel trailers on myriad camping sites. Berry pickers still gather wild blueberries that grow on the flat herb and grass plains of the Moose and Red rivers. Anglers and folks hoping to spot moose still follow old footpaths to distant ponds, and hunters continue to trod around the edges of boggy ponds, alongside streams that twist toward distant locations and over gentle and often steep pitches in their quest for a prized trophy buck.

Missing is all of Gould Paper Company's past logging activity, but a sharp-eyed woods traveler might still spot a former lumber camp clearing or some discarded tools or parts of old machinery.

This crisp new brilliance that dazzles lakes and rivers, greens trees with new leaves and delights people and wildlife alike has a history.

Remains of Wakeley Dam on the south branch of the Moose River, 2020. William D. Wakeley Sr. was a lumber man. He hewed out six miles of road into Cedar River Falls and settled there about 1868. Wakeley built a dam, a sawmill, and finally a new hotel. He named his place Cedar Falls Hotel, but it was generally known as Headquarters. Ted Aber, former Hamilton County historian, developed a four-page biography titled "Wakeely" that can be found in the Hamilton County's office in Lake Pleasant. *Author's photo*

The Moose River Plains area has been a major winter concentration area for deer since the 1890s at least. Even then, the range was severely over-browsed. Various observers reported the occurrence of starvation at that time. During the early 1900s, some studies were undertaken. The Conservation Department began a continuing investigation of the problem in 1931.

The Adirondacks' Moose River Plains, Vol. 2: The Land of the Deer, continues with the New York State Conservation Department's early Moose River deer studies; yesterday's and today's deer yards; serious and controversial dam building threats; more stories of leisure and camp life; and colorful, interesting characters.

Appendix A

Adirondack Beaver

IN 1900 HARRY V. RADFORD of New York, a noted outdoor writer, began a campaign to restore the beaver. Naturalists, nature lovers and various newspaper and magazine editors joined in the effort and in 1904 the New York State Legislature voted a small appropriation to the Forest, Fish and Game Commission for the purchased and liberation of the species in the Adirondack Park.

This Beaver lodge at Eighth Lake outlet was a tourist destination over one hundred years ago. *Courtesy Winfred Murdock*

The animals were shipped to State Game Protector Ned Ball at Old Forge in December 1904. The lakes and streams were frozen, and obviously the furry newcomers could neither build their homes nor store their winter's food. Ned constructed a beaver lodge in a cement trout-rearing pond on the State hatchery ground. There, with daily offerings of fresh cut brush, bark and a variety of succulent vegetables, he and his fellow guides succeeded in bringing the captives through the winter. They consumed an average of one cord of brush and the bark of one cord of small logs a week in addition to a bushel of mixed vegetables which included apples, carrots, turnips, cabbage, and potatoes.

Gerald Kenwell paddling on the south branch of the Moose River, circa 1950. Moose River: "Te-ka'-hun-di-an'-do" means "clearing an opening," which is what a moose does by feeding on bark and lower branches of trees. Taken from *Aboriginal Place Names of New York* by William M. Beauchamp, 1907. *Photo by Dante O. Tranquille. Courtesy Town of Webb Historical Association*

On April 27, 1905, seven men with seven beaver set out with specially constructed litters to liberate the animals on Big Moose Lake, Raquette

Lake and the south branch of the Moose River. That was the first attempt to restore the species to natural habitats of the Adirondacks, and the effort soon resolved itself into a distinct achievement. The seven rapidly multiplied, and sought other waters in which to build and propagate. Several more shipments followed, which were released at various lakes and streams between Old Forge and Tupper Lake. Ten years later a census of Adirondack beaver placed their number at 20,000. They continued to increase until the Conservation Department, in 1924, by declaring an open trapping season on the species, adopted what was proved to be a successful policy of control.

Two private letters, written by D.F. Sperry and G. Frank Gray, which are the property of Mr. John N. Drake, of New York City, shed additional historical light of on the attempt to restock the Adirondacks with beaver. The following letters first appeared in the April 28, 1906 edition of *Forest and Stream*.

Weehawken, NJ, April 14—John N. Drake

Dear Sir:
You ask me to give you a history of the attempt to restock the Adirondacks with beaver, by the State and the Brown's Tract Guides' Association.

Colonel Fox and Superintendent Midddleton, of the Forest Fish and Game Commission, purchased seven beaver to be liberated at the end of the Louisiana Exhibition, Dec. 1, 1904. That being too late in the season for them to prepare for winter, A.M. Church, secretary and treasurer of the Brown's Tract Guides' Association, agreed that the Association would care for and turn them loose at the proper time. So they were shipped to Old Forge, at the foot at the Fulton Chain of Lakes.

There the Association built three houses in a small pond of the Fulton Chain fish hatchery and hired one of the pioneer guides to feed and care for them during the winter of 1904–05. They did very well with one exception. One was ugly and could not get along with the rest, so he was put in a pen alone, with a screen of heavy wire to separate him. But about April 20 he gnawed through the screen and in the morning he was missing. On making a search of the pond his body was found buried under the refuse; he had been killed and buried by the rest.

The latter part of April the ice and snow were gone enough for them to care for themselves, so the Association hired five guides to take two of them to Otter Brook, on the head of the South Branch of the Moose River, to where there was a lone beaver living that T.L. Woodruff, Esq., had released several years before.

We did not know what gender the hermit was, so we tried to pick male and female and started on the "journey of liberation," as the great Adirondack enthusiast, Harry V. Radford, styled it. He came from New York [City] to see them liberated. I tried to persuade him not to make the trip to the South Branch, but he was game and when we got off at 6 A.M. at the head of Fourth Lake, for a twelve-mile tramp over three of the high ranges in that part of the Adirondacks, with provisions for two days and two beaver and a crate weighing 125 pounds, with the streams and swamps overflowing with water, when we reached Frank Gray's camp at 12 P.M., your humble servant was tired. The younger fellows would not own to being tired, but I noticed it was hard work to get them started at 5 A.M. to go on two miles further.

We found where the other beaver had felled a tree, within two or three days at the farthest. They stayed in that vicinity all summer, and the accompanying letter from Frank Gray is the first I have heard from them this spring. As soon as I can learn how the other four wintered I will give you a history of their liberation. D.F. Sperry

Gray Camp, May 28—Frank Sperry, Old Forge:
Dear Sir—I thought you would like to hear from the beaver you brought here last April.

644

SUMMER
EXCURSIONS

From 6th Lake Dam Thro' 6th, 7th and 8th Lakes
AND RETURN

The Launch "SPRAY" is now ready to carry Passengers from 6th Lake Dam to the head of 7th Lake, where a walk of three-quarters of a mile over one of the finest carries in the Adirondacks brings you to 8th Lake, where the Launch "ANONA" will carry passengers around 8th Lake, one of the most beautiful lakes in the whole country, and give them ample time for Lunch before leaving 8th Lake.

For further information write or phone

DON A. C. MURDOCK, Capt.
INLET, N. Y

Inlet Lumber Co. Phone.

TICKETS 75c Round Trip
covering a distance of 16 miles

Don't Fail to See At 8th Lake **BEAVER DAM**

Lyon DeCamp continues: "...this condition continuous on and about the headwaters of the south branch of Moose River and of Red River. Mr. Kenwell also has stated that there are numerous streams in that locality which have been dammed and the timber killed along and about the shore. I know of another stream called Third Lake Creek carrying quite a volume of water. This empties into Third Lake...which has been dammed. All of the timber is killed along its banks, to a depth of from 100 to 300 yards for over a mile or more. This condition can be seen from the top...of Bald Mountain. The condition presents the appearance of a strip of land that has been fire swept."

Courtesy Winfred Murdock

645

I went up there the other day to see how they were managing. They have adopted the country on Otter Creek [Brook] where you opened the cage door. They have been working on the poplar near there.

The author stands on a large beaver dam near Little Moose Lake in 2018. Jay talks to this day of his crazy hellish canoe ride as he raced down the Red to its junction with the south branch of the Moose River during very high water as his canoe plunged over six beaver dams. *Author's photo*

I counted seventy-five trees, from two to seven inches in diameter, they have cut and used for food and to make a log cabin. They made a house about ten feet across at the bottom and six feet high, shaped like a haystack, Gothic finish outside. Inside I suppose it is of the poplar logs. I have no doubt they have improved on the houses they had at the St. Louis Exhibition, or even the ones they had at the Old Forge hatchery, where they still owe for their winter's board.

Deer have wintered well here. I have not found one dead. Last spring a man could count 100 dead in a day.

G. Frank Gray

King of the Land at Kamp Kill Kare

ROY E. WIRES once felt as if he was "King of the Land" at Kamp Kill Kare. I kid. That's a title I anointed him with. Roy's kingdom was one of the Adirondacks' Great Camps and once upon a time, his father served as Superintendent of Kamp Kill Kare. Edwin B. Wires worked at the private estate from October 1964 until May 1975. Mrs. Francis P. Garvan was Wires' employer. The Garvans spent their summers at Kamp Kill Kare in Raquette Lake accompanied by their children, grandchildren, and other invited guests.

Roy said one of the best things about living at the camp was that a good portion of the complex had hardly changed since the days of Timothy L. Woodruff around 1900. The bridge to the island, the gardens in front of the camp, the island cabin, the swimming dock on the lake—almost everything remained as it had been minus the fish hatchery and the immense main lodge, which sustained severe damage in a 1915 fire. The Garvins called in architect John Russell Pope to help in the rebuilding. Pope's step design flowed the main lodge's construction down a knoll to the shore of Lake Kora.

Louis Rhead wrote of the grand park in his Sunday, July 31, 1910, article in the *Brooklyn Daily Eagle*, as "playground of the rich."

Rhead reported the collection of "Kamp" proper buildings was so large that:

> Such places cannot be closed in winter. The manager and at
> least fifteen people of both sexes have winter duties, so that
> when in summer or winter the host and guests arrive nothing
> is wanting for their comfort. When a large party occupies the
> camp, additional servants are engaged and I am well within
> bounds in stating that $50,000 per annum will hardly suffice
> for the up-keep of this and other beautiful camps in the vicinity.

647

Without doubt, the genial owner finds that, along with his less favored brethren, health is far more precious than wealth.

To create such a place, and thoroughly enjoy it, in addition to gaining health and keeping it, the varied advantages are well worth the cost, however large it may be.

Boat house on Lake Kora. *Courtesy Roy E. Wires*

Roy would agree with Rhead's judgment that "such places cannot be closed in winter." He would also concur that living in the extensive Adirondack camp was healthful while not always restful. Kamp Kill Kare required a considerable amount of care to keep it operating properly and attractively.

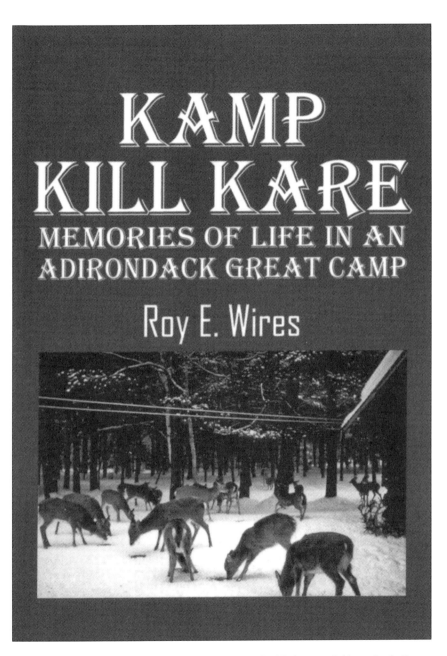

KAMP KILL KARE
MEMORIES OF LIFE IN AN ADIRONDACK GREAT CAMP

Roy E. Wires

Roy wrote *Kamp Kill Kare: Memories of Life in an Adirondack Great Camp,* not as a history, "but rather a written and pictorial accounting of the day-to-day life of a family that lived there for ten years. Books such as

Entrance to Kamp Kill Kare. *Courtesy Roy E. Wires*

Adirondack Camps, and *Durant* by Craig Gilborn, *Township 34* by Harold K. Hochschild, and *Great Camps of the Adirondacks* by Harvey H. Kaiser, do an excellent job of documenting the historical legacy of the Adirondack Great Camps," penned Wires in his Foreword.

Wires explained that his story is about "...how family dealt with living in the 'back woods' at the end of a six and one-half mile dirt road, and how the environment around us shaped our lives. Long before moving to Kamp Kill Kare, our family had always been an outdoors family. The opportunity to live in the deep woods came as an extension of a lifestyle we already enjoyed."

650

The experiences Roy relates during his family's tenure at Kamp Kill Kare are some of his most memorable and rewarding teenage reminiscences. The events relate to how his family "adapted to the changing seasonal environment," said Roy. "The stories of deer and other wildlife will heighten your appreciation for the Adirondack Mountains." His first-hand perspective brings a "never before seen overview of Kamp Kill Kare and the surrounding wilderness."

A variety of Roy Wires' original photographs used to document his accounting of Kamp Kill Kare is shared in this appendix.

Chapel at Kamp Kill Kare. *Courtesy Roy E. Wires*

Beaver Lake Crash

SOMEONE'S REPORT of an interesting find or a site that's well worth seeing has always stirred in me an interest to take off on a quest somewhere in the Moose River Plains hinterlands. And so it was when Marilyn Breakey handed me the only photo I've ever seen of the Beaver Lake plane crash.

It didn't take me long to decide I'd like to see the site of the accident. Using an old Gardenway two-wheeled lawn cart, I strapped my Grumman aluminum canoe to the cart and rolled the makeshift carrier along the yellow-blazed Beaver Lake Trail. The Moose River Recreation Area official map and guide reports the route is 2.3 miles long. The guide reads: "This trail starts at a parking area and road barrier [at Otter Brook] just west of the Moose River Bridge. The trail follows an old road to the northern shoreline of the lake. The lake is named for its odd shape, which resembles a beaver." By the time I arrived at the lakeshore I would have sworn I had lugged the 75-pound canoe more like five miles. It was a tiresome trek I wouldn't repeat, but the trip was well worth the effort.

Marilyn's prediction had been spot-on. Decades following the crash, remains of the plane's fuselage can still be seen on the sandy shallow bottom at the eastern end of the lake.

It remains as a reminder of a bit of history most users of The Plains don't know about.

Ted Harwood said he was overseas serving in the Navy at the time of the plane accident. He learned about it from his brother Bob later on. Ted said, "Bob's description of the accident was pretty much as the article stated. We know that the wind was gusting upwards of 30 mph and that the lay of the land at Beaver Lake probably caused a violent wind shear at the edge of the lake. Bob was doing the flying for Scotty then. Scotty was ready to sell the business, I believe, and was breaking Bob in. Bob had been teaching Arm pilots in Arizona. When the war ended he returned home to Inlet and started flying for Scotty.

"When Bob didn't return to the sea base from his Beaver Lake flight, Scotty and Dad thought he might have had trouble starting the plane's engine so they began walking in to Beaver Lake Lodge with a new battery. It was during their trip in when they met hunters coming out and learned what had happened. They were very lucky to survive with the injuries they came away with."

The eye lingers on beautiful views from Camp Nit, September 25, 1918. It was at the far end of the lake that the plane crashed. *Courtesy Margaret Wilcox (The Camp Nit Collection)*

The Thursday, November 1, 1945, *Adirondack Arrow* tells the story.

INJURED IN PLANE CRASH
Breakey Brothers, Supervisor's Son
Hurt in Beaver Lake

Three prominent Town of Webb young men were injured badly, but not critically, Monday afternoon when their airplane crashed in a bog adjoining Beaver Lake, near The Plains. They managed to get out of the wreck and make their way a quarter-mile to reach the only camp on the lake where they remained overnight and were flown out Tuesday to Utica for hospitalization.

The injured are:

John Breakey, 23, recently discharged AAF sergeant and holder of the Distinguished Flying Cross, the son of Mr. and Mrs. Samuel Breakey, Garmon St., Old Forge.

Francis E. Breakey, 27, brother of John and a native of Old Forge, who has been living recently in Utica.

Robert "Bob" Harwood, 23, son of Hamilton County Supervisor and Mrs. K. Leonard Harwood of Inlet.

The condition of all three men today was reported to be improved. John Breakey, holder of the DFC for 35 missions over Japan as a radar operator in a B-29, has only a fractured thumb. At first it was feared he had a fractured vertebra in his back but x-rays last night failed to disclose such an injury and he was able to move his head.

Harwood has a fractured jaw, and Francis Breakey escaped without broken bones although he was badly cut, as were his companions.

Harwood was flying the small-cabin plane owned by Harold Scott of Inlet. The trio left Eagle Bay about 2:30 p.m., and crashed about 10 minutes later.

They had planned to land on Beaver Lake and leave hunting equipment for a further haul overland to the Harwood camp, which is four miles beyond the old Kenwell camp on The Plains. The only other ways into the camp are by wagon or foot from Limekiln Lake, more than 20 miles, or from Raquette Lake village, a distance of 17 miles. The trip has usually been made by plane in recent years.

None of the three men was able to state the cause of the accident, but Scott said he believed the ship must have struck a downdraft as it circled the lake for a landing. The craft was badly damaged, and Scott said he had not yet decided about its salvage.

Supervisor Harwood and Scott became worried when the plane did not return to its Eagle Bay base, and they started the long trek on foot. They had traversed more than 10 miles when they met a party of hunters who told them of the crash and that the missing men were in the Allen Wilcox camp on Beaver Lake.

Beaver Lake plane crash. Remains of the plane's fuselage is still visible.
Courtesy Marilyn Breakey

Harwood continued on foot to the camp while Scott returned to Inlet. The hike and the nervous tension sent Scott to bed, but he telephoned Lou Lavery, who operates a plane service at Round Lake, and made arrangements for him to start out early Tuesday morning by plane with Dr. F.K.T. Warrwick, Raquette Lake. He treated the injured men and prepared them for the flight to Utica.

Lavery made the first trip to Utica with Harwood and Francis Breakey. They landed at the Utica Airport's water base on the Barge Canal and were taken to St. Luke's Hospital. Lavery then returned to Beaver Lake and on the return trip brought out John Breakey and Dr. Warrwick.

Beaver Lake is justifiably a very desirable destination for those who know The Plains. Its remote location adds to its attraction. I think about what could have happened to this delightful place each time I reach the crest of the hill just before I descend to the lake. It exists today and looks as it always has because of the efforts of Paul Schaefer and many others, and their unflagging commitment to the wilderness. Schaefer was a staunch conservationist. Paul Graodahl said of Paul in the December 1998 issue of the *New York State Conservationist*: "Schaefer's biggest fight on behalf of the Adirondacks came during the late 1940s when utility companies proposed 35 major hydroelectric dams and reservoirs that would have involved clearcutting and flooding several hundred thousand acres in the Adirondack Park— including the largest deer wintering grounds, on the Moose River Plains."

Margaret Wilcox told me Beaver Lake would have been flooded under 40 feet of water. It's that fact I ponder each time before plunging downhill. Beaver Lake is one example of Schaefer's legacy to the land that he so loved.

The Adirondacks' Moose River Plains, Vol. 2: The Land of the Deer tells about this remarkable man and his dedication to The Plains.

Acknowledgements

My Heartfelt Gratitude

MY DEEPEST THANKS to all the people who contributed to *The Adirondack's Moose River Plains Vol. 1–2* undertaking. Here, in alphabetical order, are those to whom I am particularly grateful:

Mart Allen; Rabbi Katy Z. Allen; Charles Glen Amrhein; Wayne Blanchard, Indian Lake historian; Paul Birmingham; George Blakeman; Wayne Blanchard; Peter Bruno, Jr.; John D. Casadonte; Robert "Zeke" and Ann Cummings; Eliza Jane Darling, Joan Davis; Gerald A. Dupuis; Hamilton County Historian; Helen B. Dutton; Robert J. Elinskas; Tom Gates; David Gibson; John Gymburch; Donald Hammond; Shawn Hansen; Ted Harwood; Wayne Hayes; Charlie Herr; William Ingersoll; Robert Igoe; Mary Pesez-Kames; Wayne Kwasniewski; Louis Lafforthun; Gary Lee; Mitch Lee; Nancy Long; Bill McGee; James D. Massett; Anne Meade; Catherine Mooney; Katherine K. Lewis; J. Neelly, volunteer at the Oneida Country Historical Society; Caroline Nelson; David Nelson, editor *Conservationist* magazine; David Nelson; Jacob Niziol; Bette M. O'Hern; Matt Osternaudt; Francis J. Parent; Jim Payne; Lewis H. "Lew" Payne; Mary Louise Payne; Sid Payne; Jerold Pepper; Jerry Perrin; Patti Quinn; Edward Reed; Kristy Rubyor; Brian Rudd; Gordy and Greg Rudd; Tom Thibado; Eileen C. Stegemann, assistant editor *Conservationist* magazine; Susan O. Steverman; Jack Swancott; Dianne J. Thibado; Town of Webb Historical Association; Shirley T. VanNest; John Warren; Donald Wharton; Margaret Wilcox; Elsie Wilkins; Marilyn Willems; Roy E. Wires; and Bill Zullo.

I would also like to acknowledge, posthumously, Ted Aber; Charles Glen Amrhein; William Apgar; Mrs. Gordon McAllen Baker; Farrand Benedict; Norton Bird; Donald Bowman; Hal Boyce; Ben Bradley; Cecil Brown; Charles Brown; Rose Burdick; Ken Cannan; John Chamberlain; Greenie Chase; William Christy; Margaret C. Cunningham; Robert W. Darrow; Bob Daws; Archie Delmash III; Julie H. Dennis; Maitland C. DeSormo; Richard

F. Dumas; Bob Failing; John P. Ferris; Warren Flood; Gladys Funk; Oma V. Glazier; Amedee J. Grandbois; Charles Guyer; Leonard Harris; Ray Hart; Harold Hater; Jack Higbee; MaryLee Kalil; Ora Kerber Kenwell; Tom Kilbourn; Floyd King; Stella King; Norbert Kornmeyer; Frank Lamphear; Martha Leonard; Karl Lesbrick; Charlie Levesque; Dick Long; Dr. George H. Longstaff; Daniel P. McGough; Bill Marlow; Edward Maunton; Barbara McMartin; John R. Meneilly Sr.; Robert Moore; Winfred Murdock; Marjorie Z. O'Hern; Bill Okusko; Robert O'Neal; Richard and Joan Payne; Louise Payne; Donald "Red" Perkins; Merrill and Robert Phoenix; Edmund H. Richard; Ralph Richards; Robert J. Ringle; Jane and "Red" Ritz; Bill Roden; Henry Rubyor; Gordon Rudd; Milton Rugoff; Paul Schaefer; C.W. Severinghaus; LeRoy Short; Jim Smith; Ralph Smith; Jack Tanck; Alfred "Tip" Thibado; Henry Thibado; Dante Tranquille; H. Wayne Trimm; Ethel Tripp; Joseph Van Way, Fredia Westfall; Director of the Stowe-Day Foundation; Olive Wertz; Charles Wharton; Howard Wieman; Margaret Wilcox; Elsie Wilkins; and Dick Wills.

I would also like to thank my friend and editor Mary L. Thomas for her patience, thoughtful ideas, and her unflagging concern. Mary listened and added valuable insight and good cheer, as did Neal Burdick, who showed me what it takes. He edited the final draft. His constructive comments and observations tightened and focused the story as well as suggested additional historical material.

A special thanks goes to my wife, Bette. Words will not do justice for all the time she spent traveling with me to chase down material I felt was potential historical matter for the development of this book. She is a wonderful companion on any adventure, and I hoped she had as much fun as I did.

Any omission to acknowledge the assistance of anyone who helped with this project is an unintentional oversight.

SOURCES

The material gathered together for use in *The Adirondacks' Moose River Plains, Volume 1* is extensive. Research was based on printed material and the author's collection of interviews. The detailed list of some source material I used, it is hoped, might provide a direction for future researchers.

Books

_____. Chapter Four: "The Takeover of Privately-Owned Lands in the Adirondack State Park Step One." (Title of book has been misplaced.)

Aber, Ted. *Adirondack Folks*. Prospect Books, 1982.

Aber, Ted and Stella King, *The History of Hamilton County*, Great Wilderness Books, Lake Pleasant, New York, 1965.

Beetle, David H. *Up Old Forge Way-West Canada Creek*. North Country Books, 1972.

Brumley, Charles. *Guides of the Adirondacks: A History*. North Country Books, 1994.

Donaldson, Alfred L. *A History of the Adirondacks, Part II*. Harbor Hill Books, 1977.

Gerster, Arpad Geyza. *Notes Collected in the Adirondack 1895 & 1896*. The Adirondack Museum, 2005.

Gerster, Arpad Geyza. *Notes Collected in the Adirondack 1897 & 1898*. The Adirondack Museum, 2010.

Gilborn, Craig. *Durant: The Fortunes and Woodland Camps of a Family in the Adirondacks*.The Adirondack Museum, 1981.

Gilborn, Craig. *Adirondack Camps: Homes Away From Home, 1850–1950*. The Adirondack Museum/Syracuse University Press, 2000.

Ives, V.B. Martin. *Through The Adirondacks In Eighteen Days—in 1898*. Reprinted by Harbor Hill Books, 1985.

Kaiser, Harvey H. *Great Camps of the Adirondacks*. David R. Godine, Publisher, Inc., 1982.

Longstaff, George H. *From Heyday to Mayday*. Valkyrie Publishing House, 1983.

McMartin, Barbara and Lee M. Brenning. *Discover the West Central Adirondacks: A Guide to the Western Wilderness and the Moose River Plains*. Backcountry Publications,1988.

McMartin, Barbara. *To the Lake of the Skies: The Benedicts in the Adirondacks*. Lake View Press, 1996.

O'Brien, Clara. *God's Country: Eagle Bay, Fourth Lake in the Heart of the Adirondacks*, North Country Books, 1982.

Wallace, E.R. *Descriptive Guide to the Adirondacks*. 1880 and 1894.

White, William Chapman. *Adirondack Country*. Alfred A. Knopf, 1980.

Wires, Roy E. *Kamp Kill Kare: Memories of Life in an Adirondack Great Camp*. Outskirts Press, Inc., 2005.

Magazines

Goldstein, Nathaniel L., Attorney General, State of New York. "Our Forest Preserve." The New York State *Conservationist*, April–May, 1952.

Kenwell, Gerald. "Our Forest Preserve." The New York State *Conservationist*, Vol. 6, no. 4, February–March, 1952

Lansing, Robert. "The Roman Warriors of the Iroquois: The Region's Early Sovereigns." *Watertown Daily Times*, July 3, 1976.

Wack, Henry Wellington. "Kamp Kill Kare: The Home of Hon. Timothy L. Woodruff." *Field and Stream*, February, 1903.

Wilkins, Elsie. "Woodsloafer." *North Country Life*, Summer 1956.

Newspapers

_____. "Deer Stalking in the Adirondacks." *The Saratogian*, March 10, 1881.

_____. "Deer in Adirondack Lakes." *Forest & Stream*, December 9, 1881.

_____. "The Hunting and Fishing." *Brooklyn Union-Argus*, July 22, 1882.

_____. "Big Trout-Its Hatcheries." *The Tri States Union*, April 3, 1890.

_____. "Moose River." *The Boonville Herald and Adirondack Tourist*, March 31, 1892.

_____. "From Forestport to Fulton Chain." *The Boonville Herald and Adirondack Tourist*, August 3, 1893.

_____. "Adirondack Echoes." *The Boonville Herald and Adirondack Tourist*, April 10, 1894.

_____. "Killing of Deer in the Adirondacks." *New York Herald*, February 10, 1896.

_____. "All Around Us-Big Indian Clearing." *The Otsego Farmer*, October 23, 1896.

_____. "Visit to Kamp Kill Kare." *The Brooklyn Daily Eagle*, October 7, 1901.

_____. "Adirondack Squatters Sued." *The Sun*, October 27, 1901.

_____. "Found Mr. Woodruff a Jolly Good Fellow." *The Daily Standard Union*, September 15, 1903.

_____. "Luxurious Camps in the Adirondacks." *The Sun*, Sunday, July 10, 1904.

_____. "The Politicians' Rendezvous at Kamp Kill Kare." *The Brooklyn Daily Eagle*, September 6, 1908.

_____. "Game Thrives in Adirondacks." Glens Falls *Daily Times*, March 1, 1907.

_____. "Kamp Kill Kare Costs About $50,000 A Year." *The Post-Standard*, August 1, 1910.

_____. "Kamp Kill Kare the Playground of Timothy L. Woodruff." *The Brooklyn Daily Eagle*, July 31, 1910.

_____. "Alfred G. Vanderbilt Buys Kamp Kill Kare." Amsterdam *Evening Recorder and Daily Democrat*, 1913.

_____. "Kamp Kill Kare Sale Enriches Woodruff." *The Brooklyn Daily Eagle*, August 27, 1913.

_____. "Donald Curran Killed in Woods." *Utica Herald-Dispatch*, October 24, 1914.

_____. "New Conservation Commission Outlines Plans." *New York Times*, August 29, 1915.

_____. "Camp Neodak was Burned to the Ground." *Utica Observer-Dispatch*, August 18, 1919.

_____. "Rambling Round the Adirondacks." *Utica Daily Press*, May 24, 1921.

_____. "Summer Resorts Out of Utica Invite Vacationists." *Utica Daily Press*, May 25, 1924.

_____. "Old Timers of the Adirondacks Are Gradually Disappearing Down the Trail." *Boonville-Herald*, July 1, 1926.

_____. "Where to Spend Your Summer Vacation." *Utica Daily Press*, June 19, 1926.

_____. "Adirondack Her Career." *Cazenovia Republican*, August 24, 1932.

_____. "John G. Hun Dies; School Founder, 67." *New York Times*, September 16, 1945.

_____. "Dr. John G. Hun, School Founder, Is Dead at 67." *New York Herald Tribune*, September 16, 1945.

_____. "Philip Christy, Noted Guide, Dies." Rome *Daily Sentinel*, September 6, 1947.

_____. "Hun School Ends 50th Academic Year With Reminiscences About Its Founder." *Princeton Herald*, June 24, 1963.

D.K.L "Sleeping in the Woods at Kenwells." The Oswego *Daily Palladium*, September 2, 1899.

D.K.L. "September in the Woods: The Oswego Colony is Still at Kenwell's House." The Oswego *Daily Palladium*, September 2, 1899.

Brimmer, F.E. "Deer Hunting About Limekiln Lake." *New York Evening Post*, October 7, 1921.

Reid, Kenneth A. "Effects of Beaver on Trout Waters." *The Northeastern Logger*, August–September, 1952.

Shurter, Joseph Delmarsh J. "Deer Hunting in the Adirondacks Trip to Indian Clearing." *Forest and Stream*, Vol 20, April 12, 1883.

Spears, E.A. "In the Lore of the North Country, French Lewey Was a Pioneer of the Adirondacks." Utica *Observer-Dispatch*, 1938.

Tranquille, Dante. "Mayor of Otter Brook." Utica *Observer-Dispatch*, January 27, 1952.

Interviews, Correspondence, Letters, Tape Recordings

Aber, Ted with William J. O'Hern

Allen, Rabbi Katy Z. with William J. O'Hern

Apgar, Bill with William J. O'Hern

Baker, Mrs. Gordon McAllen with William J. O'Hern September 19, 1988

Chapin, Patricia Cotter with William J. O'Hern

Coleman, Earle E. Princeton University archivist with William J. O'Hern on June 30, 1988

Delmarsh, Archibald Jr. with William J. O'Hern

Harris, Leonard with William J. O'Hern

Harter, Harold with William J' O'Hern

Harwood, Ted with William J. O'Hern between March 29, 1986–June 2016

Kenwell, Ora with William J. O'Hern

Lee, Gary with William J. O'Hern on May 31, 1987 and during 2016–2017

Longstaff, George H. with William J. O'Hern

Murdock, Winfred with William J. O'Hern

Leonard, Martha with William J. O'Hern during December 2016

Nelson, Caroline with William J. O'Hern

Payne, Lewis "Lew" with William J. O'Hern

Payne, Mary Louise with William J. O'Hern September 21, 1986

Rudd, Gordon and Greg with William J. O'Hern

Thibado, Henry Alfred and Tom with William J. O'Hern on November 21, 1986

Thibado, Dianne J. with William J. O'Hern

Wertz, Olive with William J. O'Hern

Westfall, Freda with William J. O'Hern on January 6, 1990

Wilcox, Margaret with William J. O'Hern

Willis, Dick with William J. O'Hern

Wires, Roy E. with William J. O'Hern

Youman, Leonard with William J. O'Hern

Zullo, Bill with William J. O'Hern

Unpublished Sources

Beaver Lake Hunting Club Camp Memories by Margaret Wilcox. Author's collection

Camp Nit Diaries of Charles T. Chapin (1905–1919). Author's collection

Camp Nit Diaries of Charles T. Chapin (1920–1930s). Town of Webb Historical Association

Almy D. Coggeshall's 1933 "North Recreational Adventures: Being a Journal of a Three Weeks Hike Through the Adirondacks."

Sixth Lake Reservoir by Hollister Johnson, Senior Assistant Engineer, September 6, 1933

Isaac Kenwell's April 10, 1935, letter to W.P. Wessler. Stored in Hamilton County archives.

Inlet's dedicated two-man road crew on the Rock Dam road. Shawn Hansen, left, and Don Towsend.

ENDNOTES

1. A spring wagon was an important, highly versatile, general-purpose, four-wheeled vehicle in the late horse-drawn era. It was equipped with spring interposed between the body and the axles to form elastic supports. It had a square box and between two and tour movable seat boards. It was used for the transportation of either goods or passengers. *(Introduction, p. xvii)*

2. Red & White began about 1925. Similar to IGA, the company did centralized buying and distribution for small local stores to help them to compete against large chains that were consolidating their power in the 1920s. *(Author's Note, p. xxv)*

3. See *Adirondack Logging: Stories, Memories, and Cookhouse Chronicles from Adirondack and Tug Hill Lumber Camps* (In the Adirondacks, 2016) for more history about the Gould Paper Company. Continental Can purchased the Gould Company's outstanding stock in August, 1945. *(Author's Note, p. xxxi)*

4. In 1895 the Fisheries, Game and Forest Commission was established. In 1900 the name was changed to the Forest, Fish and Game Commission. In 1911 the agency was renamed the Conservation Commission. *(Chapter 1, p. 5)*

5. Burnham, an ardent conservationist, came to the attention of New York State's Chief Game Protector J.W. Pond in 1899 when he decided to write a powerful article to the *Forest & Stream* magazine about the intolerable game law violation of 1896 that made the hounding of deer illegal. See "The Albany Years" chapter in *John Bird Burnham: Klondiker, Adirondacker, Eminent Conservationist* by Maitland C. De Sormo. *(Chapter 1, p. 27)*

6. Perhaps the action of the state as revealed in a handwritten note penned by Mary Teal, the long-standing Lyons Falls historian and authority about the Gould Paper Company, and preserved in her files was related to the news that "forever wild" mandated by the state Constitution were being enforced: "On January 2, 1919, men employed by the Conservation Commission blew up the Gould Paper Company's large dam on the Red River. The twenty-foot long dam was located near the Little (Red River) Plains. The State had given Gould permission ten years earlier to build the dam. It had been used every year since 1909 for floating softwood logs downstream to the south branch of the Moose River. The territory flooded behind the dam was not considered valuable. The destruction of the dam meant considerable loss to Gould of some 150,000 feet of logs that was to have been floated downstream during the spring of 1919. The destruction of the dam made it necessary for Gould to explore some other way to move the timber to the Lyons Falls mill. It is said Gould was given no warning that the dam would be blown up if not removed. John B. Todd of Marcy and Lewis Joslin of Boonville were sent to the site of the dam after it was blown up to assess the situation." Notes do not tell how the situation was solved. It is assumed Gould relied on the company's fleet of Linn tractors purchased in 1918 to transport the logs to their landing on the south branch of the Moose River. *(Chapter 1, p.31)*

7. "Jack" Sheppard was a well-known guide on Fourth Lake. *(Chapter 4, p. 67)*

8. Frank Warwick of North Salem, N.Y. reports "In the Moose River Country," September 13, 1883 *Forest & Stream* his deer hunting trip that included at night's stopover at Brown's cabin on the Indian Clearing. *(Chapter 4, p. 68)*

9. Much more of this can be read in *Durant*, by Craig Gilborn, The Adirondack Museum, 1981. *(Chapter 5, p. 85)*

10. An interesting description of an earlier Eighth Lake launch named Anona operated by C.R. Murdock, Capt. is found on pages 96–97 in *Through the Adirondack in Eighteen Days—in 1898*, by Martin V.B. Ives (reprinted in 1985 by Harbor Hill Books. *(Chapter 5, p. 93)*

11. Dorsey evidently owned a store. During testimony given to the commissioners investigating the state Forest, Fish and Game Department, Lieutenant Governor Timothy L. Woodruff had a telephone line built "at State expense that connected the Kenwell Place" to his Kamp Kill Kare. (See: *The Thrice-A-Week World*, Wednesday, August 31, 1910.) *(Chapter 8, p. 116)*

12. "Indian Lake" by Gretchen H. Fish (*Adirondack Memories and Campfire Stories*, 2014) details Indian Lake's history. *(Chapter 14, p. 188)*

13. Not to be confused with the Adirondack League Club's Mountain Lodge Club House on Little Moose Lake near Old Forge, N.Y. *(Chapter 14, p. 188)*

14. A few years later Woodruff purchased an additional 1,000 acres which cost him $43,000. *(Chapter 15, p. 196)*

15. In the days when Wellington Kenwell was raising a few hardly vegetables and keeping his larder supplied with fresh meat by means of his rifle and rod, the Plains homestead must have seemed like a homelike site when Timothy L. Woodruff arrived on horseback because he had learned of the region's superb reputation for good hunting and fishing. He was led by Maxam, in the company of other guides. *(Chapter 15, p. 202)*

16. The Atlantic salmon (Salmo salar) is a salmon in the family Salmonidae. It is found in the northern Atlantic Ocean, in rivers that flow into the north Atlantic and, due to human introduction, in the north Pacific. Other salmon, fiddler, or outside salmon. At different points in their maturation and life cycle, they are known as parr, smot, grisle, kelt, slink, and spring salmon. Atlantic salmon that do not journey to sea, usually because of past human interference, are known as landlocked salmon or ouananiche. *(Chapter 15, p. 206)*

17. The motto makes no sense to me. The meaning lost to time? Is it possibly "Kare Killed at Kamp"? That's the only way it makes sense to me. *(Chapter 15, p. 207)*

18. This fact is rather hard to believe—a college baseball preseason would be early April or even March, when the weather and condition of the ground in the Adirondacks would hardly be conductive to baseball. *(Chapter 15, p. 211)*

19. State Archives, State Education Department's publication number 72. *(Chapter 17, p. 221)*

20. http://www.dec.ny.gov *(Chapter 17, p. 221)*

21. The full timeline tracing DEC's history and various environmental milestones throughout the decades can be read on the PDF. Go to www.dec.ny.gov. *(Chapter 17, p. 222)*

22. "Hunting and Hunters" in *Birth of a River: An Informal History of the Black River Headwaters* by Thomas C. O'Donnell, 1952, describes the shift in attitudes. O'Donnell reports and interesting survey: "A questionnaire conducted by the *Utica Herald*, sent to guides and hotel men of this and other Adirondack areas, brought in thirty-five replies, of which thirty were against floating. Sam Dunakin, one of the all-time greats of the Fulton Chain guides, once declared that seven-tenths of the does had fawns, and that of the fawns who lost their mothers in August 'very few if any ever see the next spring.' They managed to get through to the following spring, said Dunakin, 'then die, explain the cry we hear so often of deer being so plentiful they starve. They do starve, but they are the motherless fawns that begin the winter so poor and weak there is no show for their getting through.'" *(Chapter 17, p. 227)*

23. See David Beetle's *Up Old Forge Way* (1948). *(Chapter 17, p. 232)*

24. The site of the former lumber camp is on the south side of the trail to Beaver Lake after crossing the Otter Brook double culverts. *(Chapter 17, p. 232)*

25. According to Wikipedia, the free encyclopedia, the ".303 Savage is a rimmed, .30 caliber rifle cartridge developed by the Savage Arms Company in 1894 which was designed as a short action cartridge for their popular Savage Model 99 hammerless lever-action rifle. The cartridge was designed for smokeless powder at a time when black-powder cartridges were still popular. The .303 Savage round was ballistically superior to the .30-30 Winchester, but only marginally. The .303 Savage remained popular through the 1930s. Savage Arms created the .303 Savage as part of an unsuccessful attempt at creating a cartridge for the military. Although the cartridge was never popular with the military, it did become a popular round for civilian hunters. *(Chapter 18, p. 241)*

26. The story "How Eagle Lake Got Its Name" appears in *Adirondack Memories and Campfire Stories: Honoring the Mountains and Their History*, 2014. *(Chapter 21, p. 284)*

27. Jonathan W. Miller, whose grandfather was Stanley Miller, said in October 24, 2016, "It's my understanding Leon bought his brother Frank out, but it might have been left to him directly. Leon left the [Seventh Lake] camp to his daughter Margaret, and she in turn, left it to both Miller and Leonard Harris jointly, and they subsequently left their interests in that camp to their respective children. As I understand it, at some point in the last 10 years or so, one of Miller Harris's sons, Peter, bought all of the other "children" out and is now, I believe, the sole owner of that camp." *(Chapter 21, p. 290)*

28. On Wednesday afternoon, October 24, 1925 Joseph Payne, Abner Blakeman, 54 and granddaughter Irene Bobling, 9, were driving along the South Shore road from Inlet to Old Forge when a tree was uprooted by a strong wind and fell on their automobile crashing on the heads of Blakeman and the child. Payne remained uninjured. Blakeman and his granddaughter, who he was holding on his lap, died. *(Chapter 23, p. 316)*

29. For more French Louis stories see *Adirondack Characters and Campfire Yarns*, The Forager Press, LLC, 2005; *Adirondack Adventures: Bob Gillespie & Harvey Dunham on French Louie's Trail*, The Forager Press, LLC, 2012; and *Adirondack Camp Life Around the Indian Clearing: Early Sporting and Recreation in the Moose River Plains*, In the Adirondacks, 2017. *(Chapter 28, p. 385)*

30. Eldridge A. Spears knew French Lewie and occasionally wrote about the West Canada Creek woodsman. Spears said in a 1938 article, "Lewey wasn't a writing man, not even to the extent of writing his name. It was quite indifferent to him how his name was spelled, which accounts for a variety of spellings. He said his name was Louis Seymour, but people called him French Lewey. That was all right with him. Some spell it Loui. Others have it Lewey and Lewie, because that is English and the way it sounds. In his quiet, gentle manner he said such things were for other people to bother with." *(Chapter 28, p. 385)*

31. "Johnny Leaf, an Indian and something of a hermit himself who spent a good deal of his time in the Seabury country above Noblesboro." —E.A. Spears *(Chapter 28, p. 390)*

32. Cubbies are pens or boxes that prevent the animal from approaching the bait or lure from any side except that guarded by the trap. Hollow logs or trees, stumps and drain tiles are natural cubbies. A trapper may construct others of sticks, logs, bark or rocks. Boxes with one end removed, or with holes cut in them are also types of cubby sets. *(Chapter 29, p. 398)*

33. In 1910, Woodruff was a volunteer witness who testified before Governor Hughes's commissioners who were probing the administration of the Forest, Fish, and Game Commission. On August 30, 1910 *The Saratogian* reported on its front page, "WOODRUFF EXPLAINS KILL KARE PURCHASE: Denies Imputations Concerning Adirondack Holdings." A part of that testimony revealed, "In response to questions from Mr. Clark, Woodruff admitted that while a member of the state land purchasing board he had caused $1,500 to be paid to Wellington Kenwell, who ran a twenty-room boarding house on state land eleven miles from his, Woodruff's camp, that a state protector had then been installed in the Kenwell house and a telephone line constructed between there and the Woodruff camp at state expense." *(Chapter 30, p. 406)*

34. This is the old term for the south branch of the Moose River that runs through The Plains. *(Chapter 30, p. 407)*

35. Allen Wilcox, owner of Beaver Lake in the Moose River Plains wrote, "the liberation of seven beaver in 1905 was a blow to the deer that they were to feel for many years to come." *(Chapter 30, p. 407)*

36. Gerald Kenwell always spelled his friend's name "Lewie." *(Chapter 30, p. 411)*

37. Slim was referring to a group of Syracuse hunters who bought Gerald Kenwell's Halfway camp. See "Back In: The Arrival of the Massett and Hart Hunting Party" in *The Moose River Plains*, Vol. 2. *(Chapter 31, p. 437)*

38. Charles Terry Chapin, better known to his friends as "Charley" and "Chape,"was born in Rochester, New York, February 24, 1861. After attending several private schools, he entered Rochester High School, continuing there until 1877. He was sixteen when he entered the employ of the old Bank of Rochester, of which his father was president later flourished as the German-American Bank,—still later becoming the Lincoln National Bank. Charles Chapin was employed as a bookkeeper in the Rochester bank until 1880. With valuable business experience under his belt, he was elected secretary and treasurer of the Rochester Car Wheel Works, founded by his father, Charles Hall Chapin. Later he was elected president of the corporation, and continued as its executive head until 1905, when it became an integral part of the National Car Wheel Company. His active official connection with the works then ceased, but he continued to act as special representative of the National Car Wheel Company in matters of unusual importance. *(Chapter 34, p. 457)*

39. A jack-light is simply a reflector, in front of which a lamp burns. It is secured in the bow of a boat to a stout pole, and under and in front of this reflector the hunter sits. He is in the darkness, but the lamp throws a lane of light in front of the boat and enables the hunter to shoot a deer. *(Chapter 34, p. 465)*

40. Saleratus (aerated salt) is an old word for modern baking soda. It actually was used as a name for both of the above compounds, but, like pearlash, potassium bicarbonate had an unpleasant aftertaste and fell out of use early in the nineteenth century. So "saleratus" came to mean just sodium bicarbonate (bicarbonate of soda) itself. You'll find it in nineteenth century recipe books used just as baking soda is used today.

Saleratus was first sold on this side of the Atlantic by John Dwight, who, with his brother-in-law, Dr. Austin Church, started manufacturing it in their kitchens. It was called "Dwight's Saleratus" with a cow as a trademark because of the necessity of using sour milk to activate it in baking.
Source: https://www.kingarthurflour.com/tips/quick-bread-primer.html#a1 *(Chapter 35, p. 474)*

41. William D. Wakeley (1822–1897) operated the North River Hotel. He later sold it to Scarritt & Eldridge and was soon busy hewing six miles of road into Cedar River Falls, where he built a dam, a sawmill, and finally a new hotel. He became one of the early lumbermen in Township 17 (4 District). Wakeley named his place Cedar Falls Hotel, but it was generally known as Headquarters. The spot was so remote that each night bonfires were required during his first season to keep the wolves from his tethered oxen. The impressive hotel had a three-story main building, 56 feet x 26 feet with two-story wings, each 35 feet long, and sported a bar. It was destroyed by fire in 1878. Wakeley continued his stage line while engaging in real estate. In 1879, he built a small inn and dance hall. It burned in 1893. *(Chapter 35, p. 485)*

42. Acid rain is a rain or any other form of precipitation that is unusually acidic, meaning that it possesses elevated levels of hydrogen ions (low pH). It can have harmful effects on plants, aquatic animals and infrastructure. Acid rain is caused by emissions of sulfur dioxide and nitrogen oxide, which react with the water molecules in the atmosphere to produce acids. Some governments have made efforts since the 1970s to reduce the release of sulfur dioxide and nitrogen oxide into the atmosphere with positive results. Nitrogen oxides can also be produced naturally by lightning strikes, and sulfur dioxide is produced by volcanic eruptions. The chemicals in acid rain can cause paint to peel, corrosion of steel structures such as bridges, and weathering of stone buildings and statues. —from *Wikipedia*, the free encyclopedia *(Chapter 37, 510)*

43. See Appendix C "Beaver Lake Crash" *(Chapter 38, p. 533)*

44. Lonnie Warneke, nicknamed "The Arkansas Hummingbird," was a tobacco-chewing major league Baseball player in the 1930s. *(Chapter 42, p. 574)*

45. The *Osprey* was a large excursion boat Gerald Kenwell built and operated on Sixth and Seventh lakes. Winfred "Slim" Murdock helped his Uncle Gerald prepare dinners that were served to tourists at the head of Seventh Lake. Slim remembers, "the outings and shore parties were very successful." In 1942, Norton Bird purchased Gerald Kenwell's property near Sixth Lake dam. The *Osprey* was among the assets acquired. (*Chapter 43, p. 587*)

46. Timothy Lester Woodruff (August 4, 1858–October 12, 1913) was the Lieutenant-Governor of New York State, serving in that capacity from 1897 to 1902. He was also a businessperson and a leader of the Republican Party in the state of New York. Woodruff was instrumental in removing Wellington and Elisa Kenwell from their homestead on the Moose River Plains. Microfiche #FP1619 in the State of New York Office of the State Comptroller has on record a deed between Isaac Kenwell and New York State for part of lot 56 (27 acres) located in Township #7 of the Totten & Crossfield Purchase. This is the deed Woodruff vacated. The record is unclear if Isaac Kenwell then resold or gave the land to his brother. See Chapter 8: Lt. Gov. Woodruff's Kamp Kill Kare.

Adirondack guide Isaac Kenwell built the Raquette Lake House, the first hotel on Raquette Lake. He was a timber estimator for several companies, helped in the first marked survey of the Moose River Plains country and was appointed a fish and game protector in 1890. (*Chapter 43, p. 589*)

47. Camp Neodak was built around 1902. It was purchased by Royal Rogers in the late teens and burned in 1919. It was rebuilt the following year as the New Neodak Hotel. (*Chapter 46, p. 604*)

48. Refer to Collection 2 "Old Men of the Mountains" in *Adirondack Characters and Campfire Yarns* (The Forager Press, 2005) for an extensive profile of Alvah Dunning. (*Chapter 46, p. 606*)

Heading into the Land of Deer. Deer hunting season of by-gone days. *Courtesy Jim Massett*

INDEX

675

677

681

A LOOK AHEAD AT VOLUME 2

The Adirondacks' Moose River Plains, Vol. 2
The Land of the Deer

Epigraph   Paul A. Schaefer
Dedication
Author's Note
Introduction   Bette's Dream

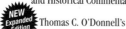